# THE ICSA CORPORATE GOVERNANCE HANDBOOK

# THE ICSA
# CORPORATE GOVERNANCE HANDBOOK

**4th Edition**

BERNADETTE BARBER
AND
BARBARA ALLEN

First published as *The Law and Practice of Corporate Governance* (Vine Publications Ltd, 2004).

Published 2010 as *ICSA's Corporate Governance Handbook* by ICSA Information & Training Ltd

Published 2011 as *ICSA's Corporate Governance Handbook* by ICSA Information & Training Ltd

Published 2013 as *ICSA's Corporate Governance Handbook* by ICSA Information & Training Ltd

This edition published by
ICSA Publishing Ltd
Saffron House
6–10 Kirby Street
London EC1N 8TS



Typeset in 10 on 12½ pt Kuenstler by Hands Fotoset, Bexhill, East Sussex

British Library Cataloguing in Publication Data
A catalogue record for this book is available from the British Library

ISBN 978-1-86072-712-2

# Contents

# Foreword

The UK corporate governance framework is well developed and robust, requiring high levels of disclosure and providing safeguards for shareholders. The need for a shareholder vote on certain matters, such as the annual vote on the appointment of directors, and the statutory and other duties directors must comply with, have put in place checks and balances to foster a healthy corporate culture for businesses in the UK. However, despite this system, which is partly legislative and partly based on regulation, the spotlight on corporate governance issues and, in particular, executive pay has intensified. There have recently been a number of high-profile corporate governance failures affecting not only listed companies but also large privately owned companies. As a result, there is a demand for steps to be taken to rebuild trust between the public and the boards of companies with the expectation that companies should be run responsibly in the interests not only of shareholders but also of their employees, customers, suppliers and other interested parties.

The challenge is identifying how the existing system can be improved. It is therefore timely for *The ICSA Corporate Governance Handbook* to be updated, providing a ready reference for boards on the sources of and historical context to the UK's current corporate governance framework and their existing obligations.

The starting point in working towards a healthy corporate culture in any organisation must be for boards to understand what their role entails, their legal obligations and the various voluntary guidelines with which they are expected to comply. In carrying out their duties, boards must be sensitive not only to the views of their shareholder base but also the perception by the general public of their actions. Boards must therefore address the public relations implications of their actions and question whether their actions may attract opprobrium.

Importantly, there is a tension between holding boards to account for their decisions and at the same time, giving them the autonomy to run a business. To date, the success of the UK corporate governance framework has relied on high levels of disclosure and the ability to 'comply or explain' with guidelines on what constitutes best practice. 'Comply or explain' has allowed companies to take decisions in the best interests of shareholders and to support the company's business strategy. Should new sanctions be introduced making directors more accountable if they breach their statutory duties? Would more disclosure and transparency lead to more accountability? Should shareholders have more rights to influence decisions or, indeed, overturn them? If they did have those rights, would they use them? Shareholders themselves need to take the role they have to play as responsible shareholders seriously and use their votes effectively, as encouraged by the Stewardship Code.

We can only speculate as to the outcomes of the current review into corporate governance reforms. If new legislation is introduced as a result of the review or the regulatory regime becomes more prescriptive, the burden on boards, in terms of time and cost, is likely to increase even though any changes might not benefit shareholders or stakeholders significantly and may actually prove to be an impediment to the effective operation of a board.

As regards executive remuneration, there has been a distinct shift in attitude by institutional investors. For example, the Investment Association, the principal body representing UK institutional investors, has endorsed remuneration committees having more flexibility to set a remuneration policy which is right for the company and which has a clearer line of sight between company performance and levels of remuneration. That said, the spiralling quantum of executive pay and the increased complexity of pay structures have attracted particular attention. As a result, it is inevitable that this area will always be somewhat regulated, at the very least, to make pay structures as transparent as possible.

In response to demands for reform of corporate governance, a balance needs to be struck between the obligations placed on boards to comply with the standards set to give shareholders and stakeholders, including employees, a voice and allowing boards to play an independent role in promoting the success of the company. While the focus has to date centred on listed companies, it is quite possible that corporate governance standards will in future also apply to larger privately owned companies. Despite a lack of visibility on what shape any reforms will take, it is without doubt that corporate governance will continue to be a focus for directors who will need to be equipped with appropriate knowledge and skills.

It has been a great pleasure for us to have had the opportunity to partner with Bernadette Barber on this fourth edition of *The ICSA Corporate Governance Handbook*. It has been invaluable to us to tap into Bernadette's practical experience of working with boards as a company secretary. She has challenged our thinking along the way and as a result, we believe that this publication provides readers with the information they need to craft a corporate governance framework which meets the needs of their own organisation.

Finally, I would like to thank my colleagues at Stephenson Harwood who assisted with the preparation of this publication and, in particular, Tom Nicholls, Joanne Wallace, Tom Page and Anika Chandra.

Barbara Allen
Partner, Head of Employee Incentives
Stephenson Harwood LLP
*June 2017*

# Preface

Corporate governance is a topic that continues to increase in importance and profile across the business community, not just within UK plc but throughout the private sector and beyond. There is a growing perception that there needs to be an effective response from all types of business and other organisations to the social issues of the day and to public expectations for greater fairness, transparency and accountability. In particular, against a backdrop of continued disquiet over disproportionate executive remuneration, the actions of those in positions of authority within the corporate world continue to be questioned.

This edition of *The ICSA Corporate Governance Handbook* has therefore been written in an environment in which there is a degree of uncertainty about the future direction of the corporate governance framework. The publication at the end of 2016 of the UK Government's Green Paper, *Corporate Governance Reform*, raised important questions about the efficacy of the existing regime and consulted on a number of different options to enhance existing requirements in order to address concerns about perceived deficiencies in current arrangements.

While this uncertainty might be viewed as somewhat disconcerting, for those who are charged with governance of their organisation or who are called upon to advise on and implement governance arrangements, an alternative view is that the debate can be helpful to stimulate such individuals to 'think deeply, thoroughly and on a continuing basis' about the work of their board.

The 'comply or explain' regime and other best practice requirements continue to task boards with exceeding the minimum standards of good governance as set out in legislation. But if enhanced practices are to be adopted, boards need to be convinced that such super-compliance is in the best interests of their company and its shareholders. Where the business case for going above and beyond statutory and regulatory requirements is unconvincing, directors are likely to be reluctant to adopt such practices. After all, a director's duty is not simply to bow to public opinion on certain matters but rather to promote the long-term success of his or her business. Board decisions, including decisions on governance practices, should be consistent with that duty.

The progress made towards demonstrating the value of responsible corporate practices is therefore to be welcomed. Adding to the existing body of evidence that a company with a healthy culture, which actively takes account of the impact of its operations on both direct and indirect stakeholders, is likely to be more sustainable in the longer term will ultimately do more to drive improvements in corporate responsibility than issuing guidance that purports to represent best practice but which is not backed up by evidence that the recommended practices will benefit the business.

It is not an easy task to challenge established thinking (whether one's own or more generally accepted wisdom) or to present alternatives to investors as the best way forward. Nor is it simple to keep abreast of current thinking, to balance the demands of a diverse range of stakeholders and to develop solutions that are appropriate for the organisation. It is the intention of this publication that, by providing clear information on the baseline requirements, pointing out areas of greater flexibility and setting out some of the arguments for and against different approaches, the reader may be helped to form their own opinions on what might work well for their own organisation.

It has been my great pleasure and privilege to have partnered with Stephenson Harwood on this fourth edition of *The ICSA Corporate Governance Handbook*. Like other company secretaries, I often work closely with legal colleagues and advisers and value the slightly different perspective and expertise that they bring to difficult issues. Stephenson Harwood's contribution has certainly enhanced this work by bringing those attributes to its drafting. I knew from personal experience that Stephenson Harwood would be an excellent choice of legal firm to work on this with me. In my 'day job' I have always found their team to be extremely knowledgeable, highly responsive and (above all) practical in their approach. I know the latter is a quality that company secretaries like myself particularly value, called upon as we are to juggle numerous issues, often to tight timescales!

Finally, I would like to thank my own colleagues who assisted in getting this publication ready in time – Bev Siddons and Tom Crowe. Their patience and ability to correctly interpret many almost unintelligible amendments made in manuscript have been most impressive!

Bernadette Barber, FCIS
Director, Chadwick Corporate Consulting Limited
*June 2017*

# Abbreviations and acronyms

| | |
|---|---|
| ABI | Association of British Insurers (now the Investments Association) |
| AGM | annual general meeting |
| AIM | Alternative Investment Market |
| CA 2006 | Companies Act 2006 |
| CBI | Confederation of British Industry |
| CDDA 1986 | Company Directors Disqualification Act 1986 |
| CIIA | Chartered Institute of Internal Auditors |
| CMA | Competition and Markets Authority |
| CSOP | company share option plan |
| CSR | corporate social responsibility |
| D&O | directors and officers |
| Defra | Department for Environment, Food and Rural Affairs |
| DTI | Department of Trade and Industry |
| DTR | Disclosure Guidance and Transparency Rules |
| EC | European Commission |
| ecoDa | European Confederation of Directors' Associations |
| EEA | European Economic Area |
| EMI | enterprise management incentive |
| EMS | environmental management system |
| EPS | earnings per share |
| ERM | enterprise risk management |
| ESG | environmental, social and governance |
| ESMA | European Securities and Markets Authority |
| EU | European Union |
| Eurosif | European Social Investment Forum |
| FCA | Financial Conduct Authority |
| FRC | Financial Reporting Council |
| FRS | Financial Reporting Standard |
| FSA | Financial Services Authority |
| FSMA 2000 | Financial Services and Markets Act 2000 |
| FTSE 100 | Financial Times/London Stock Exchange index of 100 most highly capitalised UK companies |

| | |
|---|---|
| FTSE 250 | Financial Times/London Stock Exchange index of 250 next largest UK companies after FTSE 100 |
| FTSE 350 | all companies included in FTSE 100 and FTSE 250 |
| GAAP | Generally Accepted Accounting Principles (US) |
| GC100 | General Counsel 100 (group of senior legal officers drawn from FTSE 100 companies) |
| GHG | greenhouse gas |
| GRI | Global Reporting Initiative |
| HCM | human capital management |
| HMRC | HM Revenue & Customs |
| IA | Investment Association |
| IA 1986 | Insolvency Act 1986 |
| ICAEW | Institute of Chartered Accountants in England & Wales |
| ICGN | International Corporate Governance Network |
| ICSA | Institute of Chartered Secretaries and Administrators |
| IFRS | International Financial Reporting Standards |
| IIA | Institute of Internal Auditors UK and Ireland |
| IIRC | International Integrated Reporting Committee |
| IPO | initial public offering |
| IoD | Institute of Directors |
| IR | investor relations |
| ISC | Institutional Shareholders' Committee |
| ISO | International Standards Organisation |
| KPIs | key performance indicators |
| Libor | London Interbank Offered Rate |
| LLP | limited liability partnership |
| LR | Listing Rules |
| LSE | London Stock Exchange |
| MAD | Market Abuse Directive |
| MAR | Market Abuse Regulation (596/2014) |
| MiFID | Markets in Financial Instruments Directive |
| MLD4 | Money Laundering Directive (EU 2015/849) |
| NAPF | National Association of Pension Funds |
| NASDAQ | US Stock Exchange |
| NED | non-executive director |
| NGO | non-governmental organisation |
| Nomad | nominated adviser |
| NYSE | New York Stock Exchange |
| OECD | Organisation for Economic Cooperation and Development |
| PCA | person closely associated |
| PDMR | persons discharging managerial responsibilities |
| PIE | public interest entity |
| PLC | public limited company |

| | |
|---|---|
| PR | Prospectus Rules |
| PSC | people with significant control |
| RCG | Remuneration Consultants Group |
| RIS | Regulatory Information Service |
| RLE | relevant legal entity |
| SBEEA 2015 | Small Business, Enterprise and Employment Act 2015 |
| SEC | Securities and Exchange Commission (US) |
| SID | senior independent director |
| SMEs | small and medium-sized enterprises |
| SRI | socially responsible investment/sustainable and responsible investment |
| SYSC | Senior Management Arrangements, Systems and Controls (regulatory framework) |
| UKLA | UK Listing Authority |
| UKSIF | UK Social Investment and Finance Association |

# Acknowledgements

Figure 6.2 The CSR Route Map is ©Asesoria Group and is reproduced with permission.

# Part 1

## Governance Context and Framework

# 1

# Introduction and background

## The development of corporate governance

Corporate governance is now a familiar subject for any serious commentator on corporate affairs. However, it has not always been so. Until the early 1990s, the governance of companies attracted little public debate or scrutiny. It was largely the preserve of individual boards of directors, each of which functioned as it saw fit within the broader confines of company law. All that has changed, so that, across the free market economies, regulatory and best practice regimes of varying degrees of prescription now define how companies and organisations, from all sectors, should be directed and controlled. Twenty-five years on from the *Cadbury Report*, it is indisputable that corporate governance has come of age. Politicians of all persuasions claim it as their own, press coverage of corporate governance issues is frequent and wide and universities now recognise it as a serious academic subject, with prestigious MBA courses requiring their students to 'learn' corporate governance in order to equip them for the world of business. Regulators have moved swiftly to define and set standards of governance and institutional shareholders have left companies in no doubt as to their own governance requirements. The speed of development of the governance agenda has been such that most energy has been directed at first producing and then refining the rulebooks. This process has inevitably led to some incidental reflection on the wider issues, such as the linkage between compliance with rules and enhancement in shareholder value.

### Governance and the law

Company law provides the foundational rules about the way companies are to be governed. To this extent, corporate governance is best viewed through the prism of the law. However, at least under the UK legal system, rules made by legislators (or judges) are intended to be exact and to be applied 'to the letter'. It can be argued therefore that the strictures of the law provide no basis for fostering the proper processes, even culture, that are required if a company, with its complex mix of interests and relationships, is to be effectively governed. Those who are of this persuasion favour a flexible and voluntary governance framework founded on the sensible application of broad principles, not the rigid imposition of narrow rules of law. Experience shows, however, that the lawmakers can be swift to act if that voluntary governance framework proves to be so flexible as to be ineffective. The Sarbanes-Oxley Act 2002 in the US is the most obvious example of the introduction of legislation after the failure of a voluntary approach. In the UK, the introduction in 2013 of an enhanced statutory regime governing directors' remuneration, now the subject of further review as part of the Government's 2016 Green Paper, *Corporate Governance Reform*, and the repeated threats of legislation from the Government on shareholder activism are indicative that governments will intervene, where they feel constrained to do so, on public policy grounds. The European Union (EU), following a review of corporate governance, has also continued to introduce more rigorous measures.

### Governance and the political economy

Belief in the ability of the markets as almost perfect regulators of corporate activity (sometimes termed the American Business Model, in recognition of it being followed in its purest form in the US) has been undermined by various stock market bubbles and the inevitable crashes that follow. From the internet-inspired boom of the 1990s to the inflated valuations of complex multinational banking groups that crashed so catastrophically in 2008/9, there can be no doubt that the markets are very far from always being perfect. The American Business Model also appeared to justify the significant and controversial escalation in the personal wealth of company executives. The loss of trust in public company directors and perceived lack of justification for generous executive remuneration arrangements have made the task of proponents of a voluntary and self-regulated approach to corporate governance that much more difficult. As mentioned already, in the US, the reaction to corporate failures has been swift and comprehensive. The Sarbanes-Oxley Act in 2002, and more recently the Dodd-Frank Act in 2010, provided a remarkable statement of the US conversion to the merits of greater regulation and better corporate governance. Yet in many respects it has been a counter-intuitive development. Whereas, previously, senior company executives had been able to govern their companies and pursue wealth creation autonomously, now they face a raft of controlling external regulations. At one stroke, the Sarbanes-Oxley Act forced through radical change in the US in marked contrast to the relatively unco-ordinated and less prescriptive approach adopted in other developed economies.

The UK experience has been more measured and generally less overtly political. The seeds of change were sown in the early 1990s, as corporate scandals such as Polly Peck, the Maxwell Group, BCCI and Barings hit the headlines and political opinion moved from the right towards the centre.

The subsequent emergence of 'stakeholder capitalism' into popular consciousness in the mid-1990s posed new questions about the value-creating role of the company. This was viewed in broader terms than simply enriching shareholders. Others were perceived to have a call on the company's resources, including employees, customers, suppliers and communities affected by the company's operations.

The duty of directors to take account of such factors was enshrined within the Companies Act 2006 (CA 2006) and the expectation that shareholders will take a more 'enlightened' approach to their stakeholder responsibilities has similarly gained ground. The political fallout following the global banking crisis of 2008/9 strengthened calls for account to be taken, by both boards and investors, of wider issues than just those of a short-term financial nature. A growing sense that the economy and business works for the elite few, rather than society as a whole, has added strength to those arguments. Accordingly, pressure to take a responsible stance in relation to all the possible impacts corporate activities may have on a range of stakeholders continues to increase.

### Governance, the environment and social policy

The recent identity of good governance with corporate social responsibility (CSR) means that financial criteria are no longer the sole measure of corporate health, with directors' statutory duties, other legislation and narrative reporting requirements both expressly recognising a wider set of factors. To a significant degree, retail investors who are attracted to the notion that their investments should benefit people and the environment as well as providing them with a financial return have driven this development. Ethical and 'green' funds have for some time represented a sizeable proportion of funds under management in the UK, but the degree of importance placed upon the risk of reputational, operational and financial damage resulting from a poor CSR record has also more generally increased over recent years. Increasingly, therefore, such matters are routinely considered by shareholders and their advisers in selecting and valuing their investments and, accordingly, such considerations have become a more mainstream part of asset management processes.

Beyond this, however, there are growing demands, arguably not always consistent with a system of corporate ownership predominantly based around delivering shareholder value, for corporate behaviours to recognise, and even take a leadership position on, wider environmental and social issues. Such demands are reflected in the 2016 UK Government Green Paper, *Corporate Governance Reform*, which reflects, in particular, concerns about the part that excessive executive remuneration has played in widening social divisions. The Green Paper calls upon businesses to restore 'faith in what they do, and in the power of the market economy to deliver growth, opportunity and choice for all'. The challenge this call presents is undoubtedly huge and questionably beyond the remit of private commerce.

### Corporate governance – a definition

There have been many attempts at defining what is meant by 'corporate governance'. The classic definition, which is still included in the UK Corporate Governance Code, is found in the *Cadbury Report* (see below), which said:

> 'Corporate governance is the system by which companies are directed and controlled. Boards of directors are responsible for the governance of their companies. The shareholders' role in governance is to appoint the directors and the auditors and to satisfy themselves that an appropriate governance structure is in place. The responsibilities of the board include setting the company's strategic aims, providing the leadership to put them into effect, supervising the management of the business and reporting to shareholders on their stewardship. The board's actions are subject to laws, regulations and the shareholders in general meeting.'

This definition does not recognise, however, the wider social purposes discussed above, assuming instead that the role of governance is essentially restricted only to delivering shareholder value. In contrast the G20/OECD Principles of Corporate Governance published in 2015 confirm the view that 'the purpose of corporate governance is to help build an environment of trust, transparency and accountability necessary for fostering long-term investment, financial stability and business integrity, thereby supporting stronger growth and more inclusive societies'.

This wider purpose will present challenges for boards and their investors.

## A brief history of corporate governance in the UK

Although corporate governance as a concept had its origins prior to the late 1980s and early 1990s, it was not until then that it was defined and scrutinised in a formal manner, and so became part of the common language of the UK corporate world. Adopting the luxuries of hindsight, it is possible to chart the changes that followed by reference to the publication of reports by committees of eminent governance experts, the first of which was the *Cadbury Report*, and other related developments.

### The *Cadbury Report* (1992)

Under the chairmanship of Sir Adrian Cadbury, the Committee on the Financial Aspects of Corporate Governance was established in 1991 on the initiative of the Financial Reporting Council (FRC), the London Stock Exchange (LSE) and the accountancy profession. The subsequent *Cadbury Report*, the result of a thorough review, was a defining moment for corporate governance in the UK, setting both the tone and the reference points for subsequent developments. In the preface to the report, Sir Adrian commented as follows:

> 'When our Committee was formed just over eighteen months ago, neither our title nor our work programme seemed framed to catch the headlines. In the event, the Committee has become the focus of far more attention than I ever envisaged when I accepted the invitation to become the chairman.'

This attention derived from heightening concerns about standards of financial reporting and accountability as a result of such events as the BCCI and Maxwell Group collapses and the rising controversy over directors' pay.

As suggested by its title, the Cadbury Committee's terms of reference were focused on the specifically financial aspects of governance, including in particular the effectiveness of financial controls and the auditing process. However, the climate in which the Committee operated was such that its conclusions and recommendations had wider implications than the purely financial. A review of the *Cadbury Report*'s chapter headings reveals the extent to which it defined the scope of corporate governance: namely, the structure and effectiveness of boards of directors, internal controls, the audit process, financial reporting and accountability to shareholders.

Subsequent developments in law and practice have been shaped significantly by the following three conclusions of the *Cadbury Report*:

- Corporate governance is, in essence, about 'the system by which companies are directed and controlled'. To achieve an effective system, the right structures and rules must be in place, and while they cannot of themselves raise standards, they are necessary to provide the framework to encourage good governance.
- Voluntary compliance with a Code of Best Practice provides the vehicle for putting the right structures and rules in place. Supported by principles of openness, integrity and accountability, the system of governance should be self-regulated and not forced by formal regulations imposed by Government.
- Effective standards of self-regulation can be achieved by reliance on the principle of 'comply or explain'. This requires companies to include an audited statement of compliance in their annual report and accounts, giving reasons for any non-compliance. This approach relies on the expectation that compliance levels will be high and that any exceptions will be for good and cogent reasons.

In summary, the lasting legacy of the *Cadbury Report* has been to provide a framework for understanding corporate governance based on three essential principles: the need for adequate systems of control, the preference for a voluntary approach to compliance and the merits of a 'comply or explain' approach to enforcement.

### The *Greenbury Report* (1995)

Despite (or perhaps because of) the enhanced level of disclosure required by the Cadbury Code, public and shareholder concerns about directors' pay continued unabated. These concerns centred in particular on the large pay increases and gains from share options enjoyed by directors in the recently privatised utility industries. In addition, the level of directors' compensation payments on termination of their contracts attracted much criticism. The Study Group on Directors' Remuneration was established in 1995 on the initiative of the Confederation of British Industry (CBI), and chaired by Sir Richard Greenbury. Its terms of reference were to identify good practice on public limited company (PLC) directors' remuneration, and to prepare a new Code of Practice accordingly. Having reviewed the alternatives, it concluded that:

> 'The way forward as we see it lies not in statutory controls, which would be at best unnecessary and at worst harmful, but in action to strengthen the accountability and encourage enhanced performance.'

The *Greenbury Report* included a new Code of Best Practice covering directors' remuneration and service contracts, and the level of compensation payable on termination. The Code drew on several of the principles trailed by the *Cadbury Report*, in particular endorsing the approach that voluntary compliance, and disclosure of non-compliance, would bring improved standards. A key role was handed to the remuneration committee. Under new terms of reference, it was given delegated responsibility from the board for determining both the policy on directors' remuneration (including pensions) and the specific remuneration packages for individual directors. It was also required to provide shareholders with a formal remuneration report, containing detailed disclosure on individual remuneration packages, within the annual report and accounts. The committee should consist exclusively of at least three non-executive directors (NEDs), excluding any non-executive chairman involved with the day-to-day running of the company. No member could have any personal financial interest in the committee's decisions, other than as a shareholder.

The Greenbury Study Group did not attempt to define in a prescriptive manner what specific level or type of remuneration would be appropriate for any company, but it did make two proposals, each of which has stood the test of time:

- remuneration should be linked to performance, both by the company and the individual director. Subsequent experience has shown that the proportion of PLC directors' pay which is performance-related has increased year on year;
- share and cash incentive arrangements should be designed so as to align the interests of directors and shareholders. In response to this proposal, both companies and professional consultancies have shown a remarkable capacity for developing different types of incentive arrangements and performance measures, although investor patience with some approaches does now appear to be wearing thin.

A number of now familiar phrases had their origins in the *Greenbury Report* and were for many years incorporated into the Combined Code (now the UK Corporate Governance Code): no circular to shareholders on a new incentive plan would have omitted to state that it aligned 'the interests of executives with shareholders' and no statement on remuneration policy would have been complete if it did not state that it was designed to 'attract, retain and motivate people of the highest calibre and experience'. That language, however, has now been replaced in the UK Corporate Governance Code as thinking on remuneration issues has further developed.

### The *Hampel Report* and the Combined Code (1998)

The Codes of Practice resulting from both the *Cadbury* and *Greenbury Reports* were criticised by companies for being treated as a set of prescriptive rules by shareholders. It was suggested that the result was the emergence of a 'box-ticking' approach to corporate governance, which took no account of the real circumstances or experience of companies. Accordingly, a new Committee on Corporate Governance was established in 1995 on the initiative of the FRC to take a fresh look at the issues. Under the chairmanship of Sir Ronnie Hampel, its primary terms of reference were to review the Cadbury Code against its original purpose, to pursue relevant matters deriving from the *Greenbury Report* and to address the role of directors, shareholders and auditors in corporate governance.

The Committee published its conclusions in 1998, following a review period of over two years. It was observed that the *Cadbury* and *Greenbury Reports* were responses to things that were perceived to have gone wrong – corporate failures and unjustified remuneration packages. Understandably, they had as a result focused on the prevention of abuse, and compliance with detailed guidelines and rules of disclosure. The Hampel Committee set out to shift the emphasis towards the positive contribution which good corporate governance can make to business prosperity. This contribution would require flexibility, and the repudiation of a box-ticking approach which, it was implied, applied blunt solutions to complex governance issues. The *Hampel Report* concluded that:

> 'Business prosperity cannot be commanded. People, teamwork, leadership, enterprise, experience and skills are what really produce prosperity. There is no singular formula to weld these together, and it is dangerous to encourage the belief that rules and regulations about structure deliver success.'

And also:

> 'Good corporate governance is not just a matter of prescribing particular corporate structures and complying with a number of hard and fast rules. There is a need for broad principles. All concerned should then apply these flexibly and with common sense to the varying circumstances of individual companies.'

The clear aim was to restrict the regulatory burden on companies, and to substitute principles in place of detailed rules wherever possible. The burden of achieving full compliance with the rules of governance was to be lifted with the *Hampel Report* stating:

> 'We draw a distinction between principles of corporate governance and more detailed guidelines like the Cadbury and Greenbury Codes. With guidelines, one asks "How far are they complied with?". With principles the right question is "How far are they applied in practice?". We recommend that companies should include in their annual report and accounts a narrative statement of how they apply the relevant principles to their particular circumstances.'

The main outcome of the Hampel Committee's efforts was a new Code of Practice, replacing the Cadbury and Greenbury Codes and known as the Combined Code. Structurally, it was made up of a series of corporate governance principles, which were then explained by a set of more detailed provisions. Following the recommendations of the *Hampel Report*, the Combined Code was effectively incorporated into the Listing Rules (LR) by the requirement for companies to make a statement in their annual report and accounts to show (1) how they applied the principles and (2) the extent to which they complied with the provisions of the Combined Code and, in the latter case, to justify any significant variances.

It is worth observing that the *Hampel Report* placed corporate governance firmly in the shareholder value camp, by stating that:

> 'The single overriding objective shared by all listed companies, whatever their size or type of business, is the preservation and the greatest practicable enhancement over time of their shareholders' investment. All boards have this responsibility and their policies, structure, composition and governing process should reflect this.'

However, showing awareness of the wider perspectives of governance, it was recognised that there were relationships other than those with shareholders which mattered. Such 'stakeholders' included employees, customers, suppliers, credit providers, local communities and governments. It was management's responsibility to develop such relationships, but in so doing 'they must have regard to the overriding objective of preserving and enhancing the shareholders' investment over time'.

The point is emphasised in the *Hampel Report* by drawing a key distinction: the directors of a company may be responsible for relations with stakeholders, but they are accountable to shareholders and shareholder interests (both present and future). Therefore, according to the *Hampel Report*, the performance of directors was to be measured relative to their accountability to shareholders, not to stakeholders. Endorsing the prevailing shareholder value approach, the inference was that behaving responsibly towards stakeholders should not be an end in itself; rather it was a means to the ultimate end of serving the long-term interests of shareholders.

The Combined Code was revised in 2003 (see the *Higgs Report* and the *Smith Report* below), 2006 and 2008. It was reviewed again in 2009/10, when it was renamed the UK Corporate Governance Code to better reflect its purpose. The Code is subject to a regular review and consultation process by the FRC and was most recently updated in June 2016.

### The Turnbull Guidance (1999)

After the Combined Code was published in 1998, the Institute of Chartered Accountants in England & Wales (ICAEW) agreed with the LSE that it would provide guidance to assist listed companies to implement the requirements of the Code relating to internal control. Accordingly, the ICAEW established an Internal Control Working Party in 1999 under the chairmanship of Nigel Turnbull, which published its internal control guidance later that year. Published in 1999, the Turnbull Guidance (subsequently called *Internal Control: Guidance to Directors* and now incorporated into the FRC Guidance *Risk Management, Internal Control and Related Financial and Business Reporting*) has assisted boards of directors to achieve compliance with the internal control requirements of the Combined Code.

Internal control is at root about risk management and safeguarding shareholders' investments and companies' assets. Yet the Turnbull Guidance did not view the task as being a rather negative exercise in risk containment.

Rather, it asserted that a sound system of internal control will facilitate the effectiveness and efficiency of operations, help ensure the reliability of internal and external reporting and assist compliance with laws and regulations.

The generation of profits is, in part, the reward for successful risk-taking. Accordingly, the *Turnbull Report* asserted that the purpose of internal controls is to help manage and control risk in a manner which is supportive of a company's business objectives, not to eliminate risk. Despite the passing of many years since the *Turnbull Report* was first published, the 2014 FRC Guidance on *Risk Management, Internal Control and Related Financial Business Reporting* reaffirms that adherence to good stewardship should 'not inhibit sensible risk taking that is critical to growth'. The challenge is to ensure the quality of risk decision-making is optimised and the Turnbull Guidance placed responsibility for doing so squarely on the shoulders of directors.

### The *Myners Report* (2001)

On the face of it, the Government's announcement in 2000 that it would bring forward a review of institutional investment did not appear to presage a significant turning point for corporate governance. This review was to consider what factors (if any) were distorting investment decision-making, causing institutional investors and in particular trustees of occupational pension schemes to follow industry-standard patterns which avoided investing in small and medium-sized enterprises (SMEs) in favour of quoted equities and gilts.

The review was conducted by Paul Myners, and his *Report on Institutional Investment in the UK* was published in March 2001. The conclusions and recommendations were wide-ranging, and have had a very significant impact on corporate governance in the UK. First, he proposed that trustees of pension funds should have a legal requirement, as in the US, to be familiar with the relevant issues when making investment decisions (this appeared to strike a blow against the 'responsible amateur' view of trusteeship). Secondly, he set out, Cadbury-style, some basic principles of an effective approach to investment decision-making. One of these proposed that shareholder activism should be a duty of investors, on the grounds that this would be in the best interests of the ultimate beneficiaries on whose behalf investors (and fund managers as their agents) controlled assets of huge value.

The Government's initial response to the *Myners Report* was published in October 2001, and set out revised versions of the investment principles. Subsequently it issued consultation papers both on the proposed higher standard of care required of trustees in investment matters, and also the proposals for encouraging more and better shareholder activism. Shortly afterwards, the Institutional Shareholders' Committee (ISC) issued its own *Statement of Principles* on the subject in an effort to prove that the industry could get its own house in order without being coerced by legislation. This statement was superseded in July 2010 by the UK Stewardship Code, published by the FRC, which took over responsibility for the Code following recommendations made by the *Walker Report*, published in November 2009.

The Stewardship Code, which was updated in 2012, sets out best practice for institutional shareholders (and their appointed investment managers) in relation to their responsibilities with respect to investee companies. All UK-authorised asset managers are required, under the Financial Conduct Authority (FCA) Code of Business Rules, to produce a statement of commitment to the Code or state why it is not relevant to their business.

### The *Higgs Report* and *Smith Report* (2003)

Most of the key corporate governance tasks end up on the desk of the non-executive director. Yet the role of this corporate officer has historically been relatively ill-defined, and in terms of legal status and liabilities has been indistinguishable from that of the executive director. During 2002, Sir Derek Higgs undertook a review of the role and effectiveness of NEDs. By this task, he was inevitably doing far more than examining a detachable part of the governance process. Rather, he was reviewing the foundations of that process, in the form of the unitary board and the responsibilities of and relations between those who populate it. The backdrop was a severe crisis in equity markets.

The *Higgs Report*, published in January 2003, is composed of two main parts. First, there is the main body of the Report. This is elegantly drafted, and full of finely judged and memorable phrases (such as 'corporate governance provides an architecture of accountability'). The breadth of this review places it firmly in the *Cadbury* and *Hampel Report* category. The second main part to the *Higgs Report* comprises the Annexes.

The *Higgs Report* confirmed the place of NEDs within the unitary board structure. They are the 'custodians of the governance process' and as such must exhibit high standards of integrity and probity, possess sound judgement and strong interpersonal skills and also be probing and questioning of executives by nature. In a notable phrase, it is declared that:

> 'They should question intelligently, debate constructively, challenge rigorously and decide dispassionately.'

Attempting to head off any suggestion that its recommendations were a blueprint for box-tickers, the *Higgs Report* emphasised time and again the importance of behaviours and personal attributes over and above structures and compliance with processes and rules. People and board cultures are key, and ensuring that the right people are appointed requires a 'relentless meritocracy' in the boardroom, drawing from a wider pool of talent. Higgs proposed that induction and continued professional development programmes be constructed, providing further impetus to the notion that a NED is a qualified professional, not a gifted amateur.

Sir Derek roundly endorsed the 'comply or explain' principle originally established by the *Cadbury Report*. However, his detractors baulked at the apparent increase in governance rules at the expense of governance principles in the first draft of the amended Combined Code that was appended to the report. While the version finally adopted represented something of a compromise, the *Higgs Report* led to several significant new rules relating to the composition, structure and functioning of boards and more onerous levels of disclosure for public companies. Good Practice Suggestions from the *Higgs Report* guided boards on how to apply many aspects of the Combined Code until it was replaced in 2011 by the new *Guidance on Board Effectiveness*, developed by ICSA: The Governance Institute, on behalf of the FRC.

The Co-ordinating Group on Auditing and Accounting (CGAA) was established in February 2002 as the vehicle through which the relevant Government departments and others, such as the accountancy bodies, would respond to issues of audit reform. At an early stage, the CGAA focused on the issue of auditor independence and linked to this related issues such as the provision of non-audit services by auditing firms, all of which it was recognised would not be of direct concern to the NED review undertaken by Sir Derek Higgs. Accordingly, under the chairmanship of Sir Robert Smith, a separate review group was established with the remit to examine specifically audit committees (not wider auditing issues) and the associated implications for the Combined Code. The *Smith Report* was published simultaneously with the *Higgs Report* in January 2003. Its recommendations were adopted unchanged by Sir Derek Higgs and found their way into the revised Combined Code. The headline points for audit committees related to their independence, their role in monitoring financial statements and reviewing internal audit functions and their oversight on behalf of the board of the relationship with external auditing firms.

These changes received much less attention in the UK than the audit committee changes introduced in the US by the Sarbanes-Oxley Act 2002. In part this is because the *Smith Report* was building on an existing platform, rather than (as in the US) creating an entirely new structure. The original Combined Code had required a level of audit committee independence and oversight that did not, in practice, exist in the US. Also, the whole approach to auditing in the UK, with its emphasis on substance over form and the 'true and fair' certification, has provided a more robust defence against the sort of abuses which afflicted accounting processes in the US. The guidance derived from the *Smith Report* has subsequently been revised several times, most recently in April 2016, and has become known as the FRC *Guidance on Audit*

*Committees*. Alongside this guidance is a separate document published by the FRC in 2013 – *Best Practice Guide to Audit Tendering*.

### The Company Law Review (2001) and Companies Act 2006 (CA 2006)

The publication in July 2001 of the Company Law Review Final Report on company law reform proposed major changes through the enactment of new company legislation. It contained some potentially far-reaching proposals about the governance of companies, and asked some searching questions about why companies exist and whose interests they are designed to serve. It was followed in July 2002 by a White Paper entitled *Modernising Company Law*, which included over 200 draft clauses to be incorporated into a proposed new Companies Bill. The Companies Act was finally enacted in 2006 and came into force through a phased approach during the three-year period to 1 October 2009. While many of its measures were designed to deregulate company law through the so-called 'think small first' approach, there were also many implications for governance of larger entities, such as the provisions for the statutory codification of directors' duties, the limitation of auditors' responsibility for loss, changes encouraging shareholder engagement through enhancing the powers of proxies and provisions to implement the Takeover Directive by placing the Takeover Panel on a statutory footing.

Also, in order to achieve future flexibility in company law, the legislation contains provisions which facilitate future changes to company law being made by a special form of secondary legislation (rather than by primary legislation) to produce both the reform and restatement of existing law. Despite this flexibility, some changes to the CA 2006 have been made by the Enterprise and Regulatory Reform Act 2013 and the Small Business, Enterprise and Employment Act 2015 (SBEEA 2015).

### Convergence in International Financial Reporting Standards (IFRS) (2005)

Convergence in financial reporting within the EU has for some time been a key goal of the European Commission (EC). The damage caused by accounting failures at the heart of recent corporate governance scandals, particularly those involving global companies with complex multi-jurisdictional operations, led the Commission to press ahead firmly with its agenda of convergence. The policy objective has been to ensure consistency in reporting standards across different EU jurisdictions, thereby achieving greater efficiency within the internal market. Since 2005, UK listed companies have been required to report their results under specified IFRS.

### The Turner Review and Walker Review (2009)

The corporate failures associated with the global banking crisis prompted further reviews of corporate governance. In March 2009, the Turner Review, which examined the circumstances leading up to the financial crisis, made two recommendations relevant to this context:

- that remuneration policies should be designed to avoid incentives for undue risk-taking;
- that risk management considerations should be closely integrated into remuneration decisions;
- that the *Walker Review* should consider:
  (a) whether changes in governance structure are required to increase the independence of risk management functions; and
  (b) the skill level and time commitment required for NEDs of large complex banks to perform effective oversight of risks and provide challenge to executive strategies.

The Review of Corporate Governance in UK Banks and Other Financial Industry Entities led by Sir David Walker, which reported in November 2009, did indeed consider these issues and, although its work was limited to consideration of the UK banking and financial services industry, it made a number of recommendations to the FRC for inclusion in its own review of the Combined Code. The result was a rewrite of the Combined Code, which was renamed the UK Corporate Governance Code, issued in May 2010 and most recently updated in 2016. Section A of the Code was separated into Sections A and B, focusing on leadership and effectiveness respectively, with greater emphasis on the need for robust induction, development and evaluation processes, for non-executives to commit adequate time to their role and introducing new annual re-election requirements for all directors of FTSE 350 companies. In addition, the board's responsibility for defining risk appetite was made more explicit and a new provision requiring annual reports to include an explanation of the company's business model and strategy was adopted.

### Women on boards (2011)

The issue of boardroom diversity was raised by Higgs but, concerned about the slow rate of progress towards achieving gender-balanced boards – it was calculated that at the prevailing rate of change it would take some 70 years to achieve 50% female representation in FTSE 100 boardrooms – in 2010 the UK Government initiated a review into the current situation and barriers to achieving faster change with a view to making recommendations on the way forward. The review, led by Lord Davies of Abersoch, in particular prompted a wide-ranging debate about the merits or otherwise of adopting a quota system of the type already in force in some other European countries such as Norway and Spain. A system of quotas was already under consideration by the EC at the time, although mandatory quotas have since been rejected by the Commission in favour of a system of gender equality 'objectives'. Lord Davies' final report *Women on Boards* similarly rejected the imposition of a quota system and instead recommended a series of voluntary targets, policy and reporting requirements for FTSE 350 companies which have since been reflected in the UK Corporate Governance Code and in the new strategy report introduced by The Companies Act 2006 (*Strategic Report and Directors' Report*) Regulations 2013. Although an encouraging increase in the number of women appointed to boards has since been witnessed, as confirmed in the follow-up report, *Five Year Summary*, published in 2015, the threat of introducing a mandatory quota remains if such voluntary measures prove ineffective in increasing the pace of real change.

The gender diversity debate is not seen as the only diversity issue to be addressed, however. Published in late 2016, the Parker Review, which made recommendations in relation to ethnic diversity on FTSE 100 boards, has widened the focus.

## EU Corporate Governance Action Plan (2012)

A number of EU Directives have a direct impact on company law and corporate governance in the UK and other Member States. Some of these are examined in greater detail in Chapter 15 insofar as they have been implemented through the UK LR, PR and Disclosure Guidance and Transparency Rules (DTR) and the Takeover Code. In the wake of the 2008 banking crisis, however, the adequacy of corporate governance arrangements, not just within financial institutions but across the industry as a whole, was examined by the EC. A Green Paper, *Corporate Governance in Financial Institutions and Remuneration Policies*, in 2010 raised questions in relation to the functioning and risk-oversight role of boards, the governance of risk management functions, the role of external auditors with regards to risk, the behaviour of and engagement by shareholders, the enforcement regime, accountability and liability of directors, remuneration within listed companies generally and conflict of interest rules. Following this consultation process, the EC published *Action Plan: European company law and corporate governance – a modern legal framework for more engaged shareholders and sustainable companies* in December 2012, setting out three key areas where enhancement to company law and corporate governance arrangements were to be prioritised:

- increasing the level of transparency between companies and their shareholders;
- encouraging and facilitating long-term shareholder engagement; and
- supporting European businesses and encouraging their growth and competitiveness.

Within these three areas, particular actions were identified in relation to issues such as board diversity, corporate governance reporting, transparency of institutional shareholder voting and engagement policies, directors' remuneration, employee share ownership and recognition of the concept of the interest of the group for groups of companies.

In some aspects, the existing regime within the UK is already ahead of the game and listed companies here may have found they had fewer changes to implement than companies elsewhere in Europe. Notwithstanding this, the implications for UK corporate governance practice were still potentially wide-ranging.

### *Kay Report* (2012)

Against a background of diminishing confidence in the way that companies were being run with longer-term objectives in mind, Professor John Kay was commissioned to lead a review of UK equity markets and long-term decision making. The final *Kay Report* published in 2012 made 17 recommendations on issues such as stewardship, collective engagement, shareholder consultation, narrative reporting, executive remuneration and reward structures for asset managers. In response to these recommendations, legislation was brought forward to address narrative reporting requirements and to enhance shareholder powers in relation to executive remuneration. In addition, amongst other things, changes were made to the UK Stewardship Code and, focusing on the need to develop better shareholder engagement practices, ICSA published some useful guidance, *Enhancing Stewardship Dialogue*. An investor forum was established to assist with collective engagement and the National Association of Pension Funds (now Pensions and Lifetime Savings Association (PLSA)) developed a Stewardship Disclosure Framework to assist asset management firms in setting out their approach to stewardship. The Government's 2014 review of progress towards achievement of the *Kay Report*'s recommendations welcomed such developments and set out a number of 'next steps' to improve the position still further. Alleviating a board's concerns about the short-term implications of their decision-making to the detriment of longer-term considerations is clearly an important issue in the context of effective governance.

### Corporate Governance Reform Green Paper (2016)

Reflecting concerns that UK business and the economy generally were marginalising a large proportion of the population, a Green Paper was published in 2016 to seek 'a new approach to strengthen big business through better corporate governance'. The Green Paper focused on:

- ensuring executive pay is aligned to long-term performance;
- giving greater voice to employees and consumers in the boardroom; and
- raising the bar for governance standards in the largest privately held companies.

The outcomes of the consultation could potentially introduce measures on executive pay through an annual binding shareholder vote, greater shareholder engagement, increased transparency, obligations for remuneration committees to consult with shareholders and employees when developing policies and the imposition of holding periods for shares awarded under long-term incentive plans.

The resultant proposals are expected to be published in 2017 and the FRC has already confirmed that it will then review the UK Corporate Governance Code based on the outcome of the Government's response to its Green Paper consultation. Amongst other things, the FRC's proposed changes to the Code are expected to take account of other work it has recently undertaken on corporate culture and succession planning.

While we await the outcome of the Government and FRC reviews, other initiatives might be expected, and in many cases are already underway, to drive the debate forward and perhaps persuade legislators that a voluntary approach can be effective. ICSA and the Investment Association (IA) have, for example, announced a joint project to consider how the views of employees and other stakeholders can be brought more effectively into the boardroom.

### Extension of corporate governance codes beyond the FTSE

As we have seen, the development of corporate governance practice codes began with listed companies and, for many years, those in other organisations wishing to apply corporate governance best practice principles to their own boards had little choice but to refer to guidelines designed to address the needs of large commercial companies capitalised by external investors and to apply or adapt those principles to their own organisation's circumstances as best they could. However, as recognition of the value of corporate governance as a business specialism has grown, so too has demand for bespoke guidelines aimed specifically at entities outside of the listed sector. There are now numerous examples of sector-specific guidance relevant to corporate governancc including:

- *Seven Principles for Standards in Public Life* – Nolan Committee;
- *Good Governance Standard for Public Services* – Independent Commission for Good Governance in Public Services;
- *Hallmarks of an Effective Charity* – Charity Commission;
- *Good Governance: A Code for the Voluntary and Community Sector* – The Code Founding Group;
- *Corporate Governance Guidance and Principles for Unlisted Companies in the UK* – Institute of Directors (IoD) and European Confederation of Directors' Associations (ecoDa);
- *Code of Governance* – National Housing Federation;
- *The NHS Foundation Trust Code of Governance* – Monitor;

- *Governance in Multi-academy Trusts* – National College for Teaching & Leadership;
- *Corporate Governance Code for Small and Mid-Size Quoted Companies* – Quoted Companies Alliance;
- *A Code for Sports Governance* – Sport England/UK Sport.

In this publication, generally no specific reference is made to these guidelines – the number and variety of such codes make it impossible to address them all individually. However, for board members, company secretaries and other governance practitioners working outside the listed sector, the existence of such bespoke codes makes understanding how general governance principles can be appropriately applied to their organisations that much easier. Accordingly, those working outside the listed sector will no doubt wish to refer to the specific guidance of particular relevance to their company's own circumstances. However, taking a wider approach to the guidance referred to can also be useful in exposing governance practitioners to different views and ideas and facilitating the development of practice best suited to their individual organisation.

## The catalysts for change

The brief history recounted above indicates that since publication of the *Cadbury Report* in 1992, the pace of change on governance matters has been relentless. The persistent emergence of corporate scandals over that period naturally leads to the conclusion that the main catalyst for change has been the need to react to failure in the boardroom. While the financial impact of such scandals has been immense, there is another less evident (but still powerful) imperative at work. These events have required higher standards of governance not only to restore confidence in the operation of capital markets and to protect the otherwise vulnerable investor, but also to ensure harm to society at large is limited wherever possible.

There is mounting evidence of a shift in the understanding of how a company should fulfil its essential purpose of wealth creation. In some quarters this extends to a changing perception of what that purpose is. However, the extent of this shift in emphasis should not be overstated. Major institutional investors remain fully committed to the primary objective of delivering shareholder value, even if they now recognise that this end can better be served by maintaining high standards of ethical behaviour and corporate governance.

The modern shareholder value approach to corporate governance is that, while companies exist for the benefit of shareholders, the achievement of maximum investment returns requires effective governance and responsible engagement with interested parties. Governance is viewed as the servant of shareholder interests, and is highly valued as such. It does nothing to change the classic free market view that shareholder ownership rights are primarily private in their application. Accordingly, the company remains unequivocally the commercial agency for the exercise of private property rights. If there is any apparent restraint on the exercise of absolute ownership rights, for example through the requirement to behave ethically, this is a means to the ultimate end of serving the long-term interests of shareholders.

## Conclusions

Corporate governance poses a considerable challenge of definition. The list of relevant subjects and issues includes not only matters which have an obvious relevance to the governance of companies (the law affecting directors' duties and liabilities, the effective management of business risks, the role of NEDs, etc.), but also a host of other matters, including for example wider developments in company and financial services law, concerns about the efficacy of accounting standards and auditing practices, investor engagement issues and the impact of developments in non-UK jurisdictions. Given the accelerating speed with which developments are tending to emerge, it can be difficult to recall the rationale behind the numerous codes, guidelines and statutory requirements which together make up the corporate governance framework. This presents something of a challenge to directors and corporate governance professionals, called upon as they are not to follow blindly a rigid set of mandatory requirements, but rather to consider how broad principles can best be applied to the specific circumstances of their own organisation.

In such a changing environment, the main aims of the remainder of this publication are twofold: to provide the reader with a framework in which to understand the rules and practices that make up corporate governance in the UK (including a reminder of the rationale and background which brought that framework to its present shape), and secondly, to give practical guidance on the actual 'doing' of corporate governance by those who must deal with it and effectively implement it as part of their normal working lives. While primarily referencing guidance, legislation and codes that impact listed organisations, it is hoped that an insight into corporate governance best practice in the private sector will also be of use to those engaged in the governance of other types of organisation.

# 2

# The regulatory framework

## Accessing information on corporate governance

The volume of information relating to corporate governance is already vast and is likely to continue to grow. An internet search using 'corporate governance' as the key words can prove this point. This will highlight the interested organisations with considerable resources, such as government bodies, non-governmental organisations (NGOs), shareholder organisations and regulators of professional service providers, as well as less well-resourced commentators like academics and enthusiastic lobbyists for small interest groups. An additional challenge is the inconsistency of approach. While it has relevance across the economically developed world, there is no single gold standard for governance which has universal application. The standards of good governance are, for the most part, set out in guidance and policy documents that assume voluntary adherence by companies and other organisations. Such voluntarism is widely perceived to be meritorious, as it allows for flexibility both between and within jurisdictions. Conversely, a highly regulated approach has been perceived as a drag on enterprise and, ultimately, unworkable. However, given the focus on corporate governance reform, the prospect of corporate governance becoming more regulated in the future cannot be ruled out. The typical business, particularly one operating globally, is presently faced with a plethora of governance requirements.

### Gateways to governance information

As a result of the volume of information that is available, directors, company secretaries and other governance professionals face a challenge if they are to identify, when setting priorities, those aspects that are most relevant to their particular business and its markets. At its simplest, there are two gateways for accessing and understanding the information. These are (1) the *organisations* which seek to shape governance, and (2) *the rules or guidance* that they issue. Figure 2.1 illustrates the point.

For those who must apply corporate governance in practice, such as company secretaries and directors, it is important to hold this type of framework in mind. A helpful feature of this approach is that it draws out the

**Figure 2.1** Gateways to governance information

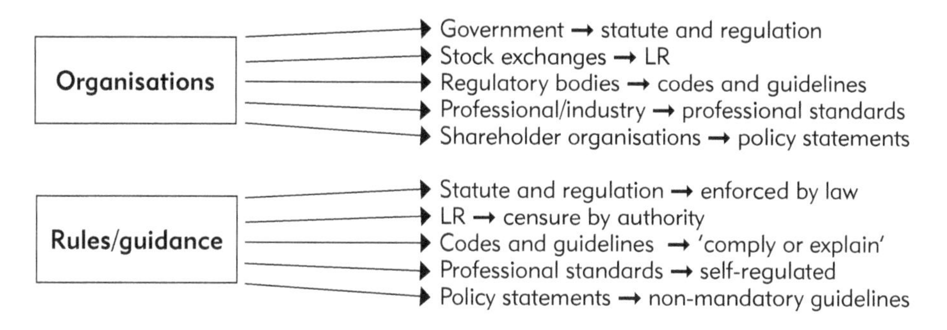


distinction between what is regulatory and therefore mandatory, and what is non-regulatory and therefore voluntary.

## The regulatory framework

The regulatory framework for companies is broadly composed of the following main parts:

- governance-related legislation and regulation;
- accounting standards and narrative reporting requirements; and
- corporate governance best practice codes.

Each of these elements is now examined.

### Governance-related legislation and regulation

In the UK there is no single coherent body of legislation that is expressly focused on corporate governance. That is not to say, however, that there are not both statutes and regulations which play a significant role in shaping UK governance. Reflecting the wide scope of corporate activities that are of relevance to the governance of companies, such legislation is diverse in both its origin and its impact. Table 2.1 contains a list of a number of the statutes which are commonly cited in the governance context, and provides a brief indication of their governance impact.

Additionally, there is a major body of legislation which imposes compliance requirements on the board, covering such areas as employment rights, health and safety, product liability, environmental risks and competition law. Although such legislation may not prescribe expressly the manner in which companies are to be governed, because the sanctions for non-compliance can be very significant, it will figure prominently in the board's efforts to maintain effective internal controls and risk management generally.

**Table 2.1** Corporate governance statutes

| Legislation | Governance impact |
|---|---|
| **CA 2006** | ■ maintenance of statutory books and records<br>■ filing returns at Companies House<br>■ preparation of annual report and accounts including narrative reporting<br>■ remuneration reporting<br>■ shareholder vote on remuneration policy<br>■ audit and auditor liability<br>■ directors' interests, duties and liabilities<br>■ shareholder communications, meetings and voting<br>■ share capital and capital maintenance<br>■ Takeover Panel |
| **Insolvency Act 1986 (IA 1986)** | ■ wrongful/fraudulent trading |
| **Company Directors Disqualification Act 1986 (CDDA 1986)** | ■ directors' misconduct<br>■ directors' unfitness |
| **Criminal Justice Act 1993** | ■ insider dealing |
| **Financial Services and Markets Act 2000 (FSMA 2000)** | ■ constitution and powers of the FCA<br>■ market manipulation<br>■ financial promotions<br>■ LR, Prospectus Rules (PR), DTR |
| **Market Abuse Regulation (596/2014) (MAR)** | ■ market abuse and insider dealing |
| **Bribery Act 2010** | ■ anti-corruption, both in the UK and overseas |
| **Public Interest Disclosure Act 1998** | ■ whistleblowing |
| **The Equality Act 2010 (Gender Pay Gap Information) Regulations 2017** | ■ gender pay reporting |

## Listed companies

### *The LR, PR and DTR*

The provisions of Part VI of the FSMA 2000 prescribe the FCA's regulatory functions as the 'competent authority' for the listing of securities in the UK.

The UK Listing Authority (UKLA) is the body through which the FCA exercises these functions and, in particular, it maintains the Official List. The regulatory objectives of the UKLA are focused around the need to maintain the competitiveness of the UK market in listed securities, and the desirability of facilitating competition in such securities and the confidence of investors generally.

The Rules and Guidance, referred to above, impose requirements on issuers, sponsors, directors and others in relation to the listing of securities on the LSE. They are designed to ensure that the LSE works fairly and efficiently for the benefit of shareholders, ensuring in particular that they enjoy generous and equal access to information. Listed companies must observe continuing obligations during the period their securities remain listed on the Official List. These include obligations with respect to major transactions, disclosure of financial information, directors' remuneration and shareholder circulars. All of these obligations have a significant governance application. The Rules also contain important requirements to be satisfied when a company's shares or other securities are to be admitted to the Official List, either on the occasion of its initial flotation or in connection with a subsequent new share issue.

***Alternative Investment Market (AIM) Rules***

The LSE established the AIM as a market designed primarily for smaller and growing companies, to which higher investment risks may be attached than is the case for larger and more established public companies. It is an exchange-regulated market, and as such is not subject to the same level of EU legislation as a regulated market. This status enables the AIM Rules to be less onerous than those for companies with a main market LSE listing. For example, there is no requirement for a company seeking admission to AIM to have a previous trading record, and the requirements for prior shareholder approval of transactions are very modest, being restricted to reverse takeovers, fundamental disposals or cancellation of listing.

However, the AIM Rules do contain important governance provisions relating to disclosures (rules 10 to 17), financial reporting (rules 18 and 19) and the requirement for a share-dealing policy for directors and applicable employees (rule 21), supplementing the provisions in the MAR, which are directly applicable.

Additionally, the key role given to an AIM company's 'nominated adviser' (Nomad) has important governance implications. A Nomad has significant obligations under the AIM Rules, the broad objectives of which are to secure compliance by the company, to guide its directors and to keep the LSE informed. The independence of the Nomad is a central and necessary part of the assurance given to investors who choose to invest in AIM. The importance of the Nomad is emphasised by the fact that an AIM-listed company which ceases to have a Nomad will have its securities suspended from trading.

In practice, when Nomads bring new companies to AIM, they will pay close attention to governance matters, often going beyond the strict requirements of the AIM Rules. Also, more established AIM companies will work with their Nomad to ensure that best governance practice is observed, taking into account the size and profile of their business. As an example, although AIM companies are not required to comply with the UK Corporate Governance Code, many will seek to achieve compliance to a greater or lesser degree, not least because in time they may want to move up to the Official List. The Quoted Companies Alliance representing smaller listed companies has published the 'Corporate Governance Code for Small and Mid-sized Quoted Companies 2013'. This useful publication identifies 12 essential guidelines which represent good practice and need to be considered. The objective of the guidelines is to apply key elements of the UK Corporate Governance Code in a way which is relevant to the needs of smaller quoted companies. The importance of directors doing what is right for their individual company is emphasised even if those actions appear contrary to best practice. Building up a relationship of trust between a company's directors and its shareholders is clearly relevant if shareholder support is to be relied upon by directors who opt to deviate in some circumstances from generally accepted best practice.

### *MAR*

MAR, which came into force in July 2016, applies to share dealings by directors and others discharging managerial responsibilities of both listed and AIM companies. This has replaced the Model Code Provisions in the LR and the AIM Rules now place an obligation on AIM companies to have in place an effective policy for share dealings by directors and other applicable employees (rule 21). A more detailed discussion of MAR is contained in Chapter 15.

### *The City Code on Takeovers and Mergers (the Takeover Code)*

The Takeovers and Mergers Panel (the Takeover Panel) is the body responsible for the contents of and compliance with the Takeover Code. Its statutory functions are established under the CA 2006. The Takeover Code is mainly concerned with regulating the conduct of parties involved in takeovers or mergers, ensuring that there is a 'level playing field' and that all shareholders in a public company subject to a takeover or merger are treated equally. It is based on six general principles, from which more detailed rules are derived.

The Takeover Panel expects both the spirit of the principles and detailed rules to be observed as well as their letter. Amongst other things, it lays down strict rules as to how companies, their directors and their advisers should conduct themselves prior to and following the announcement of a takeover, and it imposes restrictions on dealings by persons with unpublished price-sensitive information during an offer period. It also imposes requirements in respect of the contents of documentation prepared in connection with a takeover. It is worth noting that the remit of the Takeover Code means that it also applies to unlisted companies in some circumstances. The detail of the Takeover Code is discussed in greater detail in Chapter 15.

### Accounting standards and narrative reporting

The fundamental purpose of financial reporting was expressed by the Chief Executive of the FRC, at a conference on 7 November 2016, as being to:

> 'tell the story of your business, its position, performance and prospects. It should do so in a way that is fair, balanced and understandable. Those are the requirements of the regulations and the Corporate Governance Code'.

The governance ramifications are self-evident, and it is unsurprising that the relevant financial reporting and auditing practice standards attract immense scrutiny, both within and outside the accountancy and auditing professions. For example, all companies whose shares are listed on either the main LSE or AIM markets are required to report their results under specified IFRS. Convergence on IFRS reporting is intended to ensure consistency in reporting standards across different jurisdictions – an important corporate governance goal, particularly for listed entities. All companies must also include in their annual report and accounts certain narrative elements. Company auditors and the accounting profession generally have a significant role to play in the implementation of these governance developments.

#### *Narrative reporting*

As regards narrative reporting standards, these have been undergoing an extensive period of review in recent years in an effort to make such reporting clearer and more meaningful. There has been a plethora of consultations, guidance notes and regulations designed to improve the standard and clarity of reporting over recent years. For accounting periods ending after September 2013, companies have been required to produce a strategic report. In addition, companies must report on environmental issues, human rights and gender diversity as well as publish an annual tax strategy.

These developments and other issues of financial and narrative reporting, regulation and practice are discussed more fully in Chapter 8.

### Corporate governance best practice codes

While there is a vast body of legislation and mandatory requirements relevant to corporate governance, equally there are many voluntary standards devised by regulatory bodies and others with an interest in the development of corporate governance best practice. Although adoption of these standards may not be compulsory, the organisations to which they apply are increasingly judged and measured against them and failure to comply with these standards can attract criticism. Some of these are examined below.

## Listed companies

### *The UK Corporate Governance Code*

The UK Corporate Governance Code and associated guidance is the main source of governance best practice for UK premium-listed companies. Standard list companies are subject to less rigorous standards and the Code does not extend to AIM-listed companies although such companies may aspire to comply with the Code.

The Code has gone through a number of iterations but despite these many changes, the Code has remained loyal to its 'comply or explain' approach. The FRC's February 2012 report *What Constitutes an Explanation Under 'Comply or Explain'* provides some useful insight into this issue. When the Code was updated in 2014, the central changes related to the adoption of the going concern basis of accounting, company risk management, internal control systems, remuneration and shareholder engagement. In particular, the remuneration provisions emphasised how policies should be designed with the long-term success of the company in mind and enable the recovery or withholding of variable pay when appropriate. Minor changes, principally relating to audit committees' requirements, have been made to the Code in its latest edition which applies to companies with reporting periods beginning on or after 17 June 2016. The FRC has indicated that it expects to consult on possible further changes to the Code in 2017, following on from the Business, Energy and Industrial Strategy (BEIS) Select Committee Inquiry and the BEIS Green Paper on *Corporate Governance Reform*.

The Code's associated guidance comprises:

- FRC *Guidance on Risk Management, Internal Control and Related Financial and Business Reporting* (September 2014);
- FRC *Guidance on Audit Committees* (April 2016); and
- FRC *Guidance on Board Effectiveness* (March 2011).

The structure of the UK Corporate Governance Code is illustrated in Figure 2.2.

**Figure 2.2** UK Corporate Governance Code

**Code Principles**

| | |
|---|---|
| A. Leadership | A.1 The role of the board<br>A.2 Division of responsibilities<br>A.3 The chairman<br>A.4 NEDs |
| B. Effectiveness | B.1 The composition of the board<br>B.2 Appointments to the board<br>B.3 Commitment<br>B.4 Development<br>B.5 Information and support<br>B.6 Evaluation<br>B.7 Re-election |
| C. Accountability | C.1 Financial and business reporting<br>C.2 Risk management and internal control<br>C.3 Audit committee and auditors |
| D. Remuneration | D.1 The level and components of remuneration<br>D.2 Procedure |
| E. Relations with shareholders | E.1 Dialogue with shareholders<br>E.2 Constructive use of General Meetings |

**Code Schedules**

| | |
|---|---|
| Schedule A | The design of performance-related remuneration for executive directors |
| Schedule B | Disclosure of corporate governance arrangements |

**Associated Guidance**

| | |
|---|---|
| FRC *Guidance on Risk Management, Internal Control and Related Financial and Business Reporting* | Risk management, internal controls and reporting |
| FRC *Guidance on Audit Committees* | Audit committees |
| FRC *Guidance on Board Effectiveness* | Board leadership and effectiveness |

The UK Corporate Governance Code is, in effect, incorporated into the LR through the provisions of sub-paragraphs (5) and (6) of LR 9.8.6R. By this, the following items must be included in the annual report and accounts of each listed company:

- a narrative statement of how it has applied the main principles of the UK Corporate Governance Code, providing an explanation which enables its shareholders to evaluate how the principles have been applied; and
- a statement as to whether or not it has complied throughout the accounting period with the provisions set out in the Code, setting out provisions not complied with and giving reasons for any non-compliance and including, for requirements of a continuing nature or where such non-compliance has occurred for only part of an accounting period, a statement of the period of non-compliance.

LR 9.8.10 requires that the company must ensure that the parts of the corporate governance statement that relate to various provisions within Section C 'Accountability' of the Code are reviewed by the auditors before the annual report is published. While this falls short of a rigorous verification of compliance, it ensures an important level of auditor review. The UK Corporate Governance Code derives its authority from the 'comply or explain' principle, i.e. compliance is voluntary, but non-compliance must be disclosed and explained. A closer analysis of the statements required under each of the sub-paragraphs of LR 9.8.6 indicates that what is required is, in fact, rather complex. Figure 2.3 puts the key words in italic for emphasis.

**Figure 2.3** 'Comply or explain' principle

| | | | |
|---|---|---|---|
| Listing Rule 9.8.6(5) | How company has *applied* the *principles* of the UK Corporate Governance Code | ⇨ | Give *explanation* of how applied |
| Listing Rule 9.8.6(6) | *Whether or not* company has *complied* with the *provisions* of the UK Corporate Governance Code | ⇨ | Give *reasons* for non-compliance |

## The Stewardship Code

The Stewardship Code, first published in 2010, sets out good practice principles for institutional investors when engaging with UK listed companies. The Stewardship Code, which is discussed in more detail in Chapter 5, saw limited changes in 2012 in the form of movement towards greater clarification on how conflicts are managed and processes independently verified in companies. The FRC regularly monitors the application of the Stewardship Code and splits the signatories to it into different tiers, depending on their view of the standard of the signatories' reporting against the stewardship Code's Principles. The BEIS Green Paper on *Corporate Governance Reform* has identified possible ways to encourage shareholders to engage in the active stewardship of the companies they invest in and this may result in further revisions.

Since 2011, the FRC has published an annual report on developments in Corporate Governance and Stewardship.

## The non-regulatory framework

The non-regulatory framework for governance matters includes a diverse and influential network of best practice and policy guidelines published by an array of relevant interest groups.

### Relevant representative and other interest groups

Much of the practice of good corporate governance is about adopting appropriate behaviour, i.e. observing best practice, rather than simply meeting prescriptive rules. There are many influences upon behaviour, apart from the obvious need to be compliant with the regulatory requirements outlined in the previous section. These influences can be less formal, but they remain important to understanding current governance ideas and practice. Table 2.2 lists the principal sources.

**Table 2.2** Best practice and policy guidelines

| | |
|---|---|
| **Shareholder policy guidelines** | The IA, the Pensions and Lifetime Savings Association (previously the NAPF) (the PLSA) and the FRC through the UK Stewardship Code have published detailed statements of their requirements on a range of matters relating to the governance of investee companies. Individual institutional shareholders, including Hermes, Fidelity and Legal & General Investment Management, have published their own guidelines and several have powerful voices when it comes to corporate governance best practice. |
| **Survey results** | Consultancies routinely issue survey results comparing and benchmarking industry practice in areas such as executive pay, voting practices and board composition. Such surveys can have the effect of engineering, rather than simply recording, changes in practice. For example, surveys on executive pay and on voting practices are routinely quoted in support of a particular line on governance matters. |
| **NGOs and other interest groups** | Such groups can be quick to invoke governance principles to support the promotion of their causes. This is a natural corollary of the increasing prominence given to wider stakeholder interests. |

## Conclusion

The regulatory framework to which companies are subject is drawn from a number of diverse sources and consists of both mandatory requirements as well as more voluntary and flexible regimes. If they are to respond effectively to the range of expectations placed upon them for maintaining high standards of governance, boards and governance professionals must keep themselves up-to-date, give meaningful consideration to what is best for their own organisation within a constantly changing environment and be ready to explain their chosen approach in the context of their company's particular circumstances. The discussion contained in the remainder of this book is aimed at both explaining the requirements and their rationale and pointing those concerned with governance towards how strong corporate governance practice can be achieved in a way that is relevant and supportive of the company's business strategy.

## Governance checklist

✓ Does the board have sufficient understanding of the body of legislation, accounting and reporting standards and corporate governance codes of best practice that form the basis of the regulatory governance framework?

✓ Is there an awareness of the non-regulatory influences that are relevant to the organisation and is consideration given to how best to respond to them?

# Part 2

## The Board's Role and Directors' Responsibilities

# 3

# The board's structure and its committees

## The board's central governance role

It is almost universally the case now that corporate governance best practice codes expressly recognise the necessity for a successful organisation to be led by a strong and effective board. While the exact wording adopted may differ from one code to another, all essentially drive home this same point. A good example comes from the UK Corporate Governance Code Principle A.1, which describes in a succinct manner the board's place in the governance of the company, as follows:

> 'Every company should be headed by an effective board which is collectively responsible for the long-term success of the company.'

The UK Corporate Governance Code provides further explanation through its Supporting Principles which affirm that the role of a strong and effective board is to provide entrepreneurial leadership, to determine strategy and corporate objectives, to define the organisation's values and standards and to meet its obligations to its stakeholders – and to do all this within a framework of prudent and effective controls, which allow for risk to be assessed and managed.

Lawyers sometimes speak of the board as being the 'controlling mind' through which a company can express its legal personality. When the Code states that the company should be 'headed' by an effective board, the same linguistic concept is being employed. It might reasonably be objected that a company is an abstraction, not a person. Yet it is undeniable that it can have characteristics which lend themselves to this metaphor. For example, like any person, a company is capable of entering into complex contractual relationships, it can develop a powerful internal corporate culture and through the strength of its brand it can appear to have a character and existence independent of its abstract legal form. As the head of this corporate body, the board has vital governance responsibilities to control and lead it in an accountable and effective manner.

It is useful to examine at this stage company law which supports this view. Company law provides that the board of directors is responsible for directing the company and promoting its affairs, and has the power to bind the company in its dealings with third parties (art. 3 of Model Articles, and s. 40, Companies Act (CA) 2006). The articles of association, as approved by the shareholders, will normally provide that the board may exercise all the powers of the company, subject to any restrictions contained in its constitutional documents or directions contained in specific shareholder resolutions. The power to appoint (through re-election) and to remove directors is retained by the shareholders.

The law underpinning the structure of the board is developed further below. At this point, however, there are two main principles to be noted. First, the board's considerable powers derive from its position as the agent (through its directors) of the company, which in turn is the agency through which the shareholders exercise their ownership rights. The board will act under delegated powers as set out in the company's constitutional documents. There is a balance to be achieved here between, on the one hand, proper oversight of their assets by shareholders or other stakeholders and, on the other hand, a level of interference which curtails the efforts of boards to run the companies which have been entrusted to their care.

The second main principle to note is that the board is collectively responsible for its actions. All directors must take decisions objectively in the interests of the company, regardless of differing roles or status on the board. Again, there is a balance to be achieved. In an environment in which the roles of executive (management) and non-executive (supervisory) board members can appear to be diverging, there is a heightened need for effective corporate governance by a unified board. However, there are some inevitable strains as the distinctions in the roles become more marked, as identified in the following sections.

## The unitary board structure

While not all organisations will have both executive and non-executive members on their board, for listed companies and many other organisations which have appointed both it is vital to note that, under UK company law, no distinction is made between executives and NEDs. They share responsibility for directing the company and promoting its affairs within a unitary board structure. Accordingly, their duties as directors are identical, even if their roles may be fundamentally different.

The unitary nature of the board is supported by the rule that directors must act collectively when acting on behalf of the company, and not individually; see *Re Haycraft Gold Reduction and Mining Co* (1900) 2 Ch 230.

While the constitutional documents defining the board's purposes and powers, including in particular the articles of association, will usually appoint individual directors to the key executive posts and will allow the board to delegate its powers in defined circumstances, the default position is that the directors must act collectively, and are collectively responsible within a unitary structure.

The main perceived advantage of the unitary board is that the company (and ultimately the shareholders or other stakeholders) will benefit from a management environment in which those who have executive knowledge sit alongside and work with those who can bring their wider non-executive skills and experience to the board. The extent to which non-executives should become involved in the detailed management of the affairs of the company is a matter of some debate, particularly in view of the increasing awareness that they can be held equally accountable with the executive directors for breach of duties leading to corporate failure. See Chapters 4 and 13 for more discussion.

### Impact of heightened non-executive role

In recent years, governance initiatives have brought into sharper focus the distinction between the respective executive and non-executive roles, which has arguably posed a threat to the integrity of the unitary board. The supervisory role of non-executives is emphasised by the requirements for them to be wholly independent scrutineers of the audit process, to be responsible for setting and monitoring executive pay and performance, and to provide constructive challenge. This could perhaps lead to the perception of non-executive directors as somehow separated from the strategic oversight role of the board. However, the UK Corporate Governance Code stresses the need to ensure that collective responsibility is not undermined. Notwithstanding that NEDs are likely to devote substantially less time to the company's affairs than their executive colleagues, they are no less responsible for determination of strategy and other board matters than their executive colleagues. This point is made clear in Code Principle A.4 of the UK Corporate Governance Code which states 'as part of their role as members of a unitary board, NEDs should constructively challenge and help develop proposals on strategy'.

However, while the principle of joint responsibility is retained, it is entirely appropriate to acknowledge the distinct board status and difficulties potentially faced by non-executives, whose detailed knowledge of their company is likely to be less than those directors with executive responsibilities. In recognition of this potential for gaps in their knowledge compared to that of their executive colleagues, best practice is to ensure that non-executives receive appropriate induction when appointed and are encouraged to seek further clarification where necessary and to take their own independent legal or other professional advice at the company's expense as they see fit. The aim is clearly to remove, as far as possible, any barrier to non-executives playing a full and effective role that might otherwise result from any deficiency in their knowledge of their organisation's operations or environment.

NEDs can, of course, work effectively alongside executives, but the difference between the roles of the two and the emphasis on the scrutiny aspects of the non-executive role mean that it is necessary to be aware of the potential for tension. For example, the requirements that non-executives should meet at least annually as a group without the chairman or executives present and for committees consisting wholly of NEDs may be seen as dividing the unitary board.

### Responsibilities of the board

The board, as the company's governing body, is responsible for directing the organisation's affairs. As simple and self-explanatory as such a statement may at first appear, translating the theory into effective practice requires a fine balance to be achieved. Plainly it would be impractical for the board of a large and complex group to be involved with all the minutiae of running the business. In the preface to the UK Corporate Governance Code we are reminded that one of the key roles for the board is to establish the culture, values and ethics of the company and that it is important for the board to set the correct 'tone from the top' so as to ensure that good standards of behaviour permeate throughout all levels of the organisation. The challenge for boards is to maintain mutual respect and openness between all the directors, both executive and non-executive.

The UK Corporate Governance Code provides some guidance on how such a framework is expected to look. The starting point is that a board should 'meet sufficiently regularly to discharge its duties effectively'. How regularly that needs to be will clearly vary from one organisation to another. The framework also requires there to be absolute clarity over how the board, which has ultimate authority (subject to any restrictions in its articles of association or specific directions from its members) to manage the company, has delegated some of that authority to others in the organisation. The starting point for any such scheme of delegation is generally to determine which matters shall be retained by the board itself before deciding how other matters will then be delegated.

For this reason the UK Corporate Governance Code requires the board to establish 'a formal schedule of matters specifically reserved for its decision' (Code Provision A1.1). ICSA has provided helpful guidance on the matters which should be reserved to the board (available from www.icsa.org.uk). Other than those matters reserved to be decided by the board as a whole, other issues can be delegated either to board committees or to individual directors, managers or staff. Again corporate governance codes guide boards on what structure these delegations, in particular the delegation to the key committees, should take and these are examined below.

### Role of independent board committees

The prominence given to the role of independent board committees in the governance of companies is a tacit recognition that the unitary board must be flexible if it is to deal adequately with what is demanded of it. Best practice requires that the membership of the nomination, remuneration and audit committees is either entirely or majority non-executive. Members of such committees must be alive to the conflicts of interest which can exist within an otherwise united board. Yet, such committees remain committees of the full board and therefore do not have authority to act independently of it. Their separate existence derives from the independent characteristic of their membership, not their distinct constitutional status or powers.

To be effective, the unitary board relies on there being 'an appropriate balance of skills, experience, independence and knowledge' on the board so that no individual or small group of individuals can dominate the board's decision taking (Code Principle B.1). For most UK-listed companies (there is an exemption for smaller companies), the UK Corporate Governance Code Provision B.1.2 requires that at least half the board members, excluding the chairman, should be independent NEDs. According to the *Walker Review*, the optimum size for a sub-committee is between five and nine members. 'At five a group becomes more of a team, at seven thinking is optimised; above nine the ability of the cognitive limit of the group is exceeded.'

The demands placed on the non-executives to populate and operate the various board committees inevitably pose questions about the size of the board. So while the need to maintain balance within the unitary board is universally accepted, the prescriptive nature of the rules about the level of non-executive representation on listed company boards may have given rise to some unintended outcomes.

First, in recent years the number of executive directors on the board has often decreased in order to maintain the minimum 50% proportion of independent NEDs required by the UK Corporate Governance Code. A large board can be unwieldly and more difficult to manage and the Supporting Principles to UK Corporate Governance Code (Principle B.1) recognise that a board 'should be of sufficient size that the requirements of the business can be met' with 'an appropriate combination of executive and non-executive directors'. Having a strong executive representation on the board is encouraged. In the UK, executive representation now typically comprises only the chief executive and finance director. Reducing management team representation at board meetings could, it is argued, place too much influence in the hands of just one or two executive directors, isolate the board from the day-to-day reality of the company's business and detract from the board's ability to understand the company's affairs. To ensure that the board remains fully informed about the operational side of the company's business, the setting up of 'executive committees' comprising senior management who regularly report back to the board has become more common.

The UK Corporate Governance Code and other standards of good governance impose a system of checks and balances, treating the board as a governing body that is constrained by constitutional rules. For the unitary board to meet such governance standards, while at the same time being capable of providing entrepreneurial leadership, its directors must be engaged at every level. In recognition of this, UK Corporate Governance Code Provisions A.1.1 and A.1.2 require information about the various meetings of the board and its committees and also how the board operates to be set out in the annual report and accounts. The policy intention behind this requirement is to assist shareholders to judge the effectiveness of the leadership provided by the board.

Figure 3.1 offers a simple illustration of the various components of the unitary structure.

**Figure 3.1** Unitary board structure

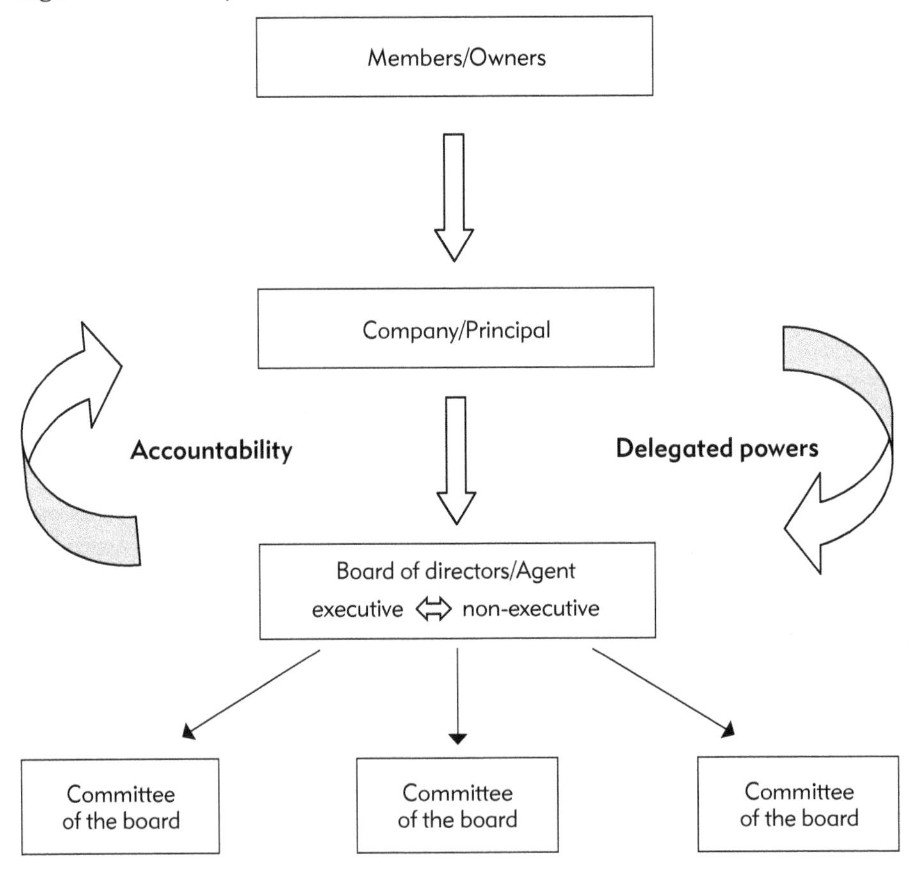

## The dual board structure

In contrast to the UK's unitary board approach, a dual board structure for the governance of companies exists in several continental European jurisdictions, where there is a separation of the functions of management and supervision. Under this dual system, these distinct tasks are allocated to separate boards – a management board and a supervisory board.

While the dual board structure sits well with the important governance principle that management and the supervision of management should be separate, critics suggest that the supervisory board, being a distinct body with its own separate agenda and reporting structures, is too far removed from the decision-making process and runs the risk of being insufficiently aware of both the substance and the details of management strategy. A dual board structure does not offer the same opportunities as are available to the non-executive directors of a unitary board for direct discussion with and challenge of the executive management. While this may be true, the management (as opposed to supervisory) boards in jurisdictions where the dual structure has been adopted tend to grant less power to the chief executive, preferring instead to operate on a more consensual basis. As is often the case in governance matters, cultural aspects, rather than theoretical debates about the most effective board structures, tend to shape the outcome.

A common feature of supervisory boards is that they can, and sometimes must, include employee representatives. These are typically drawn from unions, local community interest groups or shareholder groups. The dual structure lends itself more easily to such external representation, because members of the supervisory board receive less exposure to the details of executive management, with which they may have only limited experience.

As with many things, there is no right or wrong answer and it can be appropriate to draw upon different elements of different models in order to discover the best solution for a specific set of circumstances. For example, a dual board-type structure has been adopted in some parts of the UK public sector, for example by NHS Foundation Trusts, where the board answers directly to the governors of the trust who will include representatives of the local community. Similarly, some entities can find it useful to establish an additional advisory board to carry out a supervisory role and provide additional expertise albeit without the authority or powers of the main board. In particular, the *IoD Corporate Governance Guidance and Principles for Unlisted Companies in the UK* suggests this as a potentially beneficial interim option for smaller companies as they grow and develop into the size and type of company which would warrant the appointment of a higher proportion of independent non-executive directors.

## Board committees

### Types of committee

Companies seeking to comply with the UK Corporate Governance Code and those which aspire to list have significant outside investment or are large and/or complex businesses should have an audit committee, a remuneration committee and a nominations committee, each of which has a clear corporate governance objective and role. Tackling some of the most sensitive areas for the board, such as executive pay and the conduct of the audit, they are required to meet independently of the main board, while remaining ultimately accountable to it. Their terms of reference are now well established, as discussed below. Strong committees derive from the quality of their members, including in particular their independence of mind, rather than compliance with any rulebook or formula.

In addition to the committees identified above, universally required by all companies subject to the UK Corporate Governance Code, the *Walker Review* recommended that all banks and life assurance companies establish a risk committee with responsibility 'for oversight and advice to the board on the current risk exposures to the entity and future risk strategy'.

While the setting up of risk committees related specifically to companies in the financial services sector, such committees have become more common, particularly for companies operating in a regulated environment.

Supplementing these generic or sector-specific committees are what might be termed 'special purpose' board committees, which are routinely constituted to address particular projects or functions that are not easily managed by the whole board. Some of these will again have a clear corporate governance role (e.g. a social responsibility or ethics committee), whereas others will not (e.g. a marketing or acquisitions committee). Establishing such committees brings benefits to the board, which would otherwise find its agenda overwhelmed by numerous discrete projects and other incidental matters, deflecting it from its key strategic tasks.

UK Corporate Governance Code Provision A.1.2 requires that the identities of chairmen and members of committees of the board should be stated in the annual report, together with the number of meetings and the record of attendance of individual directors. In order to facilitate this, the company secretary should ensure that adequate records are maintained during the year.

#### *Constitution and terms of reference*

In each case, the basis of delegation from the main board should be clearly defined. As in art. 5 of the Model Articles, the company's articles of association should contain a power to delegate and establish committees. When appointing a committee, the directors should set any conditions of the delegation and establish terms of reference in writing for the committee. Procedures for giving notice of committee meetings, managing business at such meetings and keeping minutes should be as for the main board.

Boards should be careful to constitute committees in accordance with the requirements set out in the company's articles of association, as failure to do so may call into question the validity of decisions made by the committee. It is also a mark of good governance. The board is responsible for directing the company and accordingly it should ensure that those acting on its behalf do so in a manner which is defined by, and accountable to, the board. A board that fails to do so is potentially open to criticism.

It is important to emphasise that all committees appointed by the board are accountable to it, including those whose membership must exclude executive directors, to avoid conflicts of interest. For example, while the remuneration committee will formulate proposals on executive pay and benefits, it is still the responsibility of the main board to approve such proposals, subject to interested executive directors playing no part in decisions about their own remuneration. Therefore, while the committee may be independent of the executive management, it is not independent of the board itself.

Just as the committee will remain accountable to the board, so the board will remain accountable for the exercise of any powers or functions by the committee. The act of delegation by the board does not absolve the board of responsibility. For example, if the board establishes a committee to deal with the company's environmental performance, the board cannot simply wash its hands of its responsibilities in that regard, nor will it escape liability for breach of directors' duties that may arise in the event of non-compliance. In terms of internal control procedures, the board should ensure that any committee delegations are to appropriate persons, are proportionate in scope and are actively monitored with the committee reporting back on a regular basis to the full board. Where necessary, the board should revoke a delegation, which it can do at any time by the passing of a board resolution.

Regarding the remuneration of members of board committees, common practice is that each company should consider the additional amount that should be paid to non-executives sitting on committees to recompense them for the extra responsibilities of membership. For example, in view of its importance to the governance of the company, membership of the audit committee can attract a significant additional fee, with an added premium for being chairman. The *Walker Review* identified the time commitment expected of NEDs as a factor in some of the banking sector failures and recommended that for major banks, the time commitment should be increased to a minimum of 30–36 days a year. Moves towards increasing the time commitment expected of NEDs will inevitably be reflected in their fees. However, it should not be necessary to pay additional remuneration to executive members, as attendance at board committees will be required of them in the ordinary course of their director duties for which they will be remunerated under their service agreements.

## The audit committee

Reviews into the causes of corporate failures have often focused on the inadequacies of the company's audit committee on the basis that it failed to act independently and in the interests of shareholders to ensure the integrity of the financial statements. Most recently, failures in the banking sector have again shifted the audit committee centre stage. Capital markets cannot function properly if investor confidence in the financial information flowing from investee companies is undermined, but maintaining trust in such information is equally an important issue for all types of organisations. Shareholders, other stakeholders and legislators alike therefore take a particular interest in the effectiveness of the audit committee.

The role of the audit committee is to assist the board in fulfilling its oversight responsibilities by monitoring the integrity of the company's financial statements and other information made available to shareholders, as well as the company's internal controls and risk management systems. The UK Corporate Governance Code introduced a new provision in 2016 recommending that the audit committee as a whole should have competence relevant to the sector in which the company operates and that at least one member has recent and relevant financial experience. This is particularly pertinent to banks and other companies in the financial services sector. The FRC *Guidance on Audit Committees* (updated in 2016) examines the relationship between the audit committee and the board. It states that the audit committee should consider key matters of their own initiative and that it must intervene if there are signs that something may be seriously amiss. Should there be disagreement between the audit committee and the board which cannot be resolved, it is recommended that the audit committee should have the right to report the issue to shareholders in the report of its activities in the annual report.

Perhaps uniquely, the audit committee may be required to challenge a position adopted not only by the executive directors, but also by the company's professional advisers in the form of the external auditors.

A detailed review of the role and responsibilities of the audit committee and the manner in which it should discharge its functions is set out in Chapter 7.

## The remuneration committee

With increased public scrutiny of executive remuneration in recent years, the remuneration committee must carry out its functions in the full knowledge that its principal decisions will enter the public domain.

Since 2013, quoted companies have had to put their remuneration policy to a binding vote by shareholders at least every three years and have had to provide more extensive disclosures relating to directors' remuneration. The UK Corporate Governance Code also has detailed provisions on the level and components of remuneration (Section D). Additionally, guidelines are produced by institutional investor bodies and by individual institutional investors, which the remuneration committee must be mindful of.

Despite these principles and guidance, concerns continue to be raised on executive pay and this is a key element on which BEIS consulted following the publication of its Green Paper on *Corporate Governance Reform* in November 2016.

While fully accountable to the board, there is potential for conflicts of interest to arise when board members address executive remuneration and service contract issues. The remuneration committee will be required to exercise judgements which require sensitivity both to the expectations of executives and also to the interests and concerns of shareholders and other stakeholders.

A detailed review of the role and responsibilities of the remuneration committee and the manner in which it should discharge its functions is set out in Chapter 12.

## The nomination committee

It is a requirement of the UK Corporate Governance Code that all listed companies have a nomination committee consisting of a majority of independent directors, chaired by the chairman of the main board or another independent NED (Code Provision B.2.1). Its terms of reference will extend far more widely than setting the contractual terms of new director appointments. In Sir Derek Higgs' memorable phrase, it is at the forefront of promoting a 'meritocracy in the boardroom'. When discharging its responsibilities, the committee must evaluate the balance of skills, experience, independence and knowledge on the board, and prepare a description of the role and capabilities required for a particular appointment (Code Provision B.2.2). The emphasis is on establishing board recruitment processes which are based on merit, set against objective criteria and have regard to the benefits of diversity, including gender.

The Davies Review on improving the gender balance on boards launched in Autumn 2010 challenged FTSE listed companies to increase female representation on boards to 25%. Significant progress has been made, albeit principally in relation to the number of female NEDs, with the FTSE 350 overall percentage standing at 23% (2016). Building on this success, the Hampton-Alexander Review, published in November 2016, wishes to see the representation of women on boards of FTSE 350 companies increase to

33% by 2020 and proposes that action should be taken to improve the under-representation of women on executive committees and in senior management who report directly to those committees.

Board succession planning is also within the remit of the nomination committee (Supporting Principle to Code Principle B.2). This aspect of the committee's role will involve assessing the challenges and opportunities which the company faces and the preparation of a forward-looking plan to ensure that future membership of the board is aligned to company strategy, both current and future (FRC, Press Release, May 2016). This will require of the committee a notably strategic perspective on the company's future development.

A detailed review of the role and responsibilities of the nomination committee and the manner in which it must discharge its functions is set out in Chapter 9.

## The disclosure committee

A number of listed companies have put in place a further committee, commonly known as the Disclosure Committee. Previously such committees have been most prevalent amongst the larger FTSE 250 listed companies. With the advent of the new MAR (see Chapter 15 for further details) and the additional regulatory and administrative requirements this introduced, it is likely that the setting up of a disclosure committee may now be relevant to any listed company, regardless of size.

The primary role of such committees is to identify whether specific information is inside information and overseeing the treatment and disclosure of any such inside information by the company to meet its obligations under MAR and the relevant market rules. By its nature the committee may need to meet on short notice and on an ad hoc basis. Typically membership of the committee will include the CEO and finance director and may also include the company secretary, general counsel or head of investor relations. Given the need to make quick decisions, the quorum may be set at a minimum of any two members, at least one of whom would include one of the senior executive directors.

The committee's remit would typically also cover the maintenance of insider lists, deciding whether and when any announcement obligations arise and, if so, whether it may be permissible to delay an announcement as well as implementing adequate procedures, systems and controls to ensure continuing compliance with disclosure obligations.

## The risk committee

Banks and other financial institutions have had to have separate risk committees following the *Walker Review*. Following that Review, the FRC concluded that the establishment of a separate risk committee was not necessarily appropriate for all non-financial companies.

The UK Corporate Governance Code does not require a listed company to have a separate risk committee. Instead, the audit committee's role includes reviewing the company's internal financial controls and, unless expressly addressed by a separate board risk committee made up of independent directors, or by the board itself, reviewing the company's internal control and risk management systems.

Whether it is a separate risk committee or a joint audit and risk committee, that committee will have responsibility for monitoring the strategic, operational, financial and other risks to the business and to develop a strategic framework for risk management.

## Other board committees

There are no legal restrictions on the number of committees which the board can establish. The complexity of the business and the size of the board will be determining factors, as will the culture of the company.

Apart from the audit, remuneration and nomination committees, Table 3.1 provides a list of some of the additional committees that are established, sometimes on an ad hoc basis, by UK companies. Committees, such as the executive/operating committee, will comprise senior management and will be obliged to report back to the board on a regular basis.

**Table 3.1** Additional committees

| Committee | Summary terms of reference |
| --- | --- |
| **Acquisitions/ disposals** | To identify and assess potential acquisitions/disposals, to bring to the board recommendations and to progress the board's decisions in particular cases. |
| **Ethics** | To develop and draft the board's ethics policy, to support integrity, transparency and accountability and to adjudicate on matters covered by that policy as necessary. |
| **Executive/ operating** | To develop group strategy and budget, run the day-to-day operations, approve projects within capital expenditure limits and appraise senior management performance. |
| **Marketing** | To develop the marketing strategy in alignment with the overall business strategy, and to manage the marketing expenditure within set limits. |
| **Personnel/HR** | To formulate group policies on terms and conditions of employment, manage the staff training programme, design and implement staff appraisals and conduct salary reviews. |

**Table 3.1** *continued*

| Committee | Summary terms of reference |
|---|---|
| **Social and environmental** | To undertake an assessment of social and environmental risk, secure environmental impact improvements and develop the external CSR programme. |
| **Treasury** | To be responsible for implementing treasury management transactions within specified policies and exposure limits. |

## Conclusion

This chapter has highlighted the unitary nature of the UK board and the collective responsibility that directors bear for the strategy and governance of their company. Yet the board remains a collection of individuals and for the board to function at the required standard, those individuals will need to display an understanding of their duties and powers and be effective in their various roles. The following chapters pick up on the key themes relating to individual positions on the board, as follows:

- Chapter 4, the law relating to directors' duties and liabilities;
- Chapter 11, the role of the chairman;
- Chapter 12, the role of executive directors;
- Chapter 13, the role of NEDs;
- Chapter 14, the role of the company secretary.

## Governance checklist

✓ Does the board operate as the controlling head of the company, providing 'entrepreneurial leadership within a framework of prudent and effective controls'?

✓ Where there are both executive and NEDs, do they co-exist constructively within a unitary board structure or do they divide along 'us and them' lines?

✓ Are board committees properly constituted under delegated powers from the board and does the board operate effective oversight of such committees?

✓ Are the key board committees (audit, remuneration and nominations) constituted in a manner proportionate to the needs of the business, independent not only in form but also in substance and compliant with relevant corporate governance best practice?

✓ Does the company make appropriate and transparent disclosures about the board's governance practices, its membership, functions, activities and committees?

# 4

# Directors' duties and liabilities

## Directors' duties and corporate governance

It is beyond the scope of this book to provide a comprehensive narrative on directors' duties in law. Yet it is important to recognise that such duties provide the essential legal context within which directors must operate when governing their companies. The starting point is an appreciation of the wide scope of directors' powers.

### Background to directors' authority, powers and duties

Under the terms of its articles of association, the management of a company's business and assets is invariably placed in the hands of the board of directors. Acting as agents on behalf of the company, the directors will be able to exercise the considerable powers that are granted to them so as to bind the company and to deal with third parties on the company's behalf. Under the law of agency, the directors will be acting either with 'actual' authority, or with 'apparent' or 'ostensible' authority. In the latter case, even where the directors do not possess actual authority, they may be able to bind the company on the basis that it has represented to the world at large that they have the authority to act on its behalf. The CA 2006 (s. 40) provides a statutory third-party protection in favour of a person dealing with a company in good faith by providing that the power of the directors to bind the company is deemed to be free from any limitation under the company's articles.

Directors' duties act as a restraint on the abusive use of their powers, thus protecting the position of the company and its shareholders as well as other stakeholders such as the employees or creditors. Those duties originate from two sources. First, under the common law rules of equity, directors must observe onerous obligations, namely a duty to exhibit good faith, loyalty, skill and care in dealings with their companies. Secondly, duties are imposed under statute. As well as the requirements of the CA 2006 and IA 1986, there is an array of statutory duties imposing often onerous obligations on directors in such areas as health and safety, environmental hazards, product liability and competition laws. For the listed company director, there is also an additional layer of duties imposed by the regulators of capital markets, including, in particular, duties arising under the LR or AIM Rules, the PR, DTR and the Takeover Code.

Against that background, it is not surprising that the law as it applied to directors' liabilities for breach of duty was the subject of review in recent years, with commentators suggesting that the potential personal liabilities faced by directors might discourage the holding of office, particularly at a time of increasing levels of public scrutiny and litigation. The position of directors in terms of their company's ability to indemnify them was improved by the Companies (Audit, Investigations & Community Enterprise) Act 2004 and the provisions of that legislation relating to directors' indemnification were incorporated in largely unchanged form into the CA 2006.

Starting with an overview of directors' duties, including those duties which specifically apply to directors of UK listed companies, this chapter reviews the current position on directors' liabilities and includes a section on directors and officers (D&O) insurance.

## Directors' common law duties

The common law duties of directors derived from the relevant case law authorities were widely agreed to be opaque and similar duties have now been codified in the statutory directors' duties set out in the CA 2006. However, the earlier case law remains relevant to the interpretation of the codified duties and is therefore reviewed briefly below. Note that the duties of directors, both common law and statutory, are owed to the company, not the shareholders. Accordingly, it will normally be the company which must enforce the duties and not the shareholders either as a class or individually.

### Fiduciary duties

According to these, a director must act in good faith and in what he or she considers to be the best interests of the company, which will normally equate to those of the shareholders. A director should exercise their powers for the purposes for which they were conferred and must avoid any circumstance where their duties to the company are in conflict with their own personal interests. A director must take proper care of the assets of the company and must account to the company for any unauthorised gains made out of their position. They have a duty to consider how a transaction might impact on differing categories of shareholders and must not act with the purpose of discriminating against a group of shareholders.

In summary, a director is in the position of a fiduciary and should be aware that they owe trustee-like obligations to the company (see *Regal (Hastings) Limited v. Gulliver* [1942] 1 All ER 378). In governance terms, the ramifications are significant. Many governance best practice standards can be met if the director consistently satisfies the general fiduciary duties they owe to the company. Equally, a breach of such duties will cause a lapse in good governance. Table 4.1 uses some hypothetical examples to provide practical illustrations from the governance perspective.

**Table 4.1** Corporate governance – practical illustrations

| Fiduciary duty | Governance illustration of breach |
|---|---|
| **To act in good faith in the company's interests** | A director, whose appointment has been secured by a major shareholder, promotes its interests over those of other shareholders. |
| **To use powers only for a proper purpose** | A director works to block the progress of an otherwise meritorious takeover bid because, if successful, it would threaten their job security. |
| **To avoid using powers to benefit themself** | A director is paid a special success fee on achievement of a major transaction without its payment being approved according to the company's articles. |
| **To avoid a personal conflict of interest** | A director takes up a non-executive directorship with a competitor company and uses information they obtain as a director of one company to the detriment of the other. |
| **To provide accurate and timely information** | A finance director delays the disclosure of some key trading information to the board, as a result of which decisions on future strategy are flawed. |

### *Duty of skill and care*

According to the classic formulation, a director must observe the conduct of a reasonably diligent person having both the general knowledge, skill and experience that may reasonably be expected of a person carrying out the same functions as are carried out by that director in relation to the company as well as the general knowledge, skill and experience that the director actually has – see *Re City Equitable Fire Insurance Co* [1925] 1 Ch 407 and *Re D'Jan of London Ltd* (1993) BCC 646.

This standard, which mirrors the tests laid down in s. 214 of the IA 1986, does not require the director to have special skills or attributes according to an objective standard, but should not be interpreted as a purely subjective duty (where the standard to be applied is relative only to the personal skills and attributes that the director possesses). The overall effect is that a director is required to meet the higher of the objective and subjective standards. It follows that an individual should be cautious about taking up a directorship for which they are not properly qualified or experienced.

### *Standard of skill and care – executive directors*

In practice, the standard of skill and care required of the employed executive director will be defined specifically by his or her contract of employment. This will typically be drafted to take into account the detailed requirements of their job and will also contain a more general and objective 'due skill and care' requirement. Even where the contract does not contain such provisions, a contractual duty of reasonable skill and care can be implied in the contract. For example, it would be expected that a finance director would be appropriately qualified and experienced in accounting matters.

### *Standard of skill and care – NEDs*

For NEDs, who will not normally be subject to the more onerous contractual duties that will apply to executive directors, the common law duties remain relevant. As noted above, these require that all directors must satisfy a test which has both an objective and a subjective element. This raises difficult issues for the NED, particularly so for the generalist non-executive on the board of a company with a highly complex business, such as in the insurance or financial services sectors. They might not possess specialist skills relating to the company's business, and yet owe a duty of skill and care that will be measured according to an objective standard.

For all NEDs there will be a need to rely on the information provided by – and the opinions of – the executive team. This is particularly true of those who sit on the boards of complex businesses. Unless they have reason to doubt the integrity, skill or capability of the executives and provided they exercise reasonable and independent judgement, they can place such reliance on the executives. The duty of care does not infer a requirement to oversee the detailed day-to-day activities of the company, or to exercise close supervision of the executive directors. Non-executives should be aware, however, that in the event of a corporate failure for which the executives are held culpable, the diligence of their supervision of the executives is likely to be very carefully scrutinised (*Dorchester Finance Co Ltd and Another v. Stebbing and Others* [1989] BCLC 498).

A key consideration will be the level of attention that NEDs must give to their duties (note that they are unlikely to be subject to the more onerous contractual duties that will apply to executive directors). While there is a line of older authorities to the effect that a director does not need to give continuous attention to the company's business, they would now be expected not only to attend the key board and committee meetings, but also to understand the business, read the relevant board papers, be familiar with the company's financial statements and generally keep abreast of matters of relevance to their position on the board. This is abundantly evident from the heightened awareness of the non-executive role following the *Higgs Report*, the commentary on the effectiveness of the NEDs in restraining the risks taken by banks in the lead-up to the banking crisis of 2008/9 and the need for them to commit adequate time to their role, and the consequential changes to the UK Corporate Governance Code.

## Directors' statutory duties

The CA 2006 (ss. 171–177) codifies seven general duties owed by a director to the company in which they hold office. Each of these seven general duties is examined in the following paragraphs.

As these are duties owed to the company, only the company itself can bring an action against the director for any breach of duties. However, a process by which members can make derivative claims is set out in the Act. At the time of the introduction of this process, much concern was expressed that a flurry of litigation against directors for breach of duty would be caused. So far, this has not materialised, but the existence of the derivative claim mechanism will remain as an additional weapon in the shareholder activist armoury.

### Duty to act within powers (s. 171)

A company's members, by resolution or through the company's articles of association, may place restrictions on the objects of the company and the powers of the directors to manage the company. This statutory duty imposes an obligation on a director both to abide by any such restrictions and to exercise such powers as they possess for a proper purpose.

For a director to be sure they are complying with this duty, it is necessary for them to have a good knowledge and understanding of the company's constitution and to consider, in the light of that knowledge and understanding, if the powers they propose to exercise are consistent with the terms of the constitutional documents. Secondly, the director must be satisfied that they are exercising those powers for a proper purpose; in other words, in the interests of the company.

### Duty to promote the success of the company (s. 172)

This section sets out six factors which a director should 'have regard to' in considering whether or not a particular decision or course of action is likely to 'promote the success of the company for the benefit of its members as a whole'. These factors are:

1. the likely consequences of any decision in the long term;
2. the interests of the company's employees;
3. the need to foster the company's business relationships with suppliers, customers and others;
4. the impact of the company's operations on the community and the environment;

5. the desirability of the company maintaining a reputation for high standards of business conduct;
6. the need to act fairly between members of the company.

This list is not exhaustive – the legislation makes that clear – and directors may wish to consider other factors. Conversely, not all of the above factors may be relevant to the decision in hand.

The practicalities for directors obliged to comply with the duty to have regard to these factors is addressed by the GC100 in its guidance on directors' duties. In summary, the GC100 guidance, while not wishing to add unnecessary layers of bureaucracy or formality to existing procedures, recommended that:

- directors ensure they are aware of their duties;
- briefing papers or presentations for formal board and committee meetings address the relevant factors;
- minutes should not be used as the main medium for recording the extent to which the relevant factors were discussed; and
- lack of formal process (for example, where a decision is taken by an individual director under a scheme of delegation) should not lead to any inference that the factors were not considered.

In considering the relevant factors, directors should keep in mind the overarching need for a decision to be likely to promote the success of the company for the benefit of its members as a whole. The meanings of 'success' and 'benefit' in this context are open to debate and will certainly mean different things to different companies. For example, a commercial company is likely to measure success, at least in part, in terms of its profitability, whereas the success of a charitable company is more likely to be measured by reference to the extent to which it achieves its charitable objects.

### Duty to exercise independent judgement (s. 173)

Directors frequently take decisions having first received briefings and advice from both internal and external sources. Failure to obtain such briefings and advice in the first place could in fact constitute a breach of duty. However, the existence of such advice or briefings does not absolve a director from the responsibility to reach their own conclusion in relation to the matter at hand. It is not sufficient for directors to blindly follow the recommendations made to them – they are required to exercise their own judgement. Moreover a director is required to ensure that their judgement is independent. A director's judgement should not be clouded by personal considerations, for example.

### Duty to exercise reasonable care, skill and diligence (s. 174)

This statutory duty is defined by both objective and subjective tests. The objective test sets the minimum standard, being the level of 'general knowledge, skill and experience that may reasonably be expected of a person carrying out the functions carried out by the director in relation to the company', while the subjective test measures the skill, care and diligence exercised by the director against 'the general knowledge, skill and experience that the director has'. The effect of this two-pronged measure is to compare the care, skill and diligence exercised by a director not only to the care, skill and diligence which one might generally expect someone in a director's role to employ, but also to the care, skill and diligence which one might expect someone with their background and expertise to exercise.

- First, a director must be satisfied that they possess the knowledge or expertise to enable them to meet the standards of general knowledge, skill and experience which one might reasonably expect someone in their position to possess. These standards will differ depending on the type of company and the sector in which it operates, as well as the specific nature of the director's role.
- Secondly, a director must be satisfied that the care, skill and diligence they exercise is reflective of their own knowledge, skill and experience. For example, a director with an accounting or legal qualification would be measured against the standards which might be reasonably expected of someone with those qualifications.

### Duty to avoid conflicts of interest including conflicts of duties (s. 175)

There are numerous situations in which a director may find they have a conflict of interest or conflict of duties. They could, for example, be a director of two companies which it is proposed may enter into a transaction or which are competitors. This statutory duty requires directors to avoid such situations, whether the interest in question is direct or indirect, real or potential. Conflicts which involve the exploitation of property, information or opportunity (regardless of whether the company could take advantage of the property, information or opportunity) are identified in the legislation as being particularly relevant to this duty. However, this statutory duty is not infringed if the situation in question is not likely to give rise to a conflict of interest or if the matter has been authorised by the directors.

The ability of the directors to authorise conflicts of interest is an important tool facilitating the practical governance of a company, but in order to be able to take advantage of this tool, the company's articles must, in the case of a public or charitable company, enable the directors to authorise the matter. It is also important to note that the authorisation must be given in advance and that the director whose conflict, or potential conflict, is the subject of the authorisation cannot form part of the quorum or vote upon the authorisation. The GC100 has issued a number of worthwhile papers on the issue of directors' conflicts of interest and the process for authorising them.

### Duty not to accept benefits from third parties (s. 176)

This duty obliges a director to refuse any benefit from a third party which has been granted by reason of them doing (or not doing) anything as a director. Any benefit which, if accepted, could not reasonably be regarded as likely to give rise to a conflict of interest is exempted from the duty. Therefore, acceptance of a trivial benefit is unlikely to be prohibited on the grounds that it is not likely to create a conflict of interest. It would be prudent for a company to have guidance in place for its directors on what benefits may or may not be accepted, as well as a procedure for the approval of benefits where the director is in any doubt as to how the acceptance of the benefit might reasonably be viewed.

### Duty to declare interest in a transaction or arrangement (ss. 177 and 182)

A director with any direct or indirect interest in a transaction or arrangement which the company in which they hold office is proposing to enter into, or has already entered into, is required to declare the nature and extent of that interest to the other directors. The declaration may be made either at a meeting or in writing and can take the form of a general notice that they have an interest in a given entity or are connected with a specified person. The declaration must be kept up-to-date by the director as the nature or extent of their interest changes from time to time and must be made before a proposed transaction or arrangement is entered into (s. 177) or, in the case of an existing transaction or arrangement (s. 182), as soon as is reasonably practicable.

Although an exception is made in both sections for interests, transactions or arrangements of which the director is not aware, these exceptions do not apply if the director ought reasonably to have been aware of the interest, transaction or arrangement. Therefore, a director needs to take steps both to keep informed of transactions and arrangements to which their company is party and of the changing nature and extent of their own personal interests and to ensure that they make the relevant declarations in a timely fashion. The legislation also sets out various exemptions from the declaration requirements insofar as they relate to interests which could not reasonably be regarded as giving rise to a conflict, interests which the other directors are already aware of (or ought reasonably to be aware of) or the terms of a director's service contract which have been or are to be considered by a meeting of the directors or board committee appointed for that purpose.

## Other statutory duties: CA 2006

Many of the duties imposed by the CA 2006 relate to administrative matters, including in particular the filing of forms and returns with the Registrar of Companies, completing registers in relation to the company's members, directors, and the maintenance of proper accounting records and so on. Typically, the task of ensuring compliance with such duties will be delegated to the company secretary and the finance department. While such compliance is generally taken for granted, the information about the company and its activities that is thereby put into the public domain is very relevant to the governance process.

Table 4.2 sets out a summary of the more significant CA 2006 specific duties to be observed by directors.

**Table 4.2** CA 2006 corporate governance duties

| Summary of CA 2006 duties | Governance impact |
|---|---|
| **To maintain the company's statutory books and records, including the various registers, and make timely filings at Companies House.** | This provides an essential source of public information on the company and is the starting point for any review of the constitution, group structure, share capital, board of directors and shareholders. |
| **To keep accounting records, prepare the annual statutory accounts and the directors' report and lay them before the shareholders in general meeting (public companies only).** | The annual report and accounts are a key source of information on governance practice and compliance. This is particularly the case for a listed company in view of the requirements of the LR and enhanced reporting regime and for any other company which voluntarily adheres to those or a similar reporting regime. |
| **To obtain shareholder approval for substantial non-cash asset transactions with the company.** | Directors are required to make best use of the company's assets and must not abuse their position by such transactions. |
| **To observe the rules restricting loans to directors.** | Restrictions on loans to directors are required in view of the potential for conflicts of interest if directors could borrow the company's money for their own personal gain. |
| **To ensure service contracts are open to inspection.** | The principle of transparency in directors' contractual terms and remuneration arrangements is now supported by a raft of other statutory and regulatory requirements. |

### *Criminal offences*

There are numerous criminal offences in the CA 2006 which may be committed by a company, and for which a director or company secretary may also be prosecuted if he or she is in default. Being 'in default' means that the officer in question authorises or permits, participates in or fails to take all reasonable steps to prevent the contravention. From this wide definition it can be seen that directors and company secretaries need to take steps to ensure that the company's statutory obligations are met.

## Directors' duties: IA 1986

Directors of companies in financial difficulties are likely to be faced with fine judgements on matters that will be of critical importance in governance terms. While being mindful of the interests of all the key stakeholders, including in particular shareholders, employees and creditors, when seeking to keep the company in business, directors should also be mindful of the risks of committing a criminal offence or incurring personal liability. While there are several heads of liability under the IA 1986 including fraud in anticipation of winding-up (s. 206), transactions in fraud of creditors (s. 207), misconduct in the course of winding-up (s. 208), falsification of company books (s. 209), material omissions from statements relating to the company's affairs (s. 210), false representations to creditors (s. 211) and misfeasance or breach of fiduciary duty (s. 212), the two principal hazards for directors in this situation are fraudulent trading and wrongful trading. These will be scrutinised with particular care by a liquidator handling the winding-up of a company following its insolvent liquidation. Table 4.3 identifies and describes the relevant statutory provisions.

### *Fraudulent trading*

As fraudulent trading involves dishonesty, the burden of proof is the criminal standard of beyond reasonable doubt. Wrongful trading does not require dishonesty and accordingly the burden of proof is the lesser civil standard, on the balance of probabilities. In both cases, the liquidator must have the sanction of the creditors or the court to bring the legal proceedings.

### *Wrongful trading*

In the absence of their being dishonest, it is the potential for wrongful trading that will be of most concern to directors at the helm of a struggling company. While liability cannot arise until there is no reasonable prospect on an objective basis that the company can avoid going into insolvent liquidation, determining when that point is reached is a matter of judgement. Directors should be careful to take legal advice when in doubt and should ensure that they have available relevant financial advice on the company and keep proper records and minutes relating to their decisions. In the event of insolvent

**Table 4.3** IA 1986 duties

| IA 1986 duty | Statutory provisions |
|---|---|
| **Fraudulent trading**<br><br>Section 213 | If in the course of the winding-up it appears that any business of the company has been carried on with the intent to defraud creditors, the liquidator may apply to the court under s. 213 to obtain a contribution to the assets of the company from those (including directors) who were knowingly party to the carrying on of the business in that manner.<br>For the application to succeed, it must be proven that those responsible behaved with actual dishonesty. For this purpose, it will be enough if the directors are found to have taken positive steps to continue to trade and incur debts when they knew that there was no reasonable prospect to repay the debts. |
| **Wrongful trading**<br><br>Section 214 | If before the commencement of the winding-up any one or more of the directors knew or ought to have concluded that there was no reasonable prospect that the company would avoid going into insolvent liquidation, the liquidator may apply to the court under s. 214 to obtain a contribution to the assets of the company.<br>A director will not incur liability to make a personal contribution if they can satisfy the court that after the time when they knew or ought to have concluded that there was no reasonable prospect that the company would avoid insolvent liquidation they took every step with a view to minimising the potential loss to the company's creditors. |

liquidation, the liquidator has a statutory duty to submit a report under Section 7A CDDA 1986 (inserted by Section 107(2) of the SBEEA 2015) on the conduct of the directors (or shadow directors) of the insolvent company. If an adverse report is submitted, the Secretary of State may issue proceedings seeking disqualification orders under the CDDA.

While the above paragraphs refer to liquidation and winding-up, Sections 246ZA and 246ZB of SBEEA 2015 provided that an administrator appointed under Schedule B to the IA 1986 has the same powers and duties to prepare a report on directors (or shadow directors) and to bring proceedings for fraudulent or wrongful trading.

## Disqualification of directors

The Secretary for State can initiate court proceedings with a view to obtaining a disqualification order against a director whose conduct has been unfit. While the majority of such orders are made in connection with company insolvency, proceedings can be taken in a number of other circumstances. For directors, it is salutary to note that the official statistics indicate a sharp increase in the number of directors' disqualification orders granted over recent years. The coincidence of this increase with a closer scrutiny of directors' duties is notable.

The CDDA 1986 sets out four categories for the court granting a disqualification order against a director, each of which is sub-divided to cover specific heads of disqualification. Table 4.4 identifies the relevant provisions and describes their effect.

**Table 4.4** CDDA 1986 disqualification categories

| CDDA 1986 category (as amended by the SBEEA 2015) | Summary of heads of disqualification |
|---|---|
| **Sections 2–5A:** General misconduct in connection with companies | Conviction for an indictable offence in connection with company (including an overseas company) management and other prescribed actions.<br><br>Persistent breach of companies' legislation (this also applies to an overseas company).<br><br>During a winding-up it appears the director has been guilty of fraudulent trading or any other fraud or breach of duty and for certain convictions abroad (Section 5A inserted by Section 104(1) SBEEA 2015).<br><br>Conviction for an offence due to non-compliance with prescribed Companies House filings. |
| **Sections 6–8:** Unfitness to act as a director | Conduct making them unfit to be concerned in the management of a company when they have been a director of an insolvent company (including an overseas company).<br><br>On an application made by the Secretary of State on the grounds of public interest following an investigation into the affairs of the company. |
| **Sections 9A–9E:** Competition infringements | Conduct making them unfit to be concerned in the management of a company and also a prescribed breach of competition law. |
| **Sections 10–11:** Other cases | A requirement to contribute to a company's assets deriving from fraudulent or wrongful trading under the IA 1986.<br><br>Acting as a director when an undischarged bankrupt. |

In addition, s. 105 of SBEEA 2015 introduces a new disqualification for 'persons instructing unfit directors' under s. 87A–s. 87E. In this case a disqualification order may be made against a person ('P') who instructs a director or former director to do certain acts. The relevant director is known as the 'main transgressor' and they must have been disqualified on the grounds of unfitness (Sections 6, 7(2A), 8 or 8(2A)) and their disqualification must arise as a result of acting in accordance with P's directions or instructions.

CDDA 1986 sets out the detailed procedural rules that are to apply to disqualification proceedings. Several reported cases have addressed the scope and application of such rules, as well as determining the meaning of some of the key terms used in the legislation. The courts have paid particular attention to what is meant by 'unfitness'. Under s. 12C of CDDA 1986 (as amended by the SBEEA 2015), when determining whether a director is unfit, the courts shall have regard to any breach of fiduciary duty or misapplication of the company's assets. A breach of a statutory duty could also bring a charge of unfitness, for example, at the instigation of the regulators applying the health and safety or environmental protection laws. When determining unfitness in the context of an insolvency, Schedule 1 to CDDA 1986 states that the court shall have regard to the extent of the director's responsibility for both the insolvency itself and any misfeasance or breach of any fiduciary duties which could include the company's act of entering into transactions liable to be set aside as preferences or transactions at an undervalue, and also any other failure to comply with prescribed obligations placed upon them by the IA 1986.

## Implications for NEDs

NEDs should note that they are under an obligation to be familiar with the company's accounts and to inform themselves of the company's affairs generally. They should be careful not to place unquestioning reliance on information provided to them by executive directors, but rather should evaluate it in a critical manner. Accordingly, non-executives cannot avoid collective responsibility with the rest of the board where they have failed to give proper attention to their directorial duties.

## Effect of disqualification order

If made the subject of a disqualification order, an individual is prevented from acting as a director, limited liability partnership (LLP) member, receiver, insolvency practitioner or in any position, whether directly or indirectly, being concerned with, or taking part in, the promotion, formation or management of a company. Other legislation will prevent that individual from acting as a charity or pension scheme trustee. The period of disqualification is between two years and a maximum of 15 years, according to the limits contained in the applicable provisions. If a disqualified individual acts in breach of the order, he or she is liable to conviction and a fine and/or imprisonment not exceeding two years.

The primary purpose of disqualifying a director is not punitive. It is more to protect the public from the loss that might otherwise be caused by an unfit director. The policy intention behind the legislation is to prevent an abuse of the limited liability protections enjoyed by directors. Conversely, directors should be aware that a breach of their common law or statutory duties could result in their disqualification, with the consequential loss of livelihood and reputation.

### Case study: Trod Limited

Trod Limited (Trod) was an online poster and frame supplier. The Competition and Markets Authority (CMA) found that Trod had entered into an agreement with one of its competitors, GB eye Limited (GB), that they would not undercut each other's prices for posters and frames sold on Amazon's UK website. The CMA fined Trod £163,371 and commenced disqualification proceedings. Mr Aston, Trod's Managing Director who was found to have been personally involved in the breach of competition law, gave a disqualification undertaking not to act as a director of any UK company for five years. In line with the CMA's leniency policy, GB, which had initially reported the cartel, was not fined.

This is the first, and currently the only, case on disqualification for competition law breaches since the section 9A CDDA 1986 came into force but it demonstrates that disqualification of directors is not a risk that is solely restricted to insolvency scenarios. A number of other bodies, including Companies House, can apply to have an individual disqualified as a director.

### Directors' duties: 'stakeholder statutes'

The idea that companies have responsibilities not simply to their shareholders, but also to their other key stakeholders, including the community and the environment within which they operate, is now well developed. There can be no doubt that directors of companies must be aware of the corporate and personal risks which legislation seeking to address these responsibilities can entail. In the context of corporate governance, there are two important background principles of which directors should be aware:

1. where there are sanctions for breach of the legislation, it may be the case that the directors will be personally liable in their capacity as directors, sometimes on a strict liability basis (i.e. culpability does not require the relevant authority to establish any degree of intent, recklessness, neglect, blame, consent or connivance);

2. secondly, when establishing effective systems of internal control and their strategy on managing corporate risks, the directors should apply the principles set out in the *Risk Management, Internal Control and Related Financial and Business Reporting* (which revises, integrates and replaces the previous editions of the FRC's *Internal Control: Guidance for Directors* (formerly known as the Turnbull Guidance) and the *Going Concern Liquidity Risk: Guidance for Directors of UK Companies* and reflects the changes made to the UK Corporate Governance Code) to identify and address the risks to which the company is exposed as a result of such legislation. While the guidance is aimed at listed companies which are subject to the UK Corporate Governance Code, much of its content has a wider relevance.

The scope of the stakeholder legislation is very wide, covering risk areas such as bribery and corruption, fraud, competition, health and safety, employment, data protection, environmental protection, product safety and trade descriptions. Moreover, for the directors of large, complex and international groups, the challenge of ensuring effective compliance across such an organisation is not to be underestimated and will require clear policies, thorough implementation and regular review.

## Directors of listed companies

Apart from the common law and statutory duties noted above, directors of listed companies have numerous additional responsibilities to observe. These derive from the rules that apply when a company's shares are listed and traded on a regulated UK market and relate principally to the following:

- obligations on making offers of shares to the public and obtaining a listing;
- shareholder approval for major transactions by listed companies;
- the law relating to financial promotions and market abuse;
- the rules on takeovers and mergers;
- the regulation of share dealings by directors and others in management.

The UK Corporate Governance Code, through a Supporting Principle to Code Principle A.1, reinforces the general statutory duties of directors. The relevant Supporting Principle states:

> 'directors must act in what they consider to be the best interests of the company, consistent with their statutory duties'.

A footnote to the Supporting Principle confirms that the statutory duties in question are those set out in ss. 170–177 of the CA 2006.

## Directors' liability for breach of duties

If a director is in potential or actual breach of a statutory duty, he or she will want to refer to:

- the statute to confirm its exact terms;
- the party which can bring an action for its breach;
- the nature of the liability;
- the possible defences; and
- the limits of any civil or criminal penalties.

For example, health and safety legislation has been framed so that if a company commits an offence, and it can be shown that the offence was committed with the 'consent or connivance of, or was attributable to any neglect on the part of' the director, then he or she can also be liable. To that extent, a director's liability for breach of a statutory duty is well defined and, importantly, is capped at a level that Parliament has deemed appropriate.

### Liability for breach of common law duties

A director's common law duties operate in a markedly different manner. They are owed to the company rather than the shareholders. This contrasts with the position in the US, where shareholders can bring actions against directors personally for negligent management. It therefore falls to the company to take action for breach of duty, with the remedies including compensatory damages, a return of profits or other restoration of company property, a rescission of contract where the director has failed to disclose an interest, a restraining injunction or dismissal of the director. In practice this traditionally meant the action must be initiated by the board itself (this will be a new board where the former directors have departed, as in the example of Equitable Life, where the new board instigated an action against certain former directors relating to losses deriving from the policy on guaranteed annuity rights) or the liquidator, in the case of an insolvent company.

### Derivative claims

While directors have always owed their duties to the company and not to the shareholders, it has previously only been possible in limited circumstances for an individual shareholder to bring a derivative claim on behalf of the company for breach of duties (commonly known as the rule in *Foss v. Harbottle*). This was an exception to the general rule that only the company itself could bring such a claim, and was only available to a shareholder if he or she could show that a 'fraud on the minority' had been committed. This was typically in situations where the wrongdoing directors controlled the majority of the company's shares and so could prevent the company from bringing legal proceedings to address the directors' breach.

Following the introduction of a statutory derivative claim mechanism under Part 11 of the CA 2006, it is now possible for a member of a company to bring a derivative claim where the cause of action arises from an actual or proposed act or omission involving negligence, default, breach of duty or breach of trust by a director of the company. Any such claim will be on behalf of the company, with all proceeds passing to the company. An application will also have to be made to obtain the court's permission to bring the claim. The court must take into account whether the person bringing the claim is acting in good faith, the importance that a person acting in accordance with the general duty to promote the success of the company under s. 172 would attach to continuing the claim, whether the act or omission has been or is likely to be authorised or ratified by the company, whether the company has decided not to pursue the claim and whether the member could pursue the claim in their own right rather than on behalf of the company.

Despite these safeguards designed to limit claims, in response to some strongly expressed concerns that activist institutional investors might seek to make use of the provisions to bring forward unmeritorious claims with the aim of pressurising management, the Act also requires the court to dismiss any application where it appears to the court that the application and the evidence filed with it do not disclose a prima facie case for giving permission for the application to proceed. Additionally, where the court dismisses an application in this manner it will have the power to make consequential orders, which could include costs and civil restraint orders. Although the feared flood of derivative actions has not materialised, it is likely that directors, especially non-executives, will remain keen to seek independent legal advice before endorsing key issues such as corporate policies or strategies.

## Guidance for directors

At a time when the perceived risks of being a director are growing, all directors are understandably anxious to limit the scope of their liability, and to ensure that adequate protections are in place to shield them from crippling litigation, either by the company or third parties. Previous guidance attached to the Combined Code on directors' liabilities was dropped from the UK Corporate Governance Code. However, as the initial consultation document issued for the ICSA-led review of the Higgs Guidance perceptively noted, 'guidance for directors on "how to stay out of trouble – and jail" is often a much sought-after piece of advice'. In order to meet that need, ICSA has issued a guidance note on the liability of NEDs in the context of their duty to exercise care, skill and diligence. This useful guidance note is available on ICSA's website (www.icsa.org.uk) and addresses the way in which NEDs, who normally devote less time to their role than their executive colleagues, may meet the particular challenges this presents with regards to exercising their statutory duties. While primarily aimed at non-executives, many of its points are equally applicable to all directors.

### Indemnification of directors

Since 1929, Parliament has legislated to prevent companies from exempting or indemnifying their directors against liability for breach of duty, the idea being to remove the practice of companies' articles of association relieving directors from the consequences of breach of their duties with the result that shareholders were unable to obtain redress. Before the amendments described below took effect, any provision in the articles or any contract exempting or indemnifying any director (or other officer) of the company from any liability which would otherwise attach to them in respect of 'negligence, default, breach of duty or breach of trust of which he may be guilty in relation to the company' was void. This rule applied even where a director acted in good faith and in the belief that their decision was in the best interests of the company. Such provisions did not prevent the company from maintaining insurance for the director's benefit, and the company could still indemnify them for either the cost of defending any proceedings brought against them where their defence proved successful, or the cost of any application where relief was granted by the court. Accordingly, the payment of legal costs was dependent on the director being successful in the proceedings taken. Note that costs could not be paid as they accrued before conclusion of the proceedings.

It was widely believed that this legislation was unfairly weighted against directors. The CA 2006 has relaxed the statutory provisions restricting the indemnification of directors. Table 4.5 identifies the directors' indemnity and insurance provisions of the CA 2006 and provides a summary of their effect.

While these changes are significant, it should be noted that it remains impossible for a company to indemnify one of its directors for damages awarded against them as a result of a civil action taken by the company. Also, while the changes make it possible for a company to pay a director's legal costs as they accrue, in the event that they are unsuccessful in defending the action, such costs must be repaid. There is no restriction relating to the indemnification of company secretaries.

To ensure full advantage can be taken of these provisions, the company's articles of association should be checked to ensure that they contain the necessary powers permitting the company to provide to the director an indemnity (in addition to any general indemnity already contained in the articles). Where necessary, the company should bring forward a shareholder resolution to make the necessary changes to its articles of association. Any indemnity should be contained in a separate deed so that there can be no doubt as to its enforceability by the director and to ensure that it will survive cessation of the director's employment and only expire after any relevant limitation periods for bringing claims against the director have expired. Also, the issue should

**Table 4.5** CA 2006: directors' indemnity and insurance provisions

<table>
<tr><th>CA 2006</th><th>Summary of provisions</th></tr>
<tr><td>Qualifying third-party indemnity<br><br>Section 234</td><td>A company may indemnify its directors in respect of proceedings brought by third parties (i.e. other than by the company or an associated company), provided such an indemnity does not apply to any liability:<br>■ for fines imposed in criminal proceedings;<br>■ for penalties imposed by a regulatory authority;<br>■ incurred in defending criminal proceedings in which the director is convicted or civil proceedings brought by the company (or an associated company) in which judgement is given against him;<br>■ incurred in connection with an application for leave in which the court refuses to grant him leave.<br><br>The indemnification of directors by other companies in the same group is not permitted.</td></tr>
<tr><td>Qualifying pension scheme indemnity<br><br>Section 235</td><td>A company which is a trustee of an occupational pension scheme may indemnify its directors in connection with the company's activities as trustee of the scheme provided that such an indemnity does not apply to any liability:<br>■ for fines imposed in criminal proceedings;<br>■ for penalties imposed by a regulatory authority;<br>■ incurred in defending criminal proceedings in which the director is convicted.</td></tr>
<tr><td>Disclosure requirements<br><br>Sections 236 to 238</td><td>The directors' report must disclose the existence of any indemnity granted to directors of the company or any associated group company which is in existence at any time during the reporting year. Shareholders are entitled to inspect any indemnification provision or, if it is not in writing, a memorandum setting out its terms. Notification must be made to the Registrar of Companies of the location at which the memorandum is available for inspection unless it is at all times available at its registered office.</td></tr>
<tr><td>Paying legal costs<br><br>Section 205</td><td>A company may pay a director's legal costs for civil or criminal proceedings as they accrue through the granting of a loan to a director without shareholder approval, including those deriving from civil actions brought by the company, provided such costs (i.e. the loan) are repaid in the event that the director is unsuccessful. Similar provisions relate to the defence costs incurred in connection with an investigation or claim by a regulator.</td></tr>
</table>

be referred to the company's insurance brokers to provide an appropriate D&O policy.

For the listed company, it should be noted that the granting of an indemnity to a director, the provision of insurance for a director or the making of a loan to a director to cover defence costs are all exempted from the related party transaction rules (see para. 5 of LR 11 Annex 1R of the LR).

## Directors and officers (D&O) insurance

D&O insurance is designed to protect directors from the losses resulting from claims they suffer as a result of a breach of their duties. In an environment of increasing scrutiny of directors' performance and a growing regulatory burden, there is widespread agreement that the likelihood of directors facing such claims has increased. For example, the litigation involving former directors of Equitable Life, and the increased risk of huge class action claims in the US against directors of UK companies with a dual listing in the US, have provided stark reminders of the potential liabilities. Additionally, directors who are in breach of statutory duties can face considerable fines, often on a strict liability basis. As was observed in the *Higgs Report*, the risk of suffering such losses can strike NEDs particularly hard.

Under s. 233 of the CA 2006, companies are permitted to provide D&O insurance on behalf of their directors (and other officers) and to pay the premiums. While s. 233 is merely permissive, it is stated in UK Corporate Governance Code Provision A.1.3 that:

> 'the company should arrange appropriate insurance cover in respect of legal action against its directors'.

It is an essential part of any newly appointed director's due diligence that adequate D&O insurance is in place. Also, the scope and terms of any D&O insurance policies provided to existing directors should be reviewed in the light of the extension of the Companies Act indemnity provisions, referred to in Table 4.5 above.

Typically, a policy will provide cover at two levels:

- first, it will cover the amount which companies may need to pay to indemnify their directors for damages incurred as a result of claims by third parties; and
- secondly, it will cover the directors for damages they may incur as a result of claims taken against them by their own companies. However, the twin effects of increasing premiums and an apparent trend for insurers to offer

less comprehensive coverage have added to the difficulties of providing adequate cover.

Settling the terms of the cover requires specialist knowledge of the insurance market and policy terms and the board would always be advised to seek the assistance of an appropriately skilled insurance broker and/or legal adviser. ICSA has published a very useful guidance note (summarised below) on what is required. Clearly there is a limit to what can be achieved through guidance because of the specialised nature of the product and the need to tailor it to the individual needs of the policyholder. Companies should not approach their D&O insurance cover on the basis that there is a 'standardised' product. Table 4.6 draws on the ICSA guidance note to highlight the key points to be addressed in the policy.

**Table 4.6** ICSA Guidance on Protection against D&O Liabilities

| Policy term | Summary of issues |
|---|---|
| **Who is covered** | Past, present and future officers of the parent company and its subsidiaries should certainly be covered. The coverage of an associated company's officers should be reviewed. |
| **Outside directors** | The terms of coverage (if any) of officers sitting on unconnected boards should be reviewed. |
| **Acquisitions** | Policies deal with acquisitions in different ways, so careful review of the terms is required. Note that US and Canadian companies may be excluded. |
| **Period of cover** | Normally cover commences from the date of appointment. Notifications of changes in officers should be made on time. |
| **Basis of cover** | Normally policies are written on a 'claims made' basis, i.e. cover will cease when the appointment comes to an end. As liability can continue, 'run-off' cover should be provided. |
| **Run-off period** | The provision of a run-off period (normally at least six years) will require payment of extra premiums and should be negotiated before expiry of the policy. |
| **Definition of 'claim'** | This is usually defined as 'a demand made in writing'. Threats of legal action should be notified separately. |
| **Duty of disclosure** | An officer will be required to disclose to the insurer actual or possible claims. The terms relating to innocent non-disclosure and whether knowledge is ascribed jointly should be reviewed. |
| **Extent of cover** | The extent of cover should be carefully reviewed, and should include damages suffered, out-of-court settlements, costs and expenses, libel and slander and 'wrongful acts'. |

**Table 4.6** *continued*

| | |
|---|---|
| **Exclusions** | What is and is not excluded should again be carefully reviewed. Typical exclusions include penalties imposed by regulators and criminal courts, criminal defence costs, fraudulent acts, loss of earnings, taxes, etc. The ICSA guidance includes a more comprehensive list. |
| **Basis of contract** | Such a clause can cause any misstatement in the proposal form to be treated like a warranty so that an apparently innocuous error can allow the insurer to avoid any liability. If possible, it should be removed. |
| **Amount of cover** | A specific monetary limit normally applies, either per claim or per year. A careful review of the implications is required. |
| **Re-instatement** | The automatic re-instatement of sums insured has become more difficult to obtain. If possible, it should be included. |
| **Deductibles** | These are a matter of commercial negotiation and can range from nil to a large excess amount. |
| **Conditions** | These will vary, but typically include conditions about notifications, admissions of liability, conduct of claims, etc. Careful attention should be paid to the exact wording. |
| **Right of litigation** | The insurer will reserve the right to act on behalf of the insured, although the officer will be under a duty to defend the claim. |

ICSA, in its published guidance on the induction of directors, recommends that companies should supply details of the insurance cover provided to directors before they are appointed. Potential directors should take the time to study the D&O insurance policy carefully and if necessary should seek clarification on the key terms and take professional advice. Continuing directors will wish to understand the procedures for renewing the policy to ensure that adequate cover is maintained and departing directors will be interested in the level of post-retirement cover provided.

As a means of outsourcing a key area of risk, D&O insurance is certainly an important and essential product. However, companies and their directors should recognise that D&O insurance is far from being a panacea for all liability ills. Rather, it is just one of the tools available to the board if it is to manage the risks that both current and former directors will face. Following the developments in company law in relation to the indemnification of directors noted above, another important tool has been enhanced by which the company will be able to grant directors better protection from third-party liability and the right to have their legal costs paid as they accrue.

## Governance checklist

✓ Are directors aware of the extent of their authority and powers and the purposes for which those powers have been granted?

✓ Are the directors aware of the common law duties and the statutory codification of their general duties?

✓ Are directors, in particular NEDs, provided with sufficient information and advice for them to exercise reasonable care, skill and diligence?

✓ Is the information provided to directors sufficient for them to 'have regard to' the relevant factors set out in the CA 2006 when determining whether a proposed decision is likely to promote the success of their company for the benefit of its members as a whole?

✓ Are the directors able to authorise conflicts of interest and are adequate processes in place to declare and where appropriate to authorise and otherwise deal properly with directors' interests?

✓ Have the directors taken the necessary steps to ensure that the company is compliant with the relevant 'stakeholder statutes' in the employment, health and safety, environmental protection and other areas?

✓ Where key compliance tasks are delegated, do the directors review the adequacy of that delegation periodically and are they satisfied with the performance of the delegate?

✓ Are directors aware of the risks of disqualification and do they understand their responsibilities where the company is in financial difficulties?

✓ Has the company reviewed its practice on directors' indemnification and taken steps to ensure indemnification has been fully provided?

✓ Is the board satisfied that the company's D&O policy is appropriate to the company's circumstances and is it subject to regular review with the benefit of professional advice where necessary?

# Part 3

## External Perspectives on Effective Governance

# 5

# Shareholder activism and investor relations

## Introduction

Over a number of years, the standards expected in company/shareholder engagement have changed and shareholder activism – that is, responsible and active ownership by shareholders – is now generally accepted by both investors and investees alike. However, there has been renewed focus on the role and responsibilities of shareholders in light of criticism that shareholders do not fulfil their ownership responsibilities and obligations. In the words of Lord Myners (2016, High Pay Centre paper, *Restoring Responsible Ownership*):

> 'The mentality of share investors switched from that of a car owner to a car renter. . . . Institutional investors are the equivalent of renters. They are driven by the short term with qualified interest in the long term, largely as a result of client focus on short-term performance versus a diversified index or benchmark.'

The UK Stewardship Code aims to promote the long-term success of companies in a way that the share owners also prosper. The key principles set out in the Stewardship Code are designed to encourage more effective engagement between institutional shareholders and UK-listed companies. While the Stewardship Code applies on a 'comply or explain' basis, the FRC, which is responsible for overseeing implementation of the Stewardship Code, expects its signatories to publish a statement describing how they have applied each of the Stewardship Code Principles and, as appropriate, explain why they have not complied with any elements of it.

The FRC ranks the signatories to the Stewardship Code into three tiers based on the quality of their statements against the Stewardship Code's principles. Tier 1 is assessed as having the highest level of transparency and reporting while signatories in Tier 3 are at risk of removal from the list of signatories if they do not improve their standard of reporting.

The PLSA Voting Guidelines, which support the UK Stewardship Code, contain detailed voting guidance on the principal resolutions put to shareholders at the annual general meeting (AGM). Organisations such as IVIS and the ICGN also provide voting guidance for their members.

The Green Paper on *Corporate Governance Reform* issued by BEIS (November 2016) has as one of its key planks to strengthen the employee, customer and wider stakeholder voice in the boardroom. In response to this, ICSA and the IA are proposing to publish joint guidance to assist boards in improving engagement with and understanding the views of their employees and shareholders. This practical guidance is due to be published in the second quarter of 2017.

## Options for shareholder activism

Laying aside the contexts in which shareholder activism can be considered beneficial, the question may be asked, what then are the choices available to shareholders (either as beneficial owners or, more likely, through their appointed institutional shareholder agents) who wish to respond to the challenge of activism by exercising their share ownership rights? In essence, they have only three choices:

- they can vote or exercise other shareholder rights;
- they can engage;
- they can sell.

The objectives of shareholder engagement and the perceived benefit of constructive dialogue between company and investor and the exercise of voting and other shareholder rights are considered further below.

## Aims and benefits of shareholder engagement

### Building shareholder value

Institutional shareholders almost universally now view engagement as a means of building long-term shareholder value for the benefit of their clients. This outlook derives from two closely linked ideas. The first of these relates to why companies are selected as a suitable investment class in the first place. In this respect, the following statement in the Hermes Responsible Ownership Principles is instructive:

> 'Hermes' overriding expectation is that companies be run in the long-term interest of shareholders.'

At a theoretical level, this view translates as follows: a company is the commercial agency through which the property rights of the owners are exercised and its board of directors has delegated authority accordingly to operate and manage the company in the best interests of the owners. Company law recognises this to the extent that the company's constitution (the articles of association) is a matter of contract between the shareholders as private persons and the company. Therefore, to invest in a company is to promote the private property interests of the shareholders. The second notion behind the shareholder value approach to engagement is that the primary responsibility of institutional shareholders, as fiduciaries, is to manage the investments entrusted to their care in the interests of their clients, which the UK Stewardship Code seeks to support.

The shareholder value approach described above is, at its core, about the primacy of shareholder interests – the company is run for the shareholders' benefit and institutional investors are accountable as fiduciaries to their clients. While according to a traditional pure shareholder value approach, any attention given to wider public interests is incidental, a notable effect of the increased awareness of governance matters has been the emergence of fresh thinking about how shareholder interests can best be served.

### Achieving returns through socially responsible investment (SRI)

Within the shareholder value camp there are some strong advocates of the view that the level of return to shareholders can be enhanced when investee companies address environmental, social and corporate governance (ESG) factors. This belief is reflected in the IA Guidelines on Responsible Investment Disclosure, according to which returns can be enhanced 'by focusing on the need to identify and manage ESG risks to the short and long-term value of the business'. It therefore follows that it is a matter of 'good business' for boards to address the impact on corporate value and reputation that can result from the mismanagement of ESG matters.

Examples where failure to address ESG matters adequately could adversely impact long-term shareholder value – product recalls, environmental damage or poor health and safety records, to name but a few – are easy to imagine. With such considerations in mind, institutional investors may wish to consider their voting stance in relation to the report and accounts of investee companies that fail to make adequate disclosure on ESG matters.

While SRI started out as an investment style used principally by specialist 'green' retail funds, it is now commonplace in mainstream institutional fund management. A number of organisations exist to assist and motivate shareholders to adopt and implement SRI policies and in doing so to become more active shareholders. The European Social Investment Forum (Eurosif) is a pan-European group that has this goal and among its members is an array of differing organisations including fund managers, pension funds and campaigning groups. Similarly, the UK Social Investment and Finance Association (UKSIF) is an organisation which 'promotes responsible investment and other forms of finance that support sustainable economic development, enhance quality of life and safeguard the environment'. The 2016 WeConvene Extel/UKSIF Sustainability Survey noted that almost

40% of asset managers believe sustainability issues have an important influence on stock prices.

Chapter 6 focuses on CSR and responsible investment issues and notes the growing perception that the non-financial aspects of company management can matter. In the current context, the point can be made that beneficial owners that find a place for SRI considerations in investment matters will normally expect their fund managers to be active in their dealings with investee companies.

### Taming the corporate Goliath

There is, however, an alternative view: that the achievement of socially and economically just outcomes is an end in itself. Advocates of this view will arguably pay much less attention to the business case and will tend to relegate the interests of shareholders accordingly. In the absence of international regulation forcing companies to protect the rights of people and the environment, proponents of this type of activism will look to shareholders to bring about the change in corporate behaviour. Their primary concern is to make the world a better and a fairer place, so that the creation of financial value for shareholders is secondary. To such activists, the word 'value' will therefore have ethical, not purely financial, connotations. While private investors who espouse SRI policies will often find their motivation is to seek 'value' in both senses of the word, for institutional investors the investment objectives and restrictions set out in the mandate agreed with their clients will be paramount.

### Serving public policy interests

The fourth and final perspective on activism noted here expresses the view that activism is required in order to serve public policy interests. Adopting a macro-economic perspective, it tends to see the benefits of activism in terms of creating value for the public good. This view has found increasingly widespread support as a result of the perceived failure of institutional investors to adequately hold boards to account in the years leading up to the banking crisis, the huge cost of which has had to be borne by governments and, ultimately, taxpayers.

The need for more robust shareholder engagement led to the UK Stewardship Code. In the recent Green Paper on *Corporate Governance Reform* (2016), particular attention is given to ways which would strengthen the shareholder voice and thus restore trust and confidence in capitalism and free markets. To date, efforts to improve governance have been through voluntary rather than statutory means. It remains to be seen if in the future there will be legislative measures. Legislation has already been used to remove some of the barriers to proxy voting and to enhance corporate reporting and increase the influence of shareholder votes, for example on remuneration issues.

## Voting and other shareholder rights

A shareholder vote is a property right. While the general legal principle is that a shareholder may use or neglect that right as he or she pleases, holding the management of companies to account is ultimately achieved through the exercise of that right. The Government has repeatedly expressed its concerns about what it perceives to be the slow pace of change. It considers the level of voting at company meetings too low and views institutional investors who do not cast their votes as having failed in their stewardship of the companies in which they invest.

### The process of voting

The voting process itself has been the subject of reports going back to the reviews published by Paul Myners in 2004 and updated in 2007. These reports were unequivocal as to the importance of voting, observing as follows:

> 'It cannot be stated too forcefully that institutional investors in the voting process have fiduciary duties to their beneficiaries to preserve and enhance value through informed and effective corporate governance of the companies in which they invest. Voting is the bedrock of governance and should not be approached lightly. The process must be efficient, effective and transparent.'

The report contained a detailed summary of the practical steps involved in voting shares, with helpful diagrams setting out the various relationships. Figure 5.1 (overleaf), taken from the report, illustrates the voting process as between the various parties and remains relevant.

As can be seen, typically there may be up to four parties between the beneficial owner (pension scheme trustees, mutual and life insurance funds, etc.) and the issuer (the investee company). For voting instructions to be recorded, they therefore need to pass along a complex chain.

Myners' 2007 report contained several specific recommendations for the various parties involved in the share ownership chain to improve the voting process, including that:

*Issuers should:*

- carry out analyses to determine the extent to which voting instructions are being lost, the reasons why and publish their results; and
- endorse and facilitate electronic voting.

*IA and PLSA members, investment managers and custodians should:*

- follow the supporting principles to the UK Stewardship Code and take steps to ensure voting instructions are carried through in practice;

**Figure 5.1** The voting process (Myners)

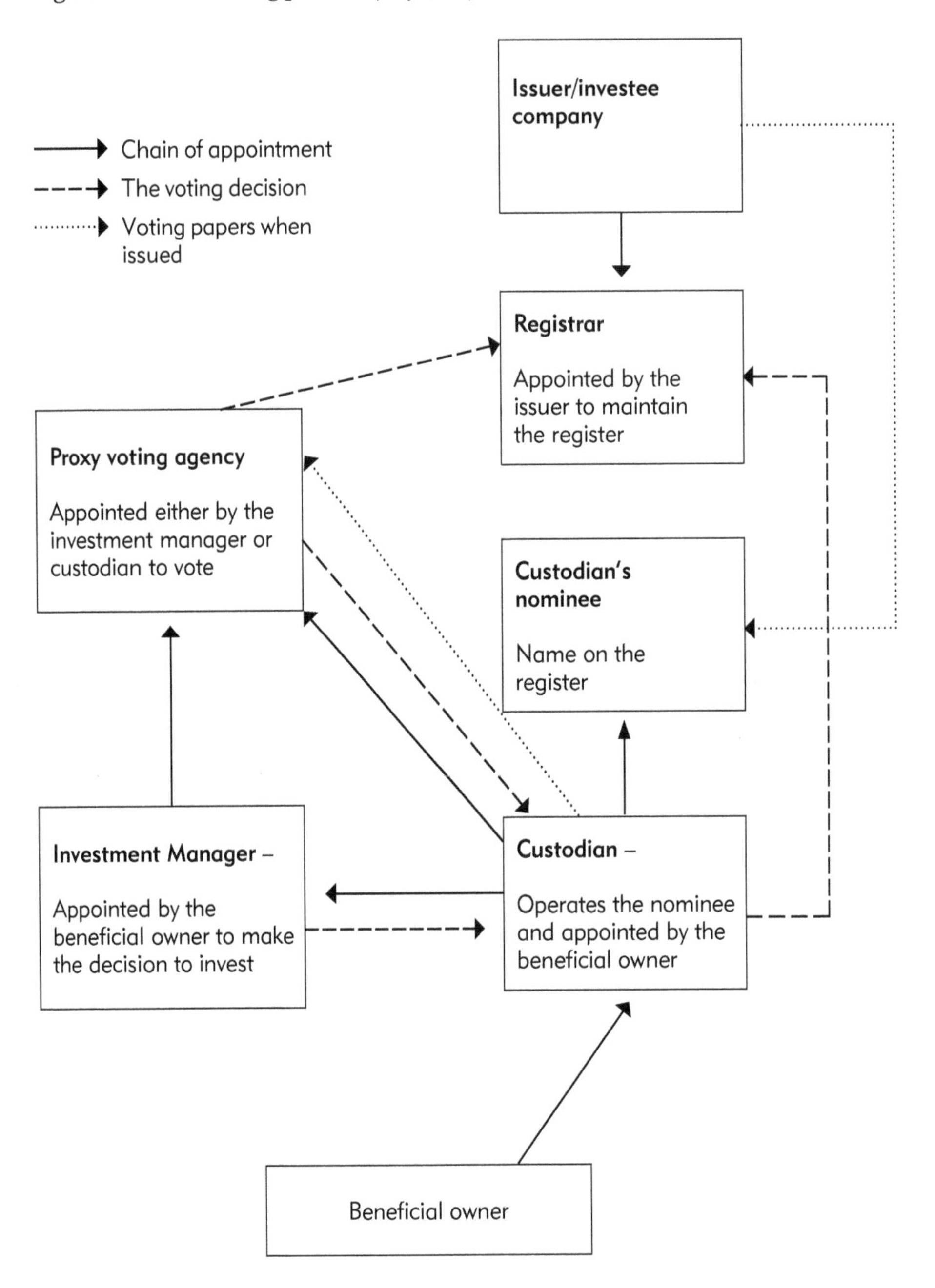

- ensure appropriate electronic voting capabilities are in place and encourage their use;
- take steps to ensure a clear audit trail and to facilitate vote tracing exercises;
- monitor stock lending risks and be aware that stock lending may affect the ability to vote the shares held in line with the policies and economic interests of the ultimate owners;
- ensure there is no disconnect between the custodian and person providing the voting instruction;
- ensure voting agents set realistic voting deadlines, i.e. not too early;
- ensure reporting meets relevant ICAEW requirements.

Alongside the voluntary codes, legislative intervention, in the form of various provisions within the CA 2006 and implementation of the Shareholder Rights Directive, has also changed the shareholder voting and general meeting environment to some extent. These changes are considered below.

### Voting rights

Under UK law, shareholders may vote at a general meeting in two ways. First, a member may attend the shareholder meeting in person in order to cast their vote directly. A corporate shareholder can attend a meeting in person by appointing someone as its 'corporate representative'. The statutory right of corporate shareholders to appoint a corporate representative provides a convenient mechanism without which a body corporate, which is a legal person but not an individual, could not in practice attend shareholder meetings. The corporate representative regime is examined further below.

Secondly, a shareholder can appoint a proxy to attend the meeting and vote in their stead. Traditionally, the rights of shareholders attending in person (whether as an individual shareholder or through a corporate representative) have been greater than those of shareholders opting to vote through a proxy.

Sections 285 and 324 of the CA 2006 enhanced the rights of proxies to remove the previous disparities. Since implementation of the relevant provisions of the CA 2006, shareholders are now permitted to appoint multiple proxies to vote different shares. In addition, s. 324A of the Act formalises the position that proxies may exercise all the rights of their appointing shareholder, provided that any votes they cast are in accordance with the instructions of that shareholder. The result is that the traditional restrictions prohibiting proxies from speaking at meetings or voting on a show of hands have been removed. Furthermore, subject to the provisions of the company's articles, a proxy appointed by more than one member, may, on a show of hands, vote once 'for' and once 'against' the same resolution if he or she has been given instructions to do so by the different members who appointed them. Equally, one member may appoint multiple proxies, so long as each proxy represents a different share or shares. Each such proxy may vote on a show of hands so that there is the potential for the vote to be skewed by the appointment of many proxies by one member who would otherwise only be able to vote once on a show of hands. Such an outcome may be anticipated by analysing proxy vote activity in advance of the meeting and, in the event of a result which does not accord with that expected based on the proxy votes received, the chairman should, of course, call a poll.

Given the flexibility of the proxy voting system under UK law, it is questionable whether companies will opt to implement the advanced voting system which was enabled under s. 322A of the CA 2006 in order to meet the requirements of the Shareholder Rights Directive.

There has also been a subtle change to the deadline for appointing proxies – the previous position required the deadline for receipt of proxies to be not earlier than 48 hours before the time appointed for the meeting. Under the CA 2006, the deadline is now calculated according to the number of working days. This is a more generous position than the strict 48-hour cut-off in earlier legislation and the traditional provisions of articles of association which, for Monday or Tuesday meetings, resulted in the proxy deadline coinciding with a weekend. As a company's articles may now validly provide for non-working days to be excluded in calculating the deadline, companies with Articles predating the 2006 Act, will, if they have not already done so, wish to adopt the statutory position by removing any provisions which are more restrictive than necessary. A similar deadline exists in relation to the requirement for traded companies to set a voting record date (s. 360B), which again may not be earlier than 48 hours prior to the time set for the meeting, excluding non-working days.

Although there is no general requirement for listed companies to provide electronic proxy appointment facilities which are accessible to all shareholders, there is a requirement for traded companies to provide an electronic address for the receipt of any documentation or information relating to proxies (s. 333A). Such documentation includes the appointment of proxy, any document necessary to show the validity of the appointment of the proxy and any notice of termination of a proxy.

The address must be provided either when sending out proxy forms or an invitation to appoint a proxy or alternatively may be provided throughout the period, commencing with the date on which the notice of meeting is given until the conclusion of that meeting, on the website on which the information required to be provided in accordance with s. 311A is made available. Arrangements for an appropriate electronic address could be made through CREST, the company or the company's registrars. It is not recommended to provide unpersonalised proxy forms through a website, as there is a danger that such forms could be returned incorrectly completed so that identification of the shareholder by the registrar is not possible. Instead, information about how to obtain a personalised proxy form should be provided on the website.

For institutional shareholders, s. 323 has created a more flexible corporate representative regime, enabling a company to appoint more than one corporate representative. The importance of this new flexibility is to enable corporate members, the shareholdings of which have more than one beneficial shareholder, to appoint a separate corporate representative for each beneficial shareholder who can then exercise the voting rights attaching to their shares in accordance with their own policies and interests. Teething problems with this regime were largely dealt with by an amendment which confirmed that where one member has appointed multiple corporate representatives, those corporate representatives may act independently of each other and vote in different ways. There remains, however, one grey area, namely whether a corporate representative appointed by more than one company has only one vote on a show of hands or whether they have as many votes as members who have appointed them with all the administrative difficulties such a scenario would entail. While this issue cannot be resolved in a company's articles, the chairman has a duty to exercise his or her discretion to call a poll in the event that the result of the show of hands does not reflect the proxy votes lodged.

In line with recent pressure to align the exercise of shareholder rights with the policies and interests of the ultimate beneficial owners of the investment, the Act now permits shareholders to nominate a third party as entitled to enjoy or exercise the rights of the member in relation to the company (s. 145). This enabling provision, however, is subject to the relevant company's articles. Given the enhanced role which may now be played by proxies, the more flexible corporate representative regime and the right of members to nominate an alternative person to enjoy their shareholder information rights, it is doubtful whether many listed companies will opt to permit their shareholders to take advantage of this regime, given the added administrative burden which it will surely involve.

## Shareholder meetings

The profile now given to the AGMs of listed companies necessitates significant pre-planning, which will certainly involve the company's registrars and may also include obtaining legal advice and consulting with other external advisers on issues such as communication, event organisation and security. Principle E.2 of the UK Corporate Governance Code states that 'the board should use general meetings to communicate with investors and to encourage their participation'. It is an important feature of the company's shareholder engagement and communication strategy.

Most general meetings are of course initiated by the directors to deal with specific items of company business which require shareholder consent.

However, members also have a right to require directors to convene a general meeting (CA 2006, ss. 303 and 305) provided that they meet certain specified criteria and that the requisition is valid. If a valid requisition is received, the directors must give notice of the meeting within 21 days of receipt of the requisition and hold the meeting within 28 days of the notice having been given. Notwithstanding the circumstances which give rise to the need for a general meeting, the meeting timetable and planning generally work backwards from the date on which notice must be given to shareholders.

Subject to the company's articles, which may require a longer period of notice, AGMs must be called on at least 21 clear days' notice although for companies which are subject to the UK Corporate Governance Code Provision E.2.4 requires the notice of AGM and related papers to be sent to shareholders at least 20 working days before the meeting. CA 2006 allows for other general meetings to be called on not less than 14 working days' notice provided that (and pursuant to the Shareholder Rights Directive) in the case of traded companies, the company offers a facility which is accessible by all members that allows voting by electronic means or provides for appointing a proxy via a website. In the case of traded companies, the company must also have passed a special resolution at a general meeting to reduce the notice period to not less than 14 days.

A key stage in the preparation for the meeting is providing the chairman with a full briefing. The briefing should cover as a minimum the business of the meeting, the proxy votes submitted, the chairman's powers and duties and any 'hot topics' or controversial items likely to be raised. Companies commonly provide some mechanism for shareholders intending to attend the meeting to provide advance notification of questions they may wish to raise and such a mechanism can prove useful in ensuring the chairman is adequately prepared. During the meeting itself, members of traded companies have a right to have questions answered relating to the business being dealt with at the meeting (s. 319A). However, it should be noted that no answer need be given if it is undesirable in the interests of the company or the good order of the meeting, if to do so would interfere unduly with the preparation for the meeting, involve the disclosure of confidential information or if the answer has already been given on a website in the form of an answer to a question. Having a comprehensive set of Q&As on the company website covering topics which are likely to be the subject of shareholder questions would be a sensible precaution, enabling the chairman to refer shareholders to the website rather than dealing with such questions in the meeting. Additionally, it would be reasonable for the chairman to undertake to arrange for the answer to a question to be provided outside of the meeting where it is not practicable for the answer to be provided on the spot.

Code Provision E.2.3 of the UK Corporate Governance Code requires not only all directors to attend the AGM but specifically for the chairmen of the audit, remuneration and nomination committees to be available to answer questions. It is therefore an integral part of the chairman's role not simply to answer shareholder questions themself, but also to refer questions to the most appropriate member of the board, including the chief executive or finance director.

The UK Corporate Governance Code also contains provisions relating to the counting and declaration of proxy votes where a vote is taken on a show of hands. Although perhaps unlikely in practice, should an equality of votes arise, the chairman may no longer be granted a casting vote (reg. 22, the Companies Shareholders' Rights Regulations 2009) and best practice would be to call a poll. Although traditionally companies have tended to first take a vote on a show of hands, in his report on the impediments to voting shares, Paul Myners recommended that best practice is to call a poll on all resolutions. This is to ensure that voting is more exact, equitable and transparent, as one vote per share is counted and declared and to encourage overseas shareholders to vote more readily. Companies may also prefer to use polls, as the default mechanism for voting on all resolutions, particularly where disruption of the meeting is felt to be a risk. Subject to a company's articles (which may provide more generous shareholder rights), under s. 321 of the CA 2006 a poll may be called by the chairman or demanded, on any question other than the election of the chairman of the meeting or the adjournment of a meeting, by:

- a minimum of five members having the right to vote on the resolution;
- a member or members representing at least 10% of the total voting rights (excluding treasury shares); or
- a member or members with shares on which an aggregate sum has been paid up equal to not less than one-tenth of the total sum paid up on the company's shares (excluding treasury shares).

ICSA provides helpful guidance on voting on a show of hands or by a poll.

### Information provided to shareholders

In Chapter 8, the contents and purposes of some of the reports required to be provided to shareholders will be considered. In addition to these, certain information is required to be made available on a website identifying the company from the date of any general meeting notice for a period of two years (s. 311A) and care should be taken to ensure it is not inadvertently removed prematurely. This information includes the matters set out in the notice of meeting, the total number of shares in the company in respect of which members are entitled to exercise voting rights (with sub-totals for separate classes of share where relevant) and the total number of votes that members are entitled to exercise at the meeting in respect of each class of share. Any members' statements, resolutions or matters of business subsequently received by the company must be included as soon as reasonably practicable. There are additional requirements for the meeting notice (s. 311) which must also be adhered to:

- the website address where the pre-meeting information described above is available;
- the voting record date;
- the procedure to attend and vote;
- details of the proxy form;
- the right to ask questions; and, separately,
- where the meeting notice is issued more than six weeks before the meeting date, an explanation of the right of members to requisition resolutions and include matters to be dealt with at the meeting.

The right of members to requisition resolutions has now been supplemented by a new right to require the company to include a matter in AGM business (ss. 338–340B). The requirements governing the exercise of these rights are as follows:

- the requisition must be made by a minimum of 100 members each holding an average of at least £100 of paid-up share capital or by members representing 5% of the total voting rights;
- the request must be received by the later of the date on which notice of the meeting is given or six weeks prior to the meeting; and
- the company must bear the cost of circulating the required resolution or matter to be dealt with at the AGM if the request is received before the end of the financial year preceding the AGM.

A requisition is not valid, however, if the subject is defamatory, vexatious, frivolous or, in the case of a resolution, it would not, if passed, be effective.

Following the meeting, there are further statutory requirements as to the publication of the results of any polls. These requirements distinguish between companies which are 'traded' and those which are only 'quoted'. All traded companies are quoted companies, but companies with shares listed on the NYSE or NASDAQ (US Stock Exchange), but not on a regulated market within the EEA, are only quoted. All quoted companies must publish the following on their company website after any poll taken at a general meeting:

- the date of the meeting;
- the text of the resolution or description of the subject matter of the poll, as the case may be; and
- the number of votes 'for' and the number of votes 'against'.

In addition to the above, the information published on the website of traded companies must:

- include the total number of votes validly cast;
- include the proportion of the company's issued share capital on the voting record date represented by those votes;
- include the number of abstentions (if counted); and
- be published within 16 days of the meeting or, if later, by the end of the first working day following the day on which the result is declared.

Members have the right to request the directors to appoint an independent assessor to prepare an independent report on the poll or polls in question (ss. 342–351). The request must be made by a minimum of 100 members each holding an average of at least £100 of paid-up share capital and entitled to vote on the matter to which the poll or polls relate or members representing 5% of the total rights to vote (excluding treasury shares) on the matter to which a poll or polls relate. The request must be made within one week of the date on which the poll was taken and the independent assessor must be appointed within one week of receipt of a valid request. Information relating to the appointment of and report made by the independent assessor must also be made available on the company website. Subject to the company's articles of association, information rights may be transferred by a nominee shareholder to the beneficial owner of the shares.

## Derivative claims

The CA 2006 provides procedures for derivative claims (ss. 260– 269) which replaced the exceptions to the common law principle that only the company, rather than individual shareholders, could pursue a claim against directors. The legislation not only makes the position on derivative claims more transparent, but common law restrictions have been relaxed to some extent. Under the statutory provisions, a member may bring a claim against a director (including a former director or shadow director) or another person (or both) in respect of any actual or proposed act or omission involving negligence, breach of duty or breach of trust by a director of the company. The member may bring the action even if they were not a member of the company at the time of the cause of action.

To guard against the potential for vexatious litigation, the claimant must seek the court's permission to pursue a derivative claim. This safeguard has proved to be effective, with the courts generally refusing to grant permission and effectively imposing further restrictions through the factors which the court takes into account in deciding whether or not to grant permission. These factors include the importance of the person acting in accordance with their duty to promote the success of the company and the availability of an alternative remedy for the member.

## The register of members

Information obtained from registers of members is clearly open to abuse. There are many examples of personal information obtained from share registers being used for unwanted direct marketing, fraudulent 'boiler room' schemes and even shareholder intimidation. With no mechanism available for preventing the inspection or copying of their register of members, companies were previously unable to restrict access to the names and addresses of their shareholders. This has now changed. Inspection requests and requests for copies of the register of members are now required to include certain information, such as the identity of the person making the request, the purpose for which the information will be used and whether the information will be disclosed to any other person. In the event that the company has concerns about the purpose for which the information will be used, it may, within five working days of receiving the request, apply to the court. The court may direct the company not to comply with the request if it is satisfied that the inspection or copy of the register is not sought for a proper purpose. Useful guidance on the proper purpose test, including examples of what may constitute proper or improper purposes, has been produced by ICSA. The guidance notes that one proper purpose might be for obtaining contact with other shareholders with regards to the exercise of members' rights, for example seeking support for the requisition by shareholders of a resolution.

## Engagement with investee companies

From the activism requirement set out in the Myners Principles and best practice recommendations of the Stewardship Code to the published policies on engagement with investee companies of individual fund managers, the need for active and meaningful shareholder engagement is widely accepted and supported throughout the institutional shareholder community. Best practice in this regard is now examined.

### Institutional shareholders' best practice guidance

Best practice for institutional investors in terms of their responsibility to engage with the companies in which they invest is set out in the UK Stewardship Code, published by the FRC. The introduction of the UK Stewardship Code followed the recommendation made by Sir David Walker that the FRC take over responsibility and oversight for the ISC's *Code on the Responsibilities of Institutional Investors*. This reflected concerns that, in the lead-up to the global banking crisis in 2008/9, institutional investors had been less effective than might have been hoped in curbing the riskier management strategies adopted by some entities within the financial services sector.

The FRC states that the aim of the Stewardship Code is 'to enhance the quality of engagement between investors and companies to help improve long-term risk-adjusted returns to shareholders'. This focus echoes that of the *Kay Review of UK Equity Markets and Long-Term Decision Making* final report and the Government's subsequent response to it.

The Kay recommendations sought to address the way in which short-term trading decisions taken by fund managers can distract company directors from the long-term strategies which they should primarily be pursuing. The subsequent Implementation of the *Kay Review: Progress Report* highlights the FRC's commitment to monitoring signatories to the Stewardship Code as part of the wider review of culture in the equity markets.

In 2016 there were nearly 300 signatories to the Stewardship Code. In 2016, the FRC introduced a system of tiering for Code signatories – three tiers for asset managers and two tiers for asset owners and service providers. These tiers seek to distinguish those signatories whose standards of reporting and commitment to stewardship are good from those judged to require improvement. The intention is to encourage better practices through public identification of those whose practices are not deemed to be up to scratch, with removal from the signatory list threatened for those who fail to improve.

The Stewardship Code strongly encourages engagement in the form of 'purposeful dialogue with companies' on strategy, performance, risk, capital structure, corporate governance, culture and remuneration, but the introductory paragraphs confirm that the Stewardship Code 'does not constitute an invitation to manage the affairs of a company or preclude a decision to sell a holding, where this is considered in the best interests of clients or beneficiaries'. Inevitably, the institutional shareholder is primarily concerned with securing value for the end-investors in line with the obligations which it owes to its clients. In theory, such a focus should not necessarily run contrary to other stakeholders' interests. However, the ability of institutional investors to sell a holding provides them with a quick and convenient damage limitation mechanism – in contrast, there may be no equivalent privilege available to wider society.

The UK Stewardship Code lists seven principles to be observed by institutional shareholders, which in summary are as follows:

- *Disclosure of stewardship policy*: to publicly disclose their policy on how they discharge their stewardship responsibilities, including how stewardship is applied with the aim of enhancing and protecting value for the end-investor, the institutional shareholder's activities within the investment chain and the responsibilities which arise from those activities (this will depend on the nature of the primary activities, for example whether the institutional shareholder is an asset owner, manager or provider of some other investment-related service), how (if activities are outsourced) the outsourcing arrangements are compatible with the proper exercise of stewardship responsibilities and what steps are taken to ensure those responsibilities are properly carried out and describe arrangements for integrating stewardship within the wider investment process;

- *Managing conflicts of interest*: to have in place a robust, publicly available policy for identifying and managing conflicts of interest which may arise in relation to stewardship. In particular the policy will need to address how matters are to be dealt with when the interests of different clients or beneficiaries diverge;
- *Monitoring investee companies*: to instigate regular and effective monitoring of companies in order to keep abreast of company performance and developments that drive the company's value and risks, to satisfy themselves that the company's leadership is effective and, through meetings with the chairman, other board members and otherwise, that the board and its committees adhere to the spirit of the UK Corporate Governance Code, to consider the quality of the company's reporting and, where appropriate and practicable, to attend the AGMs of companies in which they have significant holdings. Where explanations regarding departures from the UK Corporate Governance Code are not accepted, written and/or verbal dialogue may be appropriate. One aim of the monitoring should be to identify problems at an early stage in order to minimise loss of shareholder value. There is clear scope for such dialogue to result in an institutional investor being made an insider and, if there is a willingness on the part of the institutional shareholder to do so, this should be indicated in the policy. Companies should note, however, that notwithstanding any such general willingness, no insider information should be passed to an institutional investor without their prior agreement. The MAR market soundings and insider list requirements are relevant here;
- *Intervening when necessary*: regardless of whether the investor is following an active or passive investment policy, to define the circumstances when they will intervene, for example when they have concerns about strategy, performance, governance, remuneration or risk matters and to regularly assess the effectiveness of doing so. Initial intervention will be undertaken through confidential discussions but there should be a willingness to escalate the issue in the event that an investee company board fails to respond constructively. Such escalation might include holding additional meetings with management or board members, expressing concerns to the company's advisers, making a public statement, submitting resolutions to or speaking at an AGM or requisitioning a general meeting, for example to

propose a change in board membership. Such escalation may involve intervening jointly with other investors;

- *Acting collaboratively where appropriate*: to have a publicly disclosed policy on collective engagement, indicating their willingness to work with other investors through formal and informal groups, in particular where the issues identified are ones of significant corporate or wider economic stress or which are thought to present a risk to significant value. The policy should identify the sort of circumstances in which collective engagement would be considered;
- *Voting*: to seek to vote all shares, abstaining or voting 'against' where appropriate and to publicly disclose voting records, the use made (if any) of proxy voting or voting advisory services, the scope and providers of such services and the extent to which they follow or rely on the recommendations made. Disclosure should also be made on their approach to stock lending and to recalling such stock. Where institutional shareholders intend, having engaged unsuccessfully in active dialogue, to abstain or vote against a resolution, they should inform the company of their reasons for doing so beforehand; and
- *Reporting back*: to regularly provide to clients/beneficial owners clear qualitative and quantitative information about their stewardship activities, subject only to confidentiality issues. Asset owners should also report annually on their stewardship policy and how it has been executed. Institutional investors should obtain and publish an appropriate independent opinion on their voting and engagement processes.

The FCA Handbook has endorsed the Stewardship Code as the default standard for institutional investors by placing an obligation on all UK-authorised asset managers to disclose the nature of their commitment to the Code or, where they do not commit to the Code, their alternative investment strategy. It should be noted that when publishing the UK Stewardship Code, the FRC stated its intention to undertake annual monitoring of the take-up and application of the Code. The IA also publishes an informative annual report on how the Code has been implemented. The report not only looks at how many investors are signatories to the Code, it also provides examples of specific engagement activities and their outcome.

Both the 2016 FRC report and the June 2015 IA report highlighted, amongst other things, the importance of corporate culture and board leadership.

Barriers to stewardship include lack of resources and the ability to influence companies where the institutional investor's holding is relatively small. Such barriers threaten the effectiveness of stewardship. The establishment of effective practices by companies to maximise the efficiency of institutional investors' efforts in this regard must therefore be a priority if regular and purposeful engagement is to be realised.

To promote the establishment of such practices, ICSA has produced guidance *Enhancing Stewardship Dialogue* containing a number of practical recommendations aimed at improving the engagement process. These recommendations are divided into four categories – developing a strategy for engagement, getting the housekeeping right, strengthening the conversation on strategy and long-term performance and providing feedback – each of which are now examined.

## Developing a strategy for engagement

The starting point for developing an engagement strategy is, according to the ICSA guidance, the establishment of a programme of engagement activities for the year, taking account of the expectations of their key institutional investors and the type of activity which will help them achieve their engagement objectives. Activities are likely to be mixed, including one-to-one meetings with larger institutional investors as well as group meetings and collective engagement. The programme should not just be centred around the announcement of results but should also take account of issues that may arise at the AGM or of strategic developments that are in the pipeline. This programme should be reviewed annually by the board based on a clear understanding of what level of communication is considered necessary by investors. The ICSA guidance incorporates a suggested framework for an engagement programme.

The process for engaging with institutional investors should be regular and consistent, rather than simply event-driven, so that over time relationships between the company and key investors, if possible always involving the same individuals, can be established. At the outset and until such relationships are well established, the company's approach and other background information should be provided to ensure a good understanding is developed between the parties. Laying the foundations of a constructive relationship can facilitate the discussion of difficult or urgent issues and this is particularly relevant in respect of those investors which have long-term objectives rather than those involved in short-term trading.

## Getting the engagement process housekeeping right

The first point is clearly to engage with the right parties and the appropriate representatives of each. In determining which investors to invite to presentations, factors such as those investors with strong engagement track records or with which the company has developed a constructive engagement relationship are likely to be considered. Certainly smaller investors should not automatically be disregarded. Consistent with the preface to the UK Corporate Governance Code which encourages companies to recognise the contribution made by other providers of capital and to listen to the views of such providers, some thought should be given to including investors in non-equity securities which, as providers of capital, are still relevant to the engagement process. Thought will also be necessary in respect of who should be present from the company itself, including whether executive and/or NEDs should attend. It may be appropriate for executive directors to leave meetings at some point to allow time for investors to speak with NEDs without the executives being present. An appendix to the guidance provides some suggestions on these issues. Clear records of engagement activity should be kept.

### Strengthening the conversation on strategy and long-term performance

In line with the recommendations of the Kay Review and the Government's position on the necessity of improving the alignment between institutional investor pressures and directors' responsibility for long-term strategy and performance, opportunities to discuss the company's strategy and performance and the governance arrangements in place to sustain that performance should be available to investors annually. The dialogue should be centred on the company's value creation approach and issues such as executive remuneration should be considered in that context. The agenda for discussion at these sessions should be appropriately wide, not necessarily restricted to the matters generally covered when reporting results, but perhaps extending to succession planning, board effectiveness, culture, risk and reputation. An appendix to the guidance suggests a possible framework for the content of such discussions.

### Providing engagement feedback

Without two-way feedback, it is difficult to see how the effectiveness of the engagement activity can be judged and what improvements to the processes could be made. Feedback should be accepted in an open-minded and professional manner. The process for obtaining feedback should be mutually agreed and may comprise both oral and written feedback, as well as formal and informal views. Feedback is likely to cover issues such as whether the right people were involved, whether the right subjects were addressed, whether discussions raised any concerns or delivered any surprises, whether anything had been learnt from the engagement activity and whether it had influenced the views of investors.

### Annual general meetings (AGM) and shareholder activism

The AGM is the key event in the annual shareholder dialogue calendar. It is frequently the focus of shareholder discontent and several major UK corporate names have made the headlines as being the target of sustained shareholder activism: these include HSBC, BG Group, BP, Tesco, Sports Direct and Alliance Trust. Some have observed that these rather public displays of 'dirty washing' by boards and shareholders may not be in the interests of the companies concerned and are evidence of a failure of governance to the extent that the issues were not addressed privately. This criticism is somewhat less relevant, however, where the action is the result of activism by smaller shareholders, for whom the AGM is arguably their only mechanism for meaningful interaction with their company's board. Whatever the rights or wrongs, it is clear that shareholders are prepared to be assertive, sometimes fiercely so, where they believe that boards need to be brought to account.

It is difficult to see how incidents of controversial companies being targeted by activists seeking publicity for their cause could be halted without detriment to the rights of shareholders to address their directors on issues of importance to them. With the statutory hurdle required to requisition a resolution set at just 100 shareholders, each holding on average at least £100 of paid-up share capital, getting your resolution onto an AGM agenda is easily achievable and never more so than since the advent of the internet. Although the Act does contain provisions to enable the directors to disregard a requisition, the rights of shareholders to requisition resolutions have, to some extent, been strengthened. The risk to shareholders of having to pay for circulation of their resolution has been removed for those who submit the necessary request on time and the small shareholder has been empowered thereby. The following two case studies are illustrative of the difficulties which shareholder requisitioned resolutions can create.

### Case study: BP

In April 2015 a coalition of major investors in BP, known as the 'Aiming for A' Coalition, successfully requisitioned a special resolution to be added to the business of the BP AGM. 'Aiming for A' is a group of asset owners and mutual fund managers notably including the £150bn Local Authority Pension Fund Forum and members of the £15bn Church Investors Group. It aims to promote engagement with the largest UK-listed extractive and utilities companies, to promote a focus on companies' climate performance.

The aim of the resolution was to direct that routine annual reporting from 2016 includes further information about ongoing operational emissions management, asset portfolio resilience to the International Energy Alliance's (IEA's) scenarios, low-carbon energy R&D and investment strategies and public policy positions relating to climate change. This is to build upon disclosures already made within the Company's *Energy Outlook, Sustainability Review and Annual Report*.

This AGM experience highlights the power of campaigns to play a positive stewardship role. The board of BP supported the resolution, which was passed with a landmark 98% shareholder approval. The engagement of 'Aiming for A' with BP prompted an unprecedented response by a major utilities company and its institutional shareholders. It is reasonable to conclude from this outcome that ensuring management take into account increased transparency and accountability was a significant reason for support from institutional investors.

In contrast, in 2010 shareholders successfully requisitioned a resolution to highlight the proposed extraction of Canadian oil sands but the resolution was decisively defeated. Notwithstanding this apparent failure, the issue was widely covered in the press, raising the profile of the issue and securing valuable publicity for the campaigners. While the resolution was not passed, it is reasonable to assume that the publicity in itself represented something of a success for the activists.

### Case study: Tesco

***Tesco plc has a history of difficult AGMs***

Tesco's board and in particular its chief executive, Sir Terry Leahy, came in for a rough ride over controversial pay proposals which, depending on the success of Tesco's expansion into the US, could have been worth up to £11 million to him.

The resolution approving this potential pay package appeared in stark contrast to the call, made through a shareholder-requisitioned resolution, for Tesco to pay a 'living wage' to workers in the developing world. In the end, despite almost 18% of shareholders refusing to vote in favour, Sir Terry Leahy's incentive scheme was approved. The shareholder-requisitioned resolution was defeated, but not before a very public and potentially damaging debate on the acceptability of the practices used by some of Tesco's overseas suppliers.

There was no respite for Tesco the following year, with TV chef Hugh Fearnley-Whittingstall taking his 'Chicken Out' campaign to the meeting through a self-funded resolution demanding better welfare conditions for UK-farmed chickens. Again the resolution was defeated, this time with just under 19% of shareholders either abstaining or voting for, but the publicity achieved by Fearnley-Whittingstall was considerable.

The year after there was yet another shareholder-requisitioned resolution at the AGM, this time submitted by the trade union Unite. The resolution called for an undertaking to be given to take certain steps to ensure workers within the Tesco supply chain would not be exploited. Even before the meeting itself, circulation of the resolution and supporting statement guaranteed the campaigners national press coverage for their cause. Although the resolution was defeated, the requisitioners achieved significant publicity.

### Collective engagement

The calls for collective engagement have, particularly following the global banking crisis, been gathering increasing support. The *Walker Review* encouraged a collaborative approach, highlighting the greater likelihood of success for shareholder engagement, particularly in securing the attention of the investee company board, if investors acted collaboratively rather than individually. The logic for this assertion is clear. However, traditionally investors may have been deterred from entering into arrangements for collective shareholder engagement by concerns that as a result of such collaborative engagement they might be considered 'persons acting in concert' and in so doing might fall foul of various regulatory traps. Probably the most serious of those traps was that of rule 9 of the Takeover Code, under which persons 'acting in concert' may be required, depending on the percentage of shares they hold and voting rights they can exercise, to make an offer to the holders of the other shares in the company.

To address these concerns, the Takeover Panel issued Statement No. 26 – Shareholder Activism in September 2009 confirming that it did not believe 'the relevant provisions of the [Takeover] Code have either the intention or the effect of acting as a barrier to cooperative action by fund managers and institutional shareholders or of constraining normal collective shareholder action'. The Statement confirmed the limited circumstances in which collective shareholder engagement could fall foul of the mandatory offer requirements, being, in summary, that the collective engagement was both in order to pursue a 'board control-seeking' resolution and that after agreement had been reached by the activist shareholders, the relevant shareholding/voting rights percentage levels were reached or further exceeded.

By providing this clarification, a significant perceived barrier to shareholder collaboration was effectively removed. However, further barriers were also perceived by cautious investors to be present by virtue of other regulatory restrictions on parties 'acting in concert'. In August 2009, the Financial Services Authority (FSA) (now FCA) provided the following comfort in a letter to the Chairman of the ISC:

> 'There is nothing under FSA rules that prevents investors discussing matters when it is for a legitimate purpose.'

The FSA set out its approach on the three key areas of its rules:

- The market abuse rules do not prevent investors from engaging collectively with the management of an investee company. However, trading on the basis of knowing another investor's intentions or working jointly to avoid disclosure of shareholdings could constitute market abuse.
- FCA rules on disclosure of major shareholdings require that investors who have agreed to pursue the same long-term voting strategy should aggregate their shareholdings when considering whether their shareholdings reach the threshold for disclosure (3% of a company's shares). However, this disclosure would be unlikely to be triggered by ad hoc discussions between investors on particular corporate issues.
- Under the EU Acquisitions Directive, where investors are 'acting in concert' they require FCA approval if they reach a controlling shareholding (10% or more of a company's shares) in a regulated firm. 'Acting in concert' is not defined in the Directive, but the FCA does not view the requirement as preventing ad hoc discussions or understandings between investors that are intended solely to promote generally accepted principles of good corporate governance in firms in which they have invested.

The FSA letter did not constitute official guidance, however, and it may therefore not have been quite so effective in allaying the fears of institutional investors as might have been hoped. Nevertheless, it has provided some comfort and, taken with the Takeover Panel practice statement, was expected to reduce some of the concerns that act as a barrier to greater collective shareholder engagement. However, particularly for investors who are subject to multi-jurisdictional requirements, the risks of a regulatory breach are even more complex and off-putting. Whether or not such risks are the real cause of investor reluctance to engage in collective engagement, and notwithstanding that some best practice assistance did exist including the guidance accompanying Principle 5 of the Stewardship Code and suggestions within ICSA's *Enhancing Stewardship Guidance*, it was apparent that work was needed to develop effective collective engagement mechanisms. Principle 5 of the UK Stewardship Code requires signatories to the Code to 'be willing to engage collectively with other investors' and International Corporate Governance Network (ICGN) *Global Stewardship Principles* employ similar language on the issue.

The *Kay Review* final report, published in 2012, recommended the establishment of an investor forum to facilitate such collective approaches. Accordingly in 2014, The Investor Forum was launched with the core objective of creating long-term value and to tackle the obstacles to long-term engagement identified in the *Kay Review*. The Collective Engagement Framework developed by The Investor Forum seeks to facilitate collective engagement, whether proposed by its members or a company, on issues that have a long-term focus. Provided the Framework's other criteria are also met, members can choose to opt in to the process, thereby ensuring no member is obligated to participate in engagement on an issue on which they do not wish to do so.

The Stewardship Code guidance advises that collective approaches may be the most effective form of engagement at times and that in particular it might be appropriate 'at times of significant corporate or wider economic stress or when the risks posed threaten to destroy significant value'. This guidance appears to place collective engagement in some form of crisis management category but the ICSA guidance shines a more positive light on collective engagement as offering greater cost-effectiveness, a facility for exchanging a range of views and enabling deeper analysis than might be possible in one-to-one meetings and a forum for reaching consensus on a particular issue. As such, while not dismissing collective engagement as a tool by which investors can collaborate to lend weight to significant concerns they might wish to raise with the company, the ICSA guidance also carves out a place for collective engagement within the business-as-usual investor dialogue processes.

Engagement with companies, whether on a one-to-one or collective basis, requires both commitment and resources. In particular cases, dedicating those resources to engagement may not be the preferred route or the benefits of engaging may not be perceived to be sufficient to judge it worthwhile. If so, selling the shares may be the step taken, as now examined in the following section.

## Selling shares

Activism policy statements will usually state that the underlying objective is the achievement of long-term returns. Therefore, the investment required to implement such policies needs to be justified in cost–benefit terms. Where the cost–benefit equation is negative, then selling a holding in an underperforming company will be the natural choice. The UK Stewardship Code confirms that a decision to sell a holding is not precluded where this is considered in the best interest of the end-investor. However, there has been some criticism of the readiness with which institutional shareholders trade their investments, the charge being that they are too short-termist in their perspective. Yet no one would deny that share trading in this manner is inevitable. If a fund manager considers the shares in a particular company to be under-priced relative to the market, then he or she will consider purchasing it. But equally, if it is overpriced and the manager considers it unlikely that its future performance will correct the position, then they will sell.

There are other factors at work which tend to encourage a short-termist approach. Brokers and analysts, who are the main source of investment information to the markets, will routinely measure the relative performance of sectors and individual companies over a short time frame. The recommendations 'buy', 'hold' or 'sell' are expressive of the tendency for the capital markets to demand trading activity – 'hold' does not usually mean hold for the long term and engage with the company's management. Also, there is a commission to be made by brokers making the trading recommendation. An additional factor has been the propensity for consultants to measure fund managers' performance against relative, not absolute, benchmarks. Typically, performance against the benchmark will be reviewed on a quarterly basis and fund managers will be conscious of the risk of being over/underweight in a particular stock in case this might put them out of line with the benchmark.

For boards of companies the message is also a little confused. They will hold meetings with brokers and analysts on a regular basis and, where there is underperformance, discussions will naturally focus on how this is to be addressed in the immediate future. It is rare for boards to communicate directly with the beneficial owners, whose perspective may be different from that of their intermediaries. Also, even if beneficial owners want to be involved at that level of detailed communication, FSMA 2000 rules designating the management of investments as a regulated activity which cannot be conducted by unauthorised persons may in practice constrain them from having day-to-day dealings with their investee companies. Given the pressures under which both boards and fund managers operate, however, there is an increasing onus on beneficial owners to impose their own longer-term perspective on the investment process through clear mandates to their investment managers.

As can be seen, there is a clear tension between the demands of the capital markets and the aspiration that shareholders should invest for the long term. The government-commissioned Kay Review examined these tensions and found evidence that, although boards tended to focus on long-term strategy and performance, they were subject to short-term pressures from investors. While the government has stated that, in many areas, it considers best practice and cultural change to be preferable to regulatory policy (and has indicated it does not intend to disenfranchise short-term shareholders), the *Corporate Governance Reform* Green Paper published in late 2016 demonstrates that the Government is committed to keeping an open mind to introducing legislative requirements where voluntary approaches are perceived to be ineffective.

## Conflicts of interest

The fund management industry relies significantly on trust and a failure to deal adequately with conflicts of interest can erode that trust. Recognising the problem, the UK Stewardship Code requires that institutional shareholders define how they will minimise or deal with such conflicts. This is clearly important to the integrity of the shareholder control process. *The Company Law Review Final Report* worryingly reported that there was 'completely convincing evidence' from fund managers of instances where company management had sought to create and/or exploit conflicts of interest by threatening to withdraw or withhold business opportunities from their institutional investors or associates (e.g. in relation to the investment of the company's pension scheme assets). Additional conflicts can arise with respect to the manager's in-house funds or where it holds shares in more than one party to a transaction or holds within its portfolio shares in its parent company. The 2003 revelations about the mishandling of conflicts by mutual funds in the US are illustrative of the problems that can arise.

Investment management agreements will typically deal at some length with conflicts of interest arising in relation to in-house funds and where shares are held for more than one party to a transaction. The FCA Handbook requires fund managers to identify and manage conflicts of interests between them and their clients or between one client and another so as to avoid any material risk of damage to the interests of their clients (see SYSC10, contained in FCA Handbook, available at www.fca.org.uk).

## Resources available to institutional shareholders

Major institutional shareholders will commonly have a team of several people dedicated to corporate governance. They will need to bring a broad range of skills to bear, including investment analysis, accounting and management consultancy. The external resources available to such in-house governance teams include shareholder representative bodies and network organisations, the services offered by proxy voting agencies and the information provided by corporate governance indices.

### Shareholder representative bodies

There are several UK shareholder representative bodies which function in many respects as trade associations for the professional investor community, including the Association of British Insurers (ABI), the PLSA, the IA, the Association of Investment Companies (AIC) and the Local Authority Pension Fund Forum (LAPFF). Each of these is, to a greater or lesser degree, an exponent of more and better shareholder engagement as set out in their corporate governance policies. As well as speaking for their members in formal consultations and discussions with Government and regulators generally, they provide significant resources to their members through research and best practice guidance.

### Shareholder network organisations

Several other organisations function as global alliances of shareholders with a keen interest in corporate governance matters from the shareholder perspective. Perhaps the most established and influential of these is the ICGN, which brings the investment community together to debate and agree major policy issues and to develop and encourage adherence to governance standards and guidelines. Its members are estimated to hold assets totalling around US$26 trillion. Other shareholder network organisations exist to promote social, environmental and ethical considerations through the adoption of SRI policies and place considerable emphasis on shareholder activism as a result.

### Proxy voting advisers

There are various service providers, such as the Institutional Voting Information Service (IVIS), Pensions Investment Research Consultants (PIRC) and Manifest, which offer investors research and voting recommendations on the corporate governance credentials and performance of investee companies. In 2013, following a report by the European Securities and Markets Authority (ESMA), an industry-led group was formed which worked to establish a code of conduct for proxy advisers, namely the Best Practice Principles for Proxy Voting Research and Analysis. The Principles address ESMA's main concerns about conflicts of interest and transparency as well as some secondary issues and can be summarised as follows:

- Principle one – services should be delivered in accordance with agreed client specifications and signatories should have, and publicly disclose, their research methodology and, if applicable, 'house' voting policies;
- Principle two – signatories should have and publicly disclose a conflicts-of-interest policy that details procedures for addressing potential or actual conflicts of interest; and
- Principle three – signatories should have and publicly disclose policies for communication with issuers, shareholder proponents, other stakeholders, media and the public.

A significant amount of guidance accompanies the Principles explaining in greater detail what is expected.

### Delegation of stewardship arrangements

Under asset management arrangements, end-investors will frequently delegate their stewardship activities to the investment manager mandated to look after their holdings. Local authority pension funds have been at the forefront of schemes that are committed to the merits of shareholder engagement. In March 2012, the LAPFF issued an updated guide on shareholder engagement,

*Best practice guidelines: Assessing asset managers*, to assist administrators of local authority funds to develop their policies on activism and to improve their evaluation of the performance of their fund managers.

The Stewardship Code is clear that asset owners must set out their expectations clearly within the mandates given to their investment managers if their intention is that the investment manager should engage with companies on their behalf. Alternatively, they may engage directly with the companies in which they have holdings but, even where a direct approach is taken, the investment manager will have a role to play. Investment managers are required under the Code to account to their clients how they have carried out those responsibilities, providing both qualitative and quantitative information. The asset owners will want to discuss the precise format and content of that report with their investment managers in order to ensure it meets their information needs. Based on that information, the asset owner should then report annually to those to whom they are accountable on their stewardship policy and its execution.

## Relations with shareholders

Some might suggest that much shareholder activism, particularly of the more confrontational type, is simply filling the void left by poor investor relations (IR) by companies. Communication is, of course, a two-way process and shareholder communication is no exception. It requires mechanisms, therefore, not only for the company to inform shareholders about how it manages and governs the organisation and its business, but also to enable shareholders to share their views and expectations with management. The FRC *Guidance on Board Effectiveness* sets the tone for best practice in this area and the priority with which companies should treat shareholder dialogue by stating:

> 'communication of a company's governance presents an opportunity for the company to improve the quality of the dialogue with its shareholders and other stakeholders, generating greater levels of trust and confidence'.

The UK Corporate Governance Code emphasises the board's collective responsibility for shareholder relations. Accordingly, Code Principle E.1 states as follows:

> 'There should be a dialogue with shareholders based on the mutual understanding of objectives. The board as a whole has responsibility for ensuring that satisfactory dialogue with shareholders takes place.'

Notwithstanding this collective responsibility, certain directors will have more active roles to play than others. The chairman will take a lead in ensuring effective communication with shareholders and stakeholders and should ensure that his or her personal narrative in the annual report on board leadership and effectiveness provides a clear picture of the board's governance arrangements and how they are carried out in practice. Even the process of considering those disclosures can be of benefit as the FRC *Guidance on Board Effectiveness* points out:

> 'thinking about such disclosures can prompt the board to reflect on the quality of its governance and what actions it might take to improve its structures, processes and systems'.

This idea fits well with the chairman's board evaluation responsibilities. Chapter 11 on the chairman explores his or her role in 'representing the company to its principal audiences' in greater detail. The Supporting Principles to Code Principle E.1, while recognising the important role of the chairman (and senior independent director (SID)), note that most shareholder contact will be with the chief executive and the finance director. They will be active in the important process of continual communication with major shareholders, will present the interim and preliminary results and will have appropriate questions referred to them during the AGM. The company secretary will clearly also need to be closely involved with various aspects of shareholder communication and best practice, in terms of stewardship dialogue, has already been covered earlier in this chapter. The emphasis in the following paragraphs, therefore, is not on the individual roles of the various board members or on the nature of shareholder dialogue, but rather on other aspects of a successful IR programme to support the achievement of effective relations with the company's shareholders.

### The IR manager

IR matters include the broad range of activities through which a quoted company communicates with its current and potential investors and other stakeholders. In view of the demands of disclosure, transparency and corporate governance compliance, it is now accepted that IR is an area of specialism that needs to be recognised in its own right. Its practitioners, whether they work in-house or in an advisory capacity, have a vital role to play in helping companies to manage these issues and to communicate more effectively with the investment community. While the company secretary will often have an overall responsibility for IR matters, especially in the smaller quoted company context, the advent of the director of corporate communications as a distinct role, plus the creation by many companies of a specific IR manager role, indicates that effective communication with shareholders requires rather more than has historically been the case.

To be an effective IR manager will require the role holder to have a thorough understanding of the company's business and strategic objectives and the capacity for communicating these to the market. This will require not only good communication skills, but also an understanding of the regulatory background and relevant financial, legal and accounting issues. These issues are likely to require periodic working with the company's key advisers.

The IR manager should keep the company's shareholder register under regular review to spot trends and material changes in its composition and in this respect will want to work closely with the company secretarial team and registrars. The IR manager should also be aware of developments affecting the investor community generally. For example, when designing the company's communications and reporting programme, the IR manager should have in mind the engagement demands and expectations of institutional investors.

## The fundamentals of an effective IR programme

The introduction to the LSE's publication *Investor Relations – A Practical Guide* describes the purpose of an IR programme in the following terms:

> 'the aim of embarking on an ongoing investor relations programme is that it enables the investment community to have greater awareness of the company's investment case and commercial activities so that shareholders, potential investors and traders, can each take an informed view and a decision as to their involvement with that particular company'.

The publication notes that a successful IR programme should be designed to achieve three main outcomes:

- a fair market valuation for the company;
- access to capital in the future; and
- a reasonable level of liquidity in its shares.

As can be seen, the intended benefits are significant and have the potential to contribute significantly to both the company's performance financially and its wider reputation in the market. The main components of an effective IR programme are illustrated in Figure 5.2.

## Useful resources on IR matters

The LSE's previously mentioned publication, *Investor Relations – A Practical Guide*, provides detailed advice on putting IR into practice, for example on the content of the IR section of the company website, and sets out the

**Figure 5.2** Components of an IR programme

|  | |  |
|---|---|---|
| Financial reporting | → | Dissemination of trading updates, interim and preliminary results and the annual report, ensuring the reports tell the company story effectively and clearly. |
| General meetings | → | Planning for the AGM, predicting likely shareholder issues and preparing board briefings. |
| Investor and analyst briefings | → | Preparation of presentations for delivery of key business messages at briefing meetings or site visits with investors, private client brokers, sell-side analysts, etc., fielding issues on strategy and governance and addressing investor queries. |
| Press releases | → | Drafting releases, setting embargoes and managing market impact and dealing with financial journalists. Building relationships with the press over time can bring significant value. |
| Corporate governance | → | Communicating governance arrangements clearly, explaining non-compliance with the UK Corporate Governance Code, managing investor concerns. |
| CSR disclosures | → | Drafting disclosures on CSR matters, including environmental impacts and ethical investment matters, ensuring that disclosures provide a clear link to strategy. |
| Regulatory compliance | → | Researching key regulatory developments relating to disclosures, market abuses, financial information, etc. |
| Corporate website and social media | → | Creating and maintaining the corporate website, facilitating web casts and other internet-based communications. |
| Crisis management | → | Ensuring the chief executive and other board members communicate openly and effectively during a major crisis to protect the company's reputation and prevent unwarranted falls in share price. |
| Communication with the board | → | Ensuring the board is well briefed on shareholder views and directors have the information they need to gauge the likely shareholder perception of potential decisions. |

regulatory background and the expectations of different parties for whom the IR programme is relevant.

The Investor Relations Society is a further source of useful materials on IR matters. It aims to promote best practice in IR; to support the professional development of its members; to represent their views to regulatory bodies, the investment community and government; and to act as a forum for issuers and the investment community. The Society publishes its views on best practice on its website (www.irs.org.uk).

IR is not an exclusively internal activity and is likely to involve a variety of outside parties and advisers including the company's registrar, brokers, financial PR firms, IR advisers and sometimes legal advisers. For an AIM-listed company, the advice of the company's Nomad will also be critical.

### Financial and narrative reporting

A company's IR programme clearly needs to extend far beyond issuing its financial results. However, the report and accounts remains a fundamental document and its style and content is often used as a yardstick against which to measure a company's commitment to clear and transparent disclosure. Commitment to the highest disclosure standards, particularly in the ever-developing arena of narrative reporting, engenders trust and confidence in an organisation and its board amongst those stakeholders to whom the board is ultimately accountable. This important link is increasingly well recognised.

Specific reporting requirements are discussed in greater detail elsewhere in this book, but it is worthwhile noting here the general value which may be gained through high-quality disclosure. The focus should be on ensuring that reports communicate effectively with shareholders. To do this they need to be open and honest, easily understandable and free from unnecessary disclosures which obscure the real messages, as well as interesting and engaging to the reader. The FRC's focus on 'cutting clutter' is relevant here and the associated reports it has published contain some useful ideas for discussion and disclosure aids which may assist companies to achieve these aims.

### Online investor communications

The internet is widely recognised as a very useful IR tool and best practice now requires that companies with a public shareholder base develop their own website containing relevant corporate and IR information. Companies subject to the DTR are required to announce on their website where the annual financial report, half-year financial report and interim management statement are published and traded companies are also subject to various statutory requirements for the publication of information on websites. With the CA 2006 enabling the use of websites as the default mechanism for providing documents and information to members, online investor communication, already widely used for some years, is now firmly established as the principal means of disseminating reports and notices to shareholders.

The Investor Relations Society, while endorsing the use of online communication, cautions 'it should not be seen as a replacement for direct communications or as a means to keep shareholders at arms' length'. This is not to say, however, that it should just be used as an archive of published corporate information. The use of audio or video webcasts and the provision of supplementary information about how the company is managed and governed on behalf of its shareholders can make the IR website a useful resource for investors, both those who already own shares and those who are considering doing so. CSR disclosures should also receive comprehensive treatment in the corporate website.

In accordance with the UK Corporate Governance Code, key governance information, including terms of reference and membership for the key board committees, should be available. Directors' photographs and biographical details should be included and this could also be extended to senior executive within the business.

Financial information for shareholders such as historical dividend payments and share price information, key upcoming dates in the corporate calendar and useful shareholder contacts such as the registrar will also be included.

The LSE's *Investor Relations – A Practical Guide* contains some helpful thoughts on both these issues of content but also on usability and functionality matters.

Alongside the company's website, an IT social media policy may be relevant provided that care is taken to ensure that even informal tweets are compliant with regulatory requirements!

## Measuring IR success

As outlined above in relation to stewardship dialogue, a good IR programme will leave investors, analysts and other interested parties in a position to make informed judgements and decisions. As an indirect corollary, it may lead to better results when the company seeks to raise fresh capital or to communicate new business objectives. It will also have a vital role to play under the 'comply or explain' regime where the board chooses not to comply with a particular provision of the UK Corporate Governance Code and to communicate its reasons to shareholders accordingly. Such explanations are more likely to be positively received if a relationship of trust and confidence in the company has been established over time with shareholders. Success may ultimately be measured, however, as much by the absence of IR problems as it is by achievement against clearly quantifiable outcomes.

## Conclusion

Ultimately, with increasing powers being given to shareholders, such as the advisory vote on the remuneration report and the binding vote on the remuneration policy, engagement between companies and shareholders has never been more important. It may not always be the case that the strategy and outlook of the investee company fully reflects the objectives of the investor, and so, to avoid adverse criticism and, potentially investor activism, engagement on key decisions is paramount. It is acknowledged that there is not always a clear process for engaging with shareholders and, to address this, corporate governance bodies are working towards putting in place guidance on how to facilitate engagement. It will, no doubt, take time to perfect the level and quality of the dialogue between investors and investees. In the meantime, the push for improved disclosures, transparency and timely reporting should help to bridge any disconnection.

## Governance checklist

✓ Are the motivations for shareholder activism well understood as well as the mechanisms by which shareholders can exercise their rights?

✓ Is the AGM well planned and integrated in the company's overall investor engagement strategy?

✓ Does the board consider and annually review an investor engagement programme, taking account of relevant best practice, the expectations of shareholders, potential developments during the year and previously received feedback on the company's engagement approach?

✓ Does the company get the housekeeping right for its engagement strategy, ensuring the right people are invited and that the events are attended by the right individuals from the company?

✓ Does the company's shareholder dialogue programme provide a range of opportunities for one-to-one and collective meetings to consider long-term strategy and performance and are there opportunities for engagement provided to investors of non-equity asset classes?

✓ Has an appropriately experienced IR manager been appointed to oversee the IR programme for the company in its dealings with shareholders?

✓ Is narrative reporting open and transparent and of a sufficiently high standard to engender faith in the company and enhance the company's reputation amongst its stakeholders?

✓ Is the company's website up-to-date with current best practice and regulatory requirements and is it the natural point of reference for stakeholders seeking information about the company?

# 6
# Corporate social responsibility

## Definitions, aims and perspectives

Corporate social responsibility (CSR) is now embedded in the mainstream of corporate governance thinking. This chapter begins by setting out the background and attempting a definition of what this type of corporate activity and reporting is all about.

### Political and corporate background

Over the past decade or so, the momentum behind CSR has escalated significantly. At the UN Millennium Summit in 2000, participating governments adopted a series of Millennium Development Goals which were in part aimed at setting a framework for private sector businesses to act in partnership with governments on matters ranging from tackling poverty to protecting the environment. These goals were reaffirmed in a 2010 review, which noted that progress could be accelerated by the promotion of effective public-private partnerships. In particular, Goal 8 on the development of a global partnership for development invites the private sector to cooperate on providing new technologies to assist developing countries (for example, by pharmaceutical companies donating essential drugs at affordable prices).

The World Summit on Sustainable Development in Johannesburg in 2002 and its follow-up summit in Rio de Janeiro in 2012 gave further impetus to the principle that corporate entities should take responsibility for addressing social and economic development needs and environmental protection matters. The resulting measures built upon the pre-existing *OECD Guidelines for Multinationals*, with a view to enhancing their impact and relevance. More recently, the UN Human Rights Commission has published a number of reports on the human rights responsibilities of corporate enterprises and in particular *United Nations Guiding Principles on Business and Human Rights* provides helpful clarification of the universal human rights responsibilities of businesses. In 2016 the World Economic Forum published a guide for businesses to achieve both corporate and societal value through innovation.

Within the EU, the political momentum behind CSR and the principle of sustainable development has also been significant. The EC has a history of giving greater political visibility to CSR and CSR goals are reflected in both the Europe 2020 Strategy, which includes targets on relevant issues such as the environment, poverty and social exclusion, as well as in the EU CSR Strategy 2011–14. The 2011 communication on that strategy promoted a strategic approach to CSR by businesses as 'increasingly important to the competitiveness of enterprises' citing potential risk management benefits, cost savings, enhanced access to capital, better customer relationships, improved human resource management and increased innovation capacity. The communication observed that CSR 'concerns actions by companies over and above their legal obligations towards society and the environment' but that, while CSR is therefore essentially voluntary, regulatory measures can 'create an environment more conducive to enterprises voluntarily meeting their social responsibility'. EU regulations on CSR reporting in the form of changes to the Accounting Directives were announced in 2014 with a view to requiring larger companies (those with 500+ employees) to report relevant and material information on policies, results and risks concerning environmental aspects, social and employee-related matters, respect for human rights, anti-corruption and bribery issues and diversity on the boards of directors. In accordance with the Directive, the Commission will publish non-binding guidelines on the methodology for reporting non-financial information.

Many of these themes were already covered in the strategic report requirements. Indeed much of the current focus both at home and further afield is on the need for effective narrative reporting in relation to CSR issues and in particular on the need to make clear connections between financial and non-financial disclosures. Of particular relevance here is the work of the International Integrated Reporting Committee (IIRC) which has developed a strategy to achieve a meaningful shift towards adoption of an international integrated reporting framework. The IIRC's objective is to establish integrated reporting and thinking within mainstream business practice. The IIRC's vision is 'to align capital allocation and corporate behaviour to wider goals of financial stability and sustainable development' through that integrated reporting and thinking. The IIRC believes that, by reinforcing such connections through integrated reporting, business will be helped to take more sustainable decisions and investors and other stakeholders will be better able to understand how an organisation is really performing.

In the UK, there have also been a number of other significant initiatives of relevance to CSR issues, including the introduction of various measures in the CA 2006, regulations on SRI matters for pension scheme trustees, the adoption of environmental targets such as those on reductions in greenhouse gas (GHG) emissions, the introduction of wide-reaching anti-corruption measures through the Bribery Act 2010 and regulation of reporting on modern slavery.

Directors' duties in relation to the wider impact of their company's activities, set out in s. 172 of the CA 2006, specifically embrace the idea of 'enlightened shareholder value' whereby long-term success is made more likely by having regard to stakeholders generally. The 2016 Green Paper, *Corporate Governance Reform*, is looking at additional ways to strengthen this regime.

There have been several other developments in the corporate world that have pushed the CSR agenda forward. Accounting standard setters are giving more attention to the valuation of intangible non-financial assets of companies. NGOs' agendas increasingly focus on the role of companies as servants of wider social and public interest objectives. Investors, including pension scheme trustees and other fiduciaries, are paying more regard to the link between shareholder value and sustainable and responsible investment (SRI) strategies. Moreover, consumers, employees and society at large are being encouraged to view themselves as key stakeholders alongside shareholders.

## Definitions and perspectives

'CSR' is commonly used as a shorthand term to describe responsible corporate behaviour in the broadest sense. However, an appreciation that there are wider issues to corporate responsibility than the purely social has caused some users to drop CSR as a descriptive term. They generally prefer 'corporate responsibility', with a view to highlighting that what is involved is the full range of responsible internal and external behaviour, including, but not limited to, behaviour that has a social impact. For convenience and adopting the majority view, CSR is the preferred term throughout this chapter. Whatever descriptive term is used, there is no universally recognised definition of what it means. Those who approach the subject can have in mind a wide range of different corporate aims: for some it has a moral appeal to the extent that it is about sustainability and ethical investment, for others it is about managing risks and safeguarding corporate reputation and brands, whereas for others it is about marketing strategy and building profits and competitive advantage.

In its communication, *A Reviewed EU Strategy 2011-14 for Corporate Social Responsibility*, the EC defined CSR as:

> 'the responsibility of enterprises for their impact on society.'

The explanatory narrative that accompanies that definition is clear that compliance with regulation and legislation is only the starting point. Beyond this baseline of good behaviour, organisations are expected to develop a process 'to integrate social, environmental, ethical, human rights and consumer concerns into their business operations and core strategy'. They should do so 'in close collaboration with their stakeholders'. The twin aims of this are to:

- maximise shared value creation for owners, other stakeholders and society generally; and
- identify, prevent and mitigate potential adverse impacts.

In other words, in addition to the underlying legal framework, a kind of 'super compliance' is expected on a self-motivated or voluntary basis. There is a fairly fine distinction to be drawn here between regulatory and voluntary compliance. The latter relies upon companies recognising the business case for CSR.

It is difficult to arrive at a crisp and settled definition mainly because the CSR community contains such a diverse group of constituents. Each of these has their own perspectives and priorities and tends therefore to view CSR issues accordingly. Table 6.1 summarises their typical perspectives and aims.

**Table 6.1** Perspectives and aims of the CSR community

| Group | CSR perspectives and aims |
|---|---|
| **Government** | Views CSR as integral to a larger strategy for sustainable development; emphasises business case for CSR and supports wider stakeholder involvement; traditionally light touch on regulation; aims to build supportive regulatory and market framework. |
| **Corporate enterprises** | Affirm that CSR is voluntary in nature and should not stifle business creativity; fundamentally, about managing business risk and winning competitive advantage; CSR imperatives must fit with the overall business objectives. |
| **NGOs** | Vocal representatives of special interest groups; architects of numerous best practice codes; work closely with regulators and professional bodies; provide an informal monitoring role and a level of informal independent verification. |
| **Trade unions** | Advocate a regulatory framework establishing minimum standards; companies to work in partnership with stakeholders; particular focus on labour and human rights abuses; want mechanisms ensuring accountability by companies. |
| **Institutional investors** | Seek improved disclosure and transparency; need more consistent verification of performance and objective 'triple bottom line' reporting; looking for sustainable performance and well-managed business risk. |

Table 6.1 *continued*

| Group | CSR perspectives and aims |
|---|---|
| **Private investors** | Have an appetite for ethical pooled investment funds; expectation that companies will exhibit ethical behaviour beyond mere legal compliance; increased pressure on trustees of pension funds and other fiduciaries. |
| **Consumer groups** | Underline the importance of trustworthy information, including labelling; 'fair trade' concerns about conditions in which goods are produced and traded; seek responsible advertising; linkage of brand with corporate reputation. |

With so many different perspectives, it is useful to focus on some of the common areas of agreement about CSR. In particular, there is now a consensus about the business case for CSR.

## The business case for CSR

In the 2014 Department for Business, Innovation and Skills (BIS) report, *Corporate Responsibility – Good for Business and Society*, the voluntary nature of good corporate behaviour, beyond what is required by law or regulation, was recognised. The need for that behaviour to be driven by commercial benefits was therefore acknowledged. The business case for CSR must be based on having the potential to increase a company's performance and shareholder value.

The 2014 report noted that such value might be created through enhanced staff recruitment and retention, managing supply chain risk, driving innovation, productivity and new markets or even through development of new business models. The role of the State in this regard is mainly one of leadership, supporting and promoting good CSR practices generally and providing the frameworks through which businesses can undertake their activities responsibly. Such support and leadership will include working with businesses to reduce poverty and promote human rights overseas, providing support to businesses operating in different sectors, promoting corporate responsibility on the international stage, encouraging companies to engage in CSR practices that will tackle disadvantage in the UK, improving standards of health and safety and investment in workplace skills, facilitating the transition to a low-carbon economy and encouraging volunteering, charitable giving and social enterprise. Some different elements of the business case for CSR are now examined.

## The business case for CSR: enhanced reputation

Surveys and polls have consistently confirmed that companies with a business stance that is expressly focused on their social, environmental and ethical performance can enhance their reputation and thereby their brand. Perhaps the greatest incentive for preserving reputation in this manner is the damage that can be done to the brand where CSR issues are handled badly. By way of example, note the damage done to the reputation of BP following the 2010 Gulf oil disaster, the immediate identification of Primark as the customer of the unsafe Bangladesh factory which collapsed in April 2013 or the 2015 outcry over the use of 'defeat devices' in VW cars to produce better emissions testing results.

Such criticism, however, is not always entity-specific and can extend to entire sectors or number of organisations. The damage done to the banking sector by scandals such as that caused by Libor manipulation practices, public criticism over unacceptable invasions of privacy by certain members of the press and accusations of nepotism aimed at industries who traditionally draw their staff from amongst those who have attended top fee-paying schools are all examples of broad-brush censure that can impact companies by association rather than necessarily resulting from any actual 'wrong-doing' on their part.

To counter such perceptions, there has been an advent of what has been described as cause-related marketing, whereby companies have been attracted to the benefits of forming partnerships with charities so as to associate their name or a product or service with good causes. One example is Pampers' partnership with UNICEF, donating a tetanus vaccine for each pack of nappies sold. More quirky is Innocent Smoothies' 'Big Knit' campaign, whereby bottles sold with a hand-knitted woolly hat generated a 25p donation to Age UK. Not only did this generate funds for the charity, but by bringing people together to knit the hats, social exclusion was also tackled.

Damage limitation is not the only driver. Taking account of the impact of the business on communities and the environment and initiating positive action in relation to those impacts, for example a supermarket chain acting to reduce food waste and to distribute surplus stock to those in need, can be a powerful way of making an organisation's values 'real'. A strong CSR stance can make a brand stand out from the crowd and to this extent CSR can be seen as an important marketing and brand-management tool. For example, in its July 2014 Values and Ethics Poll of more than 74,000 customers, employees and other stakeholders, 84% of respondents identified the bank's ethical policy as a key reason for opting to have their account with the Co-operative.

Like many issues of culture, however, care should be taken to ensure consistency of attitude. A business which builds a reputation for being socially responsible, for example through cause-related marketing, could find itself accused of hypocrisy if it was, for example, found to be avoiding taxes.

Enhancing brand and reputation through CSR initiatives can entice customers willing to pay a premium for products and services which they regard as socially or environmentally responsible, improve employee satisfaction, make the company more appealing to new recruits and attract shareholders looking for SRI opportunities. However, linking CSR performance issues with the preservation or enhancement of corporate reputation without real evidence can cause the quality of reporting to be compromised. CSR reports, which are replete with fine but ultimately bland statements and that are more about image than substance, may be perceived as nothing more than window-dressing.

### Case study: Vodafone

In October 2010, protestors forced several branches of Vodafone to close, including the flagship Oxford Street store. Their protest related to the perceived 'tax dodging' practices of the group following agreement reached with HMRC to settle tax on a historic purchase of a German business via a Luxembourg subsidiary.

Protestors compared the £1.25bn settlement to an alleged sum of £6bn that they believed Vodafone actually owed to HMRC. At a time of welfare cuts and other austerity measures, the protestors' claims had a sympathetic reception, with anti-Vodafone media reporting added to the pressure.

Despite HMRC confirming that the £6bn tax figure was nothing more than an 'urban myth', the UK National Audit Office was brought in to carry out an investigation which concluded that the settlement was reasonable and, in one aspect, may have been better than reasonable for the UK.

The case highlighted not only the risk that could arise from taking an aggressive approach to tax efficiency, but also the reputational risks that can arise from protracted disputes that result in high-profile settlement of significant cases.

While ultimately Vodafone was found to have reached a reasonable settlement with HMRC, by that point the reputational damage had already been done.

Vodafone are far from being alone in terms of receiving unwelcome attention in relation to their tax affairs. Google, Starbucks and others have all been publicly vilified for failing to pay their 'fair share' of tax.

### The business case for CSR: competitiveness

There is mounting evidence that companies that run sustainable businesses with an explicit CSR strategy will prove more competitive and therefore profitable in the long run. Nielson's 2015 *Global Corporate Sustainability Report* found not only that CSR issues were a driver in a significant proportion of consumer purchasing decisions, but also that 66% of those surveyed were willing to pay a premium for sustainable goods. That percentage was both higher than in previous years and reflected a greater tendency for consumers in developing markets to pay more for a sustainable product.

Moreover, with ever-more mainstream brands adopting high-profile ethical stances, for example the move to Rainforest Alliance certified tea by PG tips and the use of Fairtrade ingredients in certain supermarket own brand products, companies which fail to meet similar standards may begin to find themselves marginalised compared to their peers and losing market share as a result. Public dissatisfaction with, for example, Sports Direct's practices, particularly its treatment of workers, has arguably started to weaken its competitiveness.

For companies engaging in lifelong learning programmes for their employees, enhancement of workplace skills can lead to greater efficiency and improved innovation. Improved relationships with suppliers, brought about through the deployment of fairer terms of business, and the imposition of minimum standards in relation to issues such as bribery, health and safety and terms of employment, for example, can also bring the competitive advantages of a more secure supply chain. There can also be little doubt that there is scope for CSR activities to improve competitiveness in areas where the internal costs are more measurable, e.g. with respect to improved efficiency in the use of energy, reduction of waste and other indicators connected to resource management. While some benefits may only seem intuitive, the *KPMG International Survey of Corporate Responsibility Reporting* 2011 found that innovation and learning were consistently identified by the big businesses they surveyed as key drivers for CSR reporting and, importantly, that a significant proportion of the companies could identify financial advantages from their CSR activities.

Overall, the competitiveness aspects of CSR present a complex picture. A serious challenge for proponents of CSR is the relative absence of sufficient clear-cut evidence on non-financial returns for these to become standard parameters in the financial modelling of professional analysts. If standard valuation frameworks were to take account of CSR factors and increase the value placed by capital markets on businesses who demonstrated socially responsible behaviour, the business case for CSR as providing competitive advantage would be strengthened. Developments in this area in relation to the valuation placed upon CSR activities by investors are explored further below.

### The business case for CSR: risk management

The requirement to manage financial, legal and operational risks to achieve the delivery of optimum returns to shareholders has long been high in the consciousness of boards. A requirement to manage non-financial business risks related to the company's intangibles has also been on board agendas for some time. For example, included in the list of potentially significant risks in the former Turnbull Guidance were those related to health and safety, the environment, corporate reputation and business probity. However, the attention of boards of quoted companies will no doubt have been sharpened in this regard by the CA 2006 requirements in relation to the reporting of CSR issues in the strategic report.

That report must now include 'a description of the principal risks and uncertainties facing the company' and contain information on environmental matters, employees, human rights and social and community issues, including information about any policies on those matters and the effectiveness of those policies. Such developments have caused boards to reassess their processes for managing and disclosing non-financial risks.

The 2006 position paper on narrative reporting from the ABI (now the Investment Association) made the point that where social, environmental and ethical issues are material, 'they should be fully integrated into the Board's overall strategic approach to management of risks and opportunities and not treated as a separate "add on" consideration. The Investment Committee feels this will help investors see these issues in the proper context of the development and direction of the business.' The 2011 KPMG Survey put it another way, citing the adage 'what gets measured gets managed' to support the argument that reporting of CSR issues is itself a driver for ensuring their better management, including the management of associated risks. It is apparent that dealing with such sources of risk through the development and implementation of an effective CSR response now falls within the mainstream of effective business management.

### The board's response to CSR

For company directors, theoretical debates about the merits or otherwise of CSR are of less interest than the realities of operating their businesses in an environment in which regulator, media and consumer perceptions on business and moral issues are constantly developing and they need to react accordingly. Many companies will feel that they simply cannot afford to ignore CSR issues, irrespective of the strength or otherwise of the perceived business case. Companies that will feel this most keenly include:

- those with dominant market positions (e.g. former state-owned utilities);
- those dealing directly with consumers (e.g. banks and retailers);
- those producing essential staples (e.g. food and medicines); and

- those that exploit natural resources or that depend on supply chains in developing countries (e.g. mining, oil and clothing companies).

Figure 6.1 illustrates the various CSR-related pressures that businesses now face.

**Figure 6.1** CSR pressures

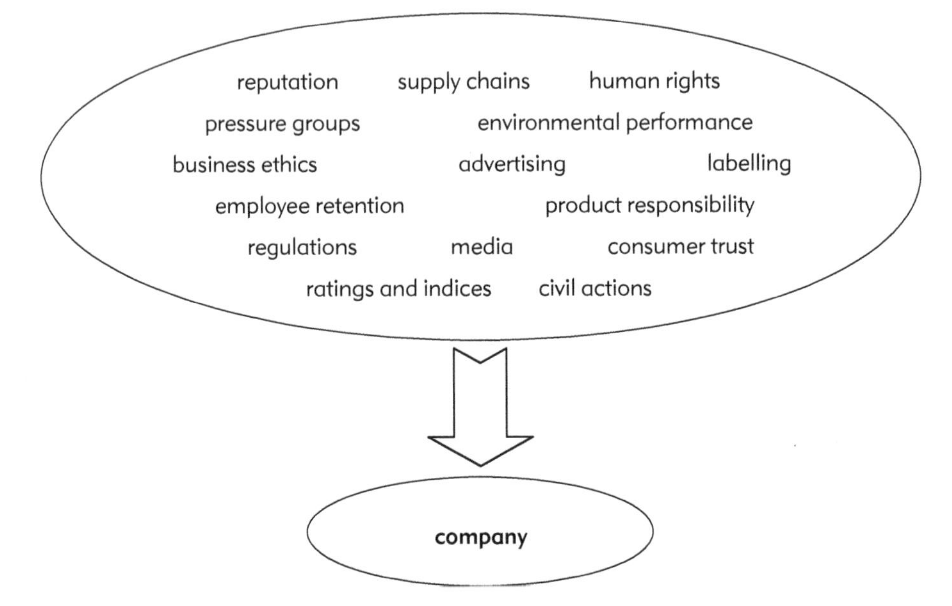


While boards will be constrained to respond to such pressures, when doing so they can draw on the now quite compelling evidence of research about the possible, even inevitable, benefits to the business of doing so and the risks that might increase in the absence of a cohesive CSR strategy. Having considered and understood the business case, the board will wish to develop a CSR strategy.

## Creating a CSR strategy

With limited regulatory CSR requirements, adoption of a CSR strategy will to a large extent be voluntarily based on the perceived business case. The main impetus for taking CSR seriously is not the threat of legal sanctions, but rather serving the long-term interests of the business. This is consistent with the principle that good governance is best achieved by fostering responsible behaviour by companies. Faced with a combination of legal obligations, media and consumer pressure and shareholder activism, the boards of the majority of larger companies view the development and maintenance of a CSR strategy as essential.

Without surrendering its overall leadership responsibility, the board will generally set up a committee with terms of reference to develop and maintain the strategy. It will be tasked with establishing a CSR strategy that is specific to the company's business. It is beyond the scope of this book to describe in any depth how the board should do this. There are, however, several resources available to companies seeking to implement or improve a CSR strategy. *The Corporate Social Responsibility Route Map*, published by The Virtuous Circle and replicated in Figure 6.2, describes some of the key steps.

**Figure 6.2** CSR Route Map

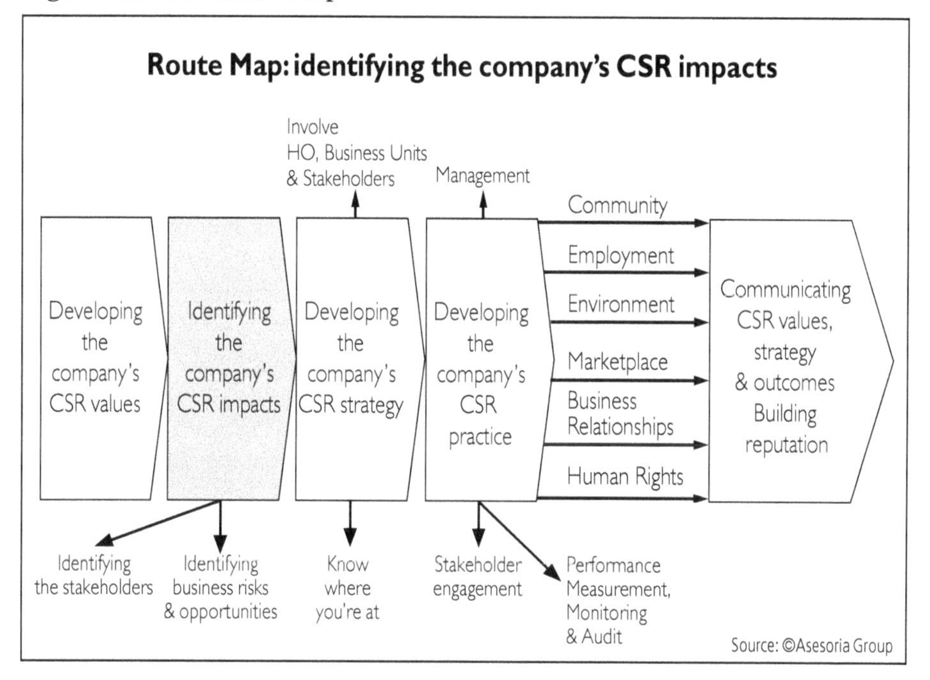


Taking account of the appraisal of the company's corporate values should be undertaken under each of the following headings:

- community;
- employment;
- environment;
- marketplace;
- business relationships; and
- human rights.

Depending on the nature of the business, some of these will be more relevant than others and in many cases there will be overlap and linkage to take account of. In all cases, the workforce and environment are likely to be necessary.

Once the strategy has been determined, it needs to be implemented and regularly reviewed. A phased approach to the introduction of operational changes is often necessary. Like other aspects of the company's values and culture, leadership from the board is essential if the CSR strategy is to be properly and effectively embedded across the organisation. Even where a phased approach is necessary, by defining clearly from the outset where the company wants to get to in terms of its CSR practices and its impact on the environment, employees, community and other stakeholders, embedding of the board's strategy on CSR will not be undermined.

As discussed, the voluntary approach of CSR activity is about corporate behaviour that is over and beyond compliance with normal legal requirements. However, the legal dimension of CSR should not be overlooked.

## CSR and the management of legal risk

Where public policy requires, for example, to outlaw environmental hazards or anti-competition or corrupt practices or to introduce employee protection or health and safety rights, the Government has been quick to change the law to meet the policy objective. In the process it has created internal obligations within companies to address the otherwise unrecognised cost of externalities (for example, adverse environmental impacts). Managing legal risks through the adoption of effective CSR policies requires the in-house legal function to work closely with a range of other internal functions. Figure 6.3 illustrates the link between the various internal disciplines and makes the point that CSR risk spans a number of potential legal risks for the company.

**Figure 6.3** Managing CSR risk

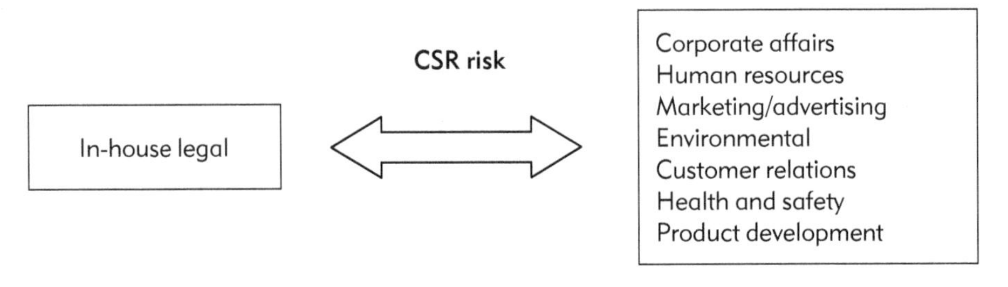


The following paragraphs explore the extent to which the law has the capacity to give enforceable remedies against companies who mismanage their corporate citizenship.

### Directors' duties and liabilities – the CSR context

Chapter 4 relating to directors' duties and liabilities notes the potential for both civil and criminal sanctions if, for example, companies:

- cause environmental damage;
- fail to prevent bribery;
- breach health and safety regulations; or
- adopt discriminatory employment policies.

These are defined by legislation and can be managed as part of the normal internal control processes. However, in the context of CSR, it is useful to consider the impact of s. 172 of the CA 2006, which imposes a duty on directors for the promotion of the success of the company. It requires directors to have regard to six factors relating to the interests of various stakeholders (e.g. employees, suppliers, customers, the community and the environment) and the need to maintain a reputation for high standards of business conduct. Accordingly and consistent with the objective of enhanced shareholder engagement and a long-term investment culture, directors' duties are expressed in terms of a social, ethical and environmental framework. This clarification of the scope of directors' duty of care arguably extends their duties to cover what are essentially CSR performance indicators and indeed, for quoted companies, reporting on non-financial key performance indicators (KPIs), environmental and employee maters, is now part of the strategic report.

### Civil law actions against the company

In the US, the threat of innovative civil law actions has presented companies with an unpredictable type of CSR risk. The fast food business whose products cause obesity, the drinks business whose brand becomes associated with under-age alcohol abuse or the bank whose lending policies are linked to high levels of personal debt may feel vulnerable to claims for damages. Following the BP Gulf oil spill, for example, the company had to make provisions for the cost of the disaster and faced a huge number of expensive civil lawsuits.

While civil law remedies of the type experienced in the US may differ from those available to complainants under English law, companies can be subjected to damaging and potentially libellous campaigns by well-organised pressure groups. These can prove difficult to counteract.

#### Case study: McLibel litigation

Fast food company McDonald's brought a libel claim against two UK resident environmentalists. McDonald's alleged that they had distributed a six-page leaflet entitled *What's wrong with McDonald's?* which contained libellous statements. The subsequent defamation trial, the longest in English legal history, attracted significant media attention and resulted in an 800-page judgement. McDonald's won the case and several of the statements were held to be libellous, although other statements made in the leaflet, including that McDonald's exploited children with targeted advertising and that some workers were paid poorly at that time, were upheld. Most commentators were of the view that the damage to its reputation far outweighed the relatively minor monetary damages it obtained. It has been reported that only 40 copies of the disputed leaflet were distributed, yet more than 183,000 people read it on a website where it was published.

## Law and global trading practices

Companies that operate globally, particularly in higher-risk industries such as mining and oil extraction, were some of the first to give serious attention to their CSR policies. They face obvious CSR challenges on account of the potential environmental impact of their operations and their need to source labour in non-developed and poorly regulated countries. However, the global nature of trade means that companies with apparently local/national businesses may also face similar challenges. The supply chain for commodities (e.g. timber, coffee, clothing, footwear) and outsourced services (e.g. call centres) can stretch well beyond national boundaries and be multi-layered. The key legal question for companies operating in this environment is whether they could face liability in their home jurisdiction for failing to ensure that foreign practices meet appropriate international standards. The cases that have been brought have generally been in the US where the Alien Tort Claims Act 1789 gives the US courts jurisdiction where injuries have been caused outside the US on account of 'violation of the law of nations or a treaty of the United States'.

There are, however, risks of legal penalties from other sources. A prominent example is the 1997 OECD Convention, by which companies, including those with a UK residence, can be prosecuted for bribing a foreign public official of any jurisdiction worldwide. The Bribery Act 2010 modernised the UK's anti-corruption laws and includes criminal offences in relation to the offering or acceptance of bribes whether in the UK or abroad. With directors potentially liable for their company's failings and even their company's suppliers' failings under this Act, boards will want to ensure practices right across their organisation are regularly reviewed to ensure robust anti-corruption policies not only exist but are effective. Transparency International UK, the Serious Fraud Office and the Ministry of Justice have all published guidance in this respect.

It is noteworthy that the environmental management standard ISO 140001, addressed separately below, makes demands of international supply chains in the context of environmental impact. The boundaries between responsible corporate citizenship and international law are relatively undeveloped and there are difficult issues of public policy and legal jurisdiction to resolve. The uncertainty of how the law will develop in this respect is a key risk that companies need to manage.

### Advertising law

Companies whose products or activities carry a higher than usual risk of negative social impact, in particular in relation to vulnerable groups such as children, need to be on their guard to avoid using irresponsible advertising. For example, additional rules apply to the alcohol, tobacco, gambling and weight loss industries under the Advertising Practice Codes published by the Advertising Standards Authority and those Codes also make specific provision in relation to the use of environmental or health claims in advertising as well as addressing issues of privacy. Irresponsible advertising, marketing or products (for example, children's clothing which sexualises its young wearers) may also result in negative media coverage and damaging campaigns by pressure groups. Therefore, ensuring that the company's advertising is appropriate may require attention not only to legal compliance, but also to thoughtful drafting, an appreciation of potential interpretation, wider issues of appropriateness and implementation of relevant ethical policies.

This challenge is all the greater in an age of fast-moving social media campaigns which can perhaps lack the disciplined and extensive planning that is given to more traditional advertising and can therefore be less well thought out. In addition, criticism can spread quickly, making damage limitation all the more difficult.

### Social labelling regulations

There are many rules and schemes for informing consumers on product quality or health and safety. There is an opportunity for companies to allow their CSR policies to shape some of their product labelling or to gain competitive advantage. The number of social, fair-trade and environmental labels is increasing. Unlike organic or safety labels, these do not provide information about the characteristics of a product, but rather its production and trading conditions. Bodies such as the Fairtrade Labelling Organisations International and the Forest Stewardship Council exist to regulate and certify the labelling criteria. A UK environmental labelling code is available in the form of Department for Environment, Food and Rural Affairs (Defra) guidance published in 2016, *Make an Environmental Claim for your Product, Service or Organisation*, which contains useful tips on environmental labelling, including the use of the EU Ecolabel. The Advertising Practice Code is also relevant and other schemes such as the recycling symbol (Mobius loop) and Energy Savings Trust energy-efficiency labelling may also be relevant. Companies that take steps to use such labelling may gain a competitive lead by taking advantage of the increasing interest of consumers in the way goods and services are produced, delivered and marketed but care must be taken to use such labelling clearly and only in respect of substantiated benefits.

### CSR codes and guidelines

The OECD *Guidelines for Multinational Enterprises*, updated in 2011, provide a voluntary framework of 'principles of good conduct' in all the major areas of business ethics, including:

- human rights;
- employment and industrial relations;
- environment;
- combating bribery;
- consumer interests;
- science and technology;
- competition; and
- taxation.

The Department for Business, Energy & Industrial Strategy is the body responsible for promoting such behaviour by UK multinationals in conformity with the OECD Guidelines.

In the field of business ethics, there are many other codes of conduct published by transnational bodies. These include the International Labour Organisation's *Declaration of Principles and Rights at Work* and *Tripartite Declaration of Principles Concerning Multinational Enterprise on Social Policy* and the UN *Global Compact*, corporate signatories to which have pledged to respect and support human and employment-related rights. Also, shareholder organisations and individual institutional investors publish their own guidelines addressing CSR matters. While these will not have the force of law, their status is not far short of legal when they are backed by a significant level of political and shareholder opinion and also when the growing majority of companies see compliance as essential. Sanctions for breaching codes may result in demands for corrective actions and perhaps the ending of a sourcing contract.

## Shareholders and CSR

Shareholder interest in the CSR performance of companies was, for some time, largely confined to private individuals investing in the specialised market for pooled ethical investment funds. These funds are managed according to a policy of either 'negative' screening to exclude unwanted companies from the portfolio or alternatively 'positive' screening to pick out those with the appropriate social and environmental credentials. Institutional investors have responded to private shareholder demands to develop such products for the retail investment market. Several developments have caused institutional shareholders to develop their interest in SRI beyond the market for ethical funds. The consequence for companies is that their CSR performance is now the subject of careful scrutiny by their major shareholders. The key developments are now described. As is noted, there is substantial overlap with the treatment of these developments in Chapters 8 and 5 with respect to narrative reporting and shareholder activism.

## Institutional investors and the business case for CSR

The uncertainties inherent in both identifying and then assessing the financial implications of companies' CSR performance present institutional investors with significant challenges. Without derogating fundamentally from the view that a company is the commercial agency of private property rights, their 'enlightened shareholder value' approach acknowledges that a company that has a good CSR record presents a more attractive long-term investment opportunity than the company that does not. Indices such as the FTSE4Good Index and MSCI KLD 400 Social Index measure the investment returns of companies which meet certain CSR standards and enable comparisons to be made between the long-term investment performances of companies with active CSR policies versus the performance of other entities. However, valuation of ESG factors now extends beyond specialist 'ethical' funds and has become a mainstream investment analysis issue.

The 2016 PwC report, *It's Not Just About Financials – The Widening Variety of Factors in Investment Decision Making*, examined the value that providers of capital place upon non-financial information when assessing a company and its prospects. One of its conclusions was that, far from considering ESG information as 'greenwashing', such details are now considered by investment professionals as capturing important aspects of corporate performance. Investors are increasingly looking to learn about all capitals of the business, namely financial, manufactured, intellectual, human, social and relationship and natural capital.

Professional analysts require clear evidence of non-financial returns before they will routinely include them as parameters in their financial modelling. The EC, in its Europe 2020 Strategy, made a renewed commitment to promote CSR; however, the lack of a clear framework for the valuation by investors and analysts of non-financial factors is seen as an impediment to successfully encouraging businesses to take CSR matters more seriously. Better rewarding companies for behaving in a sustainable and socially responsible manner through higher market valuations is seen as a key driver for encouraging such behaviours. The EC is therefore actively seeking ways in which CSR information can be better integrated into market valuations. The EC sees its interest in this matter as being aligned to the interests of the relevant investment markets who should wish to take account of CSR issues to get the most accurate market valuations of the companies in which they are investing their funds. If within such a framework CSR factors became standard financial modelling parameters, companies who failed to adopt appropriate CSR policies would potentially:

- have difficulty in raising capital from new share issues;
- find the cost of borrowing increases; and
- be generally 'frozen out' by larger institutional shareholders.

One effect of such a development would be to cause public statements on CSR issues issued by companies to be prepared with a view to better informing analysts in the institutional investor community. In this respect, the quality of CSR reporting is critical.

### Institutional shareholder SRI policies

Following the IA's lead (see below), several significant institutional shareholders have stated their position on CSR matters in their own published guidelines and have appointed internal teams dedicated to developing their SRI policies. Where institutional investors perceive CSR underperformance, their stated position tends to be one of engagement with the relevant board of directors and if necessary positive intervention through the exercise of their shareholder voting rights. While the latter may be seen as a last resort, as understanding of the financial importance of environmental and other externalities grows, the possibility of such shareholder activity increasingly cannot be discounted. A prime example of this was the public statement by significant institutional shareholders criticising the governance failings and poor labour practices of Sports Direct. A Union-proposed resolution at the company's 2016 AGM calling for an independent review was passed by a majority of shareholders.

### Pension scheme regulations

Subject to some limited exceptions, the trustees of all UK occupational pension schemes must prepare and publish a statement of investment principles, in which they set out a broad summary of the investment policies they apply to the schemes for which they are responsible. Regulations prescribing the form and content of the statement provide that such statements must state the trustees' policy on the following:

- the extent (if at all) to which social, environmental or ethical considerations are taken into account in the selection, retention and realisation of investments; and
- their policy (if any) in relation to the exercise of the rights (including voting rights) attached to investments.

The point has been made that trustees are faced with a difficult quandary. Their legal responsibilities, based on established case law, require them to act only in the best interests of the beneficiaries of their schemes, which has been interpreted to mean their best financial interests. When setting their investment policies there was concern that trustees might run the risk of being in breach of their duties if they promoted social, environmental or ethical considerations ahead of the achievement of investment returns.

The requirement to address social, environmental and ethical issues and voting matters in the statement of investment principles does not seek to change the law as it applies to trustees' investment duties, however, and such concerns are lessened by the growing body of evidence that ESG practices are entirely relevant to financial valuations and are increasingly a part of mainstream investment decision making.

The focus is on greater disclosure, with the clear intention that this will change the investment environment. While there is little evidence that such disclosure has fundamentally changed the approach of trustees, it has certainly made both them and pension scheme members more aware of the issues. For many trustees, the missing ingredient is completely compelling evidence that an attention to the CSR credentials of their investee companies will enhance investment returns. In this respect, the generally positive findings of research on CSR matters merit consideration and may, if they are further substantiated, cause trustees and other fiduciaries to conclude that it would be a dereliction of their duties not to give due regard to the CSR performance of their investee companies.

## IA disclosure guidelines

The IA (previously the ABI) has published *Guidelines on Responsible Investment Disclosure* which set out the CSR disclosures on ESG matters that its members (i.e. institutional shareholders) would expect to see included in a company's annual report and specifically in the reporting of 'board responsibilities and to policies, procedures and verification'. Notably, the guidelines are stated to be a response to the need to 'identify and manage ESG risks to the long- and short-term value of the business' and by doing so to 'enhance value'.

The guidelines require the annual report to state whether the board of directors:

- takes regular account of the significance of ESG matters to the business of the company;
- has identified and assessed the significant risks to the company's short and long-term value arising from ESG matters, as well as the opportunity just to enhance the value that may arise from an appropriate response;
- has received adequate information to make this assessment and that account is taken of ESG matters in the training of directors; and

- has ensured that the company has in place effective systems for managing and mitigating significant risks, which, where relevant, incorporate performance management systems and appropriate remuneration incentives.

With regard to 'policies, procedures and verification', the guidelines require that the report should:

- include information on ESG-related risks and opportunities that may significantly affect the company's short and long-term value and how they might impact on the future of the business;
- describe the company's policies and procedures for managing risks to short and long-term value arising from ESG matters and – if the annual report states that the company has no such policies and procedures – the board should provide reasons for their absence;
- include information, using KPIs where appropriate, about the extent to which the company has complied with its policies and procedures for managing material risks arising from ESG matters and about the role of the board in providing oversight;
- where performance has fallen short of the objectives, describe the measures the board has taken to put it back on track; and
- describe the procedures for verification of ESG disclosures, provided that the verification procedure should be such as to achieve a reasonable level of credibility.

The guidelines also require that the remuneration report should state whether the remuneration committee:

- is able to consider corporate performance on ESG issues when setting the remuneration of executive directors. If the report states that the committee has no such discretion, then a reason should be provided for its absence; and
- has ensured that the incentive structure for senior management does not raise ESG risks by inadvertently motivating irresponsible behaviour.

The best practice recommended by the IA in these guidelines, which are intended to apply to SMEs as well as larger organisations, requires that the information provided in relation to significant ESG risks is included in the main body of the narrative reports within the report and accounts rather than on a separate website. The guidelines promote verification of such disclosures through either external or internal procedures to ensure that they are credible. Companies should ideally explain the reason for choosing a particular method of verification. The issue of verification is explored later in this chapter.

The guidelines end with lists of compliance questions which shareholders will ask when reviewing the ESG practices of companies and investment trusts. The thrust of these questions is to uncover if the board has taken steps to ensure that ESG risks are identified and managed through the adoption of robust internal control systems. The IA is cautious about being unnecessarily prescriptive on these matters and wants to avoid the imposition of costly burdens. However, it is clear that, although detailed work might be undertaken by a committee, consideration of CSR matters should receive regular main board attention and careful thought should be given to reporting on CSR matters. The reporting of CSR matters is considered next.

## CSR reporting and disclosures

The trend in CSR reporting is unquestionably upwards. The 2011 international survey by KPMG referred to previously found that 95% of Global Fortune 250 companies published corporate responsibility reports, with the highest proportion of CSR reporting companies to be found in Europe. The sections below set out current environmental reporting requirements and the main non-financial reporting standards and techniques available to companies.

As already discussed, the level of scrutiny by shareholders and the public generally is increasing. In an environment where compliance with best practice is the norm, non-compliance is only an option for companies that are prepared to risk shareholder or public challenge. Therefore, a CSR report contained in the company's annual report or on its website sets a benchmark standard against which the company's performance will be measured. While the risk of legal penalties may be remote, if such benchmark standards are not maintained in practice the risk of greater scrutiny and public criticism is apparent. Reporting practices are developing in relation to non-financial disclosures including CSR. Responses to the EU public consultation on *Disclosure of Non-financial Information by Companies* indicated support for the concept of integrated reporting of the type being developed by the IIRC. Responses to the consultation indicated that further and more uniform integrated reporting requirements for larger businesses could be useful covering:

- whether or not the company has a CSR policy (and if so, how it is implemented);
- the principal business risks and opportunities arising from social and environmental issues and how these are taken into account in company strategy; and
- key information on other specific issues such as employee engagement, customer satisfaction, public perception of company, environmental issues

and innovation, but also in the field of human rights and corruption and bribery.

While developments in narrative reporting are likely to be ongoing, what will not change is that the principal reason for all reporting within the company's annual report and accounts is to inform investors about the company's performance, position and prospects. CSR reporting within the annual report should be seen in this context so that a disclosure should only be made via this medium if it is material to the business. CSR information within the annual report must be tested against this measure to ensure its relevance to shareholders. Information that does not meet these criteria may still be of general interest to the wider public and could warrant disclosure through some other means. However, to include such disclosures within the annual report obscures from investors the material information which they require in order to make their judgements as shareholders. A planned and disciplined approach is therefore required.

Reporting guidelines such as those published by the IA (*Guidelines on Responsible Investment Disclosure*) and the IIRC are available as sources of reference and are examined below together with specific issues in relation to environmental, human capital and modern slavery disclosures.

### Environmental reporting

The importance of environmental issues and in particular GHG emissions, both globally and at home, needs no explanation. The issue is no longer relevant only to heavy industry or sectors more traditionally associated with environmental concerns. Quoted companies are already required to provide, within their strategic report, information about environmental issues including the impact of the company's business on the environment. In addition to this mandatory reporting, many companies also report voluntarily on their carbon footprint, environmental strategies and action plans under initiatives such as the Carbon Disclosure Project (CDP). The Climate Change Act 2008, which commits the UK to reducing its carbon emissions to 80% of their 1990 levels by 2050, introduced a number of initiatives to achieve this objective. Relevant to the issue of CSR reporting is the introduction of mandatory GHG emission reporting by all quoted companies listed on the main LSE. Based on the internationally accepted GHG Protocol, guidelines have been published by Defra (*Environmental Reporting Guidelines: Including mandatory greenhouse gas emissions reporting guidance*) to assist organisations to measure and report their so-called 'carbon footprint'. Such measuring and reporting will, of course, also enable directors to assess their company's progress towards reducing their corporate carbon footprint.

The guidance also addresses the issue of reporting on environmental KPI's which are likely to fall into one or more of the following categories:

- GHG emissions
- Water
- Waste
- Materials and waste efficiency
- Biodiversity and ecosystem services
- Emissions to air, land and water.

Other guidance including Defra's *Environmental Key Performance Indicators: Reporting Guidelines for UK Business and Guidance on Measuring and Reporting Impacts* will also be relevant. It's important to bear in mind that reporting will vary significantly from business to business depending on the nature of the activities involved.

### Reporting on human capital management (HCM)

HCM refers to a strategic approach to people management. The assumption (now widely accepted based on the evidence of research) is that the way an organisation manages its people impacts on its performance and that there are opportunities for it to be more competitive and to create value through harnessing the skills and commitment of its people.

The *Accounting for People Report*, published in 2003 as a result of a government initiative, concluded that the link between HCM policies and performance is a material factor, the disclosure of which may influence the assessment of an organisation's value. Therefore, HCM should be reported not only for the benefit of employees, but also for shareholders and stakeholders generally. It notes that the link between HCM and performance makes such reporting highly relevant to debates about responsible ownership (and active voting) by institutional investors.

As noted previously, s. 414C of the CA 2006 requires, in relation to the publication of a strategic report by quoted companies, that information is provided about the company's employees 'to the extent necessary for an understanding of the development, performance or position of the company's business' and about the male/female split of directors, managers and employees generally. While the gender data is merely statistical, the analysis of employee matters is expected to be supported by KPIs. The FRC *Guidance on the Strategic Report* provides some guidance on reporting employee-related matters. Also of interest will be the UK Commission for Employment and Skills report, *Encouraging Employers to use Human Capital Reporting*, which includes a review of current practice requirements and relevant literature. The *Accounting for People Report* includes some fuller recommendations and reveals that the most common indicators used by larger companies relate to:

- workforce profile;
- turnover;

- retention rates;
- absenteeism;
- employee performance and productivity; and
- employee engagement.

Others used include training (e.g. the amount, cost and effectiveness), leadership/career development, revenue/profit per employee and remuneration policies. The LAPFF 2007 trustee guide *Unlocking Human Capital* also includes some useful pointers on narrative reporting, core indicators of good practice, risk assessments and KPIs.

The most recent developments in HCM reporting include the introduction of gender pay gap reporting (see Chapter 8) and a review of executive pay and employee boardroom influence as part of the Government's 2016 Corporate Governance Review. Further regulatory measures relevant to HCM practices and reporting could well follow.

To support the auditing process of disclosures on HCM matters, companies need methodologies to enable them to assess and monitor performance against the selected indicators. Various HCM valuation and assessment models have been identified. The better known of these include the Balanced Scorecard and Economic Value Added models. For external reporting purposes, some of this information relating to employees will be commercially confidential. Companies will be anxious about revealing it to competitors, for fear it might risk misinterpretation by analysts or lead to unhelpful media reporting. Directors will be required to make some difficult judgements when approving the contents of the HCM disclosures to be included in the company's narrative reporting.

**Case study: Nike**

In 1998 Marc Kasky, a labour rights activist, sued the sports equipment company Nike under California's unfair competition laws, claiming that Nike's public statements defending its labour practices constituted false advertising. The California Supreme Court found in favour of the claimant in 2002, but Nike appealed to the US Supreme Court, arguing that its statements were in the nature of commercial advertisements and should be protected by the free speech rights granted under the US constitution. The Supreme Court refused to rule on the California judgement and Nike eventually settled and agreed to donate $1.5 million to a US labour association.

The case raises difficult issues not only about CSR performance, but also about the extent to which businesses should disclose their CSR activities. Nike was a pioneer of transparency before the case, publishing its internal audit of factories on its website and breaking down the cost of a shoe from manufacture to retail. In the aftermath of the Kasky case, it withdrew from any form of CSR reporting, anxious about the legal ramifications of transparency in this area. However, in April 2005 Nike issued its first public CSR report since 2001, describing in considerable detail its supply chain practices, addressing such sensitive matters as workforce diversity, the environment, community programmes and SRI. Difficulties experienced in areas such as ending contracts with suppliers, factories' non-compliance with labour, environmental and health and safety standards were discussed frankly and openly. An independent review committee of individuals from trade unions, NGOs, academia and the business community was invited to comment on the report to lend it credibility.

Adopting what has been described as a 'warts and all' approach to reporting, Nike's 2005 CSR report arguably set a new standard for CSR reporting in terms of the amount and frankness of the information portrayed and the range of subjects covered.

## Modern slavery

The Modern Slavery Act 2015, through its supply chain transparency provisions, seeks to address slavery, servitude, forced or compulsory labour and human trafficking. Abusive treatment of foreign labour may be measured against the standards defined in human rights laws and international codes.

The Act requires business with an annual turnover of £36m or more to publish a slavery and human trafficking statement for each financial year, setting out what steps the business has taken during the year to ensure that modern slavery is not occurring within the business or its supply chain. The statement can simply confirm that no steps have been taken to do this but it is likely that such a statement would be negatively received.

A practical guide to the transparency requirements has been published by the Home Office. Reporting of these issues is intended to apply pressure to businesses not only in respect of their UK practices, but also in respect of the company's international and/or indirect treatment of workers and working conditions.

## Global Reporting Initiative (GRI)

The GRI Standards aim to represent global best practice for reporting on a range of economic, environmental and social impacts. Organised into modules, the interrelated GRI Standards, used as a set, can assist in preparing a sustainability report focused on material topics. There are three Universal Standards applicable to every organisation (Foundation, General Disclosures and Management Approach) plus further topic-specific Standards (divided between Economic, Environmental and Social) designed to be selected dependent on the company's material impacts. The Standards are available online and are for voluntary use by organisations of all types that wish to report on their social, economic and environmental performance. They are not designed to provide a set of principles of conduct or a performance standard, but rather to give a reporting framework relating to sustainability issues.

The GRI Guidelines are divided into two parts. Part 1, *Reporting Principles and Standard Disclosures*, covers:

- Principles to define report content: materiality, stakeholder inclusiveness, sustainability context and completeness.
- Principles to define report quality: balance, comparability, accuracy, timeliness, reliability and clarity.
- Standard disclosures: strategy and analysis, organisational profile, material aspects and boundaries, stakeholder engagement, report profile, governance, ethics and integrity, management approach and indicators.
- Criteria to be met in order to prepare a report 'in accordance' with the Guidelines.

Part 2 describes how to implement the Principles. The Principles are intended to serve as tools for self-diagnosis, but not as specific disclosure items to report against. The Principles on the quality of information are designed to enable stakeholders to make sound and reasonable assessments of performance and take appropriate action.

## Verification of CSR reporting

In the IA (previously ABI) *Guidelines for Responsible Investment Disclosure*, verification of narrative reporting on ESG issues is roundly encouraged in the following terms:

> 'Independent external verification of ESG disclosures would be regarded by shareholders as a significant advantage. Credible verification may also be achieved by other means, including internal audit. It would assist shareholders in their assessment of ESG policies if the reason for choosing a particular method of verification were explained in the annual report.'

However, independent verification is perhaps one of the biggest challenges to the credibility of CSR reporting. Under s. 496 of the CA 2006, the auditor must state in their report whether in his or her opinion the information given in the strategic report is consistent with the accounts. This test, however, does not require the information in the strategic report to be audited as the test is merely one of consistency. When expressing their opinion, the auditor will be guided by the terms of the relevant reporting standard.

The intention behind these provisions is not that the auditors should second guess the directors' judgements on the contents of the strategic report, nor are they required to verify its contents beyond the limited requirement to note inconsistencies with the audited financial statements. There are therefore two main choices for independent verification: either verification by an external party, such as the company's auditors or other specialist adviser, or internal verification by the company itself. These are now examined in turn.

## External verification

AccountAbility has developed the AA 1000 Standards, a series of principle-based standards and framework to guide organisations in their approach to sustainability strategy, governance and operational management.

The standards start with AA 1000 APS AccountAbility Principles Standard, designed to help companies develop an accountable and strategic response to sustainability. The Principles are as follows:

- *The Foundation Principle of Inclusivity* – for a company that accepts its accountability to those on whom it has an impact and who have an impact on it, inclusivity is the participation of stakeholders in developing and achieving an accountable and strategic response to sustainability.
- *The Principle of Materiality* – materiality is determining the relevance and significance of an issue to an organisation and its stakeholders. A material issue is an issue that will influence the decisions, actions and performance of an organisation or its stakeholders.
- *The Principle of Responsiveness* – responsiveness is a company's response to stakeholder issues that affect its sustainability performance and is realised through decisions, actions and performance, as well as communication with stakeholders.

The AA 1000 Assurance Standard was introduced with the express aim of bringing more credibility to CSR reporting by the application of robust accountability principles to both the internal and external 'audit' process. It requires that the verifier brings to the task principles of integrity, objectivity and independence, professional competence and behaviour, confidentiality and due care to stakeholders. AA 1000 AS Assurance Standard provides a way of holding a company to account for its management, performance and reporting on sustainability issues.

The standard requires the assurance provider to look not just at the reliability of data contained in published reports but also at how the Principles described above have been adhered to in practice. Finally, AA 1000 SES Stakeholder Engagement Standard provides a framework for the design, implementation, assessment and communication of quality stakeholder engagement. AccountAbility works closely with other developers of specialised standards and the AA 1000 series is designed to be complementary to and aligned with other standards including the GRI on sustainability reporting examined above.

The AA 1000 Assurance Standard recognises the need to enhance the legitimacy of auditors and addresses this need by proposing a professional qualification for social and ethical auditors. Companies may be well advised to retain specialist professional advisers to review CSR reporting in areas where technical expertise is required. For example, experts may be retained to verify management processes in environmental or health and safety matters or to measure performance against selected indicators. Such third-party verification will be essential if the objective is certification according to one of the recognised standards, such as ISO 14001 (environmental management) or OHSAS 18001 (occupational health and safety assessment series).

### Self-verification by companies

Only the largest companies will have the internal resources to undertake verification on any sort of scale. Additionally, internal verification will not lead to certification against recognised standards. This is a developing area. While companies may continue to frame their CSR policies and to make the links between performance and CSR initiatives, the trend is towards more and better third-party verification that offers the additional assurance of independent assessment.

## International standard: social responsibility

An international standard on social responsibility, ISO 26000 *Guidance for social responsibility*, was published in 2010. It aims to provide guidance to all types of organisations on:

- concepts, terms and definitions, backgrounds, trends and characteristics, principles, practices, core subjects and issues related to social responsibility;
- integrating, implementing and promoting socially responsible behaviour throughout the organisation and, through its policies and practices, within its sphere of influence;
- identifying and engaging with stakeholders; and
- communicating commitments, performance and other information related to social responsibility.

### International CSR management standards

The three international standards summarised in Table 6.2 do not define specific performance criteria, but rather focus on the internal systems over which the organisation has control. In this respect, they are useful as a means of ensuring compliance with relevant laws and regulations and to assure conformity with internal environmental policies. Also, they are all capable of certification by an independent third party, which provides important verification for reporting purposes. Such certification can provide the platform for both measuring and reporting improvements in the relevant CSR KPIs. Table 6.2 sets out the aims and content of each of these international standards.

**Table 6.2** International CSR standards

| Standard | Summary of aims and content |
|---|---|
| **ISO 14001 and ISO 14004: environmental management** | ISO 14001 and 14004 are part of the ISO 14000 series of international standards on environmental management. ISO 14001 provides the requirements for an environmental management system (EMS) which enables management to identify the environmental impact of their company's activities, to continually improve environmental performance and to develop a systematic approach to setting environmental targets, achieving them and then demonstrating that the targets have been achieved. ISO 14004 provides practical guidance on the elements of an EMS and its implementation and maintenance. Many companies now report on their compliance with ISO 14000 in the CSR section of their annual report. |
| **SA 8000: labour practices** | SA 8000 has been developed by Social Accountability International as an international standard for voluntary adoption by organisations that wish to audit and certify their labour practices, as well as those of their suppliers and business associates in the supply chain. It is based on the principles of international human rights, particularly as championed by the International Labour Organisation. It specifies a framework management system for companies in the following main areas: forced and child labour, health and safety, free association and collective bargaining, discrimination, disciplinary practices, working hours and compensation. |
| **OHSAS 18001: health and safety** | OHSAS 18001 is the major international standard on occupational health and safety management. Its aim is to enable an organisation to control its health and safety risks and improve its performance in the process. It is particularly relevant to companies operating businesses with a high risk of occupational hazard. |

## Conclusion: the current position with CSR

CSR is a diverse and, it might be said, rather ill-defined subject that offers both users and observers few fixed reference points. This lack of clarity reflects the real difficulty of attempting to deal with matters that are non-financial in nature and are not subject to conventional international accounting and reporting standards. Even its most enthusiastic proponents will concur that, notwithstanding the strides made in research and reporting, there remain gaps in understanding of the impact of CSR initiatives and that there is a pressing need for more and better quantitative data. Although the credibility of the CSR business case continues to improve, until these gaps are filled, the debate will continue to be unresolved and financial analysts will retain a level of scepticism about the precise value to place upon ESG factors.

However, despite such apparent deficiencies, there are clear indications that CSR is firmly established within the corporate governance lexicon. Table 6.1 lists the main constituents making up the CSR-interested community. It is notable that the overwhelming opinion of those who speak for these constituents (e.g. the CBI for businesses, the IA for shareholders, the OECD for international development interests, the Chartered Institute of Personnel and Development (CIPD) for employees) is that CSR has become a core aspect of business behaviour, whether from the perspective of effective risk management, improved competitiveness, enhanced reputation or any other relevant barometer of good governance. Where CSR is proving to be remarkable is that it continues to encompass some quite radical perspectives on the legitimacy of stakeholder interests without diluting the conventional view, both in law and practice, that a company's responsibility to its shareholders remains paramount.

## CSR checklist

- ✓ Is the board informed about recent developments in CSR matters?
- ✓ Has the board debated and reached conclusions on the business case for CSR, with particular reference to the risk management and competitive issues, and determined its CSR strategy accordingly?
- ✓ Has the board shown clear leadership on the company's CSR values and culture so as to maximise the embedding of those values throughout the organisation?
- ✓ Is CSR integrated into the business at all levels, with the focus on delivering improved performance over the longer term?
- ✓ Are there any specific legal risks for the company on CSR-related issues, taking into account the nature of its business and its shareholder base?
- ✓ Has the board identified the relevant KPIs with respect to the company's non-financial assets?

✓ With respect to measuring performance against these indicators, is there a need to instruct specialist advisers and what approach will the auditors adopt?

✓ Has the company taken steps to ensure modern slavery does not occur within the business or its supply chain? Does it report annually on the steps taken?

✓ Is the company's CSR reporting meaningful to shareholders and is any attempt made to link explicitly CSR performance and financial performance?

✓ What is the understanding of, and response to, investor perception of the company's ESG practice?

# 7
# Audits, accounts and financial statements

## Introduction

Corporate governance scandals, such as those at Enron and Worldcom, which have been traced back to failures in the auditing process, have inevitably led to very damaging and usually very sudden loss in shareholder value and confidence. Shareholders will be particularly frustrated if formal enquiries conducted after the event reveal that there were significant and continuing problems leading up to the collapse which, for whatever reason, were not spotted and/or disclosed adequately through the audit. At the same time it must be emphasised that it is the directors who are responsible for the financial statements and have primary responsibility for the reliability of the information provided. It is the auditors' responsibility to give an unbiased and honest professional opinion to the shareholders about the financial statements.

### The purpose of the audit and the auditors' duty of care

Past auditing failures have thrown some doubt on the integrity of the audit process and beg two linked questions:

- What is the purpose of the audit?
- To whom do the auditors owe a duty of care?

In 2003, the Department of Trade and Industry (DTI) Inspectors' report on the collapse of Transtec plc noted that 'company accounts are the major means by which the company publicly communicates performance and through which management is held accountable'. The achievement of a high-quality audit is clearly a critical investor issue. In its 2011 consultation paper *Effective Company Stewardship: Enhancing Corporate Reporting and Audit*, the FRC summed it up by declaring that the system of company stewardship 'is dependent on the provision of robust and reliable information by companies to investors and on audit assurance of that information'.

There is little scope to argue with such logic. Some commentators have identified the integrity of the audit with a fundamental 'public interest'. The notion of public interest is relatively ill-defined but is generally understood to be broad in scope and cover issues such as misconduct, wrongdoing or risks to the public.

There can be no doubt about the shareholder interest in the audit. In the House of Lords case of *Caparo Industries Plc v. Dickman and others* ([1990] 1 All ER 568) it was held that:

> 'The central purpose of the audit report was to enable shareholders to exercise their proprietary powers as shareholders by giving them reliable intelligence on the company's affairs, sufficient to allow the shareholders to scrutinise management's conduct and to exercise their collective powers to control the management through general meetings.'

This line of accountability from the auditors is reinforced under UK company law to the extent that shareholders have the power both to appoint and to fix the remuneration of auditors. While the board will negotiate the auditors' detailed terms of engagement, the shareholders' role in the appointment and remuneration aspects is more than symbolic.

Notwithstanding the legal position, when the external audit process has failed to reveal underlying problems, critics of the auditing process have suggested that, in practice, auditors will often be more beholden to the managers of the companies they audit than to the investors. It is argued that because the firms have traditionally been geared up to sell high-margin non-audit consultancy services to the companies that they audit, they can be subject to significant conflicts of interest so that the identity of the 'real' audit client (i.e. the shareholders) can become blurred. Accordingly, in recent years, changes to the regulatory framework within which auditors are required to operate have sought to address issues of audit independence and effectiveness.

In the wake of the 2008/9 banking crisis, there has been further focus on the role played by external auditors. Recent reviews of existing audit standards were initiated in response to failings within the financial services sector and the responsibilities of auditors within that sector. However, lessons from the reviews are not confined to banking sector audits and have been extrapolated to the audits of non-financial sector companies. In particular, the need for 'auditor scepticism' and how to ensure adequate levels of such scepticism without rendering the audit process unworkable have been examined. The willingness of auditors to challenge management assertions and to blow the whistle when appropriate are seen as key to achieving investor and wider-stakeholder confidence that financial statements do indeed provide a 'true and fair view' of the company to which they relate.

## Regulatory framework

The clear purpose of the accountancy and audit regulatory framework is to support the delivery of good corporate governance and stewardship. In 2003, the Government decided that the regulatory regime for audit and financial reporting should be strengthened and made more independent. Building on the existing legislative framework, a number of 'light touch' statutory provisions necessary to implement such measures were enacted in the Companies (Audit, Investigations and Community Enterprise) Act 2004. More recently, the CA 2006 and the Statutory Auditors and Third Country Auditors Regulations 2007 made further alterations to this framework.

The FRC's mission is 'to promote high-quality corporate governance and reporting to foster investment'. It has various responsibilities in relation to accounting and audit regulation pursuant to the statutory powers granted to it. The Board of the FRC is now supported in discharging its responsibilities by three governance committees (audit, nominations and remuneration) and by two business committees, namely the Codes and Standards Committee and the Conduct Committee.

The legislative and regulatory framework contains provisions aimed at improving the reliability of accounts and the efficacy of the accounting investigations regime. In summary, such provisions have the following effect:

- Auditors have powers under ss. 499 and 500 of the CA 2006 to require a wide group of officers and employees to provide information and explanations to them. It is a criminal offence knowingly or recklessly to provide the auditor with misleading, false or deceptive information. In each annual report the directors are required to state that they are not aware of any relevant information that has not been disclosed to the company's auditors which they know or ought to know to be relevant to the auditors' tasks (s. 418(2)). The FRC's Financial Reporting Review Panel (FRRP) can advise the FRC's Conduct Committee to apply to the court to amend defective accounts.
- The Secretary of State can make regulations requiring disclosure by companies of the nature of non-audit services provided to the company by the auditors and its associates and also the amount of remuneration to be paid for those services. This requirement is also addressed below.
- The FRC's Conduct Committee is responsible for supervising the accounting aspects of the reports and accounts of companies to ensure that they comply with the accounting aspects of the Companies Act. Supervision of the application of the LR by listed companies is the FCA's responsibility as UKLA.
- The Secretary of State has comprehensive powers to require information and to appoint investigators and inspectors who themselves have

comprehensive powers. There are also provisions overriding confidentiality arrangements and giving immunity to persons disclosing certain types of confidential information in specified circumstances and powers of entry and search are available.

### Disclosure of auditor remuneration

The Companies (Disclosure of Auditor Remuneration and Liability Limitation Agreements) Regulations 2008 (as amended) require disclosure by companies of the nature of non-audit services provided to the company by the auditors and its associates (carefully defined in the Regulations) and also the amount of remuneration to be paid for those services. Remuneration includes expenses and benefits-in-kind as well as fees. Attention should also be paid to the prohibitions on the provision of non-audit services by auditors set out in the Auditing Practices Board *Ethical Standards*.

There is an exemption for SMEs under the CA 2006 definition (ss. 381, 465 and 467(1)), but all other companies, whether public or quoted, must comply. The disclosures must be made in the notes to the accounts and the auditors themselves are under a duty to provide the relevant information to the directors. Criminal sanctions can apply if a director fails to make the required disclosures. ICAEW guidance (Tech 14/13FRF) on the application of the disclosure of auditor remuneration provides detailed information.

### Auditors' liabilities and accountability in a competitive market

The huge, but of course unsuccessful, negligence claim against Ernst & Young in its capacity as auditor of Equitable Life brought the issue of auditor liability into sharp focus. The major accounting firms claimed that providing a mechanism by which auditor liability could be limited would boost competition by encouraging smaller rivals to bid for the audits of the UK's larger listed companies. Notwithstanding evidence to the contrary, ss. 534–538 of the CA 2006 introduced provisions enabling companies to enter into liability limitation agreements. Such an agreement can limit the liability owed to the company by the auditor in respect of negligence, default, breach of duty or breach of trust occurring in the course of the audit of accounts.

In order to be valid, the terms of the liability limitation agreement must meet certain requirements as set out in the Act and Regulations made under the Act. Section 535 of the CA 2006 requires that the agreement must not apply to the audit of accounts of more than one financial year and must specify that financial year. In addition, the agreement must be authorised by the members by passing a resolution either approving the principal terms of the agreement prior to the agreement being entered into or, if the agreement has already been entered into, approving the agreement itself. The members' authorisation may be withdrawn by resolution at any time before the agreement is entered into or, if the agreement has already been entered into, at any time before the beginning of the financial year to which the agreement relates. The legislation defines 'principal terms' as meaning the kinds of acts or omissions covered, the financial year to which the agreement relates and the limit to which the auditor's liability is subject. The limit may be framed in any way – it need not be a sum of money or a formula.

A liability limitation agreement is not effective, however, to the extent that it limits the auditor's liability to less than such amount as is fair and reasonable having regard to his or her statutory responsibilities as an auditor, the nature and purpose of the auditor's contractual obligations to the company and the professional standards expected from them.

In addition, a company may indemnify its auditor against any liability incurred by him or her in defending proceedings in which judgement is given in their favour or they are acquitted or in connection with an application under s. 1157 of the Act (power of the court to grant relief in case of honest and reasonable conduct) in which relief is granted to them by the court.

Regulation 8 of the Companies (Disclosure of Auditor Remuneration and Liability Limitation Agreements) Regulations 2008 sets out the requirement for any company which has entered into a liability limitation agreement to disclose its principal terms and the date of the relevant shareholder resolution in a note to the company's report and accounts for the year to which the agreement relates.

The ISC has produced a statement setting out the expectations of institutional investors in relation to companies seeking shareholder approval of auditor liability limitation agreements. This statement, together with the FRC *Guidance on Auditor Liability Agreements*, offers useful assistance for any company, the directors of which are considering entering into such an agreement, on both the principal terms of the agreement and the issues to which the audit committee and board should give consideration.

## Auditors' accountability to shareholders

The CA 2006 also contains provisions designed to enhance the accountability of auditors to shareholders. The most significant points to note are as follows:

- Disclosure of terms of audit appointment (s. 493): the Secretary of State has power to require disclosure of the terms of the auditor's appointment, remuneration and duties. These disclosures will enable third parties (particularly shareholders) to understand better the scope of the audit and the terms on which it has been undertaken. Disclosure requirements in relation to auditors' remuneration have already been set out.
- Audit lead partner's signature on audit reports (ss. 503–504): where the auditor is a firm, an individual referred to as the 'senior statutory

auditor' must sign the audit report in their own name. This requirement is intended to improve audit standards by encouraging further personal responsibility for actions taken by the audit teams in large audit practices. Exemptions apply in certain circumstances in which the publication of the individual's name is considered likely to create a serious risk of violence or intimidation.

- Quoted company shareholders' right to require website publication of audit concerns (ss. 527–530): Members of quoted companies holding either 5% of the voting rights or numbering at least 100, each of whom holds on average £100 paid-up shares, may ask the company to publish on its website a statement raising concerns about the accounts or the departure of an auditor, which they propose to bring up at the next meeting when the accounts are discussed. A copy of the statement must be given to the company's auditor, published on the website within three working days, and remain there until after the relevant meeting. Quoted companies are required to draw attention to this right in the notice of general meeting at which the accounts are to be laid.
- Publication of auditor resignation statements (ss. 519–520): a departing auditor of a quoted company is required to make a statement on his or her resignation and to deposit it with the company. This statement must explain the circumstances connected with their ceasing to hold office. For other public companies and all private companies, the auditor need not deposit such a statement if they consider that there are no circumstances in connection with their departure which need to be brought to the attention of the shareholders or creditors. In that case, a statement should be made that there are no such circumstances. Within 14 days of receipt of such a statement, the company must send a copy to every person entitled to receive a copy of the company's report and accounts. A court process is available through which a company may apply to be excused from the requirement to circulate the statement and the court may direct that copies need not be sent out and order the auditor to pay the company's costs if it is satisfied the auditor is using the statement for defamatory purposes or to secure needless publicity.

These provisions reflect the desire of institutional investors for auditors to be made more accountable to shareholders in relation to their terms of appointment. The audit profession has also responded to this desire with FRC publication *The Audit Firm Governance Code* which was updated most recently in 2016. The Code encourages, through its Principles F.1, F.2 and F.3, dialogue between audit firms and the shareholders of the listed companies they audit as well as those companies and their audit committees so as to improve understanding by all parties of the others' concerns and opinions. Audit Firm Governance Code Principle F.3 also promotes to shareholders their responsibility to utilise these dialogue processes to inform their voting decisions.

## International accounting standards

All companies whose shares are traded on a regulated market within the EU, including all UK companies whose shares are listed on the LSE including AIM companies, are required to report their results under specified IFRS. The development of IFRS financial reporting means that financial reporting by EU companies is more consistent than ever before, regardless of the entity's home country. This greater consistency and comparability should lead to more efficient markets and reduce the cost of capital so that, at least in theory, the adoption of IFRS should provide companies with an economic advantage.

Convergence of IFRS with the Financial Accounting Standards Board's (FASB's) Generally Accepted Accounting Principles US (GAAP), so as to remove the requirement for companies with US listings to reconcile their financial statements to US GAAP, has also been the intention on both sides of the Atlantic for some years. Since March 2008, the US Securities and Exchange Commission (SEC) has accepted from non-US issuers financial statements prepared in accordance with IFRS without reconciliation to US GAAP, subject to certain conditions. These conditions include a requirement for the financial statements to be accompanied by an unqualified auditor's report opining on the compliance of the accounts with IFRS as issued by the International Accounting Standards Board (IASB). The convergence work has taken longer to complete than was expected and remains ongoing.

These developments are just part of the significant progress which has been made by the IASB towards its stated objective of producing a single set of high-quality global accounting standards. More than 100 countries already require or permit the use of IFRS and all remaining major economies have committed to timescales for the adoption of – or convergence with – IFRS.

## The audit committee

Best practice on audit committees is contained in the FRC *Guidance on Audit Committees*. ICSA's *Guidance Note on the duties of the audit committee* is also a valuable starting point for the development of good audit committee practice. For listed companies, the DTR also impose requirements in relation to the appointment and functions of an audit committee. DTR 7.1.7G confirms the view of the FCA that compliance with the sections of the UK Corporate Governance Code relevant to audit committees will result in compliance with the DTR requirements as set out in DTR 7.1.

## Membership of the audit committee

UK Corporate Governance Code Principle C.3 states that:

> 'The board should establish formal and transparent arrangements for considering how they should apply the corporate reporting and risk management and internal control principles and for maintaining an appropriate relationship with the company's auditors.'

The board will discharge this obligation by setting up an audit committee with appropriate terms of reference. Code Provision C.3.1 requires that the board should establish an audit committee of at least three (or two, in the case of 'smaller' companies, as defined) independent NEDs. When establishing the committee, the FRC Guidance suggests that the board must tailor the committee's terms of reference to the particular circumstances of the company, for example its size, complexity and risk profile. Code Provision C.3.1 also requires that the board should satisfy itself that at least one member of the committee has 'recent and relevant financial experience'. This will usually mean one member, normally the committee chairman, will hold an accountancy qualification. Although the degree of financial literacy required of other members will depend on the nature of the company's business, the FRC Guidance anticipates that other audit committee members will normally need to have some degree of experience of corporate financial matters. Where a company's business involves specialist financial activities, this will need to be reflected in the degree of financial expertise within the committee.

For listed companies, the DTR also impose an obligation for the audit committee to have at least one independent member and one member with 'competence in accounting or auditing or both'. The rules clarify that the independence and financial competence requirements may be met by one member or by different committee members. In addition, the members of the audit committee as a whole are required to 'have competence relevant to the sector' in which the company is operating.

The FRC Guidance provides that appointments to the audit committee made by the board, at the recommendation of the nomination committee, should be made in consultation with the committee chairman. As with appointments to the full board, the nominations committee will need to take account of the balance of skills, experience and knowledge within the committee and address any gaps through the appointment process. Committee members should be deemed independent and, in particular, should be considered to bring an independent mindset to the role. Without the ability to think independently, assessment of the work of management and the assurance provided by internal and external audit could be compromised. The maximum term that audit committee members have served on the board should therefore normally be nine years following which independence may be compromised. Other than in smaller companies, the chairman of the company should not be a member of the audit committee and in no cases should he or she be chair of the audit committee.

The company should provide a tailored induction programme for new audit committee members. This should cover the audit committee's role and terms of reference, the time commitment expected from members and an overview of the company's business model and strategy, identifying in particular its main business and financial dynamics and risks. It is also likely to include meeting some of the company staff. Ongoing and timely development and training on relevant financial, accounting and corporate reporting matters, the regulatory framework for the company's business, the role of internal and external audit and risk management should also be provided. The provision of both the induction programme and training is likely to be the responsibility of the company secretary, possibly working with the internal HR team and external trainers as appropriate.

## Procedures, resources and relationship with the board

### Procedures

The frequency of formal audit committee meetings is a matter for its chairman, who in this respect will work closely with the company secretary. The FRC Guidance recommends at least three meetings each year, to coincide with key dates in the financial reporting cycle. In practice, the committee is likely to meet more often than this, particularly where the company's activities involve complex financial matters. Such complex matters will require sufficient time for consideration and debate and the amount of meeting time scheduled should reflect that requirement.

Meetings should also be held so as to leave sufficient time before the next board meeting to carry out, and report to the board, any work arising from the committee's meeting.

Non-members may be invited to attend committee meetings, depending on the business to be transacted. It is to be expected that the external audit partner and the finance director should attend regularly. Meetings with the internal audit team and external audit partner, without executive management, should take place at least annually. Often the opportunity for the committee to meet with the auditors in the absence of management will be included as a standard agenda item for each meeting that is attended by the auditors.

Also, more frequent informal meetings with the key people involved with the company's governance will almost certainly be required. The chairman of the committee will take the lead on such matters.

## Resources

The audit committee is likely to have the heaviest workload of all the board committees. The board should therefore ensure that it has at its disposal the necessary resources to fulfil its obligations. These will include access to the company's secretariat, which most importantly will mean the availability of the company secretary and appropriate support staff. The company secretary's role in this regard will include aiding the chairman in the proper planning of the audit committee's work, drafting the agenda, collating and disseminating high-quality papers and information to the committee in a timely manner, taking minutes of the committee's meetings and providing any other practical support that the committee, its members and chairman may require. The company secretary, or member of the secretariat nominated to work with the audit committee, will also be closely involved in the preparation of the committee's annual report about its activities as described later in this chapter.

The FRC *Guidance on Audit Committees* also determines that the audit committee should have access, where it reasonably considers it appropriate, to independent legal, accounting or other advice. The board should ensure funds for this are therefore available.

An additional resource matter is the amount of remuneration to be paid to committee members and the chair. Given the workload of this committee and the necessary time commitment that its members must dedicate, the payment of additional remuneration to its members is the norm and, in view of the nature of the responsibilities and skills required of members, such additional fees are usually at a higher rate than applies to membership of other committees.

## Relationship with the board

It is important to note that the critical requirement for the audit committee to be independent of the executive does not imply a departure from the principle of the unitary board. The FRC *Guidance on Audit Committees* contains a clear reminder that as a matter of law all directors are equally responsible for the company's affairs. This is reiterated in the FRC *Guidance on Board Effectiveness* which confirms that, while the board may make use of committees to assist its consideration of issues such as audit and risk, 'it retains responsibility for and makes the final decision on' such areas. In order to ensure this distinction is maintained in practice, the FRC *Guidance on Board Effectiveness* goes on to recommend that sufficient time is allowed after audit committee meetings for it to report to the board on its discussions and on their recommendations and on actions to be taken. The FRC *Guidance on Audit Committees* recommends that the audit committee reports to the board as a minimum on:

- the significant issues that it considered in relation to the financial statements and how these issues were addressed;
- its assessment of the effectiveness of the external audit process and its recommendation on the appointment or reappointment of the external auditor; and
- any other issues on which the board has requested the committee's opinion.

The minutes of committee meetings will be circulated to all board members (unless inappropriate to do so) and the company secretary so as to ensure that the board is comprehensively briefed on the audit committee's work.

As with so many things, establishing the right culture is as important, if not more so, than procedural issues. The board should foster an internal culture of co-operation with the committee, making it clear to all directors and staff that enquiries from the audit committee should be handled efficiently and promptly. While the executive directors will be under a duty to keep the committee informed on relevant matters, the relationship with the main board cannot be reduced to a set of best practice rules. The FRC Guidance states that the essential features of the interaction between the committee, board, executive team and internal and external auditors will be:

> 'A frank, open working relationship and a high level of mutual respect. The audit committee must be prepared to take a robust stand and all parties must be prepared to make information freely available to the audit committee, to listen to their views and to talk through the issues openly.'

If there is disagreement with the other members of the board, adequate time should be set aside to discuss and resolve the disagreement at board level. This will require leadership from both the board's and the committee's chairmen. If the disagreement remains unresolved, the committee should be able to make a report to shareholders in the annual report. Clearly, this will be a last resort and is likely to be interpreted by shareholders as a governance failure by the board as a whole.

The committee is encouraged to conduct a review of its own effectiveness and of its terms of reference annually and, based upon those reviews, to make recommendations to the board as appropriate. In addition, the board should review the audit committee's effectiveness annually. The FRC *Guidance on Board Effectiveness* recommends that the review covers not only the committee's remit but also the process of interaction between committees and between the committee and the board.

Of relevance here will be the areas of interaction between the audit committee and, if there is one, the risk committee. In the absence of a risk committee, the audit committee may also interact with the remuneration committee with regards to the impact of remuneration and reward policies on risk. Such annual reviews will also require input from both the executive and non-executive members of the board.

As the chairman of the board, other than in small companies, should not be a member of the committee, he or she is likely to take a prominent role in assessing the effectiveness of such a key board committee. Ernst & Young LLP (EY) has published a useful resource, *Assessing the Performance of the Audit Committee,* including a detailed checklist to help audit committees identify areas which could benefit from improvement or strengthening.

## Role of the audit committee

The audit committee's responsibilities are several, but they can be summarised in terms of monitoring the integrity of the company's financial statements, overseeing the company's internal control and risk management systems, reviewing the adequacy of the company's whistleblowing arrangements and monitoring and reviewing the audit functions (both internal and external). These relate to areas where a governance vacuum can too easily be filled by an over-dominant management and accordingly the audit committee is under a particular duty to act independently of the executive directors. The audit committee is also required to report to shareholders within the company's annual report and accounts.

Committee members must also be clear that, while on occasions the committee may be required to grapple with matters of detail, it is not tasked with carrying out executive functions, such as the preparation of financial statements or the day-to-day management of the external audit. Therefore, an important distinction should be drawn between the monitoring and assessment of a particular financial function and its actual delivery and implementation.

The audit committee's express responsibilities are set out in some detail in Code Provision C.3.2, as follows:

- To monitor the integrity of the financial statements of the company and any formal announcements relating to the company's financial performance, reviewing significant financial reporting judgements contained in them.
- To review the company's internal financial controls and, unless expressly addressed by a separate board risk committee composed of independent directors or by the board itself, the company's internal control and risk management systems.
- To monitor and review the effectiveness of the company's internal audit function.

- To make recommendations to the board, for it to put to the shareholders for their approval in general meeting, in relation to the appointment, re-appointment or removal of the external auditor and to approve the remuneration and terms of engagement of the external auditor.
- To review and monitor the external auditor's independence and objectivity and the effectiveness of the audit process, taking into consideration relevant UK professional and regulatory requirements.
- To develop and implement policy on the engagement of the external auditor to supply non-audit services, taking into account relevant ethical guidance regarding the provision of non-audit services by the external audit firm and to report to the board, identifying any matters in respect of which it considers that action or improvement is needed and making recommendations as to the steps to be taken.
- To report to the board on how it has discharged its responsibilities.

The committee's arrangements, including its terms of reference, will need to be tailored to the company's needs and complexity and may change, particularly at the time of its annual review. Practical guidance on the role, responsibilities and authority of the audit committee envisaged by the UK Corporate Governance Code is available from ICSA's website (www.icsa.org.uk). Adopting the above best practice principles, the audit committee's role and responsibilities can be illustrated as in Figure 7.1.

The following sections of this chapter review in more detail the following three matters for which the audit committee is responsible:

- financial reporting;
- the external audit process; and
- the internal audit function.

Chapter 10 contains a separate, more detailed review of the audit committee's responsibility for the company's internal controls, risk management and whistleblowing arrangements.

## The audit committee and financial reporting

As already noted, Code Provision C.3.2 of the UK Corporate Governance Code requires the audit committee 'to monitor the integrity of the financial statements of the company and any formal announcements relating to the company's financial performance'. The 2007 report of the ICAEW *Reporting with Integrity* looked at what is meant by 'integrity' in the context of corporate reporting and concluded:

**Figure 7.1** Role and responsibilities of the audit committee

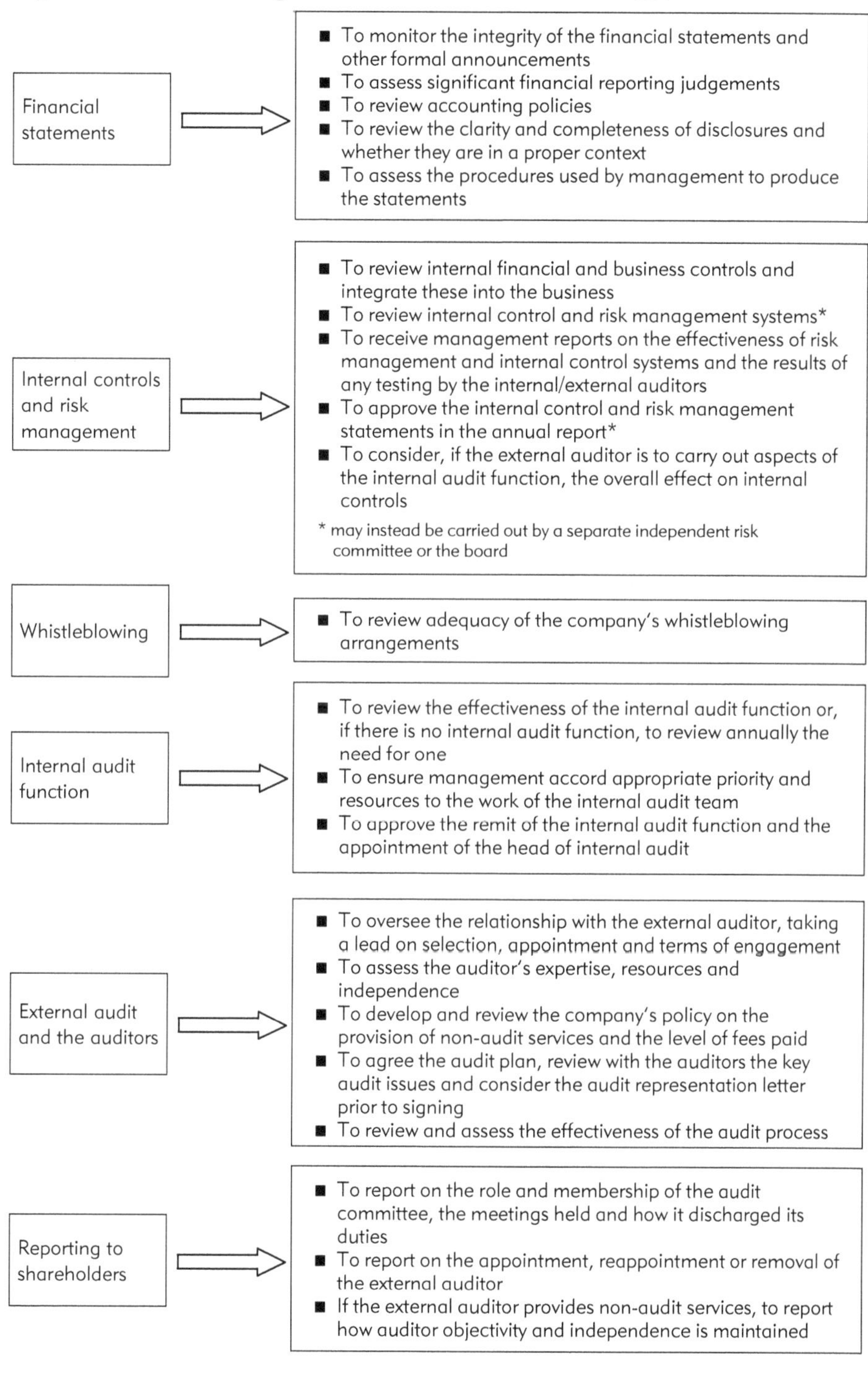

> 'Integrity in reporting needs to be underpinned by moral values such as honesty, motives such as a desire to inform, commitments to the interests of shareholders and others, qualities such as scepticism and perseverance and achievements in the face of opposition.'

The audit committee will need to review the quality of the processes adopted by executive management when preparing the statements as well as the quality of the output in the form of the financial statements. The goal is to provide to external users of the financial statements access to information which gives an unbiased, timely and complete view of the company's business. In this respect, the market impact of such statements is not to be a primary consideration of the committee and it should therefore not attempt to manipulate or manage 'bad news' in a manner which would threaten the integrity of the information provided.

### Definition of 'financial statements' and 'formal announcements'

In essence, the committee's monitoring will extend to any public statement relating to the company's business, including related information which, while not directly financial in nature, is of relevance to the external observer who is seeking to understand the company's business. The following summarises what this means for listed companies:

- the annual accounts, which must give a 'true and fair' view of the profit or loss for the financial year and state of affairs at the year end of the company or group;
- the directors' report,
- the strategic report;
- the report on compliance with the UK Corporate Governance Code as required by LR 9.8.6(5) and (6), setting out:
  - how the company has applied the Code Principles; and
  - a statement of whether or not it has complied with the Code Provisions of the UK Corporate Governance Code and if not, why not;
- the directors' remuneration report, separate from the annual accounts and directors' report, setting out details of policy and individual directors' packages; and
- any other 'formal announcements' made by the board, which would include the interim report and the preliminary announcement, summary financial statements, press releases relating to acquisitions or disposals and all other statements which contain financial or market-sensitive information.

## The review and monitoring process

The audit committee should make it clear to the executive members of the board that it needs to have the opportunity to review and comment on all such external reporting by the company. This will require the board to build time into the reporting timetable for the committee to do so. Where necessary, the committee should be ready and willing to press for clarification and hold further discussions around key issues. As part of its review and monitoring responsibilities, the committee will wish to enquire about the procedures used by executive management and the company's advisers when producing the financial statements. It is not the committee's job to scrutinise in detail every line of the statements or indeed to review every judgement made. If it can be satisfied that the executive management are adopting sound procedures and good decision-making processes, then the committee can be fairly confident that the integrity of the financial statements will be preserved. However, as the FRC *Guidance on Audit Committees* makes clear, where the committee is not satisfied that the financial statements are complete and accurate, 'the oversight function may well lead to more detailed work'. In such cases, and essential if the committee detects 'signs that something may be seriously amiss', it will need to delve more deeply to conduct a more detailed review of the procedures which lie behind the drafting of the statements. In such circumstances it will need to report its views to the board.

## Financial reporting judgements and policies

The FRC *Guidance on Audit Committees* makes the point that the focus of the committee's work on the financial reporting side should be on reviewing 'significant financial reporting issues and judgements made in connection with preparation of the financial statements', for example estimates or application of accounting policies. It is not the committee's role to check detailed compliance with relevant reporting and disclosure rules. The committee will need to use its discretion as to what may be a 'significant' financial reporting judgement, taking into account the nature of the company's business, its stage of development, the market expectations and other relevant factors including, of course, the external auditor's view.

The FRC *Guidance on Audit Committees* also notes that the committee should be aware of any significant changes to accounting policies. The litmus test for the committee is whether the proposed policies will serve the ultimate purpose of giving a 'true and fair' view to the user of the financial statements and will support the objective that the financial statements can be relied upon by users of the accounts. This will also bring into focus the well-established accounting principles of neutrality and prudence.

At the forefront of the committee's thinking should be the objective that the financial statements as a whole provide a 'true and fair' view of the company's profit or loss and its prospects as a going concern. The FRC *Guidance on the Going Concern Basis of Accountancy and Reporting on Solvency and Liquidity Rules*, as well as the FRC *Guidance on Audit Committees* and the FRC document *True and Fair*, will assist the audit committee and board in making their assessments.

In particular the consideration of the business as a going concern should be closely linked to the company's risk decision making and reporting. Chapter 10 looks at the wider issues of risk and risk management.

The committee should be careful to ensure that reporting the legal form of transactions does not hide or distort their economic substance or their real impact on the company. It should also ensure that statements are clear and complete and that any commentary is set in its proper context. A notable feature of some high-profile accounting failures has been the failure by the auditors to highlight the substance and not simply the legal form of complex off-balance sheet structures.

The UK Corporate Governance Code tasks the board with explaining in the annual report their responsibility for preparing the annual report and accounts and stating that they consider the annual report and accounts, taken as a whole, to be fair, balanced and understandable, providing the information necessary for shareholders to assess the company's performance, business model and strategy (Code Provision C.1.1). The board will generally ask the audit committee to review the narrative reports within the financial statements and to advise the board on whether they meet these requirements. The FRC *Guidance on Audit Committees* makes the point that this review by the audit committee must take account of the consistency of the narrative reporting with the accounting information provided in the back of the financial statements.

In arriving at their judgements, the audit committee will need to take account of the external auditor's views. He or she will be required by auditing standards to advise the audit committee of information which they believe will be relevant to the board and the audit committee in order to understand the rationale and the evidence relied upon when making significant professional judgements in the course of the audit and reaching an opinion on the financial statements.

## Managing the total auditing resource

The UK Corporate Governance Code and FRC guidance provide that the audit committee's responsibilities extend to the monitoring and review of the total auditing resource available to the board. As such, it is important that the committee understands the differing but complementary roles and responsibilities of both the external and the internal auditors and also has a strategy for using these auditing resources effectively.

### Internal auditors' role: summary

Assuming the company has an internal audit function, the exact role it performs will derive from the needs of the organisation. While it follows that there is no single model to be applied, the audit committee should be seeking independent and objective assurances from the internal auditors on financial and operational controls and frequently also on the effectiveness of the company's wider systems of internal control and risk management and governance processes. The committee's responsibilities and priorities with respect to the internal auditors are examined further below.

### External auditors' role: summary

The external auditors' primary role, alternatively, is to give a statutory audit opinion and to provide assurance to third parties that the audited financial statements are free from misstatements or material inconsistencies and are in accordance with legislation and accounting standards. For the listed company, the external auditors must also review the corporate governance statements in the annual report, the strategic report and the auditable parts of the directors' remuneration report. Our examination below of the external auditors' role starts with a look at the annual external audit cycle and in particular the audit committee's responsibilities within that cycle.

### Annual audit cycle

The FRC Guidance requires that at the start of each annual audit cycle, the audit committee should ensure that 'appropriate plans are in place for the audit'. This plan will be prepared by the auditors in compliance with relevant auditing standards and should set out the general audit strategy. The committee will need to be satisfied that this plan addresses the major anticipated auditing and accounting issues and accordingly sets out how the audit programme will develop.

Planned levels of materiality and the resources that will be available to carry out the audit should be reviewed. The committee will be seeking assurance that the quality of the audit will be adequate, taking account of relevant factors, and should discuss these with the auditors. The committee should also ensure that the plan is consistent with the scope of the audit terms of engagement. This might, for example, require a consideration of the proposed allocation of audit partners and other senior staff, taking into account potential problem areas identified in the audit plan.

During the conduct, and at the end, of the audit, the committee should review the findings of the audit work with the auditors. This will involve a discussion with the auditors on the major issues that arose and whether or not they were resolved and a careful review of the key accounting and auditing judgements based on the evidence they have received. The committee should also review the level of errors identified by the auditors and obtain explanations from management and where necessary the auditors, if these remain unadjusted (e.g. it might be that they are not considered material, but the committee should be satisfied that this is the case). Specifically, the committee should ask the auditors how the previously identified risks to audit quality were addressed. It is clear that the committee will need to set aside sufficient time to conduct this review of the auditors' findings, within an achievable timetable in the run-up to the making of the preliminary announcement of the results.

The FRC *Guidance on Audit Committees* makes specific reference to the audit committee's role as reviewer of the audit representation letter before it is signed off by management. In this letter the auditors will seek, from management, representations on matters material to the financial statements, such as confirmation that relevant accounting information has been disclosed and a statement of management's expectations with regard to future events and outcomes which will be relevant to the audit. Based on its knowledge, the committee will need to consider whether the disclosures requested are complete and appropriate. The committee should pay particular attention where representations have been requested which relate to non-standard issues. In this regard, the relevant International Standard on Auditing should be referred to for guidance.

At end of the annual audit cycle, the audit committee should review with the auditors the findings of their work before the auditors issue their interim findings and recommendations for change to the board.

As noted earlier, the FRC *Guidance on Audit Committees* recommends that the audit committee meet at least once per year with the external auditors without management being present. During this meeting the committee will discuss the auditors' remit and any issues that arose from the audit. A key question for the committee to ask during these sessions will be how the auditors perceived their interactions with senior management and other members of the finance team. In particular the committee will want to explore the responsiveness of executive management to the auditors' findings and recommendations and should challenge and probe the management response where necessary.

Finally, the audit committee should assess the effectiveness of the audit process. This assessment will be made as part of a wider assessment of the external auditors. The approach to and scope and purpose of that assessment is examined next.

## Annual assessment of the external auditors

The FRC *Guidance on Audit Committees* requires that the audit committee should carry out an annual assessment of the external auditors covering, amongst other things, the effectiveness of the audit process. This assessment will be an integral part of the committee's overall responsibility for monitoring the integrity of the financial statements.

The quality of the audit will need to be assessed by reference to the particular circumstances of the company. The committee should take account of the culture and mindset, skills, knowledge and character of the auditors. The chairman of the audit committee should lead the assessment process, involving the incumbent auditors as necessary. Normally, the chairman will deal with the senior audit partner to agree the parameters of the assessment. The FRC Guidance proposes that when carrying out the audit assessment the committee should:

- Ask the auditors for an explanation of the previously identified risks to audit quality and how these risks were addressed.
- Discuss the key audit firm and network level controls which the auditors relied upon to identify the risks to audit quality and enquire about the findings from internal and external inspections of their audit and firm.
- Review whether the auditors have met the agreed audit plan and understand the reasons for any changes, including changes in perceived audit risks and the work undertaken by the external auditors to address those risks.
- Obtain feedback about the conduct of the audit from key people involved, particularly the finance director and the head of internal audit. The latter will include considering reliance on internal audit.
- Review and monitor the content of the auditors' management letter to assess whether it is based on a good understanding of the company's business and establish whether recommendations have been acted upon and if not, why not.

This audit-facing review process should cover all aspects of their services (i.e. including any non-audit services) and include quality control, the judgement of the auditors and how robust and perceptive they were in making them. The audit report, together with the audit firm's report on its internal quality control procedures and its annual transparency report, should also inform the more wide-ranging assessment of the auditors' qualification, expertise and resources, effectiveness and independence that the committee is required to undertake under the FRC *Guidance on Audit Committees*.

The FRC guidance Audit Quality: Practical Aid for Audit Committees provides further detail on the key elements of the committee's assessment and how the audit committee can seek appropriate assurance and evidence that:

- judgements about materiality were made appropriately;
- the areas of highest risk were properly identified and focused on;

- effective audit procedures were chosen and carried out;
- evidence obtained during the audit was well understood, interpreted and reliably evaluated; and
- reports made were clear and candid.

While much of the assessment will be carried out at the conclusion of the audit, by linking the assessment to the risks to audit quality identified at the planning stage, the assessment will be comprehensive and ongoing throughout the audit cycle.

On the assumption that the auditors will be registered auditors, qualification should not be in doubt. The main focus will therefore be on the auditors' expertise and resources, effectiveness and independence. The audit committee will wish to assess the quality and competence of the senior audit staff, both individually and collectively, in addition to the effectiveness of their working with the internal audit team.

While the committee will want to be satisfied primarily that the statutory audit and the review of the relevant non-audited parts of the annual report and accounts have been completed competently, the level of added value derived from the auditors' work should also be assessed. In this respect, the committee may wish to consider the following:

- Did the senior audit partner bring leadership and integrity to the audit process and where necessary a capability to challenge and probe senior management? Section 505 of the CA 2006 requires the name of the senior statutory auditor (in practice, the senior audit partner) to be published on every copy of the auditor's report, unless there are reasonable grounds for considering that publication of the name might give rise to a risk of violence or intimidation. The regulatory objective of this requirement is to encourage further personal responsibility for the quality of the audit team's performance.
- Did the auditors show an understanding of the business and its sector, e.g. when advising on difficult accounting judgements?
- Were weaknesses in internal controls and elsewhere identified and were any recommendations for change useful?
- Where required to do so, did the auditors work well with other advisers, e.g. lawyers or actuaries, etc.?

The audit committee should assess, prior to reaching a conclusion, whether they have received sufficient information and evidence or need to delve further before reporting to the board on the audit quality and external audit effectiveness.

### Reappointment and tender

Having completed their assessment, the audit committee will report on their findings to the board and make a recommendation on whether the auditors should be reappointed or the contract put to tender. The formal appointment (normally reappointment) of the external auditors is made annually by a resolution of the shareholders at the general meeting at which the company's annual accounts and reports for the previous year are laid. Sections 489–491 of the CA 2006 govern the appointment of auditors by a public company. Separate provisions apply for private companies.

Code Provision C.3.7 states that:

> 'The audit committee should have primary responsibility for making a recommendation on the appointment, reappointment and removal of the external auditors. If the board does not accept the audit committee's recommendation, it should include in the annual report and in any papers recommending appointment or reappointment, a statement from the audit committee explaining its recommendation and should set out reasons why the board has taken a different position.'

When considering whether the current auditors should be reappointed, the committee will want to take account of the period since the current audit firm was first appointed.

A new requirement to put the external audit contract out to tender at least every ten years reflects concern over the length of tenure historically enjoyed by many listed companies' auditors and the domination of the listed company audit market by the so-called 'Big Four' (Deloitte, Ernst & Young, KPMG and PricewaterhouseCoopers). The concerns centre on the risk that a lack of competition in the market may lead to weaknesses in auditing practices. As noted above, while technically auditors are appointed by shareholders as the body to which they primarily owe their duty, in practice it is the directors, influenced by the concerns of management, who hold the day-to-day power over auditor appointments. This disconnect enhances the risk that auditors may be swayed by management concerns and provide a less robust form of assurance to shareholders as a result.

The Competition Commission examined the audit market and considered the issues created by the small pool of auditors with FTSE 350 contracts and the tendency for companies to retain their auditors for many years. The 2013 findings of the Competition Commission identified a number of issues in relation to the market including:

- barriers to switching auditors arising from, amongst other things, difficulties in judging the quality of audits offered by competitor firms and the

nature of the strong relationship of trust and confidence with their auditors which companies were reluctant to lose;
- the significant management time commitment required to select a new auditor and to familiarise the auditor with the company;
- experience and reputational barriers that mid-tier firms face when considered for selection for a FTSE 350 audit; and
- a misalignment of incentives between shareholders and management resulting in auditors seeking to satisfy management demands rather than the demands of the shareholders they should primarily be serving.

A notice of possible remedies was published by the Competition Commission (now the CMA), which included mandatory tendering, mandatory audit firm rotation, expanded remit and/or frequency of the Audit Quality Review Team (AQRT) reviews, prohibition of 'Big Four only' clauses in loan documentation, strengthened accountability of the external auditor to the audit committee, enhanced shareholder-auditor engagement and extended reporting requirements.

In 2014, EU legislation to reform the statutory audit market was adopted for implementation for accounting periods commencing on or after 17 June 2016. In particular, changes are introduced for the audit of public interest entities (PIEs). The definition of PIEs includes companies listed on a regulated market, credit institutions, insurance companies and other entities which the member state designates as PIEs by virtue of their size or the nature of their business.

The new EU regulatory framework goes beyond issues of auditor rotation but here only rotation provisions, including the transitional arrangements, as implemented in the UK by virtue of a CMA Order, are summarised.

**Table 7.1** EU re-tendering requirements

| Category of company | Re-tendering requirements |
|---|---|
| FTSE350 companies that have had their auditor in place for 20 or more years.* | Tender their next audit appointment made on or after 17 June 2020. No renewal of existing engagement. |
| FTSE350 companies that have had their auditor in place for 11–19 years.* | Tender their next audit appointment made on or after 17 June 2023. No renewal of existing engagement. |
| FTSE350 companies that have had their auditor in place for less than 11 years.* | Apply a ten-year tendering regime for audit appointments made on or after 17 June 2016. Existing auditor may be reappointed. |

*By reference to the time an auditor has been the appointed auditor as at 16 June 2014.

It will possibly be unwise to leave the tender to the last possible year and therefore consideration should be given to carrying out the tender exercise at least one or two years before it is strictly required. Whatever the decision, companies are required to include in the Audit Committee report within annual report and account the approach or re-appointment of the external auditor information on the length of tenure of the audit firm, when a tender was last concluded and advanced notice of any retendering plans (Code Provision C.3.8). The giving of such advance notice will enable shareholders to consider whether they wish to be consulted on the tender.

If, having conducted their assessment, the audit committee wishes to recommend a change in the auditors, it will need to bring that recommendation to the board prior to commencing a tender process. That process is now outlined.

### Audit tender process

The FRC has published *Audit Tenders, Notes on Best Practice* and the IA has also issued *Guidelines on Audit Tenders*, both of which will be useful when considering an exercise which, for many, will be one that they have never before or, only infrequently, experienced.

In accordance with the EU Audit Regulation, the audit committee will lead the audit tender process, thus ensuring that the tender is managed and directed in the interests of a company's shareholders. The committee (and the board) should be aware that a change in the auditors is likely to be expensive in terms of professional fees and the demands made on management time. Such a decision needs to be made in sufficient time to allow a selection process to be completed and a resolution appointing the proposed new firm of auditors to be included on the notice of the relevant general meeting. Working backwards from this deadline, a project timeline including an opportunity for early shareholder engagement should be established.

The company's finance team will inevitably be heavily involved in the process and will wish to ensure that, as far as possible, the timing does not distract them during the busy year-end period. It will also be sensible to arrange the timing so as to avoid the incumbent auditors undertaking too much planning and preparation work for the following year's audit which they may not subsequently be appointed to perform. For this reason, the optimum time to commence the tender process may be shortly after completion of the AGM, even though at that time the existing auditors have only just been reappointed.

Having settled on the appropriate timing, clear objectives for the tender process and a project team to lead and manage the process should be established. The tender objectives are likely to be informed to a certain extent by the assessment the committee made indicating that the auditor role should be tendered. The need to acquire audit services should be prioritised over non-audit services, the provision of which is subject to significant restrictions.

Once the scope of the audit contract has been determined, invitations to tender will need to be issued. The decision about which firms to invite to tender will be based upon criteria such as reputation, geographical coverage of the firm's network, personal prior experience of a firm or a firm's knowledge of a sector or regulation. It is interesting to note that the IA, in its published guidelines, confirms that, for all but the largest international groups, the pool of prospective auditors should extend beyond the 'Big Four' and that there should be genuine prospects of selection for all firms participating in the tender.

Interested parties will need to be provided with sufficient information and opportunities to find out more about the company in order to submit a meaningful pitch for the contract.

A review of the tender documents will enable a shortlist to be prepared of firms to be invited to present to the selection panel. The selection panel will want to meet the individual audit partner and manager who, if successful, will manage the audit. Following completion of this work, the selection panel should be in a position to make a recommendation to the audit committee. In arriving at their recommendation, the selection panel is likely to wish to consider a number of issues including:

- the firm's ability to service company-wide audit needs, experience of auditing similar organisations, creditability and references;
- audit team resources, personal fit, succession planning and time commitment;
- the proposed approach, how the team will ensure understanding of the business and organisation, how responsive to the company's specific needs the audit processes will be, how the team will work with relevant internal functions, how quality assurance will be managed, how accounting issues will be addressed and how findings will be reported;
- the proposed transition plan and the extent to which the firm has experience of managing other audit transitions; and
- confirmation of independence, details of other services already provided by the firm to the company and how conflicts of interest will be dealt with. Matters that may threaten independence, integrity and objectivity might include services that will need to be transitioned and whether an audit committee member was previously employed by the firm.

Audit fees for the consolidated accounts, individual subsidiary accounts and interim results and the basis for calculating fees for future years will be less important than assurance on audit quality.

It is important to bear in mind that, unless reappointment is prohibited under the CMA Order, the recommendation may be reappointment of the current audit firm, but care should be taken to ensure that unfair advantage is not given to the incumbent auditor in the tender process.

Investors will welcome clear and transparent reporting on the tender process including:

- an outline of timetable and stages in the tendering process;
- how firms were assessed;
- how the issue of fees was addressed;
- details as to why the firm concerned was chosen; and
- a summary of the handover process.

Before taking up its appointment, a new firm of auditors is required by professional ethics rules to obtain any information from the outgoing firm that may be relevant to its decision to take up the appointment.

An audit committee might want to consider using auditors from more than one audit network. The traditional position for multinational and complex businesses has been to appoint one audit firm which then sub-contracts with other firms within its network to provide complete audit coverage across the entire group. This approach can offer advantages including commonality of audit methodology, effective communication processes between the different auditors involved and consistent quality control and monitoring policies. However, a single-network approach is not the only option and alternatives are to appoint one firm as lead auditor to audit the parent company and consolidated accounts, with other firms separately appointed as appropriate to provide local audit requirements or to appoint joint auditors. Each approach will have its pros and cons and the FRC have produced Guidance on the Use of Audit Firms from More Than One Network to assist audit committees in considering the relevant issues.

There are some incidental aspects to the process of appointing a new audit firm that the committee will need to manage carefully. If the auditor resigns, the FRC *Guidance on Audit Committees* requires that the audit committee should investigate the issues giving rise to the resignation and consider whether any action is required. This will be unusual and may reveal governance failures of one sort or another. The auditors will also be required to make a statement under s. 519 of the CA 2006 of the circumstances connected with their ceasing to hold office and the company, within 14 days of receipt of the statement, must either send a copy to every person entitled to receive the company's accounts or apply to the court.

In addition, some termination of auditor appointments will give rise to a statutory duty for the auditor and company to notify the FRC (in its capacity as appropriate audit authority). Flow charts published on the FRC website provide guidance on these notifications.

### Terms and remuneration

The FRC Guidance provides that the audit committee should approve the terms of engagement and the remuneration to be paid to the external auditors in respect of audit services. Where the appointment is continuing, the committee should review the engagement letter at the outset of the audit process. It should define in detail the scope of the engagement, the lines of responsibility and the fee payable. When negotiating the fee, the committee should be satisfied that, while being competitive, it is sufficient to secure an effective, high-quality audit. Developments in accounting and reporting practice and changes in circumstance since the previous year will inevitably have an impact on the audit scope and fee from time to time.

While large parts of the engagement letter will follow the relevant auditing standard closely and so will, in effect, be non-negotiable, the committee should be prepared to challenge other proposed terms where necessary.

Regulations introduced following s. 494 of the CA 2006 require publication of the remuneration paid to the auditor and any associate of the auditor for both audit and non-audit services provided to the company or any associate of the company. A breakdown of the remuneration by type of service is also required. This enhances the rigor of the audit committee's scrutiny of the terms of the engagement and in view of the increased transparency it is essential for the committee to take full control of negotiation of such terms (not, for example, delegating this to the finance director).

In addition, the same Regulations require a company which has entered into an auditor liability limitation agreement, as permitted by the Act, to disclose the principal terms of the agreement in its accounts, as well as the date of the resolution approving either the agreement or its principal terms. Any proposal to enter into a liability limitation agreement with the auditor and the terms of that agreement would need to be considered by the audit committee as part of its overall recommendations to the board on the auditor's appointment.

The processes and documentation around the selection, appointment and terms of engagement of the auditors are crucial areas of governance. In view of the obligations on the audit committee in these matters, it would be advisable to take legal advice on the auditors' terms of engagement and any limitation of liability in particular.

### Independence, including the provision of non-audit services

Self-evidently, investor confidence in the audit opinion in the annual report and accounts is key to the orderly conduct of capital markets and is, therefore, of primary concern from a good governance perspective. Taking up the themes of objectivity and independence, the FRC Guidance requires the audit committee to annually review the totality of the relationship between the auditors and the company. The committee will want to take account of the views of the company's management team and internal auditors as well as those of the external auditor. The audit committee will also need to be sufficiently aware of the FRC's Ethical Standard, which is referred to on a number of occasions within the FRC Guidance and will have a direct bearing on the committee's deliberations over whether auditor independence or objectivity is compromised.

In particular the committee will need to seek reassurance, taking account of relevant ethical standards, that the auditors and their staff have no family, financial, employment, investment or business relationship with the company (other than in the normal course of business) which could impact auditor objectivity and independence. As part of their review, they will require from the auditors information about policies and processes for maintaining independence and monitoring compliance with relevant requirements, including rotation of audit partners and staff. Where a change of audit partner could, in the opinion of the audit committee, impair the quality of the audit, the FRC Guidance gives some leeway for the appointment of a new audit partner to be delayed for up to two years provided that no longer than seven years is spent in the role in total.

The audit committee should also establish, with the board, the company's policy for the employment of former employees of the auditors, in particular former employees of the audit firm who were part of the audit team. The committee should also monitor application of the policy and consider whether, in cases where former employees of the audit firm have been employed in senior positions within the company, there has been any impairment or appearance of impairment of the auditor's independence and objectivity.

The audit committee is also tasked with developing, recommending to the board and keeping under review the company's policy on the provision of non-audit services provided by the auditor, although care will need to be taken to avoid breach of the EU audit reform restrictions on the provision of non-audit services by auditors. The committee's objective in establishing its non-audit services policy must be to ensure that the external auditor's objectivity and independence are not compromised by the provision of non-audit services. The Ethical Standard sets out, in Section 5, those services which, for PIEs, are considered to be prohibited non-audit services.

The FRC Guidance advocates that a number of factors are considered by the committee including whether the audit firm's skills and experience make them the most suitable supplier for the relevant non-audit service, the safeguards which are in place to mitigate the risk that independence and objectivity are threatened, the nature of the non-audit services, the individual and aggregate amount of non-audit fees relative to the audit fee and the criteria governing the compensation of those performing the audit.

A policy should specify which non-audit services (if any) the auditor is pre-approved to supply (i.e. approval has been given in advance as a matter of policy), the non-audit services for which specific audit committee approval is required before they are contracted and those from which the auditor is excluded altogether. Only trivial non-audit services may be given pre-approval. The FRC Guidance confirms that even pre-approved non-audit services must be reported.

The prescriptive reporting requirements in relation to non-audit services will, in particular, focus the audit committee's attention on the need to publicly justify their policies. The provision of other services to their audit clients by auditors brings in each case the possibility that objectivity and independence will be jeopardised or will be seen to have been jeopardised, potentially exposing the company and its audit committee to censure. This means that the audit committee's job to review the independence of the auditors is all the more imperative.

## Internal controls and risk management

While ultimate responsibility for the adequacy of the company's risk management and internal control systems rests with the board, the audit committee has a pivotal role in reviewing the adequacy of the company's system of internal financial controls. Additionally, in the absence of a separate risk committee, it will be tasked with reviewing the company's capacity to manage the company's internal control and risk management systems. This latter responsibility will extend to both financial and non-financial risks. An internal audit function is commonly used to provide assurance on both internal controls and risk management systems. The status and role of internal audit in the context of the maintenance of internal financial controls is addressed in Chapter 10 but the specific responsibilities of the audit committee for monitoring and reviewing the internal audit function are dealt with here. Code Provision C.3.6 states that:

> 'The audit committee should monitor and review the effectiveness of the internal audit activities. Where there is no internal audit function, the audit committee should consider annually whether there is a need for an internal audit function and make a recommendation to the board and the reasons for the absence of such a function should be explained in the relevant section of the annual report.'

If no internal audit function exists, the audit committee must therefore give consideration annually as to whether an internal audit function should be established. The decision will depend on the specific nature of the company and its operations, including its size, diversity, complexity and number of employees. The committee will wish to take account of other internal functions which provide assurance on issues such as legal or regulatory matters and review whether such resources already provide sufficient objective assurance. They will also need to look ahead to see if the company's plans, operating environment, activities or other aspects have changed or are expected to change in such a way that might increase the risks faced by the company. For example, a planned restructuring or the introduction of new reporting processes might give rise to new risks that indicate a greater need for an internal audit function than was previously the case. The costs and benefits will need to be weighed up in reaching a decision. Where the conclusion reached by the committee is to continue without an internal audit function, that decision will need to be explained and justified to shareholders in the audit committee's section of the annual report.

The FRC Guidance recognises that an alternative approach to the provision of an internal audit function is to engage the external auditors for the role. PIEs may not, however, adopt this approach. Even for companies not subject to this restriction, however, the audit committee should take a cautious stance when considering such a proposal given the potential threat to the overall effectiveness of a company's internal audit arrangements that the external auditor's appointment may have in this regard. The Guidance warns audit committees that investors' views in such circumstances may be influenced by:

> 'Whether, in the absence of an internal audit function, the audit committee is wholly reliant on the views of the external auditor about the effectiveness of the system of controls relating to core activities and significant locations.'

Where an internal audit function does exist, the committee has an important role to challenge and test its effectiveness and to champion its position, role and resources within the company. In some cases, it may be necessary for the committee to educate the board as to the key role of the internal audit function as a provider of objective assurance on risk management, internal controls and governance generally. The committee should ensure that the internal auditor's role and responsibilities are set out in reference formal charter, with particular regard to its position as the provider of independent assurance to the board and that those terms of reference are regularly reviewed.

The Chartered Institute of Internal Auditors (CIIA) and the IOD have published joint guidance, *What every director should know about internal audit: essential information for boards and audit committees*, which provides some useful suggestions on how to frame the internal audit function's charter. The joint CIIA/IoD guidance also provides some helpful ideas on how to monitor and review the effectiveness of the company's internal audit activities.

The FRC Guidance suggests that, when reviewing the internal audit function, the audit committee should:

- ensure that the internal auditor has direct access to the board chairman and to the audit committee and is accountable to the audit committee;
- review and assess the annual internal audit work plan;
- receive a report on the results of the internal auditors' work on a periodic basis;
- review and monitor management's responsiveness to the internal auditor's findings and recommendations;
- meet with the head of internal audit at least annually without the presence of management; and
- monitor and assess the role and effectiveness of the internal audit function in the overall context of the company's risk management system.

With the FRC Guidance in mind, the audit committee will want to cover in its assessment such issues as the clarity of the internal audit strategy ad alignment of the internal audit plan with key risks faced by the business, the relevance of its performance objectives and adequacy of its reports on these to the committee, the level of internal audit resource including the mix of skills and experience within the internal audit team, the independence of the internal audit function and its credibility within the organisation and the degree of proactivity demonstrated by the internal audit team, in particular with regard to emerging risk identification and the highlighting of relevant issues to the committee.

The audit committee's assessment will also need to cover the links between internal audit and external audit and the way they work together to maximise efficiency of the total audit resources available to the organisation. Direct assistance from internal audit to supplement the external audit resource can compromise auditor independence and the integrity of the audit and is prohibited.

In addition, the committee should satisfy itself that the relationships between internal audit and other internal functions such as legal, finance, risk and compliance are well co-ordinated and operate effectively, with open communication.

In recognition of its overall accountability for the internal audit, the audit committee is tasked with approving the appointment (and removal) of the head of internal audit. In order to do so, it is clear that the committee must also approve the job specification and have a clear understanding of the requisite skills and attributes of any candidate.

While it is not mandatory for internal auditors to comply with professional standards, increasingly it is best practice that they should do so. The FRC Guidance assumes that appropriate standards such as the CIIA's Code of Ethics and the International Standards for the Professional Practice of Internal Auditing will be adopted. The Guidance also makes the point that the audit committee should ensure that the necessary people and any other additional resources are made available. Additionally, the committee should ensure that the internal audit function has unrestricted scope and access to appropriate information, which can be taken to include access to the skills and insights of other functions within the company, for example health and safety. The raised governance profile of the internal audit function is evident.

## Governance checklist

✓ Does the committee have the requisite skills, financial experience, resources, time commitment and robust independence of mind to undertake its tasks?

✓ Does the committee review all financial statements and related announcements prior to their release to the market by the company and can it verify the integrity of such statements?

✓ Is the committee satisfied that the company's narrative reports meet regulatory requirements?

✓ Is an external audit plan in place and does the committee review and monitor the auditors' performance against that plan?

✓ Does the audit committee meet at least annually with the external auditors and with the internal auditor without management being present?

✓ Does the committee control the process of appointing and assessing the external auditors and is it satisfied as to their independence and effectiveness?

✓ Has account been taken of the PIE audit tender requirements and is the audit committee involved in the tender process?

✓ Is there an effective and adequately resourced internal audit team and, if not, does the committee annually review the need for such a function?

✓ Is the head of internal audit appointed by and accountable to the audit committee, does he or she have unrestricted access to the audit committee and board chairman and is the management team responsive to his or her findings and recommendations?

# 8

# Narrative reporting

## Narrative reporting – an overview

The narrative reports which form the 'front end' of a company's annual report and accounts are based upon a number of legislative and regulatory requirements that set out the minimum disclosures that companies must make and the extent to which those disclosures should be subject to audit. The requirements, while prescriptive as to content, are flexible to the extent that companies largely have freedom to determine placement of the relevant information (subject to inclusion of cross-references where needed) and can exercise judgement as to materiality.

The focus is on creating a cohesive set of reports which enlighten investors and other users. To this end, in 2009, as part of its 'Complexity Project' aimed at seeking ways to make corporate reporting less complex and more relevant, the FRC published a consultation paper *Louder than Words*, which recommended that:

> '... regulators and standard-setters should adopt a consistent principles-based approach to the making and communication of regulations to ensure regulations are targeted, proportionate, co-ordinated and clear; corporate reporting should be focused, open and honest, clear and understandable, interesting and engaging.'

The consultation document made the point that company reports are now aimed at so many different users that the primary purpose of such reporting – to provide investors with the information they need to make their resource allocation decisions and to assess management's stewardship – risked being lost.

To help address the problem, the FRC subsequently issued a discussion paper *Cutting Clutter* which attempted to identify the reasons for, and the barriers to reducing, so-called 'kitchen sink' reporting. The paper argued that over-reporting obscures key messages about the company and so devalues corporate reporting as a tool for assessing company progress. The paper challenged all those involved in corporate reporting – standard-setters, regulators, auditors and companies as well as the stakeholders who use the reports – to debate what reporting is meaningful and therefore actually required and to address the behaviours, which lead to increases in the length of reports, such as the tendency to include a disclosure 'just in case'.

The *Cutting Clutter* discussion paper incorporated some disclosure aids designed to help those preparing narrative reports to visualise clearer ways in which information can be presented. They were not intended to be templates but could be used as a helpful tool to kick-start discussions within a company about the key messages it wants its reports to convey and how best to communicate those messages to its target audience. The paper urged those involved in the preparation of corporate reports to debate those key messages, the tone of the company reports, the presentation style and overall objectives for the reports at the planning stage so that there is clarity on what the final document is expected to achieve.

Building on the FRC's *Cutting Clutter* agenda, a new initiative entitled 'Clear & Concise' was developed to deliver higher-quality corporate reporting that would provide investors with more relevant information. In particular the initiative sought to address the inclusion of boilerplate or immaterial disclosures. Key focuses were:

- communication;
- placement of information; and
- materiality.

At EU level, measures to improve the transparency of larger listed and financial services PIEs (those with 500+ employees) through narrative reporting on diversity, social, environmental and anti-corruption matters have been introduced through the *Disclosure of Non-Financial and Diversity Information Directive*. On the international stage, the IIRC continues to explore development of an integrated reporting framework.

## Narrative reporting – UK Corporate Governance Code

Code Principle C.1 sets out the overriding requirement for boards to ensure that in their corporate reporting they 'present a fair, balanced and understandable assessment of the company's position and prospects'. The Supporting Principle to C.1 clarifies that this responsibility 'extends to interim and other price-sensitive public reports and reports to regulators as well as to information required to be presented by statutory requirements'.

Boards will need to bear in mind, therefore, when considering draft reports for approval, whether, both individually and combined as a whole, reports are 'fair, balanced and understandable'.

In addition to this overriding principle, the Code includes a number of specific reporting and information requirements which are considered in the relevant sections of this chapter.

### Preparing the narrative reports

When planning the preparation of its narrative reports an early task will be for the board to approve the process and then ensure its proper application. It is suggested that the audit committee should take on responsibility for this task, placing it in the company's system of internal control. Key to the process will be verifying the information put before the board. To the extent the information obtained is the product of an internal control system that is reviewed according to the standards set out in the UK Corporate Governance Code, the board can take some comfort that it is reliable. For other information, new approaches may be required.

There will be other practical drafting and design issues relating to the annual report, including placement of information bearing in mind the objectives of the narrative reports which are to:

- provide context for the related financial statements;
- provide insight into the company's business model, key objectives and strategy;
- describe the company's main risks and how they could impact its future prospects;
- analyse the company's past performance; and
- cross-reference any complementary information provided voluntarily, possibly on the company website.

All this will require careful pre-planning and quite possibly specialist advice from a corporate communications consultant, as well as legal advice. The board would be advised to delegate consideration of these issues to a committee well in advance of the deadline for drafting the annual report.

### Contents of the narrative reports

Drawn from a variety of sources, the content requirements for the narrative reports can be confusing. To assist those preparing reports, ICSA has published a simple contents list for company annual reports. The list (which is available from www.icsa.org.uk) is intended to be a helpful starting point for companies to adapt to suit their specific circumstances rather than a rigid template and the analysis provided below should be viewed likewise as an indicative framework.

The following sections examine current reporting requirements as follows:

- strategic report;

- directors' report;
- corporate governance report; and
- directors' remuneration report.

## The strategic report

Key elements of a company's narrative reporting are now pulled together within the strategic report as required by the CA 2006 (*Strategic Report and Directors' Report*) Regulations 2013. Companies, other than small companies, are required to prepare a strategic report instead of the previously required business review, putting the strategic information at the front, separate from the directors' report.

In addition, UK Corporate Governance Code Provision C.1.2 requires the directors to 'include in the annual report an explanation of the basis on which the company generates or preserves value over the longer term (the business model) and the strategy for delivering the objectives of the company'. The appropriate place to include such explanations is within the strategic report, the statutory requirements for which are now considered, drawing in particular on the FRC *Guidance on the Strategic Report*.

S. 414C of the CA 2006 sets out that the purpose of the strategic report is 'to inform members of the company and help them assess how the directors have performed their duty under section 172 (duty to promote the success of the company)'. Accordingly, that the interests of the members are paramount and a direct link is made between their interests being served and the directors observing their essential duty to promote the success of the company. However, while, according to the statute, the purpose of the report is to inform shareholders, the nature of the content requirements means that other users of the accounts, such as employees, customers, suppliers and society more widely, will also have an interest in the strategic report.

The strategic report must contain 'a fair review of the business of the company' and 'a description of the principal risks and uncertainties facing the company'. The review must contain a 'balanced and comprehensive analysis' of the development and performance of the company's business during the financial year and the position of the company at the end of the year, consistent in each case with the size and complexity of the business.

To the extent necessary for understanding and measurement of the development, performance or position of the company's business, the strategic report must also include analysis, based upon financial KPIs and, where appropriate, other KPIs including those relating to environmental or employee matters. The KPIs chosen must be ones by which the company's business can be 'measured effectively'. Non-financial KPIs could include indicators such as customer complaints, product quality or information on employee and environmental matters (such as environmental spillage and $CO_2$ emissions). While the requirements give the directors discretion to decide on the appropriate KPIs and there is, additionally, an exemption available to medium-sized companies in relation to the non-financial KPI reporting elements, certainly for directors of larger entities, the reporting of non-financial KPIs will tend to increase their focus on transparency in CSR matters.

More prescriptive requirements additionally apply to the strategic reports of quoted companies. For such companies the strategic report must, as well as the general strategic report contents referred to above, contain 'to the extent necessary for an understanding of the development, performance or position of the company's business':

- a description of the company's strategy;
- a description of the company's business model;
- the main trends and factors likely to affect the future development, performance and position of the company's business; and
- information about environmental matters (including the impact of the company's business on the environment), the company's employees and social, community and human rights issues. The information on these issues must include details of any policies of the company in relation to them and the effectiveness of those policies. If the report does not contain information on any of these matters, it must point out which matters are not covered.

For information relevant to environmental matters, a helpful resource is available in the Government's publication *Environmental Key Performance Indicators: reporting guidelines for UK business*. Defra has also published *Environmental Reporting Guidelines: Including Mandatory Greenhouse Gas Emissions Reporting Guidance* which companies may find useful.

In addition, as a result of the high-profile board diversity debate, a quoted company's strategic report must provide information on the gender split for board, management and all-employee totals. As the strategic report must be prepared on a consolidated basis, figures for both the parent company and group are required.

So for quoted companies, one implication of the legislation governing the strategic report is that, in order to enable members to develop an understanding of the development, performance or position of the company's business, it will be necessary, to some extent, to address environmental matters and to provide information about the company's employees and social, human rights and community issues. For the majority of quoted companies, it is difficult to envisage a situation in which the key environmental and employee matters would not be considered necessary for shareholders to acquire the understanding envisaged by the legislation. This brings CSR issues into the boardroom in the context of the board's responsibility for the approval of the strategic report. Reporting on CSR issues is covered in detail in Chapter 6.

The range of information to be included in the strategic report is extensive. Placement of the information so as to produce a coherent, informative and readable document is therefore an important consideration. A common approach is to disclose the information required in the strategic report across separate reports – a chairman's statement, chief executive and chief financial officer's reports, strategy review and risk report, for example – with appropriate cross-references.

The chairman's statement might include an overview of the period, a statement of the proposed dividend, comment on diversity, culture and corporate responsibility and a statement on the outlook for the business. The chief executive's review could provide a more detailed commentary on the sector and trading environment, progress in the business, strategy and KPIs while, as you might expect, the chief financial officer's report will focus on key elements of the financial results, the balance sheet, capital position, going concern assessment and dividends.

Matters that would otherwise be disclosed in the directors' report may be included in the strategic report if the directors consider them to be of strategic importance to the business. All the above reporting requirements must be completed on a consolidated basis so as to be in the form of a 'group strategic report' in all cases where the company that prepares group accounts is a parent company.

All these reporting requirements are subject to an exemption where disclosure of the information about impending developments or matters being negotiated would 'in the opinion of the directors, be seriously prejudicial to that person and contrary to the public interest'. This exemption will provide some comfort to directors who are concerned about issues of confidentiality or commercial competitiveness.

The strategic report must be approved by the board of directors (although in practice it will have been reviewed initially by the audit committee) and signed on behalf of the board by a director or the company secretary. The points made in the section 'Directors' Obligations and Judgements' later in this chapter will be relevant to this board approval.

Companies that have previously offered shareholders the option of receiving summary financial statements in place of the full report and accounts will now send such shareholders the strategic report instead, together with certain supplementary material (including information on the audit report and how to obtain a copy of the full annual accounts). While the strategic report and the summary financial statements are two quite different documents, it is indicative of the potential value of a well-crafted strategic report that the Government proposals on this received high levels of support.

Shareholders who receive the strategic report instead of the full report and accounts will retain the right to request a copy of the full document should they wish to do so.

The Companies (Receipt of Accounts and Reports) Regulations 2013 set out the process that must be followed in order to ascertain the wishes of members in relation to receipt of the full accounts or strategic report plus supplementary material. In summary, a shareholder who fails to respond to an invitation to elect and receive the full report may be deemed, in the absence of any notification to the contrary, to have elected to receive the strategic report with supplementary material instead.

## Directors' report

The matters to be dealt with in the directors' report are set out in sections 416 and 418 of the CA 2006 and in Schedule 7 to the Large and Medium-sized Companies and Group (Accounts and Reports) Regulations 2013 (as amended). The contents will include:

- the names of all directors who held office at any time during the financial year;
- the amount of any dividend recommended by the directors;
- for quoted companies, annual GHG emissions data, expressed in tonnes of carbon dioxide equivalent, from combustion of fuel and operation of any facility and resulting from the purchase of electricity, heat, steam or cooling for its own use, with prior year comparators also provided. The requirements only apply to the extent that it is practical for the company to obtain the information. Where it is not practical, a statement on what information is not provided, and why, must be included. Finally, a statement on the calculation methodologies used and at least one ratio comparing annual emissions with a quantifiable factor associated with the company's activities must be provided;
- political donations in excess of £2,000 (in aggregate);
- for any financial instruments the company uses, unless the information is not material, the risk management objectives and policies, including the hedging policy for each type of transaction for which hedge accounting is used, and an indication of the company's exposure to price, credit, liquidity and cash flow risks;
- details of any important post-balance sheet events;
- an indication of likely future business developments;
- information on the company's research and development activities (if any);
- details of any non-UK branches (this does not apply to unlimited companies);

- details relating to any acquisition of its own shares – in particular the number, nominal value and consideration paid for the shares and the percentage of called-up shares they represent; and
- for companies that employed 250+ people (on average), a description of the company's policies in relation to the employment, training, development and promotion of disabled people and of the action the company has taken to introduce, maintain and develop employee communication, consultation and participation in initiatives such as employee share schemes.

The directors are responsible for ensuring that all 'relevant audit information' (meaning information needed by the auditor in connection with his report) has been disclosed to the auditor. The directors' report must include a statement that each of the directors:

- is not aware of any relevant audit information of which the auditor is unaware; and
- has taken all necessary steps to make themself aware of the relevant audit information and to establish that the auditor is aware of it.

Those steps will include making enquiries for that purpose of their fellow directors and the auditors. That in itself, however, may not be sufficient and directors should consider whether there is anything else they need to do in this regard in order to discharge their duty as directors 'to exercise reasonable care, skill and diligence'.

## The corporate governance statement

The obligation for companies with a main market listing to publish a corporate governance statement is imposed by DTR 7.2, which also sets out a number of requirements with regards to the statement's contents. The report must be published as a separate section of the directors' report. Reflecting the chairman's responsibility for leading the board and ensuring its effectiveness, they are expected to report personally on matters of corporate governance. The aim of the corporate governance statement is to pull together in one place key information about the company's governance arrangements, including:

- the required 'comply or explain' information in respect of the UK Corporate Governance Code;
- the composition and operations of the board and committees;
- information on the group's internal control and risk management systems in relation to the financial reporting process;
- details of significant shareholders (both direct and indirect holdings), the identity of any shareholder whose shares carry special rights, certain

details in relation to exercise of share and voting rights, rules relating to appointment of directors or changes to the company's articles of association, and the details of the directors' power to issue or buy back shares; and
- diversity policy information including its objectives, how it has been implemented and the results for the reporting period. Diversity in this context should be interpreted widely and not simply in relation to gender.

The key elements of the corporate governance statement are discussed further below.

### *Comply or explain*

Central to the corporate governance statement is the company's reporting under the 'comply or explain' requirements of LR 9.8.6R. This requirement is broken down into two subtly different reporting components. The first of these components is to explain how the Principles of the UK Corporate Governance Code have been applied. It should be noted that there is an expectation that all the Principles will have been applied. This is echoed unequivocally in the section of the Code which explains the 'comply or explain' approach when it says:

> 'The principles are the core of the Code and the way in which they are applied should be the central question for a board as it determines how it is to operate according to the Code'.

In other words, boards are not to be confused with the thought that non-compliance with the Principles themselves may be explained away – those Principles are non-negotiable. It is only whether those Principles are applied through adherence to the Code Provisions or applied in some other way that is within the board's discretion.

This leads onto the second reporting component which is to confirm whether or not throughout the relevant accounting period the company has complied with all the relevant Code Provisions and, where there has been an area of non-compliance, both to provide details of the period when the non-compliance occurred and to explain the reasons for non-compliance.

It is important to note the Code's requirement for boards to 'think comprehensively' about their roles and governance arrangements in a way which a 'tick-box' requirement simply would not require. The Code is designed to reflect the fact that effective governance cannot be broken down into a one-size-fits-all set of prescriptive rules and it provides boards with discretion to find arrangements which suit their company's own circumstances through the 'comply or explain' regime. The success of this regime is dependent firstly on companies providing meaningful explanations which enable a shareholder to properly understand and evaluate their approach. Secondly, it is dependent on the commitment of shareholders to take the time necessary to carry out that evaluation and to support those boards which, although perhaps taking a different approach to that envisaged by a particular Code Provision, are nevertheless applying the Code Principles in a way which serves the needs of the company well. In the Preface to the Code, chairmen are urged to use their personal statements to provide investors with a clear picture. By providing a 'fuller context' the point is made, that investors should become more willing to accept explanations of why a company has chosen to explain rather than comply with a particular provision.

In order to understand what information shareholders need in this regard, it is useful to look at available guidance. In 2012, the FRC, based on discussion meetings between senior investors and companies, published *What constitutes an explanation under 'comply or explain'?*. The report contains a number of useful suggestions, including:

- setting out the company's approach to governance in the context of its business model;
- ensuring explanations are full and include reference to context and a coherent rationale; and
- reporting, even where full compliance can be confirmed, should be full so as to form a basis for further dialogue to engender trust.

Further insight into what might constitute best practice 'comply or explain' reporting is provided in the ABI's 2012 report, *Comply or Explain: investor expectations and current practices*, which sets out six criteria according to which companies are encouraged to:

- describe company-specific context and historical background;
- provide convincing and understandable rationale;
- detail mitigating action to address any additional risk;
- make it clear whether aspects of non-compliance with the Code are time-bound;
- specify deviations from the Provisions as well as from main Principles; and
- explain how the alternative is consistent with the Code Principles and contributes to the objective of good governance.

As well as establishing these criteria, the ABI's report provides a number of best practice examples to illustrate the type of explanations most valued by shareholders.

### *The board and its committees*

DTR 7.2.7R requires the corporate governance statement to report on the composition and operation of the board and its committees. DTR 7.2.8G confirms that the FRC considers that a company which reports in accordance with the requirements of UK Corporate Governance Code Provisions A1.1, A1.2, B2.4, C3.3, C3.8 and D2.1 will comply with DTR 7.2.7R.

We first look here at reporting on the board's composition and operations before moving on to examine reporting on the committees.

Code Provision A1.1 states 'The annual report should include a statement of how the board operates, including a high-level statement of which types of decisions are to be taken by the board and which are to be delegated to management.' The board will typically draw up a schedule of matters reserved to it and the report will also need to specifically address how the roles of the chairman and chief executive are divided and distinguished from each other. These issues are examined further in Chapters 3 and 11 respectively.

Code Provision A1.2 also sets out a number of specific reporting requirements that will be included in the corporate governance statement. In particular, the chairman, the deputy chairman (if any), the chief executive, the SID and the chairmen and members of the board committees must all be identified. Frequently these disclosures are incorporated into short biographical details for each director which enables users of the report to assess the experience of the directors, their other commitments outside of the company and their specific roles within the organisation. By providing such profiles 'side by side', a sense can be obtained, not only of the skills, knowledge and experience of individual directors but also the balance and diversity of the board as a whole.

As discussed in Chapter 9, directors must commit sufficient time to their role in order to be able to discharge their duties effectively. To enable an assessment of this to be made, the report will set out the number of meetings of the board and its committees held during the year as well as a breakdown of individual attendance by directors. While occasional absences are perhaps unavoidable for most and, therefore, are acceptable to a point, and of course there can be legitimate circumstances where longer periods of absence are understandable, for example in the event of serious illness, as a general rule, high levels of meeting attendance will be expected as the norm. Providing an explanation for any deviation from this norm would be wise. Certainly it would be difficult to recommend the re-election of a director with a poor attendance record unless justification for doing so was clearly explained.

### *The nomination committee report*

In addition to the requirement to 'make available its terms of reference' (Code Provision B.2.1), for example on the company website, Code Provision B.2.4 requires that a 'separate section of the annual report should describe the work of the nomination committee, including the process it has used in relation to board appointments'. The report will need to cover work carried out by the committee to review the structure, size and composition of the board and succession planning and the annual review of the time commitment required of NEDs.

In addition, in a year in which there has been a new board appointment, the report on the committee's activities will need to be rather fuller, including in particular an explanation if neither an external search consultancy nor open advertising has been used in the appointment of a chairman or a non-executive director. Where an external search consultancy has been used, it should be identified in the annual report and any other connection with the company made clear.

As well as reporting on these aspects, Code Provision B.2.4 also requires that the nomination committee's report should address diversity issues, including a description of the board's policy on diversity and any measurable objectives that it has set for implementing the policy, and progress on achieving those objectives. Within the Code Provision, specific reference is made to gender diversity; however, in the FRC's *Feedback Statement* announcing the introduction of this requirement, the need for reporting on the board's diversity policy and measurable objectives to relate to wider aspects of diversity was emphasised. The FRC's observation that 'companies should not focus purely on gender at the expense of other aspects of diversity' provides boards with a clear steer that issues of gender are to form only part of their overall consideration of diversity matters.

Furthermore, the requirements of DTR 7.2.8A are explicit in expanding the diversity reporting requirements beyond the issue of gender. It provides, as additional examples, age, education and professional background but frames the requirement in such a way that these aspects cannot be inferred to be an exhaustive list.

The nomination committee's reporting on the board's diversity policy and objectives should therefore reflect this wider interpretation of 'diversity' and not restrict itself to issues of gender. It goes without saying that 'boiler plate' reporting is to be avoided. Links will need to be made to the board diversity reporting required in the strategic report (see above).

The ABI's 2012 *Report on Board Effectiveness: Updating progress, promoting best practice* made a number of recommendations on the disclosures a company should make which are relevant to the nomination committee's reporting requirements. While not mandatory, they do provide a useful indication of what shareholders might consider best practice in this regard. In summary, the ABI recommendations relevant to the nomination committee report are for the inclusion of:

- clear, company-specific information about the steps the company is taking to achieve 'diversity of perspective' within the board;

- 'forward-looking and candid' disclosures on what the board is doing to ensure they have the right balance of skills and experience amongst board members;
- meaningful disclosures about the board appointment process, the barriers faced in appointing women to the board and what they are doing to address this issue;
- meaningful succession planning disclosures, including on initiatives to develop the next group of senior management, regardless of whether changes are expected in the short or long term;
- an explanation of any past relationship with any party appointed to carry out a board evaluation and how any potential conflict of interest has been dealt with; and
- an explanation of the performance evaluation process including details of any significant recommendations, changes or improvements which have been agreed to as a result of the review. An expectation that the outcomes of the evaluation will differ from year to year is explicit.

Also worth considering are the recommendations on reporting made in the joint EY/ICSA report, *The Nomination Committee – Coming out of the Shadows*, which concluded that 'nomination committee reports are less informative than audit and remuneration committee reports' and did not reflect the 'expansion of roles, practices, reach and breadth' of the nomination committee. Given the importance to investors of getting issues of board composition and succession right, the importance of the nomination committee report providing 'enough assurance to investors that relevant issues are being addressed' is evident.

The preface to the FRC Guidance on Effective Boards makes clear that an effective board thinks regularly and deeply about its role, behaviours, structures and processes and tailors arrangements to their own company's circumstances in order to best serve its shareholders and other stakeholders. The nomination committee plays a vital role in ensuring good governance by:

- keeping board balance under review so that the company is governed by individuals with the requisite skills, experience and qualifications;
- recruiting to the board individuals who can bring diversity of perspective;
- ensuring the company is not exposed unnecessarily to the risks that it could face in the absence of an effective succession plan; and
- addressing gaps and issues identified through the board's evaluation process.

A board that is able to report good governance practice to its shareholders is likely to be rewarded by them with enhanced levels of trust and confidence. However, disclosure of those arrangements through meaningful reporting is not just of value because of the messages those disclosures send to the outside world. The actual process of crafting those disclosures can itself stimulate fresh thinking about existing arrangements and how improvements might be made and so become part of the cycle of continual learning and governance enhancement.

### *The audit committee report*

The DTR7.2.7R requires listed companies to report on functions carried out by the audit committee. This requirement can be satisfied by compliance with Code Provision C.3.8 which states that:

> 'A separate section in the annual report should describe the work of the committee in discharging its responsibilities.'

Provision C.3.8 specifies that the audit committee report should include:

- a description of the significant issues considered by the committee in relation to the financial statements and how those issues were addressed;
- an explanation of how the effectiveness of external auditors was assessed, the approach taken to the (re)appointment of the auditor, information on the length of tenure of the current auditor, when a tender was last carried out plus advance notice of any retendering plans; and
- an explanation of how auditor independence and objectivity are safeguarded if the auditor provides any non-audit services.

These reporting requirements very much put the committee in the spotlight and the chairman of the audit committee will need to be present at the AGM to answer questions on the report on the committee's activities and matters within the scope of its responsibilities. The *Guidance on Audit Committees* provides further detail on the content requirements for the audit committee section of the annual report, namely that it should include the following:

- a summary of the role of the audit committee;
- how the audit committee composition requirements have been addressed and, if not provided elsewhere, the names and qualifications of all members of the audit committee during the period;
- the number of audit committee meetings;
- how the committee's performance evaluation has been conducted;
- a report on the way the audit committee has discharged its responsibilities;
- the significant issues that the committee considered in relation to the financial statements and how these issues were addressed, having regard to matters communicated to it by the auditors. Additional disclosures will be required if there has been any interaction with the FRC's Corporate

Reporting team or the company's audit has been reviewed by the FRC Audit Quality Review Team;

- an explanation of how it has assessed the effectiveness of the external audit process and the approach taken to the appointment or reappointment of the external auditor, the length of tenure of the current audit firm, the audit partner's name and how long he has held that role, when a tender was last conducted and advance notice of any retender plans; and
- an explanation on how the external auditor's objectivity and independence is safeguarded if the auditors also provide non-audit services, including a description of the committee's policy on approval of non-audit services, fees for the statutory audit, audit-related services and non-audit work, an explanation of the relevant services and why the committee determined that it was in the best interests of the company for the auditor to provide them.

In particular, the committee will need to exercise judgement in deciding which of the issues it considered in relation to the financial statements are significant and so should be included in the report.

The Guidance also advises disclosure would not normally be expected of information which, in the opinion of the audit committee, would be prejudicial to the interests of the company, for example because it relates to impending developments or matters in the course of negotiation.

In preparing their report, the audit committee should consider the Global Disclosure Guidelines which were published in October 2011 by the Enhanced Disclosure Working Group. While the guidelines are not meant to serve as a definitive guide to accounting, audit and risk control disclosures, their use is encouraged as an accompaniment to existing legislation and practice.

In accordance with the FRC Guidance, the audit committee will expect to be supported in these reporting obligations by the company secretary. As well as his or her in-depth knowledge of the reporting requirements, the company secretary, with their close involvement in the planning and contents for the whole of the report and accounts, will be able to swiftly identify information that is already disclosed elsewhere in the annual report and accounts so that, instead of repeating the disclosure, the audit committee section of the annual report can simply provide cross-references to the places where that information can be found. In drafting the audit committee's section of the annual report, attention should be paid to the need to ensure that the language used, in particular in providing descriptions of the significant issues considered by the audit committee in relation to the financial statements, is concise and readily understandable.

## Statement on risk management and internal control

DTR 7.2.10R requires companies which produce a group directors' report to include a description of the 'main features' of the group's internal control and risk management systems in relation to the financial reporting process for the undertakings included in the consolidation. This will be provided in the corporate governance statement.

Code Principle C.2 relates directly to risk management and internal control and Code Provision C.2.2 requires the board to report on its review of the effectiveness of the company's risk management and internal control system. The FRC Guidance offers assistance on what is required for this statement requiring as a minimum that the board:

- acknowledge responsibility for those systems and their annual effectiveness review;
- confirm there is a process in place for ongoing identification, evaluation and management of the company's principal risks;
- disclose that the relevant systems have been in place for the duration of the financial year on which the board are reporting and that those systems are up-to-date at the time the report and accounts are approved;
- confirm that the systems of risk management and internal control are regularly reviewed; and
- report on the extent to which those systems are consistent with the FRC Guidance.

The process used to review the effectiveness of the company's risk management and internal control systems should be described and any actions taken to address identified weaknesses or significant failings should be confirmed provided that such disclosures are not expected to be made where they would be prejudicial to the board's interests.

Appendix C to the FRC Guidance provides a non-prescriptive and non-exhaustive list of questions that the board may wish to discuss with management, covering issues including risk appetite and culture, risk management and internal control systems and monitoring and review processes.

A key question for the board will be how they have satisfied themselves that the necessary risk management and internal control system disclosures help ensure that the report and accounts are fair, balanced, understandable and informative.

To assist achieving this objective, placement of the information and the links made between the statement on risk management and internal control, the going concern assessment of material uncertainties and the principal risk disclosures in the strategic report in particular, should be considered. As elsewhere, cross-referencing to information provided elsewhere can be more helpful than repetition.

Additional requirements in relation to internal controls are placed on SEC registered companies by virtue of s. 404 of the Sarbanes-Oxley Act 2002, as implemented by SEC rule 33-8238. In order to meet these additional requirements, the annual report of a non-US company registered with the SEC must include an internal control report by management. When giving its internal control report under s. 404(a), management must make a statement identifying the 'framework' it has used to conduct the required evaluation of the company's internal control over financial reporting. The SEC has identified the Turnbull Guidance as a suitable framework for the purposes of s. 404(a).

The FRC issued a guide to summarise how the now superseded Turnbull Guidance addresses both the processes and criteria needed to satisfy the requirement that management perform a review of the effectiveness of the company's internal control over financial reporting and also the procedures to be followed in order to maintain supporting evidence of that review. The guide still merits close study by boards of affected companies. The FRC makes the point, however, that the Turnbull Guidance is a framework within which to address the requirements of s. 404(a). It does not reduce the onerous obligations imposed by the Sarbanes-Oxley rules and regulations, to which the flexibility afforded by the UK Corporate Governance Code's 'comply or explain' approach is not available.

## Remuneration reporting

Quoted companies (i.e. UK registered companies that are quoted on the LSE or on a stock exchange in the European Economic Area (EEA), the New York Stock Exchange (NYSE) or NASDAQ) must produce a remuneration report every year which needs to be set out in the annual report and accounts. The remuneration report comprises two key elements – a remuneration policy which is forward looking and a report which details remuneration paid during the year being reported.

The statutory remuneration reporting requirements that apply to all quoted companies were reviewed in 2013. Following this, tougher provisions on the disclosure of remuneration policy and executive pay, including its links to company performance, were introduced through *The Large and Medium-sized Companies and Groups (Accounts and Reports) (Amendment) Regulations 2013* which amended the *Large and Medium-sized Companies and Groups (Accounts and Reports) Regulations 2008* and in particular Schedule 8 to those regulations. Now, quoted companies are required to put their remuneration report to a shareholder vote annually and their remuneration policy to a binding vote at least every three years. The vote on the remuneration report is 'advisory' which means that if it is not approved by shareholders, there is no immediate impact.

However, a significant level of abstentions or votes 'against' could indicate shareholder dissatisfaction with the quality of disclosure or the company's remuneration practices or both. The vote can therefore prove a useful barometer of shareholder opinion and, in crafting the report, account will need to be taken, not only of the legislative regime, but of investor expectations as outlined by relevant guidelines as well.

One important point to remember is that, while the remuneration report must contain a statement by the chairman of the remuneration committee (see below) and will be reviewed by the committee as a whole, the remuneration report itself is a report of all the directors. It must be approved by the full board as required by s.422 of the CA 2006. Each director must satisfy themself that the contents of the report meet the requirements of the regulations. If a director knew the report didn't comply or if they were reckless as to whether it complied and if they didn't take steps to make it comply or to prevent the approval of the report, they could be guilty of an offence. Once approved by the board, it must be signed by a director – normally the chairman of the remuneration committee – or company secretary and put to shareholders for approval. It must then be filed at Companies House.

The company secretarial department and/or the HR department will typically supply much of the data needed to complete the statistical parts of the remuneration report. A point for the remuneration committee is that it should ensure that the information is being properly recorded during the year and that the auditors have the necessary access to and confidence in the information.

The GC100 and Investor Group issued the *Directors' Remuneration Reporting Guidance 2016*, an update of their guidance which was first published in 2013, and which provides helpful and practical guidance on the directors' remuneration report.

## Remuneration report statutory requirements

Since the new requirements came into force, quoted companies must produce a remuneration report which must include:

- a statement by the chair of the remuneration committee;
- in years where the policy is to be the subject of a shareholder vote, details of the company's policy on directors' remuneration; and
- an annual report on remuneration.

The purpose of this report is to pull together into one easily accessible report the most important information on remuneration to enable investors and others with an interest in the matter to quickly access the salient details. Additional content may also be included at the discretion of the board. Each of the three elements listed above is now described.

***Statement by the chair of the remuneration committee***

The chair of the remuneration committee will be required to include a statement setting out the major decisions on directors' remuneration, the context in which decisions have been taken and any major changes relating to directors' remuneration during the year. As the 'public face' of the company's approach to executive remuneration, the chairman of the remuneration committee will undoubtedly be even more sensitive to the potential for adverse comment about and criticism of the company's pay practices.

***Report on the directors' remuneration policy***

Where the directors' remuneration policy is to be proposed to members for approval, a separate section of the remuneration report must describe that policy. The regulations are prescriptive as to the details of the policy to be disclosed and how the disclosures are to be framed. Table 8.1 sets out a summary of the key elements of the required disclosures.

**Table 8.1** Information required in remuneration policy

| Reference in Schedule 8 | Description |
|---|---|
| Paragraphs 25–26 | A description in tabular form of the elements of the directors' remuneration package, including information on how each of those elements supports the short and long-term strategic objectives of the company, how each element is operated including whether there are any provisions for recovery or withholding of sums, the maximum that may be paid in respect of each element and what performance measures (if any) are used in relation to them, the relative weighting of these performance measures the time period over which they are measured and the minimum level of performance that results in any payment under the policy. |
| Paragraph 27 | Notes to accompany this table describing, amongst other things, any differences between the company's policy on remuneration for directors and the company's policy that applies to the remuneration of employees generally and an explanation of why relevant performance measures and conditions were chosen. |
| Paragraph 28 (c) | In respect of NEDs, the approach of the company in determining fees payable to each, together with any other items which are considered 'in the nature of remuneration'. |
| Paragraph 29 | A statement of the principles that would apply when agreeing the remuneration for a newly recruited director, identifying the elements of remuneration that would be considered and the approach of the company to each, as well as the maximum level of variable remuneration that may be awarded. |

**Table 8.1** *continued*

| | |
|---|---|
| **Paragraphs 30–31** | The disclosure of any obligations on the company under existing directors' service contracts or which are proposed to be included in future service contracts, together with details of how and where service contracts can be inspected. |
| **Paragraphs 33–35** | A bar chart for each executive director showing the minimum, on-target and maximum remuneration scenarios and separately identifying the fixed, annual variable and multi-year elements (for example, share plans). The charts must be accompanied by a narrative description of the basis or calculation and the assumptions underpinning them so as to enable an understanding of the charts. |
| **Paragraphs 36–37** | A summary of the company's policy on setting notice periods and termination payments including, in relation to the latter, how each element of a termination payment will be determined and calculated and how the circumstances under which a director leaves and his or her performance while in service would be taken into account. |
| **Paragraphs 38–39** | A statement confirming how, when setting the remuneration policy, account was taken of pay and employment conditions elsewhere in the group, whether (and if so, how) the company consulted with employees when drawing up the directors' remuneration policy and what, if any, comparison metrics were used when drawing up the policy. |
| **Paragraph 40** | A statement of whether (and if so, how) account was taken of any views of shareholders in drawing up the remuneration policy. Those views include any expressed at any general meeting or during the financial year. |

For years in which the above disclosures are not made, the remuneration report will need to include a statement detailing the date of the last general meeting at which the directors' remuneration policy was approved and informing members where on the company's website or elsewhere they may inspect a copy of that remuneration policy. Typically, companies will include details of their remuneration policy in their annual report each year, even if shareholders are not being asked to vote on it.

The policy is meant to apply for three years and therefore the policy itself must be relatively future-proof. The challenge for remuneration committees and boards will therefore be to convince shareholders through their reporting and other engagement activities that, in setting the directors' remuneration policy, they have struck a good balance between a policy which would constrain excess but which might subsequently thwart the recruitment or retention of a much-valued director and a policy which would give freedom to agree to any contract terms they felt necessary to negotiate but which would set alarm bells ringing with investors and fail to secure their support. Within the policy, companies will want to give themselves sufficient flexibility to operate without the need to revert to shareholders on major decisions.

### Report on remuneration

While information on the remuneration policy is only required in years when a new or revised policy is to be proposed to members for approval, information on actual directors' remuneration and various other relevant matters must be included in the remuneration report every year. Table 8.2 sets out a summary of the key elements of information which will be required and must be audited.

**Table 8.2** Information required in remuneration report

| Reference in Schedule 8 | Description |
|---|---|
| **Paras 4 to 12** | A table in the prescribed form setting out, for each person who has served as a director at any time during the financial year, the salary and fees received, taxable benefits, pension-related benefits, cash or other benefits received by way of a performance-related bonus for that year and cash or other benefits received under performance-related schemes covering multiple years, together with a total figure for all these elements. |
| **Para 12** | For variable elements paid during the year, details of any performance conditions and their relative weighting, the targets set and corresponding value of the achievable award, details of the actual performance against the targets set for each performance condition and, if any discretion was exercised on behalf of the company to determine the resulting level of variable pay, how that discretion was exercised and how the resulting level of award was determined. In addition, if any element of any annual award was deferred, the percentage deferred, whether it was deferred in cash or shares and whether the deferral is subject to any conditions other than performance measures must be disclosed. |
| **Para 13** | For pension entitlements under a defined-benefit scheme, details of each director's accrued benefits as at the end of the year (assuming normal retirement date) and the date on which the benefit becomes receivable, together with the total value of any additional benefit that will be receivable in the event of early retirement. |
| **Para 14** | Descriptions, for any variable pay where the value will be determined in accordance with the achievement of performance conditions in future periods, of the type of interest and basis on which the award was made, the 'face value' of the award calculated by reference to the maximum number of shares that could vest and their average market value or the share price at grant, the percentages that would vest if the minimum performance is achieved, the date by which performance conditions must be fulfilled and a summary of performance measures and targets. |

**Table 8.2** *continued*

| | |
|---|---|
| **Para 15** | Details of any money or other assets paid to past directors. |
| **Para 16** | For any loss of office payment made during the year to a director (including a past director), the total amount of the payment broken down into each element comprised in that payment, an explanation of how each element was calculated, any other payments made in connection with the termination including the treatment of outstanding incentive awards that vested on or following termination and, where any discretion was exercised, an explanation of how it was exercised. |

In addition to the above auditable information, the remuneration report must also include:

- a statement of any requirement or guidelines for the director to own shares in the company and a table detailing for each director their beneficial share ownership, interests in share schemes (identifying where relevant those with and those without performance conditions) and details of unexercised share options and share options exercised in the year;
- a comparison between the share performance of the company and that of a broad equity market index, using a line graph representing total shareholder return for each over a number of years;
- the percentages by which the chief executive's elements of pay have increased between the preceding year and the reported year, and details of the average percentage change compared to the percentage increases group employees generally have received and, if the comparator percentage used does not relate to all group employees, an explanation of why a separate comparator group of employees was chosen;
- a graph or table showing the profits distributed by dividends or share buybacks, the overall expenditure on pay for the company and any other significant distributions and payments that help show the relative importance of spend on pay;
- the names of all remuneration committee members, details of any person who provided advice or services to the committee, the nature of any other services provided during that year by that person to the company, who appointed the adviser or consultant and how they were selected, whether and how the committee satisfied themselves that the advice given was objective and independent and the amount paid to the adviser or consultant for the services provided to the committee and for any other services provided that year to the company; and
- a statement of the percentage of votes cast for or against or which abstained from voting on the last occasion on which the remuneration report was considered and the remuneration policy was approved. Where on either

vote there were a significant number of votes cast against the resolution, if the reasons for the shareholder objections are known, those reasons and the directors' response must be outlined. Both the GC100 and Investor Group Guidance and the IA Principles of Remuneration indicate that 'significant' would be more than 20%. The IA Principles provide that companies should not only understand the reasons for dissent and publish those but also outline what the board and remuneration committee are doing to address the dissent.

## Gender pay gap reporting

With effect from 6 April 2017, companies with 250 employees or more will be obliged to publish a report on their gender pay gap in accordance with the *Gender Pay Gap Information Regulations 2016*. The first reports from employers will be due no later than 4 April 2018 and reports will then be required no later than 4 April each year as long as an employer continues to have at least 250 employees. If an employer sits within a group structure, the 250 employee threshold applies in respect of each employer within the group – and multi-employer groups are not allowed to publish consolidated figures. The definition of 'employee' in the Regulations is very broad – workers and some self-employed contractors will be covered. However, employers do not have to compile information if they do not have the relevant data and it is not reasonably practicable for them to obtain it.

Employers who are covered will need to publish the following figures:

1. The difference in mean and median hourly pay between male and female employees, which should be expressed as a percentage and calculated over the relevant pay period, which should include 5 April each year.
2. The number of men and women working in each of the four quartiles of the employer's pay range. The quartiles are obtained by putting all employees in order of their pay, from lowest to highest, then dividing the employees into four equal groups.
3. For employees who receive bonuses, the 'gender bonus gap' during the 12-month period to 5 April each year. Bonus figure calculations will include profit sharing, performance, long-term incentive plans and cash equivalents for share payments. Non-cash elements of bonus are to be treated as paid when they would give rise to taxable earnings rather than at the time of award.
4. The proportion of male and female employees who received bonus pay during the 12 months prior to 5 April.

Employers may voluntarily include a narrative with their reports, but are not obliged to do so. For companies where the data reveals a gap, an accompanying narrative that explains any legitimate reasons for the gap and/or what the company intends to do to address the gap may mitigate the risk of adverse comment.

There are no formal penalties for employers who do not publish a report but it is likely that the press and probably also the Government will name and shame companies who fail to comply. The plan for Government-published league tables will also provide a relatively simple tool to encourage employers to address their gender pay gaps. In addition, the explanatory notes for the Regulations state that failure to comply will constitute an 'unlawful act' under the Equality Act 2010, which opens the door for enforcement action to be taken by the Equality and Human Rights Commission.

## Shareholders and directors' remuneration

Recent corporate governance developments have affirmed the importance of shareholder engagement when it comes to executive pay.

It follows that the remuneration committee is particularly exposed to the public scrutiny of the shareholders' general meeting. Specifically, under the LR, shareholder resolutions will be required to approve certain share and cash incentive schemes and under the CA 2006, shareholder resolutions will be required to approve the remuneration report in the annual report and accounts and the remuneration policy.

This increasingly close involvement in the determination of remuneration arrangements, albeit at a high level, makes shareholder engagement on those arrangements ever more important. Such engagement must be both timely and meaningful. When a company seeks the views of its major investors at a stage when proposals are too far developed and cannot realistically be changed, the engagement cannot be considered meaningful and companies should be wary of asking shareholders to simply 'rubber stamp' their views on executive pay matters. The timing of consultation is therefore critical to how genuinely useful it is to both sides. ICSA and the IA are working on guidance on facilitating better shareholder engagement. Greater detail of best practice in relation to shareholder consultation is discussed in Chapter 5. Here we now look at each of the specific issues on which shareholders are entitled to vote.

### Shareholder approval of the remuneration report

The CA 2006, s. 439 requires that the directors' remuneration report of every quoted company must be put to the shareholders for approval by ordinary resolution in the general meeting when the annual accounts for the financial year are to be adopted. As noted above, this resolution is 'advisory' only. This means that no entitlement of any director to be paid remuneration is conditional on the resolution being passed.

In response to criticisms that this approach alone did not have sufficient 'teeth' to exercise true shareholder control of remuneration matters, it is now supplemented by the additional binding vote on the remuneration policy outlined below. The retention of the advisory vote on the report, however, continues to provide shareholders with an annual mechanism through which to show their displeasure with the company's remuneration approach, either by abstaining or by voting against the adopting resolution. In the Pensions and Lifetime Savings Association (PLSA) *Corporate Governance Policy and Voting Guidelines 2017* it is suggested that, where shareholders vote against the remuneration report, they should, in most circumstances, vote against the re-election of the chairman of the remuneration committee if he has been in post for more than one year, and against other committee members as appropriate.

### Shareholder approval of remuneration policy

Quoted companies will have first sought shareholder approval of the directors' remuneration policy at the general meeting held in the financial year commencing on or after 1 October 2013. Unless the company opted to have the policy commence at an earlier date (for example, from the date of the general meeting), the policy will automatically have applied from the start of the next financial year. For a policy which had effect from 1 January 2015, the company will need to re-submit the policy for shareholder approval (in the same form or an updated form) at a general meeting held no later than 31 December 2017.

The consequences of failing to obtain shareholder approval to adopt a new policy are potentially severe. Remuneration paid to directors outside of the policy will be unlawful. Once a first remuneration policy has been approved, should a subsequent attempt to obtain approval for a revised policy be unsuccessful, the company could find itself relying on an outdated and unhelpful remuneration policy and as a result be more restricted in its ability to reward its directors than it might otherwise wish to be.

The restrictions in the policy apply to current directors, those who are to be appointed and those who have previously held office. Therefore the remuneration policy applies not only to current directors' pay but also to the compensation package for new recruits (including where benefits that they would otherwise be entitled to from their previous employer are bought out), severance payments and claims from past directors of the company. The remuneration policy should therefore address how such payments are to be dealt with.

The board of directors will not wish to act outside of the approved directors' remuneration policy as, in the event of payments being made outside of the policy, the directors who authorised the payment may find themselves personally liable for any losses incurred as a result. This will be the case even if the payment was made pursuant to a legal contract or obligation unless the contract was entered into prior to 27 June 2012 and the contract has not subsequently been amended or renewed.

## Shareholder approval of executive incentive schemes

UK Corporate Governance Code Provision D.2.4 requires companies to invite shareholders to specifically 'approve all new long-term incentive schemes . . . and significant changes to existing schemes, save in the circumstances permitted by the LR'.

Under LR 9.4.1R, any employees' share scheme which will or may involve the issue of new shares in the listed issuer company and (subject to the exceptions noted immediately below) any other 'long-term incentive scheme' in which one or more directors of the issuer company is eligible to participate will require the approval of shareholders by an ordinary resolution passed in a general meeting.

Under LR 9.4.2R, a long-term incentive scheme will not require such shareholder approval if:

- by its terms, participation is offered on similar terms to all or substantially all employees of the issuer or any of its subsidiaries whose employees are eligible to participate (provided that all or substantially all employees are not directors of the issuer); and
- it is an arrangement in which the only participant is, or is soon to be appointed, a director of the issuer and it is set up specifically 'to facilitate, in unusual circumstances, the recruitment or retention of the relevant individual' and provided specified information about the arrangement is disclosed in the next published annual report.

The terms of the second limb of LR 9.4.2R are demanding and the remuneration committee should be careful not to view them as providing an easy way around the normal requirement to obtain shareholder approval, particularly where the scheme relates to an existing director. Although it will be for the committee to determine whether or not the circumstances are 'unusual', it should assume that shareholders may need some convincing that they are just that and the UKLA generally take a restrictive view of 'unusual circumstances'. In incentivising new recruits the committee will also need to be mindful of the remuneration policy to ensure any elements of the remuneration package proposed to be offered are within the parameters of the approved policy.

Under LR 13.8.11R, the notice of meeting containing the resolution proposing the adoption of the incentive scheme must contain either the full text of its rules or a description of its principal terms. The result is inevitably that the notice of meeting will contain a significant amount of disclosure about the scheme and its rules. The notice must also state that the scheme provisions on certain key aspects (e.g. the participation and share dilution limits) cannot be altered to the advantage of participants without shareholder approval. Also, if the scheme's full text is not circulated to shareholders, the notice must state that rules will be available for inspection by shareholders in the run up to and at the general meeting.

## Remuneration and service contracts – reporting requirements under the LR

LR 9.8.6(7)R and 9.8.8R require the annual report of a listed company to include a variety of disclosures relating to directors' remuneration, service contracts and pension entitlements. Such companies will want to incorporate those disclosures into their directors' remuneration report to comply with the legislation that stipulates what information those reports should contain. By virtue of LR 9.8.11R, the company must ensure that the auditors review the disclosures on share options, details of long-term incentive schemes for directors and information on money purchase and defined benefit pension scheme entitlements. In the event that the auditors consider the company not to have complied with the requirements of LR 9.8.8R, the auditor's report in the annual report and accounts should provide an opinion on the non-compliance (LR 9.8.12R).

## Going concern assessment and viability statement

Code Provision C.1.3 and LR 9.8.6R3 require the directors of the company to confirm in the annual and half-yearly financial statements that the company is a going concern and to identify any material uncertainties to the company's ability to continue to adopt a going concern basis of accounting for at least a further twelve months from the date on which the financial statements are approved. In considering the company's going concern statement, the board will want to take account of the FRC *Guidance on Risk Management, Internal Control and Related Financial and Business Reporting*. The Guidance seeks (amongst other things) to implement the 2012 recommendation of the Sharman Inquiry that a going concern statement should be broader than that required to determine the accounting approach used. The Sharman Panel which looked at lessons for those involved in addressing going concern and liquidity risk, provided clarification on what was meant by the term 'going concern':

> '... a company is judged to be a going concern if, for the foreseeable future, there is a high level of confidence that it will have the necessary liquid resources to meet its liabilities as they fall due and will be able to

> sustain its business model, strategy and operations and remain solvent, including in the face of reasonably predictable internally or externally generated shocks.'

It should be noted that the term 'going concern' as referred to in the UK Corporate Governance Code and FRC Guidance should be interpreted in the context of the going concern basis of accounting for the preparation of financial statements. The use of the term 'going concern' in everyday language has a different meaning.

Before making the going concern statement, directors must clearly first assess if their company passes the above test. The FRC draft guidance prepared to implement the recommendations of the Sharman Panel contained a statement on the purpose of the going concern assessment, clearly establishing that assessment within the company's risk management processes in the following terms:

> 'The overarching purpose of the going concern assessment is to ensure that risks that would threaten the company's survival are properly identified and managed, respecting the interests of shareholders, creditors and other stakeholders.'

The assessment carried out by the board in order for a decision to be taken that the going concern basis of accounting is appropriate will also form the basis of the assessment necessary for the viability statement. Specifically, Code Provisions C.2.1 and C.2.2 require the directors to confirm within the annual report that they have carried out a review of the principal risks, including those with the potential to threaten the company's future business model, performance, solvency or liquidity, and to explain how they have assessed the company's prospects, over what period and why they consider that period to be appropriate. The directors' statement should confirm 'whether they have a reasonable expectation that the company will be able to continue in operation and meet its liabilities as they fall due over the period of their assessment', drawing attention to any qualification or assumptions as necessary.

The FRC Guidance provides some practical suggestions for boards in determining the various aspects of the statements they are required to make as follows:

- whether to adopt the going concern basis of accounting – the hurdle for departure from a going concern basis is very high and, accordingly, although a confirmatory statement is required, it is likely to be a rare occurrence for a board to determine that the going concern basis is not appropriate;

- whether there are material uncertainties – the directors should consider whether there are events or conditions that might cast significant doubt on the use of the going concern accountancy basis for future financial periods, assessing uncertainties as material by reference to whether their disclosure could reasonably be expected to influence the economic decisions of shareholders and other users of the financial statements. If an outcome is considered to be only a remote possibility, the guidance advises the uncertainty should not normally be assessed to be material, regardless of how significant the potential impact might be;
- how the prospects of the company have been assessed and why the period over which the assessment was carried out is considered appropriate – the board's assessment of whether they have a 'reasonable expectation' that the company will continue in operation and be able to meet its liabilities over the period of assessment. It will need to take account of the general rule that, the longer the period of assessment, the higher the degree of uncertainty will be. This does not mean, however, that boards should adopt a short period. The guidance indicates a minimum of 12 months to be the norm except in rare circumstances. The assessment should include qualitative and quantitative analyses as well as stress and sensitivity analyses. Reverse stress testing, starting from a presumption of failure and working backwards to identify the possible causes, should be considered; and
- whether there is a reasonable expectation that the company will be able to continue in operation and meet its liabilities – broad thinking on the factors that could threaten the business and its solvency and cash-flow will be required. It will be necessary to take account of how the company could respond to risks to reduce their likelihood or impact.

In addition, the board may wish to make additional disclosures, for example to draw attention to particular assumptions that they have used in arriving at their determination.

The IA has also issued *Guidelines on Viability Statements* (2016) in which it notes that the disclosures made under Code Provisions C.2.1 and C.2.2 are useful to its members and sets out the expectations of institutional investors in relation to such statements. The IA Guidelines urge reporting companies to:

- consider longer time frames for their assessments, noting that, while a medium-term three to five years seems to have been adopted as the norm, directors' fiduciary duties and capital markets are longer-term in nature;
- how, having taken account of the factors described in the FRC guidance, directors decided on the time frame for their assessment;
- differentiate between the assessment made of the company's prospects over the longer-term and the company's viability over the medium-term as well as the current state of affairs;

- address the sustainability of dividends;
- distinguish between risks that impact performance and those that threaten operations, focusing primarily, in the viability statement, on those risks that threaten the company's existence;
- ensure that the description given of the company's principal risks explains why they are important to the company and what the priorities are;
- provide greater transparency on the scenarios tested as part of the board's assessment and the outcomes from that stress testing as well as the risk mitigation actions that have been taken or have been identified as potentially necessary. In this respect reverse stress testing is also encouraged; and
- draw attention to the assumptions used, and any qualifications to the assessment, with an emphasis on assumptions and qualifications that are specific to the company, are likely to have a significant impact and are reasonably likely to arise.

Generic disclosures with near-universal application should therefore be avoided and only information specific to the company included. Cross-references to information provided elsewhere should be used in preference to repetition.

Clearly much of the above assessment and reporting relies on the board being assured as to the robustness and effectiveness of the company's risk management and internal control systems.

## Directors' obligations and judgements on narrative reports

The starting point is that directors are required to exercise a duty of care when preparing their company's narrative reports. Accordingly, as is the case when preparing the accounts, directors must act in good faith and with due skill and care.

A useful source of guidance to directors about their obligations and the judgements they must make when preparing the business review is contained in a legal opinion published by the Chartered Institute of Management Accountants (CIMA) in July 2005. While this legal opinion was prepared with the now-superseded statutory operating and financial review in mind, by extension it is helpful to the drafting of the strategic report. In particular, referring to forward-looking statements, an issue of understandable concern to directors, the legal opinion advises directors to ensure that such statements are appropriately couched and qualified in order to clarify the level of reliance shareholders should place on them and that they are clearly stated to have been based on information and knowledge available to the directors at the time of making the report and that they will not be updated before the next report. The following additional broad guidance points can be made:

- Directors should consider the process for preparing and agreeing the content of the narrative reports so as to exercise and be seen to exercise the requisite degree of skill and care.
- There should be a balance between historic review and the more forward-looking narrative reporting that is required to assess the company's business and the principal risks and uncertainties it faces.
- Both quantitative and qualitative information should be included, as well as, where appropriate, financial and non-financial information.
- Facts and events, probabilities, risks and opportunities may all qualify for inclusion.
- The reputation of the business should be considered in the context of risk and competitive advantage.
- The nature and size of items and also their potential future significance to the business will have a bearing on whether they should be included.
- Consistency in the treatment of items, both within the strategic report itself and by comparison with other areas of company reporting, is important for users of the accounts.
- Directors should minimise the legal risk by seeking appropriate professional advice on assessing the legal risks.

## Enforcement regime

The enforcement regime for defective accounts covers defective narrative reports as well as the financial statements. Accordingly, the Conduct Committee is authorised to apply to the court for a declaration that the strategic report or directors' report as the case may be does not comply with the relevant requirements and for an order requiring directors to provide a revised report. The court can order that certain expenses incurred by the company are to be borne by the directors. This potentially costly sanction serves as a pertinent reminder to directors of their responsibilities to ensure the contents of their company's report and accounts meet the appropriate standards.

In particular, if a strategic report, directors' report or directors' remuneration report does not comply with the statutory requirements, any director who either knew that it did not comply with the legislative requirements or was reckless as to whether it complied and failed to take all reasonable steps to secure compliance will be guilty of an offence and is liable to a fine.

Directors concerned about personal liability for negligent misstatement may be tempted to adopt a formulaic approach, using relatively standard and safe phrases which ultimately tell the users of the accounts little that they did not already know. This is likely to be particularly true when drafting forward-looking statements such as those required to comply with the requirement to include 'the main trends and factors likely to affect the future development, performance and position of the company's business' in the strategic report.

However, in order to address the concerns of directors and avoid the strategic report and other narrative reports becoming pointless boiler-plating exercises, the Companies Act provides a 'safe harbour' so that liability will only arise if the director knew of, or was reckless with regards to, untrue or misleading contents or the dishonest concealment of a material fact within the strategic report, directors' report and directors' remuneration report.

While the safe-harbour will provide directors with a degree of comfort, It is generally accepted that, in order to benefit from it, directors should ensure that all information required is included in the specified report, whether directly or by cross-reference, should be careful to take professional advice on the contents of the narrative reports and should ensure that the systems of control will pick up manifest errors.

## The role of the auditors

Under s. 496 of the CA 2006 the auditor is required to state whether, in their opinion, the information given in the strategic report and directors' report for the financial year for which the annual accounts are prepared is consistent with those accounts. The intention behind these provisions is not that auditors should second-guess the directors' judgements, nor are they required to verify the robustness of the processes adopted to produce the strategic report. The auditor's role is to apply a simple test of consistency with the accounts and the applicable legal requirements. While this test is undoubtedly limited, it needs to be taken in the context of the obligation placed upon the directors to ensure that there is 'no relevant audit information' (meaning information needed by the auditor in connection with preparing their report) of which the auditor is unaware and to include statements to that effect in the strategic and directors' reports relating to DTR rules 7.2.5 and 7.2.6.

Similarly, under s. 497A, where a company prepares a separate corporate governance report, the auditor is required to report on the consistency of the information with the accounts and whether applicable legal requirements have been met. The auditor must also report on any material misstatement and their value and provide an opinion on compliance with DTR rules 7.2.2, 7.2.3 and 7.2.7. Details about the requirements of DTR are provided above and in Chapter 15.

In contrast, under s. 497 of the CA 2006, the auditor's report to members on the auditable part of the directors' remuneration report, the auditor must confirm whether, in their opinion, the auditable part of the directors' remuneration report has been properly prepared in accordance with the Act. The auditable part of this report will therefore be subject to more rigorous audit requirements.

In the wake of the global banking crisis, the role of the auditor came under scrutiny and one of the key recommendations made by the FRC in its 2011 consultation paper, *Effective Company Stewardship: Enhancing Corporate Reporting and Audit*, was that the audit report should be expanded to include a separate section on the 'completeness and reasonableness' of the audit committee report and to identify any matters in the annual report believed by the auditor to be incorrect or inconsistent with any information either contained in the financial statements or which was obtained in the course of the audit. The intention behind these recommendations was clearly to increase investor confidence in the assurances provided by the audit process that the financial statements and narrative reports can be relied upon. The International Standard on Auditing (ISA 700) clarifies the objective of the standard is to address the need for an appropriate balance between ensuring consistency and comparability of auditor reporting globally while making sure the auditor's report is more relevant to users.

In recent years the scope of the required audit has been expanded, in particular to improve assurance and the risks and challenges faced by companies. There is a degree of concern that auditors are not necessarily specialists in forming opinions on non-financial information and that therefore the audit report may not be the appropriate place to cover such matters. The impact on companies and additional costs associated with the expanded remit of the audit are also areas of concern.

Notwithstanding these points, however, a research report commissioned by the FRC in 2016, *Enhancing Confidence in the Value of Audit*, found that the inclusion of non-financial information, for example ESG matters, in the audit scope was broadly welcomed. As one respondent to the research commented:

> 'if you look at what really moves markets now, it's often non-financial information.'

While the role of the auditors may vary in relation to different elements of the report and accounts, the onus is always on the directors, both collectively and individually, to take sufficient steps to ensure the accuracy and completeness of the information provided to the auditor. Directors need to exercise reasonable skill, care and diligence.

## Conclusion

Narrative reporting is a 'growth' industry. The trend towards improving disclosures to provide investors and other stakeholders with the information needed to be assured, not only on financial matters, but on a wide range of non-financial matters, shows no sign of abating.

This provides reporting entities and their boards with several challenges – not least the need to keep up-to-date with changing requirements. Concise, clear, meaningful, balanced, integrated, informative reporting which focuses on key, material issues is by no means easy to achieve. Combined with tight year-end reporting schedules, the need for audit and verification, the board's responsibilities for narrative reporting are considerable, creating potential difficulties for even the most diligent and experienced directors. The growth in reporting of non-financial matters in recent years has seen incredible changes in both regulatory requirements and stakeholder expectations; however, reporting needs to focus, at least in respect of voluntary disclosures, on the value that such reporting can bring to the business. Bearing in mind that 'what gets measured gets managed', that value is used as a tool for the assessment of business objectives and operational effectiveness.

## Narrative reporting checklist

✓ Does the board prepare reports which are individually and combined, 'fair, balanced and understandable'?

✓ Do reports provide context and insight into the company's prospects and business model?

✓ Does the strategic report accurately assess the principal risks and uncertainties facing the company? Does the strategic report contain all required information, including financial and non-financial KPIs, diversity and environmental information?

✓ Does the directors' report contain (or cross-reference) all the required information?

✓ Are the directors content to provide the necessary statements regarding disclosure of 'relevant audit information', having taken all necessary steps to gain assurance that such disclosures have been adequate?

✓ Has the chairman made a personal statement about his or her responsibility for leading the company's governance and is the corporate governance statement meaningful and informative about the company's governance arrangements?

✓ Are the company's remuneration arrangements described in accordance with the statutory requirements?

✓ Has the company's remuneration policy been approved by shareholders?

✓ Does the company gather and report on the necessary gender pay gap data as required?

✓ Are the directors clear on their obligations in relation to the preparation and approval of the narrative reports and financial statements?

# Part 4

## The Effective Board and its Officers

# 9

# Maintaining an effective board

## The board's role and good governance

The opening principle of the UK Corporate Governance Code requires that the company should be headed by an 'effective board' which is collectively responsible for the long-term success of the company. While the FRC *Guidance on Board Effectiveness* was issued in relation to the 2010 version of the Code, within which Principle A1 emphasised the need for 'entrepreneurial leadership . . . within a framework of prudent and effective controls', the guidance remains relevant. In particular, it places an important emphasis on compliance with not just the letter but also the spirit of the Code.

In the preface to the Guidance, the important point is made that while clarity of roles, responsibilities, accountability and transparency are all important features of effective governance, they are not on their own sufficient. An effective board is envisaged as being one which 'develops and promotes its collective vision of the company's purpose, its culture, its values and the behaviours it wishes to promote in conducting its business'. The clear message is that the board's role cannot be narrowly defined, for example purely by reference to profitability and other financial measures, but includes taking a lead in setting the company's standards and culture and ensuring that those standards and culture are applied across all aspects of the business.

The FRC Guidance sets out particular functions which it expects an effective board to perform, including:

- providing direction for management;
- demonstrating ethical leadership, displaying and promoting behaviours consistent with the culture and values it has defined for the organisation;
- creating a performance culture which drives value creation without exposing the company to excessive risk of value destruction;
- making well-informed and high-quality decisions based on a clear line of sight into the business;
- creating the right framework for helping directors to meet their statutory and regulatory duties;
- being accountable, particularly to those that provide the company's capital; and
- thinking carefully about its governance arrangements and embracing evaluation of their own effectiveness.

The Guidance attempts to paint a picture of what an effective board would look like and identifies a number of key drivers affecting a board's effectiveness. It encourages boards to think not only about the formal structures they have in place but also their roles, behaviours and group interaction. In doing so it brings into sharper focus than ever before the human side of boardroom life, recognising that processes and procedures can only ever support the collective efforts of the individuals who make up a governing body. Different directors and the company secretary have particular roles to play within the board and how those individuals carry out those roles, as well as how they interact as a group, can have an immense impact on the effectiveness of the board as a whole. Individual roles are examined in subsequent chapters and the remainder of this chapter is devoted to examining the characteristics of an effective board and how an effective board can be developed and nurtured through appropriate recruitment, development and evaluation processes. The work of the nomination committee is therefore particularly relevant and is covered in some detail.

## Corporate culture

Since 2006, the Companies Act has explicitly recognised the need for companies to take responsibility for the impacts they have on the wider world. Section 172(1) frames this need to look beyond profits by requiring every director to:

> 'act in the way he considers, in good faith, would be most likely to promote the success of the company for the benefit of its members as a whole, and in doing so have regard (amongst other matters) to –
>
> (a) the likely consequences of any decision in the long-term,
> (b) the interests of the company's employees,
> (c) the need to foster the company's business relationships with suppliers, customers and others,
> (d) the impact of the company's operations on the community and the environment,
> (e) the desirability of the company maintaining a reputation for high standards of business conduct, and
> (f) the need to act fairly as between members of the company.'

Even where there may be conflicts between stakeholders, an organisation which embodies the essence of this framework will ensure that value is created and protected, by aligning the company's purpose and strategy with values that encourage appropriate behaviours within the organisation. In this context, organisation encompasses all those who act on behalf of the company.

The responsibility for promoting such a culture increasingly falls to board directors, who are seen to play an important role in modelling such behaviour. Therefore, directors must both define the sort of behaviours they consider appropriate and then demonstrate those high standards themselves in order to be seen as setting the tone for the rest of a company's operations. In doing so, it is expected that an effective organisational culture will develop.

An effective and high-quality organisational culture is identified by the FRC's 2016 report, *Corporate Culture and the Role of Boards*, as one in which the values, strategy and business model are aligned to the purpose of the company. The board will avoid focusing just on short-term goals and will proactively focus on the preservation of the long-term value of the company, respect the interests of a variety of stakeholders and challenge behaviour which they find to be contrary to a spirit of healthy organisational culture.

In the wake of recent financial crises, such a top-down approach to responsible corporate culture has become even more pertinent. The top layers of corporate governance must be seen to encourage compliance, CSR and ethical practice. Recognising the role a company plays in society outside of purely generating profit is a useful way of considering what a healthy organisational culture looks like.

It is important to emphasise that there is no 'one size fits all' approach and cultures cannot be transplanted from one company to another. Instead, the organic development of culture within a framework is likely to be most effective. However, the FRC report, *Corporate Culture and the Role of Boards*, did make some key observations that are likely to be applicable generally:

- the value of a healthy corporate culture as an asset of the business and a source of competitive advantage needs to be recognised. The Company's purpose, values, strategy and business model must all be aligned;
- directors, and in particular the chief executive, must demonstrate leadership in embedding the culture and values determined by the board. If individuals fail to bring appropriate leadership to the organisation, in this regard, boards have a responsibility to address this shortcoming;
- good governance relies on openness and accountability at every level. In particular the board should be committed to engage with, and report to, its stakeholders in a manner that demonstrates openness and accountability and which demonstrates respect for a wide range of stakeholder interests;
- the behaviours of all staff and third-party suppliers need to reflect the values of the company. Internal functions such as HR, internal audit, compliance and risk need to be empowered to embed the company's values and to assess the organisation's culture. The board should ensure that the views of those internal functions are listened to in the boardroom;
- performance management systems and incentives should be aligned with the company's purpose, values, strategy and business model by encouraging

behaviours that are consistent with them. That alignment needs to be clearly communicated to shareholders, staff and other stakeholders;

- culture and the outcomes that the board wishes to promote should be measured so that the board has a good understanding of behaviours within the organisation and is able to challenge areas where they are not satisfied that alignment of the company's purpose, values strategy and business model are effective. This will require the board to dedicate time and resources; and
- investor stewardship, and a questioning approach to the behaviours which shareholder pressure and attitudes are encouraging in companies, is an important part of the equation. Boards and investors should engage about culture and ensure that reporting in this respect is meaningful and valuable.

The FRC report, far from seeing any conflict between an appropriate culture and long-term financial success, makes clear links between strong cultures and the long-term delivery of sustainable value. Rather than waiting for a crisis that acts as a catalyst for change, boards are encouraged to continuously underpin their decision-making and leadership with the values they have determined as appropriate.

## Providing direction and making decisions

As the governing body, it is incumbent on the board to provide direction and leadership for the organisation and its management. The board in many ways sets the tone for the entire organisation, influencing culture and behaviours through its decisions and leadership. As explained above, this culture-defining responsibility is relevant across all aspects of the board's work. The specific responsibilities which make up that work are examined in Chapter 3.

As required by the UK Corporate Governance Code, certain matters will be reserved to the board alone and a framework established for delegating other matters to committees or to management. Once that framework is in place, it should be clear which decisions and issues need to be referred to the board but it may still be necessary to nurture a culture of openness among the executive team, so that it brings those items to the board at a stage when genuine debate is still possible, rather than seeking a mere rubber-stamping exercise.

The use of committees to assist the board in its work is common practice even for non-listed companies, which are not required by regulation to maintain separate audit, remuneration and nomination committees. This is because a well-defined committee structure can be of enormous benefit, not least because it can prevent the board agenda becoming too full and facilitate more detailed consideration of important issues in a more specialised environment. However, while a committee structure undoubtedly offers these benefits, responsibility for the key areas of audit, risk and remuneration must be retained by the board and final decisions on these areas must be taken by the board as a whole. In order for the board to adequately discharge these responsibilities, it is important that sufficient time is set aside in full board meetings for the work of the committees to be properly reported and recommendations explained and to enable proper discussion of actions and board decisions which flow from their work. Moreover, regular reviews of each committee's terms of reference and the relationship between committees and the board should be carried out. The ideas provided below, on steps than can be taken to safeguard the quality of decision making, apply equally to the work of those committees and to the board decisions that flow from that work.

In order for the board to consider, in an effective manner, the issues brought to them and to minimise the risk of poor decisions being made, it is important that good processes are in place. Much of the groundwork for creating those processes is laid outside of the boardroom, starting with the preparation of agendas which cover the right issues and ensure that the board's valuable time is well spent. Once an agenda has been set, high-quality papers and, where appropriate, external advice, are required in order to ensure that board meeting attendees are well briefed and therefore well prepared to make a positive contribution to the board's deliberations. In recent times there has been much emphasis on the need for directors to commit sufficient time to their duties in order to carry them out to a high standard. Part of that time commitment needs undoubtedly to be reserved by them to read and consider the papers circulated in advance of the meeting. Papers which provide good analysis and make clear relevant timescales and the decisions required to be made by the board, as well as addressing responsibilities and the scale and nature of possible risks, ensure that directors' preparation time can be well spent.

The FRC *Guidance on Board Effectiveness* makes some suggestions for the processes which might be undertaken, particularly in the case of complex or significant issues, to optimise the chances of good decisions being made by the board. These include describing in the board papers the process that has been used to develop the proposal being presented so that directors who have not previously been involved in the proposal can assess how thorough the process for arriving at the proposal has been, as well as assessing the proposal itself.

A multi-staged process is also suggested as having possible benefits in some instances, providing boards an opportunity to consider concepts at an early stage, to be followed at a later date by the presentation of an outline proposal for discussion and then finally the proposal for decision. Other strategies include commissioning independent reports, establishing sole-purpose committees and convening additional meetings. The Guidance also recommends that past decisions, in particular those which subsequently proved to have poor outcomes, are regularly reviewed in order to learn lessons not just about the decision itself but also about the decision-making processes employed at the time.

Processes such as those described above form only one aspect of good decision making, however. In order to maximise the chances of good decisions being taken, it is imperative that a board has the right people in place – people who are appropriately skilled, knowledgeable and sufficiently experienced to understand the issues before them and bring good judgement to bear and who are sufficiently independent, proactive and critical to engage in challenging debate. Complacent or intransigent attitudes, conflicts of interest, inappropriate reliance on previous experience or an imbalanced board dominated by a small group are examples of factors which can all too easily endanger good decision making. Regular refreshing of the board and ensuring a diverse mix of personal attributes can guard against many of these factors. The issue of board diversity is examined next.

## Board diversity

Research undertaken as preparation for the *Higgs Report*, and numerous other more recent surveys, has found that the traditional plc board is 'pale, male and stale' – that is, dominated by white males, with an under-representation of directors who are either female or drawn from ethnic minorities. The findings of the 2003 *Tyson Report* which examined ethnicity as well as gender are also relevant and a persuasive case for greater boardroom diversity has been made by research that suggests that companies with more diverse boards tend to be better managed. The Equalities Office publication *Increasing Diversity on Public and Private Sector Boards* (2009) explored the benefits of – and barriers to – diversity at board level. The benefits identified include a wider portfolio of skills at the top, a better feel for and understanding of customer needs, an increased ability to recognise new markets and improved CSR.

The most frequent argument for increasing boardroom diversity is undoubtedly that doing so can help avoid so-called 'group-think', common where bodies of people share similar backgrounds, experiences and biases. For this reason, diversity in board composition is specifically identified in the FRC *Guidance on Board Effectiveness* as being an important driver of a board's effectiveness.

Much of the focus historically on boardroom diversity has tended to concentrate on the proportion of women in office but pressure to address other factors, such as ethnicity, LGBT issues or disability, is growing. The barriers experienced by these groups are significant and the benefits of increasing board diversity would be better achieved by removing all such barriers. Barriers to the recruitment of individuals from under-represented groups inherent in some selection processes can include a lack of awareness of vacancies, weak links with selection consultants, unconscious bias and unclear selection criteria.

While issues of diversity go beyond those of gender, the subject of women on boards is the most high-profile issue of the diversity debate. Since 1999, annual comparisons have been carried out by the Cranfield University School of Management in its Female FTSE Index which charts the number of female directors on the boards of FTSE companies. These reports have tended to indicate a slow increase from a low base. According to the 2016 report, 26.0% of all directors of FTSE 100 companies were female, compared with 17.3% in 2013. A significantly higher proportion of female FTSE 100 directors were non-executives (31.4%) than held executive office (9.7%). There are now no all-male boards in the FTSE 100, having reduced from seven in March 2013. Improvements in female board-level representation have also been seen in FTSE 250 companies, with only 6% of all boards being all-male. Somewhat disappointingly, however, only 90 FTSE 250 companies (36%) achieved their target of 25% women at board level. The progress towards the achievement of more gender-balanced boards in the UK owes much to the 2011 report *Women on Boards* by Lord Davies of Abersoch, the background and conclusions of which are now examined.

In response to concerns that progress in the UK towards gender-balanced boardrooms was too slow, the Government commissioned Lord Davies of Abersoch to review the situation, to identify the barriers to women attaining board appointments and to make recommendations to increase the proportion of women on private sector boards. His report *Women on Boards* published in 2011 made a number of recommendations aimed at increasing the supply of suitably qualified and experienced women candidates for board appointments and the demand for such women for those roles. Almost 90% of the respondents to the review's consultation opposed the introduction of mandatory quotas for women on boards and, as a result, the report stopped short of recommending such a measure and instead opted for a voluntary regime, under which, amongst other things:

- Chairmen of FTSE 350 companies were expected to announce the percentage of women they expected to have on their boards by 2013 and 2015. FTSE 100 companies were expected to achieve at least 25% female representation by 2015.
- Chief executives were expected to review the proportion of women they aimed to have within their Executive Committees by 2013 and 2015.
- All quoted companies are required to publish statistics for the proportion of women on their boards, holding senior management roles and employed by the organisation as a whole.

The FRC was urged to amend the UK Corporate Governance Code to require listed companies to establish, and publish annually, a policy on boardroom diversity including measurable objectives. Following a consultation on the nature of these changes, Provision B.2.4 and Supporting Principle B.6 were amended with effect from 1 October 2012 as described below. DTR 7.2.8A, which sets out reporting requirements in relation to the company's diversity policy, its aims, implementation and effect, is also relevant.

As a result of the 2012 changes to the UK Corporate Governance Code, it now contains three explicit references to diversity which are clearly intended to maintain and accelerate the pace of cultural change needed to bring about real boardroom diversity. Firstly, the Supporting Principle to UK Corporate Governance Code Principle B.2 requires that 'the search for board candidates should be conducted, and appointments made, on merit, against objective criteria and with due regard for the benefits of diversity on the board, including gender'. To increase transparency on how the board complies with this requirement, Provision B.2.4 requires the nomination committee report to 'include a description of the board's policy on diversity, including gender, any measurable objectives that it has set for implementing the policy, and progress on achieving the objectives'. Worth noting in this regard is the recommendation in the ABI's 2012 *Report on Board Effectiveness: Updating progress, promoting best practice* that such disclosures should include clear, company-specific information about the steps the company is taking to achieve 'diversity of perspective' within the board and 'forward-looking and candid' disclosures on what they are doing to ensure they have the right balance of skills and experience amongst board members.

Lastly, under Supporting Principle B.6, as part of the board's annual evaluation of its own performance the board should consider 'its diversity, including gender'. The FRC has been at pains to point out that the words 'including gender' in these Code requirements should not be taken to imply that gender is the only issue which boards need to consider. The joint EY/IA report, *Board Effectiveness – Continuing the Journey*, published in April 2015 makes the point that 'the most important objective of any effort to increase diversity should be to have a diversity of perspectives on the board – and broadening the representation in terms of gender and ethnicity are two clear ways of achieving that'. Diversity should therefore be considered in its wider sense as part of the board's thinking on how to achieve optimum board composition and in so doing maximise the board's effectiveness.

The board may consider that measurable objectives should be set on a range of diversity measures beyond those of gender. The board's work to determine diversity policy and objectives and outcomes from the board's annual evaluation will help inform the nomination committee in discharging its responsibilities insofar as they relate to diversity issues.

Notwithstanding the strengthening of the UK Corporate Governance Code requirements in relation to boardroom diversity, Lord Davies' report made it clear that, should a voluntary approach not lead to swift and radical changes in board gender balance, mandatory measures might well follow.

The 2011 *Davies Report* has since been followed by a 2015 follow-up 'Five Year Summary'. That report noted that representation of women on FTSE 100 boards had increased to 26%, slightly above the 25% target However, while noting this progress, five 'Next Step Recommendations' were made with the objective of further improving gender balance. In summary those recommendations were:

- sustained voluntary, business-led approach for a further five years;
- 33% female representations to be achieved by FTSE 350 boards within five years, including greater numbers of female chairs, SIDs and executives;
- better gender balance to be achieved within FTSE 350 executive committees and senior leadership teams;
- establishment of a steering committee to support business, act as a catalyst for change and monitor and report on progress; and
- the recommendations to be reviewed and detailed comments published by the independent steering committee.

The ambition of the 2011 *Davies Report* and threat of mandatory quotas in the absence of progress combined to drive change. The excuses that had historically been made for why change to the status quo could not readily be achieved were dismissed and, despite some challenges, have proved to be largely unfounded. Notwithstanding this success, the next stage is likely to prove challenging as the pipeline of 'board-ready' women becomes over-utilised. An even greater emphasis on developing the pipeline of women will be needed.

Achieving greater diversity in the boardroom has attracted high-profile attention not only in the UK, but further afield as well. While it is not an approach that has received widespread support in the UK, elsewhere there are some strong advocates of a quota system imposed by law. In Norway, for example, the boards of public companies must by law meet a quota of 40% female board members, with delisting being a sanction for failure to meet the target. Such quotas are now enshrined within the legislation of a number of countries and, despite initial concerns, such initiatives are showing signs of success, both in terms of increasing the number of women on boards as well as the value of their individual contributions. At EU level, changes are also afoot, with a Directive proposed to introduce an 'objective' for listed companies to achieve 40% female representation in non-executive positions by 2020. While not quite the quota system which some feared, clearly all listed companies need to continue to respond with positive action to increase boardroom diversity in a genuine manner.

What the success of Lord Davies' report shows us, however, is that greater diversity can be achieved without quotas. And there is no reason to assume that similar success cannot be achieved in tackling wider diversity issues.

In November 2016, the Parker Review Committee, led by Sir John Parker, published *A Report into the Ethnic Diversity of Boards*. Examining the FTSE 100, the report found that only 8% of directors were 'persons of colour' compared to roughly 14% for the UK as a whole with the majority of FTSE companies having no director of colour on their boards. To address this, the report made the following recommendations:

1. That the ethnic diversity on boards be increased:
   a) each FTSE 100 and FTSE 250 board to have at least one director of colour by 2021 and 2024, respectively;
   b) nomination committees to require search firms to identify qualified people of colour for consideration when vacancies arise;
   c) the Standard Voluntary Code of Conduct for executive search firms to be amended to address issues of ethnicity.
2. That candidates be developed for the pipeline and succession be planned:
   a) FTSE 350 companies should introduce mechanisms to identify, develop and promote people of colour to produce a pipeline of management, executive and board-ready candidates;
   b) led by the chairman, FTSE 350 directors should mentor and/or sponsor people of colour within the organisation;
   c) encourage and support people from diverse backgrounds to take on internal (subsidiary) and external (e.g. educational establishments, not-for-profit organisations) board roles.
3. That transparency and disclosure should be enhanced:
   a) the board's diversity policy and efforts to increase, amongst other things, ethnic diversity should be described in the company's annual report;
   b) companies that do not achieve the report's ethnic diversity targets should explain why they have not been able to do so.

Through embracing diverse board composition as the ideal, directors can also actively show leadership about the values of inclusivity that they expect to be embedded within the organisation.

## The nomination committee

The principal responsibility of the nomination committee, as already considered, is to ensure that directors with the requisite calibre, commitment and time capacity are appointed to the board. It is important to recognise, however, that this requires far more than the occasional processing of new appointments to the board. As is made clear in the FRC *Guidance on*

*Board Effectiveness*, the process of ensuring the right people are appointed should be 'continuous and proactive'. For example, under the UK Corporate Governance Code the committee will need to conduct a regular review of the shape and balance of the board, keep under review the company's leadership needs, and ensure effective succession planning. The nomination committee's remit therefore has key links with all of the issues discussed above and which are so relevant to the overall effectiveness of the board. The details of that remit will be set out in clear terms of reference.

Code Provision B.2.1 states that the nomination committee should 'make available its terms of reference, explaining its role and the authority delegated to it by the board'. This can be achieved by publication of the terms of reference on a company website. ICSA publishes guidance and model terms of reference for the nomination committee (www.icsa.org.uk). Although the committee's terms of reference will need to be tailored to the individual company and reviewed regularly, in broad terms the principal responsibilities of the nomination committee can be described as follows:

- to be responsible for identifying and nominating, for the approval of the board, candidates to fill board vacancies as and when they arise;
- before making an appointment, to evaluate the balance of skills, knowledge and experience on the board and identify any gaps and, in the light of this evaluation, to prepare a description of the role and capabilities required for a particular appointment. For example, Code Provision C.3.1 requires that 'one member of the audit committee should have recent and relevant financial experience'. There may be other specific skill requirements, such as specialist sector knowledge;
- to review annually the time required from a NED (performance evaluation should be used to assess whether the NED is spending enough time to fulfil the duties);
- to develop appointment processes which ensure there are no artificial restrictions on the pool of candidates and so enhance achievement of a diverse board;
- to give full consideration to succession planning in the course of the committee's work, taking into account the challenges and opportunities facing the company and what skills and expertise are therefore needed on the board in the future;
- to review regularly the structure, size and composition (including the skills, knowledge, experience and diversity) of the board and make recommendations to the board with regard to any changes;
- to periodically review the outcomes of its work to assess whether its vision for optimal board composition and adequate progress towards meeting diversity targets are being achieved and to revise the relevant processes as appropriate;

- to keep under review the leadership needs of the organisation, both executive and non-executive, with a view to ensuring the continued ability of the organisation to compete effectively in the marketplace;
- to make a statement in the annual report about the committee's activities, the process used for appointments (explaining if external advice or open advertising has not been used) and the board's policy on diversity. The report will also detail the committee's membership, number of meetings and attendance over the course of the year;
- to make available the committee's terms of reference, explaining clearly its role and the authority delegated to it by the board; and
- to ensure that on appointment to the board, NEDs receive a formal letter of appointment setting out clearly what is expected of them in terms of time commitment, committee service and involvement outside board meetings.

The nomination committee should make recommendations to the board which will derive from its discharging the above responsibilities. These include the board's plans for succession for both executive and NEDs, the reappointment of any non-executive at the end of the specified term of office, any matters relating to the continuation in office of any director at any time, and the appointment of any director to executive or other office. The requirement of Code Provision B.7.1 which makes all directors of FTSE 350 companies subject to annual re-election has increased the nomination committee's workload as the committee is, as a result, required in respect of each and every director to consider on an annual basis whether to make a recommendation to the board proposing them for re-election. Likewise, the increased emphasis on the importance of succession planning (see below) and ensuring diversity issues are given due consideration has added to the nomination committee's responsibilities. Given the increasing burden of work for the nomination committee, there is a trend for additional remuneration to be paid to its members, usually on a par with or slightly less than that paid to members of the remuneration committee.

A majority of the members of the committee should be independent NEDs. The chairman will normally chair the committee, bringing their vision for board composition to the committee, although the Code does allow for an independent NED to chair it as an alternative. From time to time the nomination committee may wish to invite non-members, including the chief executive, to attend its meetings, for example to express views on the appointment of additional executive directors. The attendance of other members of the board requires careful handling, to avoid the committee becoming indistinct from the board as a whole. The board should ensure that the committee has at its disposal the necessary resources to fulfil its obligations.

Apart from access to the company's secretariat, the committee is likely to require access to advice from executive search consultants and independent legal advice on the contractual terms applying to any new appointment. Lord Davies' report *Women on Boards* (2011) recommended that executive search firms should subscribe to a voluntary code of conduct addressing gender diversity and best practice and the nomination committees of FTSE 350 companies will wish to consider whether their preferred advisers adhere to the *Voluntary Code of Conduct for Executive Search Firms* and are accredited under the Enhanced Code when engaging them.

Figure 9.1 illustrates the nomination committee's role and responsibilities.

**Figure 9.1** Role and responsibilities of the nomination committee

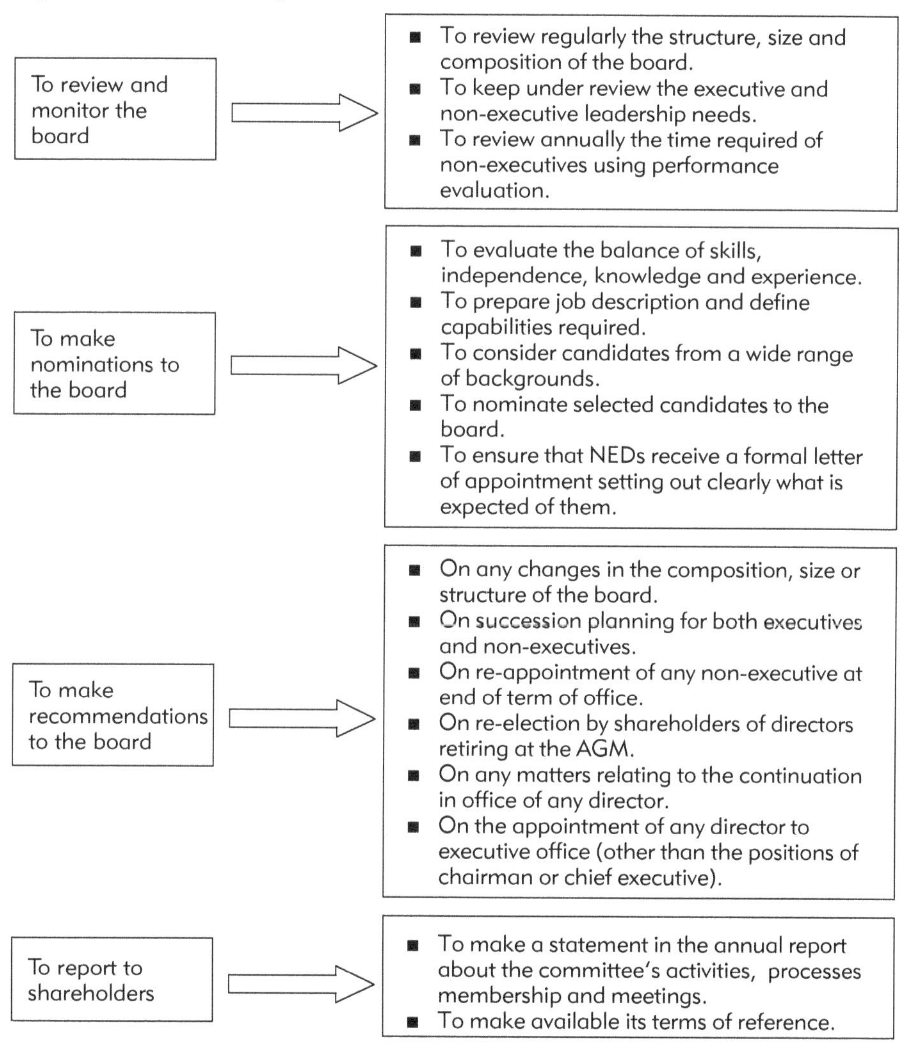

## Succession planning

A planned programme for the recruitment and retirement of board members is an essential tool for achieving a balanced board that encompasses the skills, experience and qualified individuals needed to deliver the company's strategy and objectives. Succession planning is therefore a strategic issue and not just one of periodic refreshing of the board so as to avoid an unhelpful entrenchment of views or practices or filling of occasional vacancies as they arise. Reflecting the introduction of diversity policy and target requirements proposed in the *Women on Boards* and other diversity reports and the UK Corporate Governance Code, succession planning also needs to take account of the board's diversity policy and progress towards achieving the measurable objectives on diversity which the board has set.

The Supporting Principles to Code Principle B.2 state that the board should 'satisfy itself that plans are in place for orderly succession for appointments to the board and to senior management'. Responsibility for ensuring that this is given appropriate priority and attention will be delegated to the nomination committee acting on behalf of the board. The chairman of the board, who will normally also lead the nomination committee, will have in mind an optimal board composition, taking account of the company's strategic objectives and diversity policy as well as the need to achieve a good balance between challenge and fresh thinking while still ensuring the cohesion and teamwork within the board is not compromised. This view will help inform the nomination committee's succession planning.

The joint ICSA/EY report, *The Nomination Committee – Coming Out of the Shadows*, published in 2016, gave thought to some of the issues the committee should periodically consider in relation to succession planning which are summarised below:

- What skills does the board need to support strategic delivery and the company's ability to respond to change?
- How will any skills gaps be addressed?
- How do board evaluations link to board appointment processes?
- What plan is in place to handle sudden or unexpected vacancies?
- How will the committee receive the desired degree of assurance about internal executive and management development programmes?
- Are potential executive team members known to the board and committee and are directors involved in their development?
- What policy has been adopted on executives taking on an external NED role?
- How are ongoing training and development needs identified and addressed for directors?
- How objective are the criteria used to identify potential NEDs and is the committee satisfied that the criteria will not rule out candidates that lack board experience but have the other skills and attributes needed?

- How are the character and behaviours of potential new directors assessed?
- How can reporting be improved to provide a clearer insight into the committee's role?
- How well does the committee interact with, for example, the remuneration committee, and how can it do this better?

Succession planning will not be effective unless it is based on a clear understanding of:

- the business and the skills the board needs collectively to support it;
- the existing pipeline of talent within the business and mechanisms for its development; and
- individual board members' own future plans.

Dealing with succession issues will require sensitive and skilful handling by the nomination committee, particularly in cases where the board is perceived to lack balance, the company is facing particular market challenges or there is shareholder criticism of the board's performance. However, regardless of such issues the committee should consider succession on a regular, if not continual, basis.

The implementation of executive development programmes to train and develop future directors for the company should be considered in all cases. The FRC *Guidance on Board Effectiveness* suggests that such programmes might include middle-management development programmes, facilitating engagement from time to time with NEDs and partnering and mentoring schemes. Such internal development initiatives will not create 'board-ready' candidates overnight and will require long-term vision. They should take account of the impact they can have in helping a diverse range of people overcome the barriers they face in reaching the most senior positions and should disclose what initiatives they have for developing women and what impact those initiatives are having. 'Plus one' or 'developed seat' strategies, whereby an additional director is appointed to the board enabling extra support to be given to him or her during an induction and development phase, may also be appropriate.

As can be seen, succession planning requires a long-term and continuous investment by the nomination committee and the development of a clear-sighted strategy for the future leadership of the company. While it is good practice for the committee to nurture pools of internal talent, they should also plan carefully for the occasional injection of fresh external appointments, including those who may come from outside the private sector. Most of all, the committee needs to guard against stagnation of the existing board composition. The committee should also be aware of the impact that a sudden and unexpected change in the board's composition might have. While such crisis management will not conform to the measured succession plans that will have been laid out by the committee, it should be aware of the possibility of a crisis emerging, and plan accordingly. Table 9.1 sets out five suggested steps to a well-planned senior management succession.

**Table 9.1** Succession planning

| **Step 1:** | **Plan the succession early** |
|---|---|
| | The nomination committee should encourage an environment in which members of senior management think positively and early about their own succession. Internal pipeline development has an important role to play here. Planning should include the catastrophe event, such as death or sudden illness, as well as the normal transition of management responsibility. Entrenched ideas of security of tenure should be resisted. |
| **Step 2:** | **Where possible, control the timing of the succession** |
| | The needs of the business should be paramount. A director's preferred date for succession (e.g. retirement) may not be best for the business. Where the change in leadership is caused by performance issues, the committee should consider the internal and external repercussions of the change. The pros and cons of continuing for a time with a 'wounded' leader and, alternatively, moving fast to appoint a successor, need to be carefully assessed. |
| **Step 3:** | **Appoint the successor as early as possible** |
| | Once the decision to make the change has been made, the appointment of the successor should move as early and as swiftly as possible. A long interregnum can lead to a damaging power vacuum within a business. However, enough time should be allowed for the committee to build the case for the successor and to avoid precipitous changes in management. |
| **Step 4:** | **Ensure an effective handover** |
| | The departing director should understand the need to pass on the reins of power in an orderly manner. This may involve a controlled reduction in working hours (although this may be impossible). The committee needs to avoid any suggestions of paying a soft termination bonus, but equally the departing director needs to be remunerated properly for ensuring an effective handover. |
| **Step 5:** | **Manage the public announcements** |
| | A change in a main board member will be an announceable event for a listed company. Depending on the circumstances, it may affect market sentiment. On the basis that the market abhors uncertainty, the committee should ensure that the announcement tells the full story in a transparent manner and that it gives a clear message of effective planning. The help of professional PR consultants may be required. |

## Appointing the right people to the board

As discussed above, appointing directors who are able to make a positive contribution to the board, help the board reach good decisions and maximise the chances of the company's long-term success is identified within the FRC *Guidance on Board Effectiveness* as a key element of board effectiveness. Code Provision B.2.1 requires the board to establish a nomination committee, which should 'lead the process for board appointments and make recommendations to the board'. The nomination committee therefore clearly has a vital role to play in assisting the board to discharge its recruitment responsibilities as set out in Code Principle B.2 which states:

> 'There should be a formal, rigorous and transparent procedure for the appointment of new directors to the board.'

Criticism has been levelled at the director appointment process and, despite pressure over recent years to increase the accessibility of vacancies, reports, such as *Gender Diversity on Boards: The Appointment Process and the Role of Executive Search Firms*, published by the Equality and Human Rights Commission in 2012, continue to identify weaknesses. These include lack of information on advertisement of positions and a focus when short-listing candidates on who is likely to 'fit' with existing board members, perpetuating the tendency to appoint individuals with similar backgrounds. The 2013 Female FTSE Index reported a lack of evidence that Lord Davies' recommendation of taking women from 'outside the corporate mainstream' had led to a widening of the traditional pool to encompass entrepreneurs, academics, civil servants, senior women with professional service backgrounds or candidates with experience of governing charities.

At the heart of the censure lies concern over the likely impairment of board effectiveness resulting from a failure to appoint the best available persons to the company's board. Artificial restrictions on the pool of candidates can only ever increase the likelihood that the best potential candidate may be missed. Designing recruitment processes so as to remove those artificial barriers is part of the challenge faced by nomination committees charged with overseeing board appointments. Where the appointment of an executive search firm is to be made, the committee will wish to discover whether the firm in question has committed to adhere to the *Voluntary Code of Conduct for Executive Search Firms* and is accredited under the Enhanced Code, the measures advocated by which seek to remove the barriers frequently faced by aspiring female directors.

The requirement to plan for and make recommendations to the board for new appointments is at the core of the list of responsibilities placed on the nomination committee. Once the committee has identified the need for a new appointment, whether through succession planning, the need to address a weakness or imbalance in the board's composition identified through the annual board evaluation process or otherwise, careful organisation is required in order to satisfy the requirement in Code Principle B.2 that there must be a 'formal, rigorous and transparent procedure for the appointment of new directors to the board'. Table 9.2 describes a list of the main stages involved in handling a typical new director appointment.

**Table 9.2** Stages in appointing a director

| Stage 1: | Defining the job description and capability requirements |
|---|---|
| | As a first step, the committee should evaluate the needs of the board, taking into account the balance of skills, independence, knowledge and experience, any currently identified succession or diversity issues and the company's agreed strategic priorities. For a non-executive role where it is envisaged the appointee will be a member of a particular committee, specific technical skills and knowledge may be relevant.<br>The results of this process should then inform the drafting of the capabilities and time commitment required and the job description. The appointment of an executive search firm should be considered, ensuring the firm's brief gives adequate weight to factors which are likely to encourage the establishment of a diverse candidate pool. |
| **Stage 2:** | **Advertising the post and short-listing candidates** |
| | As well as giving consideration to internal talent, the committee should know how best to attract candidates from a wide range of backgrounds. Advertising is likely to secure a better representation of candidates drawn from the public or voluntary sector, who will not be known in the normal business circles. For this reason the report *Women on Boards* encourages companies to periodically advertise board vacancies. If neither an external search consultancy nor advertising is used, this must be explained to shareholders in the annual report. A short-list of candidates should be drawn up, taking the advice of executive search firms as appropriate and giving due consideration to representation of diversity groups. Care should be taken to avoid stereotyping and making assumptions about the absolute necessity for past listed company board experience. The possibilities of recruiting from amongst internal candidates and from outside the private sector should not be ignored. |

**Table 9.2** *continued*

| **Stage 3:** | **Implementing a process to select a preferred candidate** |
|---|---|
| | Short-listed candidates should be invited to interview. The committee should prepare the interview beforehand, agreeing the points to be raised with each candidate and thought should be given to including a woman amongst the interviewers. Questioning should be rigorous, but fair. A committee member with a material conflict of interest (e.g. a prior association with a candidate) should declare it and decline to be involved. When questioning candidates the committee should be prepared to think outside the normal tramlines. In particular, the FRC *Guidance on Board Effectiveness* recommends that a diversity of personal attributes among candidates be considered including 'intellect, critical assessment and judgement, courage, openness, honesty and tact, the ability to listen, forge relationships and develop trust' as well as diversity of psychological type, background and gender. In assessing the relative merits of candidates, the focus should be on competencies. |
| **Stage 4:** | **Bringing nomination to the board** |
| | The committee's nomination to the appointment should be brought to the full board for approval. The nomination should be supported by a summary of the reasons for the committee's conclusions and should contain essential information as to the proposed contractual terms of the appointment. |
| **Stage 5:** | **Agreeing specific terms of the appointment** |
| | Having obtained the board's approval and taken such references as are appropriate, the committee should agree the detailed terms of the appointment, subject to their being formalised in writing. The committee should be mindful of the board's published remuneration policy and should take legal advice. |

Special considerations arise for the nomination committee and the board generally on the appointment of the chairman and NEDs. These are covered in Chapters 11 and 13 on the chairman and NEDs respectively.

## Terms of engagement

Approval of the terms of engagement of any new director will ultimately be a matter for the full board. The negotiation and fixing of the detailed terms with the new appointee is likely to be delegated by the board and will involve some overlap between the nomination committee and the remuneration committee. The chairman is likely to be involved in any such negotiations in their capacity as leader of the board.

When conducting negotiations with the preferred candidate, the nomination committee should be careful to observe the company's remuneration policy for directors, particularly in relation to the notice period, pay and benefits and compensation on termination including malus and clawback provisions. While the UK Corporate Governance Code is silent on who within the board should conduct detailed negotiations of terms of engagement, a high-level discussion of these with candidates will be necessary if the committee is to conduct meaningful interviews before recommendations are made to the board. Legal advice will be required on the drafting of the service agreement, which will include intricate provisions on items such as confidentiality and post-termination obligations.

More detailed overviews of non-executive terms of appointment and executive directors' service contracts are provided in Chapters 12 and 13.

## Due diligence for board candidates

Before accepting any appointment, a board candidate should undertake a thorough examination of the company, its business and the board. The FRC *Guidance on Board Effectiveness* suggests that the prospective director's due diligence should be sufficient to 'understand the company, appreciate the time commitment involved, and assess the likelihood that he or she will be able to make a positive contribution'. The implication is that candidates should satisfy themselves not only that the role is one that they want to undertake, but also that their appointment will be a good one from the company's point of view.

New directors will also want to reassure themselves that there are no material financial or other risks which might cause them to decline the offer or at least to probe more deeply. As such, they should be alert not only to what they are reading or being told, but also to whether they get a sense of openness and transparency from the communication, although prior to appointment there will, of course, be confidential or price-sensitive information which cannot be disclosed to them.

There are several potential sources of relevant information, including recent annual reports and accounts, analysts' and press reports, the company's website, rating agency and voting services reports as well as discussions with key professional advisers (the company's auditors, solicitors, corporate broker and main bankers) and in-house personnel (in-house lawyer, internal auditor, etc.). A prospective director will certainly also want to have meetings with the chairman, executive directors and the company secretary, if not all board members, before accepting the appointment and may benefit from meeting some in small groups so as to be able to better assess the dynamics between board members. Table 9.3 provides a non-exhaustive list of questions that could form the basis of a director's due diligence enquiries. More comprehensive guidance is provided by ICSA's Guidance Note *Joining the right board– due diligence for prospective directors*.

**Table 9.3** Due diligence for board candidates

| | |
|---|---|
| **Financial position** | ■ What is the company's current financial position and recent trading record?<br>■ If it is not performing well, is there potential to turn it round, and what additional time/effort/skill might be required to implement a turn-around strategy?<br>■ Are the accounts clear and unqualified, and are there any material contingencies noted in the accounts, including potential or actual litigation? |
| **Nature of the business** | ■ What is the exact nature and extent of the company's business activities?<br>■ Is there anything about those activities that would lead to concern relating to personal risk or ethical considerations and are the company's values and standards as set by the board clear?<br>■ Is there a strategic business plan?<br>■ What is the company's competitive position and market share in its main business areas?<br>■ What are the key challenges being faced by the company at the present time?<br>■ Does the operation of the business entail special regulatory compliance, licences or other permissions and if so is its relationship with its regulators good? |
| **Risk** | ■ What are the main risks faced by the company and how are they managed?<br>■ What is the company's risk appetite in the achievement of its strategic aims?<br>■ Are the internal controls adequate and given priority by the board, and is there a culture of risk management and accountability?<br>■ Is there any material litigation presently being undertaken or threatened? |
| **Board composition and processes** | ■ Are the size, structure and make-up of the board and the resources to support it satisfactory and sufficient?<br>■ Who are the current directors, what is their background and record and are they effective?<br>■ What are relationships like between the chairman, the chief executive, the chief financial officer, the SID, the committee chairmen, the other directors, the company secretary and the management team generally? |

Table 9.3 *continued*

| | |
|---|---|
| **Board composition and processes *continued*** | ■ Is the board clear and specific about the qualities, knowledge, skills and experience it needs to complement the existing directors and do your own skills, knowledge and experience fit well with the perceived gaps?<br>■ Is the information provided to the board of a high quality and delivered in sufficient time to enable proper preparation before the meeting?<br>■ How are board meetings structured and is sufficient time allowed for constructive and challenging debate?<br>■ How is strategy developed and tested and what matters have been covered in the most recent strategy away-days?<br>■ Does the board focus on the right issues? What matters are reserved to the board and what are the terms of reference for the board committees? |
| **Corporate governance** | ■ What record does the company have on corporate governance and does it articulate itself well on such matters?<br>■ Does it have a good governance reputation amongst analysts or commentators and does the board exhibit a commitment to good governance?<br>■ Is a thorough board evaluation process used and what were the key issues discovered through the most recent board evaluation? Do the board committees function effectively? How is the chairman's leadership perceived?<br>■ Are key matters such as remuneration policy dealt with in accordance with best practice and with due consideration for the impact they may have on company culture and issues of risk? |
| **Relations with shareholders** | ■ Who are the company's main shareholders and has the shareholder profile changed over recent years?<br>■ What is the company's attitude towards and relationship with its shareholders?<br>■ How often does the chairman meet with shareholders and do NEDs also have an opportunity to meet with them?<br>■ Does the chairman report personally and meaningfully in the annual accounts and are standards of narrative reporting good?<br>■ What questions were asked at the company's last AGM? |
| **Role and responsibilities** | ■ Are the role and the qualities, knowledge, skills and experience required clearly set out? Are you able to make a positive contribution in that role?<br>■ Does the role envisage you turning around poor company performance and is this something which you have the skills, desire and commitment to do? |

Table 9.3 *continued*

| | |
|---|---|
| **Role and responsibilities** *continued* | ■ Will an adequate induction process be undertaken and what form will it take? Do annual evaluations inform ongoing development processes?<br>■ How much time will the role require and can you give the necessary commitment?<br>■ Does the role place you in a position of conflicted interests? |
| **Insurance cover** | ■ What insurance cover is available for directors and what is the company's policy on indemnifying directors?<br>■ Does any cover continue after ceasing to act as a director? |

As can be seen, through such due diligence candidates should assess not just whether the company is one with which they want to be so closely associated, but also whether their skills and experience fit with the requirements of the job. With this in mind, careful consideration should be given to the likely time commitment expected of them. Finally, candidates should ask to see the terms of engagement and take independent legal advice as to such terms where appropriate. Executive directors' contracts of employment and NEDs' appointment letters are considered in Chapters 12 and 13 respectively.

## Induction and development

Although the *Walker Report* was limited to an examination of practice in UK banks and other financial services companies, it found that induction and development processes were 'variable' and described the situation as 'palpably unsatisfactory'. Comments such as these re-opened the debate about the vigour with which companies have, in practice, embraced their induction and development programmes and the measures which could make such programmes more effective. Code Principle B.4 makes no distinction between executive and NEDs when it states that 'all directors should receive induction on joining the board and should regularly update and refresh their skills and knowledge'. Notwithstanding the blanket application of this Principle to all directors, the needs of executive and NEDs will differ in some respects and will also vary from individual to individual and these differences should be reflected by creating bespoke induction and development programmes for each director. The induction process is considered here first.

### Induction

Code Provision B.4.1 requires the chairman to 'ensure that new directors receive a full, formal and tailored induction on joining the board'. The programme should be 'tailored' both for the individual and the company and such tailoring should be informed by, amongst other things, the individual's role and experience. Discussions with the new director will be necessary in order to establish their own needs and priorities. Certainly the induction will need to cover the company and its business, links with key people and an understanding of the Company's important external relationships. The rationale and need for a thorough induction programme is summed up in a Supporting Principle to Code Principle B.4 when it states 'to function effectively all directors need appropriate knowledge of the company and access to its operations and staff '. The programme will need to extend beyond the boardroom including a variety of meetings with internal and external figures.

In particular the UK Corporate Governance Code advocates that directors 'avail themselves of opportunities to meet major shareholders' (Code Provision B.4.1) but there will also be other stakeholders of which a good understanding will be important, even if the new director does not have direct meetings with them.

Key financial and strategic information plus details of significant issues for the organisation will also be required. For NEDs the FRC *Guidance on Board Effectiveness* suggests that partnering new appointees with a senior member of the executive team could 'speed up the process of him or her acquiring an understanding of the main areas of business activity, especially those areas involving significant risk'. Those areas are ones on which the newly appointed director will wish to focus additional attention in order to swiftly acquire a strong grasp of the issues. For this purpose, meetings with middle managers, as well as the more senior internal figures with whom the director might ordinarily come into contact, could prove particularly useful.

In special cases, the induction may be more fundamental. Accordingly, a new appointee taken from the public or charitable sector may need to understand the role of the commercial board generally, the obligations and entitlements of directors of listed companies and the relevant behaviours required of the job. Equally, a director from outside the UK will need to understand the working of the unitary board as well as details of the UK legal and regulatory regime in which the company operates.

Design and delivery of the induction programme will normally fall within the company secretary's remit, as envisaged by a Supporting Principle to Code Principle B5. Taking a staggered approach to induction over a number of months is advised in order to avoid 'information overload' and in any case is likely to take up to 12 months in order to encompass the full annual board cycle. During this period, a NED will need to devote extra time in order to undertake the necessary induction activity. ICSA has produced a template non-executive appointment letter which suggests ten days be committed by a new non-executive to their induction; however, the tailoring of individual programmes discussed above will mean that this amount of time, while significant, may in fact be insufficient in some circumstances and should be adjusted according to the individual's induction needs.

Discussions with the new director will be necessary in order to establish his or her own needs and priorities and to establish from the outset a mutually agreed plan of how and when each element will be covered. Careful thought should be given to this planning process in order to maximise the effectiveness of the induction but a review of the plan at the midway point should also be arranged to enable adjustments and changes to be made as appropriate. The ICSA Guidance Note *Induction of Directors* includes a full list of the kind of material to be included but Table 9.4 suggests a list of the main items which should be covered during the induction process.

**Table 9.4** Induction for directors

| | |
|---|---|
| **The role of the director** | An overview should be provided of the director's role including UKLA and other regulatory requirements, the support available from the company secretary and professional advisers, the induction and continuing development processes, D&O insurance and indemnity arrangements and relevant company policies, protocols and procedures. |
| **Board and committee issues** | A dossier of relevant information will include the schedule of matters reserved to the board, committee terms of reference and other delegation arrangements, recent board and committee minutes, future meeting dates, description of board procedures and board evaluation and development programme details. In addition, the chairman will want to convey expected behaviours and the culture, ethics and values of the company. |
| **The nature of the company, its business and markets** | To build familiarity with the company's business and environment, induction should include an overview of its corporate history, products or services and brand, significant contracts and operations, a market analysis, financial information, current strategic plan, business model and KPIs, incentive plan performance targets, risk tolerance, risk management and internal controls, disaster recovery plans and an introduction to its constituent businesses and group structure generally. |
| **Links with the company's people** | A description of the management structure and the identity and contact details for key individuals should be supplemented with meetings with the company secretary, in-house counsel, HR director and other relevant senior people. The opportunity to visit the main business locations, to attend relevant company events and to meet staff, together with feedback from employee surveys, will enable new directors to get a 'feel' for the company culture. |

**Table 9.4** *continued*

| | |
|---|---|
| **The company's main relationships** | As well as being offered the opportunity to meet with major shareholders, the new director will require a description of the shareholder base, details of key customers, suppliers and stakeholders and contact information for the main professional advisers (lawyers, bankers, auditors, registrars, brokers, etc.). In addition, information should be provided on recent IR, including recent shareholder meetings, and media activity. |

## Development

At the end of the induction process the new director should have garnered sufficient information and knowledge to facilitate his or her effective contribution to the company but their ongoing development needs will still need to be addressed. The need for comprehensive and ongoing on-the-job training and development is now widely recognised and reflected in the UK Corporate Governance Code in the context of the Supporting Principles to Code Principle B.4 on Development, which require that:

> 'The chairman should ensure that the directors continually update their skills and the knowledge and familiarity with the company required to fulfil their role both on the board and on board committees. The company should provide the necessary resources for developing and updating its directors' knowledge and capabilities.'

As with the induction process, professional training and development should be tailored to the individual if it is to be effective. The responsibility of the chairman in this context is reinforced by Code Provision B.4.2, which requires him or her to 'regularly review and agree with each director their training and development needs'.

It can reasonably be assumed, following their recruitment through 'formal, rigorous and transparent' procedures, that directors have been appointed on the basis that they already have relevant skills, knowledge, experience and ability. Therefore, the thrust of further training and development is to plug gaps in specific areas, such as risk management or new technologies and to maintain existing competencies in the face of latest developments, for example those relating to legal and regulatory obligations. Code Principle B.4 and its Supporting Principles place the company under an obligation to provide the necessary resources for such training. While the chairman is charged under the Code with the responsibility for ensuring effective development programmes are in place, in reality the major responsibility for making sure those programmes are delivered will fall on the company secretary, perhaps supported by the HR director. It follows that their personal objectives and budgets should reflect these requirements.

For their part, directors must commit to active participation in their development. The FRC *Guidance on Board Effectiveness* makes this point plain, urging NEDs in particular to 'devote time to developing and refreshing their knowledge and skills, including those of communication, to ensure they continue to make a positive contribution to the board'. While there is no current requirement to hold any professional qualification as a condition of taking up a director appointment, accredited courses are now increasingly available, for example the IoD Chartered Director programme. External training courses more generally can form a valuable part of a director's development programme and can range from the one-off and brief induction courses through to the rigours of a specialist MBA course. There are many organisations offering such training services, including most of the larger accounting and legal firms, the academic business schools, ICSA, the IoD and several specialist training consultancies.

However, while external courses are likely to form part of the available training resources, the board should not underestimate the benefits of on-the-job training; for example, when the audit committee is learning from its advisers on new accounting standards and practices or a board report on cyber risk is preceded by an educational presentation to bring all directors up-to-speed on the background. Directors should also be given access to the company's operations and staff in order to develop and maintain an appropriate knowledge of the company. The increasing focus on boardroom behaviours and personal attributes means that the development of appropriate behaviours by directors should also be assessed and where weaknesses are identified, addressed through training.

Permitting an executive director to take on a non-executive role within another organisation can also provide him or her with useful learning opportunities. Conflicts of interest are clearly one issue to be considered if such an approach is to be used, as are the requirements of Code Provision B.3.3. This requires boards to permit only one FTSE 100 company non-executive appointment per executive director, which should not be a chairmanship. The intention behind this restriction is to ensure directors are able to give adequate commitment to their roles. Concerns over the ability of individuals to adequately commit to multiple roles were also addressed in the 2011 Green Paper, *The EU Corporate Governance Framework*, which mooted the idea that a limit on the number of non-executive positions held by one person might be imposed. Certainly the number of other directorships will need to be disclosed in the Company's reports and multiple appointments may attract criticism.

## Evaluating the performance of the board and directors

Code Principle B.6 states that:

> 'The board should undertake a formal and rigorous annual evaluation of its own performance and that of its committees and individual directors.'

The use of the word 'rigorous' can leave the board in no doubt that the process needs to be taken very seriously. However, the consultation carried out as part of the 2009 *Walker Review* into the governance of UK banks found that 'not all boards have hitherto given the process the attention and seriousness that it deserves'. It would seem safe to assume that the same could be said of other companies.

The FRC *Guidance on Board Effectiveness* describes the evaluation process as 'a powerful and valuable feedback mechanism for improving board effectiveness, maximising strengths and highlighting areas for further development', leaving the reader in no doubt as to its importance. The chairman has overall responsibility for the evaluation process and as such should take the lead in selecting the approach to be used and for acting on its results. They will share the overall results with the board as a whole but keep the details of individual directors' evaluations confidential. The results should also be used to inform the board and nomination committee's consideration of issues such as board composition, succession planning and induction and development. The FRC Guidance also suggests that to complete the loop, consideration should be given, once the evaluation has been completed, to how effective the process was. The outcome of this will assist in future considerations about what approach to take in conducting board evaluations.

Code Provision B.6.1 requires that the board should state in the annual report how performance evaluation of the board, its committees and its individual directors has been conducted. Although the 2009 Combined Code review decided against including more prescriptive requirements as to the contents of that report, in the Preface to the UK Corporate Governance Code, chairmen are urged 'to report personally in their annual statements how the principles relating to the role and effectiveness of the Board . . . have been applied'. The intention behind this is to make sure investors have a clear picture of what the board is doing to ensure it operates effectively.

Clearly, meaningful reporting on board evaluation is required; however, a report published by ICSA *Board Evaluation* in April 2013 on the results of a review of the board evaluation reporting of the UK's top 200 companies noted that 'examples of boiler plate drafting, including resort to the tired assertion that "a formal and rigorous" evaluation has been undertaken' were still to be found.

The 2015 EY/IA report, *Board Effectiveness – Continuing the Journey*, emphasised how useful investors find disclosure of the board evaluation findings. However, the report also noted that 'due to sensitivities over confidentiality or potential litigation' the disclosures are frequently less informative than they would like. The report recommends that the disclosures should encompass:

- the evaluation process, including detail of the scope and key areas of focus;
- any significant recommendations; and
- action taken and improvement the board has committed to. It should be recognised that actions may need more than a year to implement fully.

### The choice of approach for evaluating the performance of the board, its committees and directors

The nomination committee, usually led by the chairman of the board, is under an obligation to evaluate the balance of skills, independence, knowledge and experience on the board when planning for new appointments and it is therefore likely that this committee will have a similar responsibility for formulating the policy for evaluating the board generally. Traditionally there has been no prescription as to what form the evaluation process should take; the assumption has been that the disclosure obligation will of itself ensure that the board does what is required. However, the findings of the *Walker Review* noted above led to a recommendation in the report that board review required under the UK Corporate Governance Code should be carried out using external facilitation every second or third year. In its final report following the 2009 review of the Combined Code, the FRC accepted this recommendation and it is now a requirement of Code Provision B.6.2 for FTSE 350 companies to carry out an externally facilitated board evaluation at least every three years. Unless the board submits itself to evaluation by an external consultancy, there is the obvious risk that by making itself the judge and jury in its own case, the objectivity of the results of the evaluation will be questioned.

Whatever the approach used, the evaluation needs to be undertaken at three levels:

- firstly, at the main board level;
- secondly, its committees, including the processes for interaction between committees; and
- thirdly, the individual directors including specifically the chairman, covering in each case a number of areas.

The FRC *Guidance on Board Effectiveness* suggests the following list, although it emphasises that the list is neither prescriptive nor exhaustive:

- the mix of skills, experience, knowledge and diversity on the board, in the context of the challenges facing the company;
- clarity of, and leadership given to, the purpose, direction and values of the company;

- succession and development plans;
- how the board works together as a unit and the tone set by the chairman and the CEO;
- key board relationships, particularly chairman/CEO, chairman/SID, chairman/company secretary and executive/non-executive;
- effectiveness of individual non-executive and executive directors;
- clarity of the SID's role;
- effectiveness of board committees and how they are connected with the main board;
- quality of the general information provided on the company and its performance;
- quality of papers and presentations to the board;
- quality of discussions around individual proposals;
- process the chairman uses to ensure sufficient debate for major decisions or contentious issues;
- effectiveness of the secretariat;
- clarity of the decision processes and authorities;
- processes for identifying and reviewing risks; and
- how the board communicates with and listens and responds to shareholders and other stakeholders.

Other than using external evaluation consultants, the evaluation of the board and its committees can be achieved by a number of other means, including self-assessment questionnaires to be completed by directors, feedback from the investor community, professional advisers and other stakeholders. In deciding on the approach to be used, desirability of including feedback from external stakeholders and other parties should be borne in mind.

In view of the adoption of the requirement in the UK Corporate Governance Code for external appraisal every three years, the board will need to periodically consider employing a specialist consultancy firm to advise on the best approach, and to highlight the issues that need to be addressed. There are many organisations offering such services. The use of an external consultant may in any case be the board's preferred approach, particularly at a time of change or if a fresh perspective is needed, and will enable the board to report that there has been an independent analysis of its operational effectiveness. Even prior to the recommendations on external appraisal in the *Walker Report* and 2009 Combined Code Review, there was some evidence that the use of external facilitators in the board evaluation process was becoming increasingly common.

Existing board advisers may be preferred for undertaking this kind of evaluation work if the chairman and the board generally are wary of allowing a previously untried and untested adviser to undertake a sensitive board review of this nature. However, if existing advisers are employed, for example the board's retained headhunting firm, there can be some doubt on the objectivity of the results. Such firms are unlikely to declare the board ineffective in a situation where this might jeopardise their mainstream headhunting work. To address the potential for such conflicts of interest, UK Corporate Governance Code Provision B.6.2 on the engagement of external board appraisal advisers includes a disclosure requirement in relation to any other connections between the company and the reviewer. This statement may be made available on a website. The ABI took a stronger line, however, in *Report on Board Effectiveness: Updating Progress, Promoting Best Practice*, recommending that board evaluations should be carried out by an independent party not subject to a conflict of interest and clarifying that 'this should preclude those who provide other services to the company'. This stance is explained by the assertion in the report that 'the greatest value of this experience is drawn from the independence and objectivity of the evaluator, and the fresh insight that they have to offer the board'.

In the 2015 EY/IA report, *Board Effectiveness – Continuing the Journey*, the importance of developing a robust board evaluation strategy is emphasised. A three-year evaluation strategy is suggested as follows:

Year 1 – externally facilitated evaluation
Year 2 – review of actions taken and changes made as a result of the external evaluation process
Year 3 – internal evaluation, perhaps consisting of a series of interviews.

The report cautions that annual use of external consultants, far from enhancing the value obtained, may in fact detract from it by reducing the evaluation to 'more of a compliance exercise'.

The Supporting Principles to Code Principle B.6 clarify that individual evaluation should 'aim to show whether each director continues to contribute effectively and to demonstrate commitment to the role'. The chairman is likely to have a role in conducting appraisals with individual directors and obtaining 360-degree peer reviews. Best practice would suggest that such feedback be channelled through an independent third party (perhaps the company secretary) and collated on an anonymous basis. Special considerations arise with respect to evaluating NEDs. These are addressed separately in Chapter 13 on NEDs. For executive directors, it should be noted that the evaluation in this context should focus on their contribution to the board rather than their performance in their management role.

However the evaluation is carried out, the chairman is required by the Supporting Principles to Code Principle B.6. to act on the results 'by recognising the strengths and addressing the weaknesses of the board'. The agreed objectives of the board and individual directors should be revisited and refreshed based on the outcome of the evaluation process and, where appropriate, the chairman may wish to propose that new members be appointed to the board or seek the resignation of individual directors. Such an outcome, together with other aspects of the evaluation results, will specifically inform areas of the nomination committee's work that have been explored earlier in this chapter.

## Governance checklist

- ✓ Does the board perform the leadership functions expected of an effective board and does it develop and promote its collective vision of the company's purpose?
- ✓ Are board processes and structures in place to maximise the chances of the board taking good decisions?
- ✓ Does the board have the right balance of skills, experience, independence and knowledge and do its members work well together, engaging in fresh thinking and challenging debate?
- ✓ Does the board have a policy and measurable targets on boardroom diversity, including diversity in the wider sense?
- ✓ Has a succession plan been formulated and is it kept under regular review? Is it consistent with the board's diversity policy and vision for the optimum board and does it support the regular refreshing of the board's composition?
- ✓ Is recruitment activity undertaken using advertising or executive search firms who are committed to the Voluntary Code of Conduct for Executive Search Firms? Do recruitment briefs take account of potential barriers to recruitment which may be experienced by women or those from ethnic minority backgrounds?
- ✓ Is the process for selecting new directors rigorous, transparent and focused on competencies rather than experience? Are candidates drawn from a wide and diverse talent pool including candidates from the public and charitable sectors? Is there a programme for internal development of potential candidates?
- ✓ Does the nomination committee work well with the remuneration committee and do the terms of appointment negotiated with directors reflect the company's HR and remuneration policies?
- ✓ Is there an effective and objective process for evaluating board, committee and individual director performance?

- ✓ Where there are weaknesses in the board's composition or skill-set, how can these be addressed?
- ✓ Is the statement in the annual report on the nomination committee and its activities clear and informative? Does it include meaningful reporting on the board's diversity policy and measurable targets as well as the board evaluation process, outcomes and action plan?
- ✓ Are the terms of reference of the nomination committee available publicly and subject to regular review?
- ✓ Do new directors receive a thorough, tailored induction and are ongoing development needs identified and addressed?

# 10

# Effective internal control and risk management

## Risk management and business objectives

Following the banking crisis and the subsequent *Walker Review*, the UK Corporate Governance Code tightened the wording about the board's responsibility for risk. Code Principle C.2 now states:

> 'The board is responsible for determining the nature and extent of the principal risks it is willing to take in achieving its strategic objectives. The board should maintain sound risk management and internal control systems.'

The FRC guidance, *Risk Management, Internal Control and Related Financial and Business Reporting*, which includes the earlier separate guidance, *Internal Control: Guidance to Directors* (formerly and still sometimes referred to as the Turnbull Guidance) sets out best practice guidance on risk management and internal control with the aim of assisting companies in applying Code Principle C.2.

The earlier Turnbull Guidance stated that the conduct of an entrepreneurial enterprise must involve taking business risk and accordingly, the purpose of raising standards of corporate governance was not to eliminate risk but to manage it effectively. Shareholders invest in a company's shares instead of investing in a cash deposit or similar low-risk investment because they expect that the reward for doing so will outweigh the risk, i.e. the equity risk premium. By definition, therefore, a company must be a risk-taking enterprise and the goal should be to maximise shareholder value. However, as both the upside and the downside impacts of risk can materially affect the achievement of that goal, a well-governed company will take steps to manage risk effectively.

In its widest sense, it might be said that all corporate governance initiatives are the response by the stakeholder community to the risk inherent in equity investment. This view is supported by the evidence that potential investors will choose to invest in companies that have a good governance record, in preference to those that do not, and by the increasing emphasis placed on ESG issues by the investment management profession. By exercising this type of investment choice, investors are seeking reassurance and greater accountability from management.

Various corporate failures and in particular the global banking crisis have forcefully made the point that, unless business risk is managed effectively, the result can be very serious indeed. *The Walker Report* into the banking industry concluded that the crisis was in part attributable to inadequate attention to risk management:

> 'Serious deficiencies in prudent oversight and financial regulation in the period before the crisis were accompanied by major governance failures within banks. These contributed materially to excessive risk-taking and the breadth and depth of the crisis.'

Effective risk management and internal control therefore are essential components of good corporate governance. The board should take risk into consideration when it makes strategic business decisions choosing policies which are expected to be profitable, but should limit risks to those necessary to achieve the business strategy and that can be kept to an acceptable level as illustrated by Figure 10.1.

**Figure 10.1** Risk management

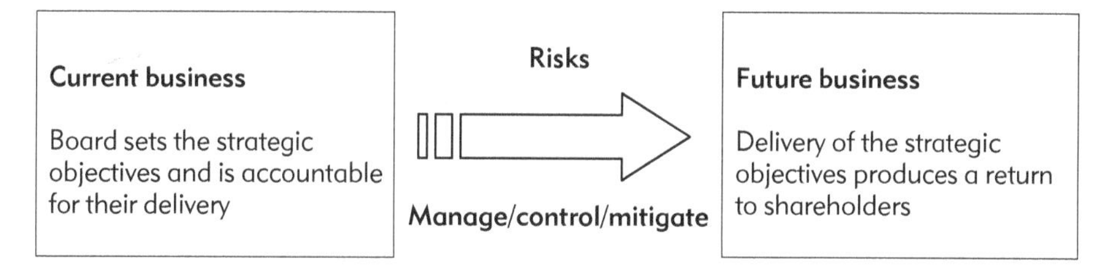


## Risk management and organisational culture

The relevance of organisational culture to risk management was summed up in the foreword to the FRC's 2016 report, *Corporate Culture and the Role of Boards*, in the following terms:

> 'A strong culture will endure in times of stress and mitigate the impact. This is essential in dealing effectively with risk and maintaining resilient performance.'

The FRC guidance, *Risk Management, Internal Control and Related Financial and Business Reporting*, also makes it clear that the 'culture and behaviour' that the board promotes is of 'crucial importance to high quality risk management'. Organisational culture and behaviours will help shape the attitude of the management and staff to risk management and the extent to which risk management systems and processes are embraced by the organisation. Like other aspects of corporate culture, it is important that the board set the tone and seek to embed an appropriate culture throughout the company.

The FRC Guidance also advises that 'risk management and internal control should be incorporated within the company's normal management and governance processes, not treated as a separate compliance exercise'. To a significant degree, this embedding will be a natural by-product of the conduct of continuing review by management, but also requires an organisation-wide approach so that the board should take steps to educate employees generally about the internal control standards that are required.

Effective leadership on risk requires the board and the executive team to be clear and consistent about the levels of risk which are acceptable, to actively and systematically manage risk and embed its consideration in decision-making, and to discourage the taking of inappropriate levels of risk. There has been much debate since the banking crisis about risk-taking behaviours that were incentivised through inappropriate remuneration structures. Such remuneration structures are a good example of dysfunctional risk culture.

In a well-run business, employees will already be aware that effective internal control is required to avoid breach of statutory duties in such areas as health and safety, employment, discrimination and data protection. There may be less conscious awareness amongst employees that internal control will apply equally where the risk is not legal sanction, but rather loss of business competitiveness and efficiency, for example:

- the maintenance of business probity;
- business reputation;
- customer relations;
- service levels of outsourced activities;
- the security of intangible assets; and
- business continuity.

The challenge for the board is to embed in the culture of the company an understanding that managing the risks in all such areas requires the application of effective internal control at every level including external relationships. To achieve this outcome, it is suggested that the board will first need to communicate to the employees the business objectives, both at the company level and also at the level of the business units within which the employees work. Against that background, the board must then raise awareness of the business risks and the internal control processes required to manage such risk successfully. Steps which the board can consider include the following:

- enlisting the HR function and giving it the necessary budget to involve and train employees in risk management;
- communicating to employees through statements of policy or codes of practice what is expected of them and any limitations on their freedom to act;
- establishing clear lines of authority, responsibility and accountability to ensure that the correct people take decisions and actions relating to managing risk;
- reviewing the company's remuneration policies to ensure that performance-related pay is aligned with the company's risk policies and systems and to enable variable components to be reclaimed in certain circumstances. The aim of performance-related pay is to reward appropriate behaviour (and to ensure that inappropriate behaviour is not rewarded); and
- introducing straightforward self-assessment processes so that internal control compliance by employees can be measured in a non-bureaucratic manner.

Embedding the internal control system into the culture of the business in this manner may require a change in behaviour by employees. This is likely to be the product of a prolonged process of 'bottom-up' engagement with employees, not the result of 'top-down' diktats from senior management. The implied observation in the FRC Guidance is that the end result will be the achievement of a high-quality system of internal control, without the imposition of a large number of bureaucratic internal control processes throughout the business.

## Enterprise risk management (ERM)

Since the publication of the Turnbull Guidance, UK listed companies have taken steps to implement what the guidance terms a 'risk-based approach'. This more co-ordinated approach is widely referred to as 'ERM'. ERM has become something of a science, with its own special language and place in the corporate governance world and well-governed companies will expend much time and effort on ensuring that their ERM frameworks operate efficiently. The remainder of this chapter will develop this theme, yet before doing so, the following note of realism taken from the Turnbull Guidance is worth repeating:

> 'A sound system of internal control reduces, but cannot eliminate, the possibility of poor judgement in decision-making; human error; control processes being deliberately circumvented by employees and others; management overriding controls; and the occurrence of unforeseeable circumstances.'

## Risk management standard – ISO 31000

Given the importance of risk management to the achievement of corporate objectives, it is no surprise that an international standard has been developed to provide principles, a framework and processes for the management of risk and to enable organisations to compare their own practices with a recognised benchmark. *A structured approach to Enterprise Risk Management (ERM) and the requirements of ISO 31000*, which is available from the Institute of Risk Management (IRM) website (www.theirm.org), describes the establishment of an effective ERM through an ongoing and iterative process of planning, implementation, monitoring and review. The planning stage includes the design of risk architecture, risk strategy and risk protocols to provide a policy and framework by which risk management processes are supported. Each of these three elements of the framework is now briefly described.

### Risk architecture

The company's risk architecture will encompass the structures by which the company's risk processes will be delivered. The risk architecture will describe the roles, responsibilities, communication and risk reporting arrangements and will typically cover the responsibilities, communication and monitoring arrangements of the board, audit/risk committee, executive risk committee and business units. By the communication and monitoring arrangements, those holding responsibilities in relation to risk, including ultimately the board, will receive assurance on risk matters. The efficacy of those arrangements will therefore need to be verified.

### Risk strategy

The risk strategy will define the objectives which the board is seeking to achieve through the organisation's risk management activities. It will encompass the risk appetite and culture.

The terms risk appetite and risk tolerance are closely related, frequently used but perhaps not always well defined. The IRM guidance paper *Risk Appetite & Tolerance* describes risk appetite as the level of risk that a company is willing to take in the pursuit of its objectives and risk tolerance in terms of the outcomes or deviations from the expected results, which are acceptable/unacceptable to the business.

### Risk protocols

Risk protocols for the business will incorporate risk guidelines, relevant rules and procedures, methodologies, tools and techniques. These protocols describe how the risk strategy will be implemented and the procedures by which risks will be managed.

## Risk policy

The company's risk framework as described above will be set out in its risk policy. It is worth noting that a balance needs to be struck. Internal controls which are too stringent and which reduce risk exposure to so low a level that the entrepreneurial ambitions of the company are thwarted could be viewed as being just as damaging to achievement of a company's objectives as internal controls which are too lax to address risks that are unacceptably high. Of course, not all risk is negative. There is a possibility that events might turn out more positively than planned.

The policy should be reviewed and updated each year to take account of changes in the company's circumstances and objectives as well as developments in best practice. The annual review process is outlined later in this chapter.

## Risk management processes

The key processes in a risk management system are risk:

- identification;
- evaluation;
- management measures; and
- control and review.

These processes are examined next.

## Identifying and categorising risks

There are several types of risk that can threaten a company's business and the directors need to be mindful of the potential impact of each of them. There are various ways of categorising risk. Here the following risk categories are examined:

- business;
- financial;
- operational;
- compliance;
- extended enterprise; and
- reputational.

### Business risk

The company's business strategy will shape and define the company's business objectives. That strategy will be played out against a general background shaped by the prevailing political and economic circumstances. Threats to the business objectives may be posed by changes in government policy or developments in the global or local economy. Equally, the business strategy will be influenced by developments in the market in which the company operates, the technology on which it relies or the capital markets in which the company raises capital.

Clearly the directors will not be able to control such general or specific influences on the company's business, but systems and procedures should be in place to identify, assess and review potential risks and plan how the company will react and adapt to them. When formulating and reviewing the business objectives (e.g. business acquisitions or investments in technology) the directors should do so in response to their assessment of the identified business risks and if necessary should be prepared to change the strategy.

### Financial risk

The directors are responsible, under s. 386 of the CA 2006, for maintaining the company's accounting records. To meet this responsibility they must maintain a system of internal control over the financial management of the company which is likely to include an internal audit function.

The risk of not doing so is apparent: breakdown of the accounting system, failure to identify liabilities, misleading the market through publication of false financial statements and, ultimately, susceptibility to fraud.

Financial risk from external sources can also affect the company. For example, for nearly all companies there will be treasury and interest rate risk and for the company with global operations or suppliers, currency risk will be of material concern.

As with business risk, the task is to have appropriate systems of control in place to identify and assess such risks. They will then be in a position to take informed decisions with the aim not simply of containing the risks, but also managing them for the company's benefit, for example when hedging against currency movements.

### Operational risk

The FRC Guidance makes clear that effective risk management is not about eliminating risk, but about pursuing business objectives through business processes which manage and control risks appropriately. The management of operational risk is primarily on that wavelength. While it is impossible to provide an exhaustive list of what such risk might entail, the broad areas for consideration by the board include the following:

- lack of business innovation;
- failure to manage internal change;
- insufficient investment to achieve business objectives;
- degradation of capital assets;

- failure to manage brand or other intangible assets;
- poor project planning;
- lack of diversification in suppliers and customers;
- failure to set and manage cost budgets;
- employee relation problems;
- poor record in employee recruitment and retention;
- under-investment in training;
- technology or systems failure;
- natural catastrophe, fire or terrorist activity;
- inadequate product/service quality control;
- failure to instruct professional advisers effectively; and
- lack of attention to business ethics and reputation.

Identifying the list of relevant operational risks for the company will be a continuing task for the board and is likely to require a degree of lateral thinking. The operational risk that might prove to be the crucial one may not fit into a neat category.

### Compliance risk

It should be straightforward for the board to identify the laws, regulations, rules and practices with which the company should comply to operate legally. These will include legislation linked to direct trading activity such as health and safety, product or public liability, data protection, environmental protection, competition and fair trading practices, law and regulation around employment such as health and safety, employment rights, corporate manslaughter and also, those which are more focused on non-operational compliance, such as areas of company law, accounting standards, the LR and UK Corporate Governance Code, the market abuse regime and institutional shareholder guidelines.

Having identified the full extent of the regulatory requirements to which the company is subject, internal systems are required to ensure compliance is achieved and a suitable culture will be needed to emphasise the importance of good compliance and the unacceptability of non-compliance. The scandal where traders in certain banks manipulated the Libor rate is just one example where inappropriate culture gave rise to serious compliance failures.

Control of compliance across complex groups, particularly where regulatory regimes of multiple jurisdictions must be considered, can be far from simple. Sound subsidiary governance processes (see Chapter 16) and extension of an appropriate compliance culture across the whole business will be key.

### Extended enterprise risk

A company's operations, finances and reputation can all be endangered by failure of external parties. The Institute of Risk Management (IRM) report,

*Extended Enterprise: Managing Risk in Complex 21st Century Organisations*, examined the way in which an organisation's activities are underpinned by a complex network of relationships and how risk can be managed in that context. The external party risks to which a company is exposed will not simply be elements of supply chain risk, but are likely to extend to IT security, outsourced services, advisers, banking arrangements, joint venture partners, licensees and many others. The report points out that risk management is only as strong as 'the weakest link'. Analysis of the external network is the first step that should be undertaken.

The IRM report makes the point that in a complex system of external relationships, stronger controls need to be balanced with influencing of relationships, attitudes and behaviours and building of trust. The IRM report points to the BS11000 Collaborative Business Relationship series as providing a systematic approach to managing the risks and opportunities of external relationships. The approach is likely to need to incorporate:

- sound business cases for each relationship;
- appropriate policies and resources for partner selection and collaborative working;
- a focus on resolving conflicts;
- a commitment to continued improvement;
- monitoring and relationship management; and
- an exit strategy.

### Reputational risk

Linking all these areas of risk is the company's reputation. That is, what is perceived and believed about the company by its stakeholders. It is one of the most valuable corporate assets. According to one poll, conducted for the CBI in 2007, well over half of consumers will pay a premium to the company they believe has the best reputation, even if they can buy a product or service more cheaply elsewhere. It is also arguably one of the most vulnerable. Research by the Economist Intelligence Unit, published at the end of 2005, revealed that while reputation is now seen as a major source of competitive advantage, changes in the business environment, development of global media and communications and increased scrutiny from regulators all expose companies to increased reputational risk.

A 2010 workshop, which included representatives from the Association of Insurance and Risk Management (AIRMIC), GC100, the Institute of Internal Auditors UK and Ireland (IIA) and ICSA, opined that responsibility for reputational capital should be at board level and, since investors are involved, boards should consider reporting more explicitly on reputational matters. Specific reputational risk analysis will highlight risks which would not normally appear on a traditional risk map and will help to identify blind spots.

### Finding solutions to identified risks

The possible solutions available to eliminate or reduce risk to the business are likely to be as many as the identified risks and, for many risks, a combination of solutions may be appropriate.

Solutions to identified risks can often be generated by internal initiatives. For example:

- preventative training programmes can be used to address health and safety and employment law risks;
- enhanced use of software applications can support better management and financial reporting; and
- the adoption of effective employee appraisal and career development programmes can address the risks to the business of staff absences and succession.

The added benefit of such internal initiatives is that they can help to embed the internal control system in the culture of the business.

Other solutions can be bought in external markets, so that the risk, particularly residual risk remaining after the mitigating effect of other available control measures, is in effect outsourced at a cost. Most obviously, a company will use the insurance market to purchase cover in respect of easily insurable risks such as product, employee and third-party liabilities. The financial markets can also provide risk-reduction tools in the form of various types of derivative instruments, for example to protect against exchange or interest rate exposure.

Consultants and other external suppliers can also be retained on contractual terms that have the effect of shifting out of the business the risk of managing non-core functions. It may also be possible to manage risk through encouraging partnership arrangements with suppliers, so improving the quality of the supply chain.

### Cycle of risk management

Figure 10.2 overleaf illustrates the steps required to both maintain and review the internal control system as a continuing cycle of risk management tasks.

## The board's responsibilities

Following the banking failures of 2008/9, the focus on the board's risk management responsibilities increased considerably. As noted above, Code Principle C.2 has been amended to place squarely with the board the overall responsibility for setting the level of risk which is acceptable to the organisation and for maintaining appropriate systems of internal control, both financial and non-financial, and this responsibility should underpin the

**Figure 10.2** Risk management cycle

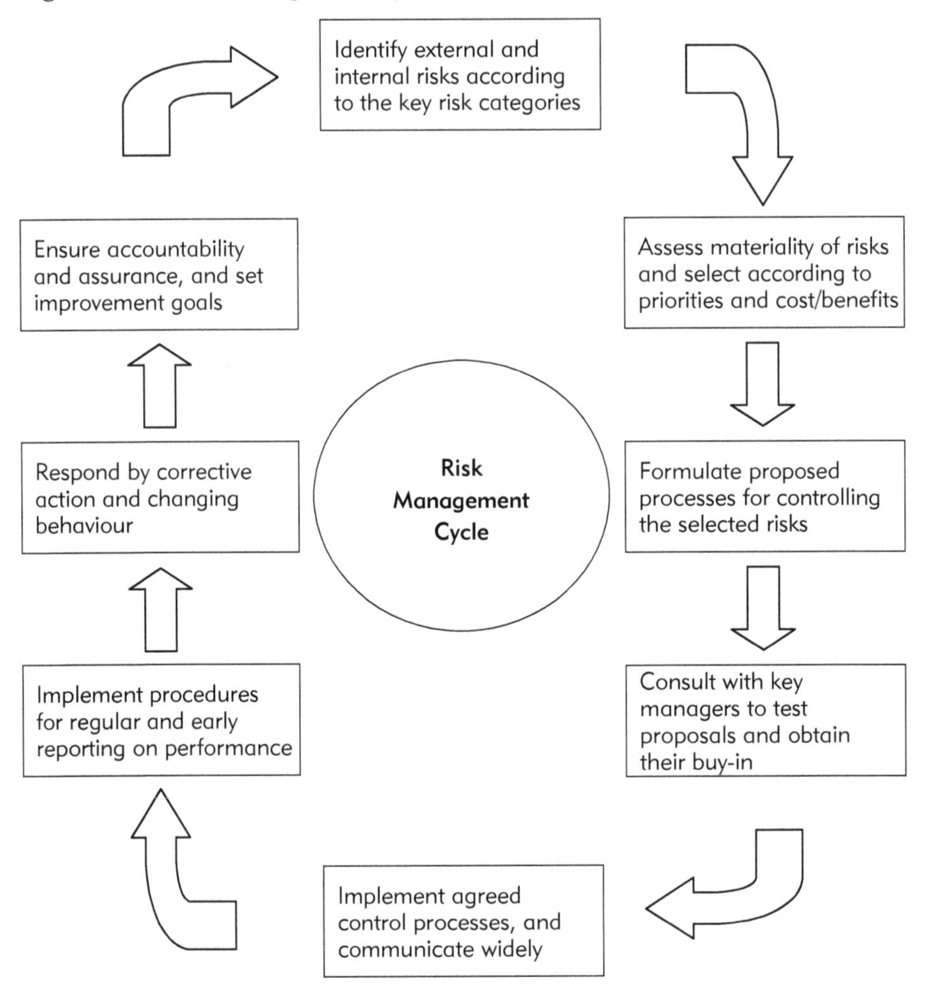


company's risk architecture. The system of internal control must start with a clear understanding of the nature and extent of the risks which exist (and are evolving) and the level and categories of risk that are to be tolerated. Without an understanding of these, it is not possible to judge whether an internal control system is appropriate and effective in achieving its aims.

The line of accountability runs directly to the shareholders. Code Provision C.2.3 underlines this line of accountability, requiring the board to:

> 'monitor the company's risk management and internal control systems and, at least annually, carry out a review of their effectiveness, and report on that review in the annual report.'

This requirement is in addition to the need to describe the main features of the internal control and risk management systems in relation to the financial reporting process pursuant to DTR 7.2.5R.

The monitoring and review of the risk management and internal control systems should cover all material controls, including financial, operational and compliance.

### The role of the audit/risk committee

Without detracting from the board's overall responsibility, the FRC guidance anticipates that the tasks of monitoring and reviewing the company's risk management and internal control systems will be delegated to one or more committees. The extent of that committee role may depend on factors such as 'the size and composition of the board, the scale, diversity and complexity of the company's operations and the nature of the significant risks that the company faces'.

Commonly, the audit committee will be given the task of acting for the board in these matters. However, with the already considerable burden placed on the audit committee, adding responsibility for risk could perhaps both overload its agenda and also compromise the very management of risk.

Although they did not attempt to extrapolate their findings to other industries, both the *Turner* and *Walker Reviews* following the global banking crisis concluded that the independence of risk committees and their relationship with senior risk managers needed to be strengthened within the banking sector. Although the *Walker Report* was of course restricted to UK financial institutions, it made the point, applicable to all companies regardless of sector, that the audit committee's responsibilities for oversight and reporting to the board on the financial accounts, accounting policies, internal control and compliance are largely backward-looking. In contrast, risk identification and monitoring is, by its very nature, forward-looking.

There is some logic therefore to separating out these two functions and establishing a separate risk committee with responsibility for the functions recommended by Walker, namely oversight and advice to the board on the current risk exposures and future risk strategy, including strategy for capital and liquidity management and the embedding and maintenance of a supportive culture in relation to the management of risk alongside established prescriptive rules and procedures. Certainly for FTSE 100 financial services companies, a separate risk committee will be required. Model terms of reference for a risk committee are available from ICSA's website (www.icsa.org.uk).

In view of the importance of the finance function to risk management, the finance director will typically be a key member of any specially constituted risk committee. He or she will be supported by representatives of the company's various subsidiary or divisional executive managers and will typically have a line report to the chief executive on the committee's business.

It is worth commenting here that the board's risk committee should not be confused with the executive risk committee common in many organisations. The role of the executive risk committee, normally chaired by the chief executive or finance director, is to implement on a day-to-day basis the risk management strategy agreed by the board and/or its risk/audit committee. While the executive risk committee and audit/risk committee will work closely together, their roles should be distinct and clearly defined.

Given the heavy emphasis, both in the UK Corporate Governance Code and the FRC Guidance, on the board's collective responsibility for risk management and internal control, the results of the audit or risk committee's work should be presented to and considered by the full board.

## Internal control systems

Code Principle C.2 requires the board to maintain sound systems of internal control. When establishing and maintaining a system of internal control the board must give consideration to the following three factors:

- how the principal risks will be managed or mitigated;
- which controls will be put in place; and
- what constitutes a significant control failing.

### Management reports

It is for management to provide information and assurances and for the board to ensure that it receives and reviews regular reports on internal control. The FRC guidance advocates that thought be given to how 'the expectations of the board are to be communicated to staff and what training may be required.' The board should confirm to management the scope and frequency of the reports it requires on internal control matters but management should also take the initiative in supplying information when relevant rather than always awaiting the board's requests.

It should be clearly understood by management that their reports will inform the board's risk assessment policies and decisions, as well as the statement on internal control systems to be included in the annual report. To assist management, it is advisable that the board provides guidance as to the required contents of the reports. In particular, such guidance should confirm that the main aim of the reports will be to provide a balanced assessment of significant risks, details of any control failings or weaknesses and the steps taken to address such shortcomings. Open communication is, above all, the essential guiding principle and a key part of the desired culture and behaviour.

While the board and its committees are primarily responsible for high-level oversight and the general rule is that the executive management, rather than the board, are responsible for carrying out detailed functions, the FRC *Guidance on Audit Committees* rightly notes in relation to the audit committee's role that, the audit committee should consider 'key matters of their own initiative and the oversight function may well lead to detailed work'. This exception to the general rule could be applied to a variety of board issues, but is particularly relevant in the context of internal control in the event that the board or its committees sense that something is seriously amiss.

### Evaluating effectiveness

Having established a system of internal control, the board is then required to evaluate its effectiveness. This is made explicit by Code Provision C.2.3, which requires the directors to conduct an annual review. This is to cover controls relating to both financial and non-financial risks.

The FRC Guidance places significant emphasis on the need for the board to come to a view on the effectiveness of the risk management and internal control systems, i.e. to keep them under regular and close review, describing these reviews as 'essential components of sound systems of risk management and internal control'. The purpose of the review is to enable the board to determine whether the systems are aligned with strategic objectives and are being developed, applied and maintained appropriately to address the company's risks.

Therefore, in addition to regular monitoring of risks that will be ongoing within the business, the board should undertake an annual assessment of the system of internal control as a whole. In this respect, it is recommended that the board should consider the following:

- the company's risk appetite, desired culture and whether the culture is embedded;
- how the risk management and internal control systems operate, including their design, implementation, monitoring, review, risk identification and determination of which risks are 'principal' risks;
- how risk management and internal controls are integrated, taking account of strategy, business model and business planning processes;
- how the nature, likelihood and impact of principal risks may be changing and how the company is able to respond to developments in its business and environment in which it operates;
- the extent, frequency and quality of management's communication to the board of its monitoring so that the board can develop a picture of the state of control of the company and how effectively risk is managed and mitigated;

- incidents of significant control failings or weaknesses and other issues that have been identified and reported during the year and the extent to which they have, or could have, resulted in an unforeseen impact; and
- the effectiveness of the company's public reporting processes.

Appendix C to the FRC Guidance sets out a helpful list of questions which the board may wish to consider when assessing the effectiveness of the company's risk and control processes.

## The internal audit function

The IIA describes the internal audit function in the following terms:

> 'Internal auditing is an independent, objective assurance and consulting activity designed to add value and improve an organization's operations. It helps an organization accomplish its objectives by bringing a systematic, disciplined approach to evaluate and improve the effectiveness of risk management, internal control and governance processes.'

The monitoring and review of the internal audit function is a responsibility of the audit committee and is addressed in Chapter 7 in the context of the audit and financial statements. This section deals with the status and role of the internal audit in the context of maintaining internal controls.

Apart from its financial control role, the internal audit function also has a key part to play as the provider of independent assurance to the board on the internal control system and wider risk management. It should have the necessary skills and resources to advise the board and management generally on the internal control processes and be able to verify and test reports submitted to the board. Best practice demands that it will develop its internal audit plan taking account of the key risks faced by the business. It should be clear, however, that the role of internal audit is one of providing assurance, advice and challenge. It is not responsible for taking or implementing risk management decisions or setting the organisation's risk policy.

Exactly how the board will seek to employ and deliver the internal audit function will depend upon several factors, such as the nature of the company (e.g. its size and resources) and of its business (e.g. its sector, complexity and geographical reach) and these factors should be subject to regular review. The board might, for example, seek to outsource some or even all of the internal audit function to a specialist provider rather than employing a full-service in-house team. There is no 'one size fits all' approach. So, for example, the directors of a financial services company with international operations will face very different challenges in this respect when compared with the directors of a smaller UK-based property development company.

The challenge for the board is to avoid the pitfall of relegating the internal audit function to an isolated position with little status within the business. Rather, the audit committee and the wider board should bring it within their sphere of influence and should satisfy themselves that it is capable of delivering the necessary level of independent and objective assurance. The FRC *Guidance on Audit Committees* sets out a number of specific safeguards to ensure sufficient weight is given to internal audit. For example, the Guidance requires the appointment and resignation of the head of internal audit to be a matter for the audit committee and for the internal auditor to have access to the audit committee and board chairmen, for the function to have unrestricted scope and the necessary resources and professional skills to fulfil its mandate.

### What if there is no internal audit function?

Code Provision C.3.6 requires that, where there is no internal audit function, the audit committee should consider annually whether there is a need for one and make a recommendation to the board accordingly. The FRC *Guidance on Audit Committees* sets out the considerations to be taken into account when conducting such a review. These can be summarised as any internal or external factors affecting the company that have or are expected to increase the risks faced by the company. An increase in unexpected incidents or internal factors such as restructuring may be sufficient reason to prompt a decision to introduce an internal audit function.

The reasons for the absence of such a function should be explained in the corporate governance section of the annual report. In the absence of an internal audit function, the board will need to apply other monitoring processes to secure an effective system of internal control. A key challenge in this respect is whether the board has at its disposal the necessary quality of objective assurance.

### Whistleblowing

Whistleblowing is an informal term to describe the reporting of concerns about wrongdoing by an organisation. An organisation with an appropriately open culture will encourage employees to be 'the eyes and ears' of the business and welcome whistleblowers who report their concerns internally (as opposed to the media).

Such reports provide an opportunity for the organisation to learn about control failings that might otherwise have serious consequences and, after investigation of the allegations, to address any wrongdoing that is discovered. The importance of effective whistleblowing arrangements to a company's internal control and assurance processes is therefore clear.

Accordingly, Code Provision C.3.5 requires the audit committee to:

> 'review arrangements by which staff of the company may, in confidence, raise concerns about possible improprieties in matters of financial reporting or other matters. The audit committee's objective should be to ensure that arrangements are in place for the proportionate and independent investigation of such matters and for appropriate follow-up action.'

The 2015 DBIS publication *Whistleblowing: Guidance for Employers and Code of Practice* provides helpful suggestions on issues such as culture, training and staff awareness and response to whistleblowing reports.

Whistleblowers are generally employees and are protected in law provided that they believe that:

- they are acting in the public interest; and
- the alleged wrongdoing falls into one of a number of categories that include criminal offences, such as fraud, or other failure to comply with the law, miscarriages of justice, endangerment of an individual's health and safety, damage to the environment or action to cover up any of these types of wrongdoing.

While such protection exists, it is likely that potential whistleblowers may still be fearful of the consequences that may arise for them. Accordingly, a whistleblower is less likely to act if he or she fears retribution or that nothing will be done to address the wrongdoing once reported. Such fears are likely to be exacerbated by high profile cases involving problems for whistleblowers or failure by companies to ensure their protection. The April 2017 report that Barclay's chief executive attempted to 'unmask' an anonymous whistleblower is a recent example. The company's policies and procedures should therefore ensure that employees have confidence that, if they make a genuine disclosure, they will be supported.

From time to time the audit committee, in line with the UK Code on Corporate Governance, should seek direct assurance on whistleblowing arrangements. This assurance may come from the internal audit team. However, if the internal audit team is itself performing an integral part of the company's whistleblowing procedures, external assurance should be sought in order to maintain independence. In either scenario, the CIIA Guidance *Whistleblowing and Corporate Governance: The Role of Internal Audit in Whistleblowing* will be useful to the audit committee in considering how to obtain assurance on the effectiveness of the company's whistleblowing arrangements. Additional whistleblowing requirements apply to banks and larger insurance companies under FCA/PRA rules.

## Governance checklist

- ✓ Has the board determined a risk policy setting out its risk architecture, strategy and protocols?
- ✓ Are appropriate structures in place for monitoring and reporting risk management matters and is assurance provided to the board appropriately verified?
- ✓ Are the main risks to the business identified and managed under a process of continuous review, taking into account the changing business environment?
- ✓ Is there a chain of reporting on internal risk from management to the board and are weaknesses identified and addressed?
- ✓ Does the culture of the business support the ERM framework established by the board, i.e. is it embedded?
- ✓ Is the internal audit function used effectively to provide objective assurance to the board on the key risks?
- ✓ Does risk management and internal control reporting to shareholders comply with the requirements of the DTR, LR and FRC Guidance and does it do more than simply 'tick the box'?
- ✓ Does the company have an appropriate whistleblowing policy and effective procedures that are well communicated and supported by an open and responsive culture?

# 11
# The chairman of the board

## The chairman's role in governance

In governance terms, the importance of the role of the chairman of the board (and similarly the chairman of a board committee) cannot be overstated. In the words of the FRC *Guidance on Board Effectiveness*, 'good boards are created by good chairmen'. For this reason the role merits examination in its own right, separate from the other NEDs. Setting the chairman apart in this manner reflects the heightened emphasis now placed upon his or her position as the leader of the board. While the doctrine of the unitary board requires that he or she is subject to equal duties and liabilities with the other directors, in practice the developing profile and stature of the role has elevated the chairman to the key position of responsibility on the board.

Company law places full responsibility for directing the company and promoting its affairs on the board. It follows, therefore, that the chairman, as leader of the board, is pivotal to creating the conditions necessary for the board to be effective in providing entrepreneurial leadership for the organisation. By the same token, where the company underperforms, particularly where this derives from a failure in governance, it is the chairman's effectiveness that will come under close scrutiny. Although this judgement may appear harsh, the logic of current thinking on these matters compels the conclusion that an ineffective chairman will result in an ineffective board, with the associated risk of corporate underperformance.

It has been observed that a board is not a natural decision-making organism (assuming it is not dominated by an imperious executive personality). Yet it is the board's responsibility to reach a consensus and then to make a decision. The chairman is the person who needs to lead the board through that process, extracting, from a variety of views, a single decision and a clear strategy. A good chief executive is not bound to have a consensual approach, but a good chairman must govern the board in a manner that ensures that consensus is achieved without impairing the board's effectiveness as a decision-making body. In the same context, Sir Adrian Cadbury, who likened the chairman's role to that of a good conductor of an orchestra, directing and controlling without imposing their own views or stifling individual contribution, commented that:

> 'Taking the chair at board meetings is the aspect of the job of chairmen which is furthest from the public eye, but the one where their personal contribution is decisive.'

The 2009 *Walker Review* observed that 'good corporate governance overall depends critically on the abilities and experience of individuals and the effectiveness of their collaboration in the enterprise' and that deficiencies in the boards of banks and other financial institutions 'related much more to patterns of behaviour than to organisation'. The ability of the chairman to enhance the effectiveness of the board by influencing the board members' collective behaviour means the role of chairman is uniquely powerful. While the earlier focus of corporate governance developments on chairmen tended to relate to their responsibilities, more recent work, such as the FRC *Guidance on Board Effectiveness*, has highlighted some of the personal and behavioural attributes required to carry out the role effectively.

## The chairman's selection and appointment

There are no special rules in the UK Corporate Governance Code governing the process for selecting and appointing the chairman. However, having observed that, not only can the pool of talent for people to fill the role of chairman be small, but able candidates can be difficult to identify. The *Higgs Report* set out three guiding principles (not rules) about the process. These are as follows:

- the SID or the deputy chairman, if independent, should normally lead the appointment process, not the incumbent chairman;
- a systematic approach should be taken to identify the skills and expertise for the role and a job specification prepared; and
- a shortlist of good candidates should be considered, rather than possible individual candidates being considered in turn.

As with other board appointments, the recruitment process will be led by the nomination committee. The first of the Higgs guiding principles described above is now enshrined within Code Provision B.2.1 which requires that 'the chairman should not chair the nomination committee when it is dealing with the appointment of a successor to the chairmanship'.

Higgs also noted that the process of selecting candidates would almost certainly benefit from external advice, provided by a specialist executive search agency. The UK Corporate Governance Code requires that an explanation should be provided where neither an external search consultancy nor open advertising has been used in the recruitment of a chairman (Code Provision B.2.4). For appointments to the chairman's position it will be difficult for the nomination committee to provide such an explanation given the last of the three principles from the *Higgs Report* set out above and the increasing focus on the need for transparent recruitment criteria for board appointments generally.

Subject to the provisions of the company's articles of association, the appointment of the chairman will be formalised by a resolution of the full board, taking into account the recommendations of the nomination committee. Once approved, it should be confirmed by written terms in an appointment letter, setting out the specific job requirements as well as the normal NED terms (see Chapter 13).

If the chairman is new to the board he or she will be required to retire and offer him or herself for re-appointment by an ordinary resolution of the shareholders at the first available AGM of the company. Under Code Provision B.7.1 the chairman, in common with all directors of FTSE 350 companies, is required to stand for annual re-election. Reflecting the chairman's status as 'board representative', the Pensions and Lifetime Savings Association (PLSA) has identified a number of general governance issues, the occurrence of which might warrant an investor deciding to vote against the re-election of the chairman.

The level of remuneration paid to the chairman will vary considerably according to the time commitment and the size of the company. As with non-executive remuneration generally, the trend is upwards on account of the greater demands and concerns over the risk/reward ratio. Guidelines from the IA (previously issued by the ABI) state that shareholders consider it inappropriate for chairmen to receive performance-linked incentives as this could impair their impartial oversight.

### The independence of the chairman

It is a prerequisite for the chairman being able to secure an effective and united board that they should be independent in both form and substance. Yet this has proved a very difficult principle to reduce to a simple statement about independence. The chairman sits in a pivotal position on the board, bridging the gap between the executive and NEDs. If they are to fulfil all the demands of the job, they will need to work closely with both categories of directors, winning their confidence in equal measure.

The UK Corporate Governance Code has settled on a sensible solution. Code Provision A.3.1 requires the chairman to meet the test of independence when they are first appointed, but in view of the degree of involvement with the executive team that the job will entail, having been appointed they will no longer need to remain independent. The thinking behind this approach is that the chairman will bring to the board the necessary objectivity and fresh thinking. Also, he or she will better be able to win the confidence of shareholders if they are independent of executive management and free from any pre-existing business or other relationship which could interfere with the exercise of their judgement.

### Former chief executive as chairman

A direct consequence of the chairman's independence requirement is that a former executive director, including in particular the chief executive, should not normally become the chairman. This restriction is provided for in Code Provision A.3.1. Critics of this provision point out that a former chief executive will have knowledge of the business which will assist them to contribute more incisively to debates on strategy and will give them more credibility with both members of the board and the shareholders. The counter-arguments are apparent: a former chief executive can find it difficult to make room for their replacement; he or she may be identified too closely with the executive team in the minds of the other NEDs on the board; and they may take for granted their inside knowledge and fail as an 'informational bridge' to the NEDs.

Given these contrary views, the Code does accept that there may be circumstances where an exception to the rule is justified. The PLSA, in its *Corporate Governance Policy and Voting Guidelines*, opines that the succession of chief executive to chairman will be 'acceptable only on rare occasions'. To deal with such occasions, the Code sets out the procedures to be followed by boards wishing to appoint a former chief executive to the role of chairman (Code Provision A.3.1). These procedures include advance consultation with major shareholders and the provision of an explanation to shareholders both at the time of the appointment and in the next report and accounts. It should be noted that, where a valid case can be made, shareholders will accept a former chief executive becoming chairman. As an example, this occurred when Barclays Plc appointed its former chief executive as chairman in September 2004. However, it should also be noted that the PLSA guidelines specifically dismiss the complexity of a business as sufficient argument in favour of this type of appointment and expressly set out the expectation that external candidates will also have been considered prior to the appointment.

## The chairman's role on the board

In the early 1990s Sir Adrian Cadbury described the chairman's role in the following terms:

> 'Chairmen are primarily responsible for the working of the board, for the balance of its membership subject to board and shareholders' approval and for ensuring that all directors, executive and non-executive alike, are enabled to play their full part in its activities.'

The *Hampel Report* endorsed this description without adding to it further, but subsequent guidance, starting with Higgs in 2003 and more recently the FRC *Guidance on Board Effectiveness*, has also attempted to provide more detailed descriptions of the role and personal attributes required of an effective chairman. While not mandatory under the UK Corporate Governance Code, the FRC *Guidance on Board Effectiveness* is intended to assist boards when considering how best to implement provisions of the Code relating to the chairman's responsibilities. Table 11.1 provides a summary of the key responsibilities of the chairman's role.

**Table 11.1** Chairman's responsibilities (based on the FRC *Guidance on Board Effectiveness*)

| | |
|---|---|
| **Demonstrating leadership** | The chairman should, by their leadership, create the conditions for overall board and individual director effectiveness. They should demonstrate ethical leadership, maintaining the highest standards of integrity and probity and setting clear expectations about the company's culture, values and behaviours. |
| **Developing good governance arrangements** | Together with the company secretary, the chairman should periodically review the company's governance processes and consider any improvements or initiatives which could strengthen them. They should ensure that the chief executive supports this work by taking steps to permeate appropriate governance standards throughout the company. They must ensure that the board's committees are properly structured with appropriate terms of reference. |
| **Setting the board agenda** | With the help of the executive directors and company secretary, the chairman is responsible for setting the agenda for the board's deliberations. The agenda should be primarily focused on strategy, performance, value creation and accountability. The chairman should ensure that issues relevant to these areas are reserved for board decision. |
| **Providing information to the board** | With the support of the company secretary, the chairman should ensure a timely flow of high-quality supporting information to the board. They should ensure that executive directors' views, including any divergence of opinion, are explained to the board by the chief executive and that the chief financial officer delivers high-quality information to the board on the company's financial position. They should also ensure that all directors are made aware of the views of those who provide capital. |
| **Procuring quality board debate and decision making** | The chairman should set clear expectations about the style and tone of the board's discussions and make certain that the board has effective decision-making processes and applies sufficient challenge to major proposals. Sufficient time should be allowed for debate, especially for complex, contentious or business-critical issues. They should encourage all board members to engage in board and committee meetings by drawing on their skills, experience, knowledge and, where appropriate, independence. |

**Table 11.1** *continued*

| | |
|---|---|
| **Ensuring consideration of risk** | The chairman should make certain that the board determines the nature and extent of the significant risks the company is willing to embrace in the implementation of its strategy and that there are no 'no go' areas which prevent directors from operating effective oversight in this area. |
| **Fostering relationships** | The chairman should foster relationships founded on mutual respect and open communication – both in and outside the boardroom – between the NEDs and the executive team. They should seek to develop productive working relationships with all executive directors and the chief executive in particular, providing support and advice while respecting executive responsibility. They should also consult the SID on board matters in accordance with the UK Corporate Governance Code. A relationship of mutual trust with the company secretary, who should report to the chairman on all board governance matters, should be developed. |
| **Director induction and development and board evaluation** | The chairman should take the lead on issues of director development, including through induction programmes for new directors and undertake regular reviews with all directors, ensuring that induction and development activity is tailored to the individual director. The chairman should act on the results of board evaluation and be aware of and respond to their own development needs, including people and other skills, especially when taking on the role for the first time. |
| **Succession planning and board appointments** | The chairman should regularly consider succession planning and the composition of the board and have a vision for achieving optimal board composition. They should help the nomination committee, which they will usually chair, to review the skills required and identify gaps within the board and to develop transparent appointment criteria. This process should be continuous and proactive and should take account of the company's agreed strategic priorities and the need to achieve diversity of psychological type, background and gender in order to avoid 'group think' and encourage challenge, fresh ideas and new thinking. |
| **Shareholder engagement** | The chairman should play a key role in representing the company to its principal audiences and ensure effective communication with shareholders and other stakeholders. In particular they should report personally in the annual report's corporate governance statement about board leadership and effectiveness. |

In the joint EY/IA report from 2015, *Board Effectiveness – Continuing the Journey*, it was noted that, as boards are changing, so is the chairman's role evolving. It described the chairman as 'the lynchpin' of areas such as diversity, succession planning and information flows.

The following issues were highlighted:

- Diversity – the chairman needs to be an inclusive leader in order to 'harness the benefits of diversity' and in particular may need to focus more on supporting and developing less experienced board members on appointment.
- Board recruitment – drawing on their wealth of experience, a chairman's insights can be of great value in selecting the right people to appoint to the board. In addition, the chairman is likely to play a vital role in communication with shareholders on new appointments and succession planning.
- Decision making – the chairman will play a key role not only in ensuring that the right strategic issues are included on board agendas (potentially being the same issue on multiple occasions in order to allow non-executive views to be sought at various stages of a proposal's development) but they also set the tone and culture of the boardroom. They should take the lead in encouraging a transparent forum where frank and open debate is the norm.
- Time commitment – a chairman needs to be satisfied that they have the 'bandwidth' to contribute as required in times of crisis and difficulty, not just having sufficient availability to meet the demands of 'normal' times.

As part of this evolution in the chairman's role, their leadership responsibility in respect of the development, embedding, reporting and assessment of an appropriate corporate culture is now more fully recognised. In particular, the chairman will have a pivotal role to play in ensuring the board takes account of issues of culture when it debates and delivers strategy, considers business proposals and sets objectives.

### Reporting lines and performance appraisal

The chairman is formally appointed by and reports to the board. The non-executive directors, led by the SID and taking account of the views of the executive directors, are responsible for the chairman's performance evaluation (Code Provision B.6.3). This will take place at least annually but potentially also on other occasions if deemed necessary.

### What makes a good chairman?

The evidence is that the role of chairman is not one for which many incumbents have a natural ability. Equally, the traditional route to chairmanship the climb up to senior executive management with the addition of some non-executive experience – does not appear to provide an adequate training ground. The role requires, in summary, a unique set of skills, but there is little by way of formal preparation. The report *What Makes an Outstanding Chairman* by Directorbank Group attempted to establish some of the characteristics which could lead to a chairman underperforming. The list included lack of impartiality, poor leadership, lack of involvement in or knowledge and understanding of the business, arrogance, poor control of the board, inability to make difficult decisions and poor communication skills. Research annexed to the *Walker Review* final recommendations identified the behaviours required of an effective chairman. These are reproduced in Table 11.2.

**Table 11.2** Behaviour of an effective chairman – the *Walker Review*

**1. Integrating the board's collective thinking**
This is possible when a chairman excels at seeking and sharing information; building ideas into concepts; analysing and considering multiple perspectives and different alternatives; and can subvert his or her individual needs for commitment to a common goal.

**2. Empathy and promoting openness in board members**
The ability to listen at multiple levels is critical to successful chairmanship and team dynamics. Listening to what is not being said is as critical as listening to the words that are spoken. Only with this ability can a chairman engender deep trust and respect.

**3. Facilitating interaction**
This requires that a chairman's behaviour moves seamlessly depending upon who needs to be in the conversation, rather than 'managing' the process. It requires that skills and expertise (authority) are valued and respected regardless of hierarchy or power dynamics.

**4. Developing others**
Undertaking active coaching, mentoring and development of talent within the board, in particular with new board members.

**5. Communicating complex messages succinctly**
Effective communication, through written and spoken means, reduces the cognitive load on the board, freeing more time for analysis, exploration and learning.

**6. Collaborating across boundaries**
The ability to identify boundaries and successfully navigate across and within them is critical to creating a culture of collaboration and efficiency.

**7. Continuous improvement**
Good behavioural objectives include continuous evaluation against internal and external benchmarks. The continual focus on improvement is as much a mindset as a behaviour.

Similarly, a 2014 report by Alvarez & Marshal, *What Makes an Exceptional Chairman*, which drew upon the experiences of a number of current and past chairman together with feedback from other board members from a diverse range of companies, identified the following eight characteristics common to effective chairs:

i) understanding the business;
ii) preparing for the future;
iii) building and getting the best from the board;
iv) working successfully with the CEO;
v) taking command of difficult situations;
vi) taking tough decisions;
vii) inspiring and energising leadership; and
viii) communicating effectively with stakeholders.

It is worth noting again here that those appointed to chair a committee will need to demonstrate similar behaviours to those described above in order to create the right conditions for the committee to be effective in its work.

### Selecting and appointing the chairman

Uniquely amongst the non-executives, it is the personal qualities of the chairman that matter. Other non-executives may be selected on account of the specialist skills they bring to the board, their business sector knowledge or their capability to enhance the diversity of perspectives of the board. The chairman needs, above all, to have qualities of personal leadership, with clear objectives for the board and sufficient personal authority to ensure that they are realised in both clement and inclement circumstances. Account will need to be taken of these qualities in the selection and recruitment process for a chairman.

### The chairman's key relationships

A particular challenge for the chairman is that a rather different form of leadership is required to that which he or she will typically have learned as an executive director or equivalent elsewhere. Unlike the hands-on role of the executive director, the chairman is required to be a facilitator. Like any other NED, much of his or her effectiveness will depend on exercising influence rather than giving orders, on establishing trust and credibility with the executive team rather than relying on the power of the office. However, considerably more demands will be placed on the chairman to the extent that they will be responsible for creating the conditions for overall board and individual director effectiveness. This pivotal position requires the chairman to foster 'relationships founded on mutual respect and open communication – inside and outside the boardroom – between the non-executive directors and executive team'. Considerable skill and fortitude of character will be needed to forge productive working relationships with all the executive team, without either competing with their executive roles or surrendering in the process the chairman's essential characteristic as the leading NED. Of all these relationships, however, the chairman's relationship with the chief executive is of particular importance.

## The chairman and the chief executive

### Separation of roles

Code Provision A.2.1 requires that the roles of chief executive and chairman should be separated. The rationale for this is that it avoids concentration of power in one individual and differentiates leadership of the board (the chairman's job) from running of the business (the chief executive's job). Advocates of this separation point out that it is part of the board's role to have oversight of management and that, if led by a member of that management team, the board's oversight is likely to be less effective. The separation of powers and the maintenance of balance on the board are key tenets of UK corporate governance.

The PLSA, in its *Corporate Governance Policy and Voting Guidelines*, suggests that the combination of the roles or the designation of an executive chairman 'would cause significant concern' although the guidelines do recognise that temporarily combining the roles may be justified, in particular when a chairman 'bridges the gap' between departure of a chief executive and appointment of a successor.

The strength of investor unease over any attempt to combine the roles was clearly demonstrated when Sir Stuart Rose was promoted from chief executive to executive chairman of Marks and Spencer Group Plc in 2008. Despite the company's attempt to justify the rationale for combining the roles, shareholder opposition was evident at subsequent AGMs and in 2010 the selection of an independent chairman brought the combined role to an end.

### The key board relationship

Ever since the *Cadbury Report*, it has been recognised that, in spite of their markedly different roles, the effectiveness of the board will in large measure depend upon the strength of the relationship between the chairman and chief executive. Matters relating to the relationship between two (usually single-minded and commanding) individuals cannot be determined by rules of governance. However, there are some factors which can create the right environment for such a relationship to prosper:

- *Complementary attributes*: the board should seek to appoint individuals to fill these posts who have a mix of different but complementary skills and experiences.

- *Chairman as non-executive*: the chairman should understand clearly that it is not their role to seek executive responsibility and they should allow the chief executive to take the credit for their achievements in the running of the business.
- *Chief executive and the board equally*: the chief executive should recognise that it is not their role to run the board and they should be careful not to dominate board proceedings or to withhold from it relevant information.
- *Chairman as partner*: the separation of powers should not prevent the chairman from being an 'informed, experienced and trusted partner' of the chief executive and 'the source of counsel and challenge' which is designed to support, rather than limit, their performance.
- *Clear boundaries of responsibility*: in compliance with the UK Corporate Governance Code, the division of responsibilities between the chairman and the chief executive should be set out in writing and agreed by the board (Code Provision A.2.1). Particular attention should be paid to potential areas of overlap.

The chief executive reports to the chairman. The board, led by the chairman, is responsible for setting the chief executive's objectives and similarly the board collectively will retain a close interest in the evaluation of the chief executive's performance. However, it is the chairman who will need to communicate the board's judgements to the chief executive on his or her performance and, if necessary, to challenge and identify areas requiring renewed effort or improvement.

In order to facilitate their relationship, it is important that the chairman and the chief executive find the time to meet regularly. A natural catalyst for such meetings will be discussion of the agenda for regular board meetings, which is likely to lead into consideration of both long-term strategic objectives and short-term operational matters. While the chairman will be guided by the chief executive's views, it is important that they retain the ultimate say on which items are placed on the board's agenda. The chairman should also ensure that supporting board papers are of a high quality, presenting the directors with sufficient background and analysis of the various choices available to the board and ensuring that the board is made aware of any differences of opinion amongst the executive directors on particular proposals.

## The chairman and the company secretary

Governance and the role of the company secretary are examined separately in Chapter 14 but relevant to the current context is the ability of the chairman and company secretary to establish a relationship of mutual trust. In the 2014 report for ICSA, *The Company Secretary – Building Trust through Governance*, it was observed that both chairmen and company secretaries indicated that 'their relationship with each other is critical to the way in which the company secretary ultimately makes a full contribution'. The chairman will need to have confidence in the company secretary and their ability to provide effective support to the chairman and the board and its committees. Four areas in which the chairman and company secretary will routinely work particularly closely are laid out in Table 11.3.

**Table 11.3** The chairman and the company secretary

| | |
|---|---|
| **Procuring the flow of board information** | The Supporting Principles to Code Principle B.5 state that 'under the direction of the chairman' the company secretary is responsible for ensuring good information flows within the board and its committees and between senior management and NEDs. This will include, but is unlikely to be limited purely to, handling the meeting agendas and papers. |
| **Implementing programmes of director training and evaluation** | The same Supporting Principles also refer to the chairman's direction of the company secretary to secure delivery of induction and professional development training for directors. The chairman is responsible for procuring board and director evaluation annually. In practice, the chairman will delegate the detailed delivery of this task to the company secretary. |
| **Managing shareholder general meetings** | More intense scrutiny of the annual report and accounts and greater levels of shareholder activism generally require careful pre-planning of shareholder meetings and the thorough briefing of the chairman. The chairman will rely significantly on the company secretary to manage shareholder meetings effectively. |
| **Advising the board on governance** | The Supporting Principles to Code Principle B.5 state that the company secretary's responsibilities should include advising the board 'through the chairman' on all governance matters. The FRC *Guidance on Board Effectiveness* expects the company secretary and chairman to work together to periodically review governance processes and to consider any improvements or initiatives which could strengthen them. |

In practice, the chairman is likely to work closely with the company secretary in other contexts, including, for example, preparing the agenda, settling the minutes of the board and its committees, agreeing the terms of appointment and remuneration of directors, advising on board procedures and governance matters, including the annual review of the board's effectiveness and assisting in dealings with the company's advisers (particularly the legal advisers). It is not surprising therefore that the FRC *Guidance on Board Effectiveness* also draws attention to the importance of the relationship between the chairman and company secretary.

## The chairman and the SID

In the *Walker Review*, the role of the SID was summed up as:

> 'to provide a sounding board for the chairman, for the evaluation of the chairman and to serve as a trusted intermediary for the NEDs as and when necessary. The SID should be accessible to shareholders in the event that communication with the chairman becomes difficult or inappropriate'.

Code Provision A.4.1 of the UK Corporate Governance Code confirms the need for such an appointment and the nature of the role using similar language to Walker. Table 11.4 summarises the SID's responsibilities under the UK Corporate Governance Code.

In major part, the policy intention behind the UK Corporate Governance Code Provisions is that the SID should ensure that the chairman remains accountable and effective and that he or she should be available at a time of difficulty in relations with shareholders (which itself may well indicate a problem with the chairman's performance). Although this is not stated expressly in the UK Corporate Governance Code, in the event that the chairman had to be removed, it would be the SID's job to lead that process.

**Table 11.4** Responsibilities of the SID

| Code Provision | Responsibility |
|---|---|
| A.4.1 | To provide a sounding board for the chairman and to serve as an intermediary for other directors when necessary. |
| A.4.1 | To be available to shareholders if they have concerns which contact through the normal channels of chairman, chief executive or other executive directors has failed to resolve or for which such contact is inappropriate. |
| A.4.2 | To lead the NEDs to meet without the chairman present at least annually to appraise the chairman's performance and on other occasions as deemed appropriate. |
| B.6.3 | To lead the NEDs when conducting the chairman's performance evaluation. |
| E.1.1 | To attend sufficient meetings with a range of major shareholders in order to develop a balanced understanding of their issues and concerns. |

As noted in the table above, one responsibility of the SID is that of chairing an annual meeting of the non-executives, without the chairman being present, to appraise the chairman's performance (Code Provision A.4.2). This provision, which also requires the SID to chair such meetings if other occasions arise in which it is deemed appropriate, was originally suggested by the *Higgs Report* and has been the subject of some lively debate over the years.

While the specific functions of the SID – supporting and leading the appraisal of the chairman, leading, when appropriate, the other NEDs and being a point of contact for shareholders when normal channels of communication are not deemed effective – may seem somewhat limited, closer consideration of the nature of the SID's role highlights the importance of the responsibilities with which he or she is charged. It is no surprise therefore that having an effective SID is considered to be vital to ensuring an effective board and that the role is addressed in the FRC *Guidance on Board Effectiveness*.

The Guidance considers not only the 'business as usual' functions of a SID, for example supporting the chairman in the delivery of their objectives, leading the annual evaluation of the chairman on behalf of the other directors and taking responsibility for an orderly succession process for the chairman's appointment, but also the heightened role which the SID might play in more difficult circumstances. Boards need to have a clear understanding of the types of occasions when the SID might be expected to 'intervene in order to maintain board and company stability' and the FRC Guidance helpfully provides the following examples:

- there is a dispute between the chairman and chief executive;
- shareholders or NEDs have expressed concerns that are not being addressed by the chairman or chief executive;
- the strategy being followed by the chairman and chief executive is not supported by the entire board;
- the relationship between the chairman and chief executive is particularly close and decisions are being made without the approval of the full board; or
- succession planning is being ignored.

The FRC Guidance emphasises that the SID is expected to work with the chairman and other directors and/or shareholders to resolve such issues, but the use of the word 'intervene' in the guidance makes it clear that the SID must be willing to challenge practices which are causing concern and to take a lead to find a resolution. Addressing and resolving such potentially difficult issues without escalating them will require not only good judgement but also significant people skills, as well as the ability to earn people's trust and respect. The SID will need to be able to carry out their role sensitively, particularly during times of change or stress. Given these descriptions, there is an obvious requirement for there to be a strong working relationship between the chairman and the SID. The SID is often an obvious candidate for the position of deputy chairman.

The role of the SID should be set out in writing.

## The chairman and shareholders

### Chairman's report

Principle A.3 of the UK Corporate Governance Code recognises the important leadership role of the chairman and his or her potential to impact the effectiveness of the board as a whole by setting out in unequivocal terms his responsibility in this regard. Meaningful reporting on the effectiveness of the board is key to the ability of shareholders and other stakeholders to assess the commitment of the board to implement corporate governance measures which best support that effectiveness. The preface to the Code therefore encourages chairmen to report personally within their annual statements in the report and accounts on how the Principles in sections A (on leadership) and B (on board effectiveness) of the Code have been applied.

The intention is clearly to reinforce the Chairman's responsibilities for application of these important governance principles and to ensure that he or she is clearly in the spotlight when it comes to shareholders' assessment of the company's arrangements. Making the requirement one of personal reporting by the chairman rather than collective reporting by the board was hoped to be a catalyst for 'attacking the fungus of "boiler-plate"'. While such tick-box reporting is undoubtedly an easy option, particularly when addressing sensitive issues, it neither properly informs shareholders of the true position nor engenders faith that the chairman and board have thought 'deeply, thoroughly and on a continuing basis' about the board's practices and effectiveness.

The ABI's (now the IA) 2012 *Report on Board Effectiveness: Updating progress, promoting best practice* supported this reporting by the chairman through one of its key recommendations 'that all chairmen should outline in their annual report their role in creating an effective board' but also goes further by recommending that the report by the chairman should also address 'how the board has been set up to respond to the business structure and to any challenges which the company faces'.

Reactions from shareholders and shareholder bodies support the view that investors are more likely to accept explanations when a company does not comply with a Code Provision if faith in the board effectiveness has been established by a history of meaningful reporting. The chairman's reporting has a clear role to play in securing this valuable relationship of trust.

#### *Shareholder dialogue*

In a similar vein, the chairman's remit clearly includes, as a representative of the unitary board and ambassador for the company, acting as a focal point for shareholder dialogue. The Supporting Principle to Principle E.1 recognises that the normal channels of contact between the board and the shareholders are through the chairman, the chief executive and the finance director. The chairman is well positioned to fulfil this role in view of his or her independence from the executive directors. One of the chairman's responsibilities is to ensure 'all directors develop a proper understanding of their major shareholders' issues and concerns' and to 'ensure that the views of shareholders are communicated to the board as a whole' (Code Provision E.1.1). In order to do this he or she should discuss governance and strategy with major shareholders and is specifically required under the Supporting Principles to Code Principle D.2 to ensure the company maintains a dialogue with its principal shareholders about remuneration. Other NEDs may wish to attend meetings with major shareholders in order to keep abreast of those shareholders' views, but the Code encourages boards to use whatever ways are most practical to keep up-to-date with shareholder opinion.

The chief executive and the finance director may be better able than the chairman to discuss the specific concerns of institutional shareholders attending briefings on the announcement of financial results, proposed new share issues, etc. However, while the important roles of the chief executive and finance director in shareholder dialogue are well recognised, the requirement for the chairman to engage with major shareholders and to lead the process by which the board can respond to shareholder concerns remains. Guidance published by ICSA, *Enhancing Stewardship Dialogue,* provides some suggested engagement strategies including informal roundtable discussions and one-to-one meetings with leading shareholders which the chairman might attend to communicate and discuss significant live issues, company strategy, long-term performance, risk appetite, governance arrangements and ESG matters. This type of engagement would be consistent with guidance in Principle 3 of the UK Stewardship Code which encourages shareholders to monitor investee companies. The guidance advocates that such monitoring should include meeting the investee company's chairman.

There will also be a role to play for the chairman of a company in any collective approach by the company's leading shareholders. A collective approach might perhaps be made where the shareholders have non-routine concerns they wish to raise. These could arise when the executive directors are subject to a conflict of interest on a matter affecting shareholder interests, for example on the proposed adoption of new executive share incentive arrangements. They may also arise when shareholder activism has placed the board's performance under scrutiny by shareholders. In such cases, the chairman may well face a situation of 'crisis management' and he or she will have a vital role as leader of the board to ensure that the shareholder concerns are addressed, while at the same time maintaining the unity and effectiveness of the board. Taking the advice of the company's professional advisers is likely to be a priority for the chairman in such circumstances.

### AGM

Finally, the chairman will have a key role to play in the company's principal shareholder meeting, its AGM. With greater institutional shareholder activism, the AGM can present the chairman with very significant challenges. These are examined in more detail in Chapter 14, in the context of the role of the company secretary and Chapter 5 on shareholder activism and IR.

## Governance checklist

✓ Does the chairman have the necessary personal attributes to create the right conditions for the board and individual directors to be effective? Does he or she have the capacity to lead and exercise influence while maintaining trust and balance on the board?

✓ Is the chairman clear about their role and familiar with their responsibilities for providing ethical leadership, optimising board decision making and ongoing development of governance processes?

✓ Does the process for selecting and appointing a new chairman meet the best practice requirements and are their terms of appointment clearly described?

✓ Does the chairman set the board agenda and chair meetings effectively?

✓ Do the chairman and the chief executive work well together, acting as 'trusted partners' with a mutual respect for each other's roles without overlap?

✓ Is the company secretary available to the chairman and do they work together to ensure the board has the support and resources it needs, including high-quality information, access to external advice, successful induction and development programmes and effective annual evaluation?

✓ Has a SID been appointed with an appropriately defined role and with the necessary experience and attributes to deal effectively with potentially difficult circumstances?

✓ Does the chairman support engagement with shareholders effectively, acting as an ambassador for the company and taking part in a range of dialogue opportunities – including the AGM – and is the board well briefed on shareholder views?

✓ Does the chairman report personally in the report and accounts how the principles relating to the role and effectiveness of the board (in Sections A and B of the UK Corporate Governance Code) have been applied?

# 12

# Executive directors

## The role of executive directors

As discussed in Chapter 3, within a unitary board structure, executive directors have the same duties as NEDs. These duties extend across the organisation as a whole and are restricted to neither a particular part of the business nor area of responsibility encompassed within their individual executive role. This important principle is emphasised in the FRC *Guidance on Board Effectiveness*. The Guidance also cautions executive directors against perceiving themselves, when they are carrying out their duties as a director of the company, as acting only as part of the chief executive's team. It is essential that executive directors understand their company-wide role and are able to distinguish between situations where they are engaged on board business and are required to act as a director versus situations where they are performing executive functions.

The chairman, as part of his or her responsibility for ensuring there are adequate induction and development processes in place, should make certain that each executive director understands this principle clearly. The FRC Guidance suggests that it may be useful for an executive director to take up a non-executive position in order to help broaden their understanding of the wider board responsibilities.

It is natural for executive directors to possess much greater depth of knowledge about an organisation and its operations. They will be responsible for developing proposals to present to the board, particularly on strategic issues. This detailed knowledge can benefit from challenge at an appropriate stage by the non-executives who, by the very nature of their role, may be able to bring the fresh perspective that those who have not been closely involved in the issue have. Executive directors should understand the valuable nature of the challenge non-executive board members provide and welcome the ability of non-executives to question proposals brought by the executive team to the board using the knowledge they have gained from their wider experience outside of the company.

### Chief executive

The chief executive holds the most senior executive office and has key responsibilities which may directly impact the effectiveness of the board as a whole. Those responsibilities will be set out in writing and agreed by the board as a whole. In particular the chief executive has a responsibility to support the chairman and their relationship will be extremely important. This point, including the need to clearly separate their respective responsibilities, is covered in detail in Chapter 11.

The chief executive will be responsible for presenting proposed strategies to the board. By virtue of his or her responsibilities, seniority amongst the executive directors and a unique relationship with the chairman, the chief executive will be able to exercise an enormous amount of control over the flow of information to the board. The adverse impact that a dominant personality in the chief executive's role could have on board effectiveness is self-explanatory.

In order for good decision making to be facilitated within the board, it is therefore important that the chief executive encourages a balanced presentation of information, analysis and views to the board and that non-executive challenge and debate is welcomed. To aid this process, the chief executive should ensure that the opinions of the executive team, including any divergence of those opinions, are explained to the board. There may also be occasions when the views of employees are relevant to the issue under consideration and the chief executive should ensure that the board is adequately briefed on these when appropriate. Regardless of the source or nature of the information provided to the boards, the chief executive should check that it is of sufficiently high quality and is readily available to the board to support its deliberations.

The chief executive will also have responsibility for the flow of information out of the boardroom into the wider organisation and for overseeing that the company's strategy and values, once agreed, are implemented and delivered. The FRC *Guidance on Board Effectiveness* makes it clear that the chief executive has 'primary responsibility for setting an example to the company's employees and communicating to them the expectations of the board in relation to the company's culture, values and behaviours'. He or she will need to be supported by the whole executive team in this to ensure that good standards of governance are maintained throughout the organisation but this will not detract from the chief executive's role as the person expected to lead this effort. In the FRC report *Corporate Culture and the Role of Boards* it was noted that the chief executive in particular 'must embody the desired culture, embedding this at all levels and in every aspect of the business'. The corporate culture is about how the company is run but should also be a key output against which the chief executive's success is measured.

### Finance director

The finance director (often called the chief financial officer) will have primary responsibility for delivering information to the board on the company's financial position. In recent years, the general trend has been one of decreasing numbers of executive directors and the finance director may therefore be the only executive director other than the chief executive. His or her contribution is therefore of significant importance to the overall effectiveness of the board.

A joint report by the Association of Chartered Certified Accountants and the Institute of Management Accounts, called *Future Pathways to Financial Leadership*, surveyed the top management skills required by a finance director. Leadership skills were identified as the most important, followed by communication, strategic thinking and change management.

The finance director is likely to lead some of the most prominent internal functions within the company and will be closely involved in preparing many of the reports that are provided to the board. The finance director will be instrumental in proposing, and subsequently reporting progress against, key objectives and targets including, of course, the budget. Accordingly, he or she will have significant scope to influence the implementation of corporate values and culture in any proposals and to provide assurance on the extent to which they are delivered in practice.

## Directors' remuneration and corporate governance

With obvious relevance to achieving good corporate governance, issues of remuneration and reward are naturally addressed in the UK Corporate Governance Code. Code Principle D.1 provides the following guidance:

> 'Executive directors' remuneration should be designed to promote the long-term success of the Company. Performance-related elements should be transparent, stretching and rigorously applied.'

Executive pay continues to hold centre stage in the corporate governance debate. In part, this is because it is by nature a headline-grabbing subject which offers significant scope for lively political debate. Increases in executive pay which outstrip increases in average earnings and/or the returns enjoyed by investors are obvious sources of controversy. The upward pay curve and generous incentive schemes enjoyed by directors and senior executives in recent years have attracted a higher level of scrutiny and, increasingly, overt criticism and a lack of support from shareholders. The perspectives and responses of institutional investors, the Government and the wider international community on issues of remuneration and compensation, which have been shaped by the global banking failures, are examined below.

## Shareholder perspectives

It is recognised that shareholders have a legitimate interest in influencing the structure of executive pay. There are three main reasons for this. Firstly, when remuneration is delivered in the form of share-based incentives, it is frequently dilutive of shareholders' equity interests and therefore potentially destructive of shareholder value. Secondly, shareholders want to mitigate the conflict of interest that arises within boards where directors determine their own remuneration. Thirdly, shareholders want to see that remuneration policies are clearly aligned with company strategy to promote value creation and do not encourage any form of behaviour that is contrary to the company's interests.

Active engagement with the boards of investee companies on directors' remuneration is viewed as a mark of responsible share ownership and shareholders have in recent years demonstrated an increased readiness to challenge boards by resisting 'excessive' executive pay packages or the payment of compensation which is a 'reward for failure'. Since the so-called 'shareholder spring' of 2012, institutional shareholders have been more willing to take a tough line against compensation packages that they view as being unwarranted. In this regard, shareholders have been able to take advantage of the new voting powers on remuneration that came into force in October 2013. The details of those powers (and the need to consult with shareholders on remuneration issues) are dealt with in greater detail in Chapter 8.

## Government perspectives

The consensus view is that the structure of executive pay is for shareholders to decide. As a result, the Government's regulatory intervention has traditionally been limited to bringing forward measures to increase the level of transparency and public disclosure and to facilitate the responsible exercise of votes on pay issues. However, in the wake of the financial crisis in 2008/9, there was considerable focus on the link between the payment of large city bonuses and risk taking. Regulation of pay in financial institutions became inevitable. Financial institutions are now subject to Remuneration Codes introduced and policed by the Prudential Regulatory Authority and the FCA. Different codes apply to financial institutions, in different regulatory levels based on their size with large banks subject to the most restrictive provisions, including a bonus cap. Others, such as private equity and asset managers, are subject to regimes which more accurately reflect their business activities and appetite for risk-taking.

The underlying aim is to ensure that firms subject to the Codes 'have risk-focused remuneration policies, which are consistent with and promote effective risk management and do not expose them to excessive risk'.

Looking back, the steps taken after the global banking crisis to more closely regulate executive pay signalled a new willingness on the part of the

Government to intervene through legislation in matters previously regulated primarily through voluntary codes and best practice guidance.

More recently the Government issued a Green Paper on *Corporate Governance Reform* in November 2016, inviting views on possible further reforms of the corporate governance regime which includes provisions relating to executive pay. Examples of proposals made include the introduction of an annual binding vote on pay and disclosure of pay ratios.

## International perspectives

Concerns over remuneration policies have not been limited to the UK.

Since 2004, the EC has adopted a number of Recommendations on directors' remuneration. Most recently, in 2014, the EC adopted measures to strengthen shareholder engagement and introduced a 'say on pay' for Europe's largest companies. The measures require clearer disclosure on companies' remuneration policies and how these are put in practice, with an explanation of the links to the long-term interests and sustainability of the company.

On the wider international stage, the Financial Stability Board (FSB), established in the wake of the worldwide financial crisis to develop and implement strong global regulatory, supervisory and other policies in the interest of financial stability, issued the FSB *Principles for Sound Compensation Practice* in April 2009. The FSB Principles were followed up, with a set of Implementation Standards at the request of the G20. Since then the FSB has issued regular progress reports on the implementation of compensation practices, the most recent in November 2015. While the FSB Principles are aimed solely at major financial institutions, a company in another sector may also consider some elements of the principles as relevant to its own remuneration policies. In summary, the FSB Principles require:

- effective governance of compensation by the board committee which is responsible for actively overseeing the compensation system's design and implementation and for monitoring and reviewing compensation, to ensure it operates as intended. Financial and risk control staff must be independent, have appropriate authority and be compensated independently of the business areas which they oversee;
- effective alignment of compensation with prudent risk-taking, with compensation adjusted for different types of risk and payments which are reflective of risk outcomes and sensitive to the time horizons of risks. The mix of cash, equity and other forms of compensation must be consistent with risk alignment and the board must be prepared to explain the rationale for the mix chosen; and
- effective supervisory oversight and engagement by stakeholders, with rigorous and sustained reviews of compensation practices, and prompt action to

address deficiencies and constructive engagement facilitated through clear, comprehensive and timely information on compensation practices.

In the USA, the Dodd-Frank Act contains pay disclosure requirements, independence requirements for compensation committees, non-binding 'say on pay' voting rights and, from 2017, disclosure of the ratio of the compensation of the chief executive to the median compensation of employees.

The direction of travel both at home and further afield is clear. As is often the case with high-profile governance issues, while the origin of the concerns may be restricted to one sector, the implications are often felt elsewhere. The remuneration committee has been uniquely in the eye of this particular storm.

## The remuneration committee

UK Corporate Governance Code Principle D.2 states that:

> 'There should be a formal and transparent procedure for developing policy on executive remuneration and for fixing the remuneration packages of individual directors. No director should be involved in deciding his or her own remuneration.'

The board will discharge this obligation by setting up a remuneration committee which, in accordance with Code Provision D.2.1, will comprise at least three members, or in the case of smaller companies (i.e. those below the FTSE 350 throughout the year immediately prior to the reporting year), two members, who should all be independent NEDs. If the chairman was considered independent on appointment, he or she may be appointed as an additional member of, but may not chair, the remuneration committee.

The IA Principles of Remuneration (the 'IA Principles') last reissued in 2016 are widely perceived to set the industry standard on shareholder requirements relating to remuneration. The IA Principles supplement the requirements of the UK Corporate Governance Code by stating that NEDs should have at least one year's experience before becoming chair of the remuneration committee. The corporate governance guidelines issued by major institutional investors also support, in the main, the principle that listed companies should appoint remuneration committees comprised of independent NEDs to determine the remuneration packages of executives.

### Procedures, resources and relationship with the board

The increasing scrutiny of the remuneration committee's role and competence has brought about a commensurate increase in the expectation that its procedures are proper and that it operates in a fully independent manner. While there is no prescribed recommendation as to the frequency of its meetings, the committee will be required to meet several times each year to fulfil its responsibilities. Details of the number of meetings held and the individual attendance of directors should be disclosed in the annual report under the Code. At least one meeting to approve the contents of the remuneration report for the annual report and accounts will certainly be required. Other meetings will be necessary on a regular basis to address issues such as the setting and reviewing of executive directors' salaries, pensions and benefits and approving new share and/or annual bonus awards and setting appropriate performance targets. The remuneration committee will inevitably have to meet more frequently when they are undertaking a review of the company's remuneration policy which may involve the adoption of new share incentive plans. For the committee of a global company, there will also be complex issues relating to international pay structures.

Non-members will routinely be invited to attend the remuneration committee's meetings, depending on the business to be transacted. It is to be expected that the chief executive and/or (if not already a member) the chairman will attend regularly to assist in the committee's consideration of the remuneration of other executive directors. Under the Supporting Principles to Code Principle D.2, the committee should 'take care to recognise and manage conflicts of interest when receiving views from executive directors or senior management, or consulting the chief executive about its proposals.'

As for all committees, the remuneration committee should be provided with 'sufficient resources' to undertake its duties (Code Provision B.5.1). Such resources will include the company secretary, who is responsible for good information flows within the board and its committees or another representative from the company's secretariat. The HR function may also attend depending on the size of the company either regularly or periodically to support the work of the committee.

In order to determine policy on remuneration and to navigate a path through the regulatory and tax complexities of the various components of executive remuneration packages, the committee will routinely need access to specialist advice including that of remuneration consultants, lawyers and accountants. Where remuneration consultants are engaged, they must be identified in the annual report and a statement made as to whether they have any other connection with the company (Code Provision D.2.1). The potential for conflicts arising from other connections with the company is clear.

The Remuneration Consultants Group (RCG) established a Code of Conduct for remuneration consultants in 2009, as recommended in the *Walker Report*. The RCG Code of Conduct aims to set out the role of remuneration consultants and the professional standards by which they advise remuneration committees. It is reviewed every two years and was last updated in December 2015. Companies are encouraged to disclose whether any remuneration consultants they have used are RCG members.

The FRC *Guidance on Board Effectiveness* contains a clear reminder that, as with other board committees, the remuneration committee will act under delegated authority from the board and will be accountable to it for its actions. The board must be clear that it retains ultimate responsibility for remuneration issues and sufficient time must therefore be given to the remuneration committee to report to the board, with all directors and the company secretary receiving copies of its minutes unless it would be inappropriate to do so, and to allow discussion at board level. The committee's functioning in this manner should not create any fissures within the unitary board structure, however, the committee should ensure that it is not only independent under the UK Corporate Governance Code requirements, but is also seen to be independent. Its members will need to exhibit the full range of requisite non-executive behaviours, such as independence, sound judgement, integrity and willingness to challenge and probe. Given the increasing burden of work for the committee, it has become standard practice for additional fees to be paid to its members and over the last few years there has been a significant increase in the level of fees for remuneration committee chairmen.

## Role and responsibilities of the remuneration committee

It is the responsibility of the remuneration committee to develop the company's policy on executive remuneration and for fixing the remuneration packages of the executive directors (Code Principle D.2). It also recommends and monitors the level and structure of remuneration for 'senior management' (Code Provision D.2.2). The board decides what is meant by 'senior management' but as a minimum it should normally include the first layer of management below the main board level. Figure 12.1 illustrates the remuneration committee's role and responsibilities.

Code Provision D.2.1, states that the remuneration committee should 'make available its terms of reference, explaining its role and the authority delegated to it by the board' (see below). Specimen terms of reference are available from the ICSA website (www.icsaglobal.org.uk). These should be tailored to the specific circumstances of the company. For example, financial institutions which are regulated by the Prudential Regulation Authority (PRA) or FCA will wish their remuneration committee's terms of reference to reflect the wider responsibilities expected of remuneration committees of such firms. Terms of reference should be reviewed periodically.

The FRC *Guidance on Board Effectiveness* recommends that as well as regularly reviewing the committee's remit, the remuneration committee's processes for interaction with the board and other committees, for example the nomination committee, are also reviewed.

**Figure 12.1** Role and responsibilities of the remuneration committee

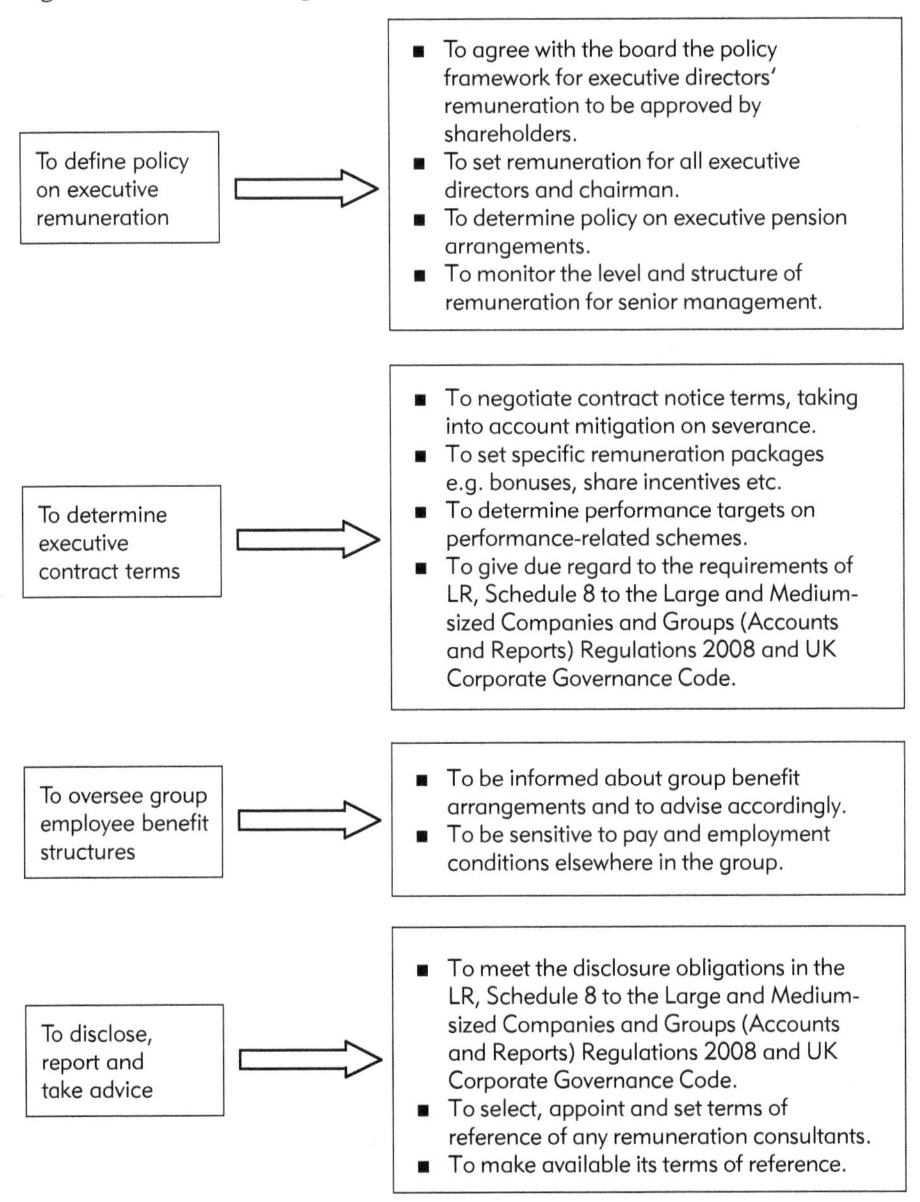


The fees payable to NEDs will be set by the board itself or, where required by the articles of association, by the shareholders (Code Provision D.2.3). Where permitted by the articles, this responsibility may be delegated to a committee, which may include the chief executive. Limits on non-executive fees are normally specified within the articles of association.

## Determining the directors' remuneration policy

The remuneration committee is tasked with determining a policy on executive directors' remuneration which, since October 2013, must be approved by shareholders. It is worth noting that a quoted company may only pay its directors as permitted by its remuneration policy. Where a company remunerates a director outside of the approved policy, directors could find themselves personally liable. The potential ramifications are therefore very significant and the remuneration committee will need to formulate the policy with care. As a starting point, the IA Principles (2016) highlight four areas to be addressed:

1. the remuneration policy should be set to promote value creation through transparent alignment with the agreed corporate strategy;
2. the remuneration policy should support performance, encourage the underlying sustainable financial health of the business and promote sound risk management for the success of the company and to the benefit of its stakeholders;
3. the NEDs, particularly those on the remuneration committee, should oversee executive remuneration. The board should ensure that the chairman and the whole board are appropriately engaged in the remuneration setting process;
4. a remuneration committee needs to exercise independent judgement and not be over reliant on their remuneration consultants. Non-executive directors should generally serve on the remuneration committee for at least a year before starting to chair the committee and should have sufficient skill and experience to manage the remuneration setting process.

Decisions relating to individual executives must be taken within the limits of the remuneration policy approved by shareholders.

Code Principle D.1 stipulates that 'executive directors' remuneration should be designed to promote the long-term success of the company'. This sentiment is echoed in the IA Guidelines which state that remuneration should be structured 'to promote value creation' and by the PLSA Guidelines that remuneration policy should be 'driving long-term strategic success'. These statements more closely reflect the statutory duty imposed on directors by the CA 2006, to 'promote the success of the company for the benefit of its members.'

The NAPF (now the PLSA) in conjunction with Hermes EDS, BT Pension Scheme, RPMI Railpen and USS Investment Management published in 2013 *Remuneration principles for building and reinforcing long-term business success*. These set out four overarching principles:

1. management should make a material long-term investment in shares of the business they manage;
2. pay should be aligned to long-term success and the desired corporate culture throughout the organisation;
3. pay schemes should be simple, understandable for both investors and executives and ensure that rewards reflect long-term returns to shareholders;
4. remuneration committees should fully explain and justify how their decisions operate to deliver long-term business success.

A company's remuneration policy should be clearly linked to the company's strategy and objectives and performance targets should be aligned with the company's strategy. Code Principle D.2 provides that 'performance-related elements should be transparent, stretching and rigorously applied'. This is particularly relevant in relation to incentive awards which are explored in more detail later in this chapter.

The UK Corporate Governance Code recognises that the remuneration committee will need to have regard to pay comparisons and market forces in establishing its remuneration policy, but advises the committee to 'use such comparisons with caution, in view of the risk of an upward ratchet of remuneration levels with no corresponding improvement in corporate and individual performance'. The PLSA Guidelines do not endorse over frequent re-benchmarking as that may result in the ratcheting up of remuneration. In a similar vein, the IA Principles do not support annual pay increases in excess of inflation or those awarded to the rest of the workforce.

### Process to formulate the remuneration policy

Since the changes which came into effect in 2013 under the CA 2006, the emphasis, and indeed requirement, is for quoted companies to develop a forward-looking remuneration policy. Provided the policy remains unchanged it is only necessary to obtain shareholder approval for it every three years. When formulating the company's policy, there is an expectation that the policy will be able to 'stand the test of time' (PLSA Guidelines).

Code Principle D.2 requires the remuneration committee to adopt 'a formal and transparent procedure for developing policy on executive remuneration' and that process is examined next.

Table 12.1 sets out a suggested process for how the remuneration committee should go about formulating the policy.

The remuneration committee must take into account the provisions in the UK Corporate Governance Code on the design and structure of executive pay as well as the guidelines issued by the IA, PLSA and other institutional investors. Crucially, with increased public interest in executive pay, the remuneration committee should be mindful of the reaction not only of shareholders but also of the public if its proposals are seen as potentially delivering

**Table 12.1** Formulation of a remuneration policy

| Step 1: | **Due diligence on current practice** |
|---|---|
| | The committee should be fully conversant with both the content and recent development of the existing remuneration packages for senior management. This is an essential due diligence exercise. |
| **Step 2:** | **Consult internally** |
| | It should then consult with the main internal parties, including the chief executive (and where appropriate the finance director) and the HR director. If the policy is to promote the long-term success of the company, it must be aligned with the company's business strategy. |
| **Step 3:** | **Appoint remuneration advisers** |
| | To ensure its independence and to ensure that its decisions take account of market and best practice, the committee should appoint its own remuneration advisers. These will be able to provide the essential remuneration data, e.g. executive pay surveys, although benchmarks should be used infrequently and should be only one element informing the review. Advisers will also act as a sounding board for the committee's own views. In appointing such advisers, consideration needs to be given to any conflicts of interest. The RCG Code of Conduct is relevant here. |
| **Step 4:** | **Consult with shareholders** |
| | There is an expectation that the head of the remuneration committee will consult with major shareholders before material changes are implemented. This should focus on the major strategic remuneration issues rather than minor pay details and be used as a means of understanding the views of shareholders (IA Principles). |
| **Step 5:** | **Undertake regular review of policy** |
| | The policy should be kept under regular review, notwithstanding the three-year rule. It is possible to seek earlier shareholder approval of amended policies should the committee believe it necessary to do so although investors expect the policy to apply over a three-year period. |

excessive amounts and/or are not linked to the performance and success of the company.

## Executive director remuneration packages

The remuneration committee is primarily responsible for the design and make-up of executive directors' packages. The package must be permitted under the policy approved by shareholders. Remuneration paid to directors is also the subject of an annual advisory vote of shareholders.

For a number of years, simplicity around remuneration structures has been advocated and 'complexity is discouraged' (IA Principles). In recent years, it has become less common for companies to operate multiple executive incentive plans, and typically, there is now only one long-term incentive plan and one annual bonus plan.

The IA's Executive Remuneration Working Group, which issued its final report in July 2016, stressed the growing concern from both companies and shareholders with the current levels of executive pay and complexity. In response to this, the most recent IA Principles (2016) have recast their guidelines.

The IA encourages remuneration committees to 'select a remuneration structure which is appropriate for the specific business, and efficient and cost-effective in delivering its longer-term strategy'. Remuneration committees are also urged to adopt 'the structure which is most appropriate for the implementation of their business strategy'.

The IA is moving away from the notion that the long-term incentive plan is the most appropriate share incentive arrangement within listed companies. As a result, in future, a company will have much more flexibility in designing its remuneration components and a remuneration policy which supports its business strategy and provides alignment of executive reward with the interests of stakeholders. That said, it is likely that a traditional long-term incentive plan will continue to be widely used.

## Pay components

An executive director's remuneration will typically be made up of three elements:

- Basic pay
- Annual cash bonus
- Long-term incentive.

## Basic pay

There continues to be a focus on getting the quantum of basic salary right. The importance of doing this is because firstly basic salary is intended to be the primary reward for the role and responsibility undertaken. Paying basic salaries at too high a level is contrary to Code Principle D.1 which requires companies to 'avoid paying more than is necessary'. Secondly, the value of other benefits such as annual bonus and LTIP grants, which are predicated on basic salary, are inflated.

In the past, basic salaries have frequently been determined by reference to the 'median' pay established in a peer benchmarking exercise. The continual chasing of median pay has resulted in a ratchet effect. Shareholders are alive to this and the level of pay should be capable of being justified and be commensurate with the executive's duties.

Taking a sensitive approach to pay and employment conditions elsewhere in the group, in particular when agreeing annual pay rises, is advocated as a Supporting Principle to Code Principle D.1. The widening pay differentials between directors' pay and that of other employees has been focused on by the media and by the Government. The PLSA Guidelines note that such differentials are 'often difficult credibly to justify and boards should be mindful of the possible negative impact on corporate culture and staff morale'.

## Annual bonuses

The IA Principles recognise that annual bonuses incentivise performance but add the caveat that they should 'reward achievement in line with the agreed corporate strategy'. This means that bonuses should not be paid unless they are to reward a contribution in excess of that which can be expected by virtue of already having received a salary. In order to measure the level of contribution made, performance objectives linked to business targets should be defined, ideally by reference to the KPIs, both financial and non-financial. Where performance targets are not linked to the reported KPIs, shareholders will expect the other measures chosen to be properly explained and justified. Where commercial sensitivities may limit or prevent full disclosure of the targets at the start of the performance year, investors still expect to have sufficient detail of the 'main performance parameters, both corporate and personal' for the financial year being reported on.

Following payment of the bonus, companies should provide a full analysis in their remuneration reports. The IA expects bonus targets to be disclosed no later than two years following the payment of any bonus award, and, preferably, within one year. Disclosure of maximum participation levels also need to be made.

To facilitate adjustment of the levels of bonuses actually awarded within a bonus plan, a level of discretion should be incorporated into the plan design. Discretion should be retained to ensure that a payment that is inappropriate in all the company's circumstances is not made. Shareholders do not support the payment of annual bonuses to executive directors where the business has suffered an exceptional negative event, even if some of the targets have been met (IA Principles).

Some annual bonus plans include a requirement for a proportion of any cash bonus to be deferred and paid in shares. The intention is to create a further linkage with long-term performance. This is now expected by the IA, which views deferral as creating a greater alignment with shareholders, especially if there is no long-term incentive. In deciding on whether such a requirement is appropriate, the remuneration committee will want to take account of the company's other long-term incentive arrangements. Share incentive plans are considered next.

### Share incentive plans

There is a wide variety of plans. While the IA has recently endorsed greater flexibility in the design of incentive plans, it seems likely that most companies will choose from the present menu of plans. As mentioned earlier, there is a lack of support for companies adopting multiple share incentive plans. The principal exception is where companies operate all employee tax-advantaged share plans in addition to plans designed for executive directors and senior management. The following analysis does not cover arrangements designed to encourage widespread employee ownership which are more commonly found in private companies. Table 12.2 summarises briefly the key features of the main share incentive plans currently used by companies.

**Table 12.2** Types of share incentive scheme

| **1. All employee plans** | |
|---|---|
| **Share incentive plan** | A tax-advantaged plan under which participants can receive free shares for no cost (£3,600 p.a. limit), partnership shares paid for out of pre-tax salary (£1,800 p.a. limit) plus matching shares for no cost (up to two for each partnership share). Dividends used to buy additional shares are tax free if the shares purchased in this way are retained for 3 years. No income tax and national insurance charge arises on the share value subject to retaining shares in the plan for at least 5 years and no capital gains tax is payable on shares which are held in the plan until disposal. The plan is operated by a trustee and normally an external administrator is appointed. |
| **Sharesave scheme** | A tax-advantaged option plan under which the option granted to a participant is linked to an approved savings contract operated by a savings institution. Maximum saving is £500 per month. The option period is 3 or 5 years with no performance targets.<br>Subject to the option being held for at least 3 years, no income tax or national insurance is payable on exercise although any gain made on sale of the shares acquired is subject to capital gains tax. If the shares are, within a specified period of being acquired, transferred into an ISA or pension scheme, any gain will be exempt. |

**Table 12.2** *continued*

| **2. Executive plans** | |
|---|---|
| **Tax-advantaged share option plan** | There are two types: a company share option plan (CSOP) and an enterprise management incentive (EMI). Typically, performance targets are imposed.<br>Under a CSOP, participants are granted options with an exercise price equal to the market value of a share at the date granted, with a £30,000 cap on the value of shares under option. No income tax or national insurance is payable on exercise but any gain made on sale of the shares acquired is subject to capital gains tax.<br>Under an EMI, eligible employees can be granted options over shares with a value of up to £250,000. At exercise, the gain is not subject to income tax and national insurance provided the exercise price was at least the market value of a share at the date of grant. Any gain made on sale of the shares acquired will be subject to capital gains tax. Limitations apply, amongst other things, to the company's assets, which must not exceed £30 million, meaning that EMIs are only suited to smaller businesses. |
| **Non-tax advantaged unapproved share option plan** | Similar type of plan to the tax-advantaged share option plan, save that all option gains will be subject to income tax and national insurance at exercise. Greater flexibility in design is possible although typically such plans will have similar features to tax-advantaged plans. |
| **Deferred or share bonus plan** | A non-tax advantaged plan. These involve the participants deferring all or a portion of a cash bonus in return for an award of shares which are released after a defined holding period. Income tax and national insurance will arise on all gains. |
| **Performance share plan** | A plan alternatively described as a long-term incentive plan. These involve the grant of a nil cost award over shares, pursuant to which shares are released to participants at the end of a specified period provided performance targets set are achieved. Often shares to satisfy the awards will be held in an employee trust. Income tax and national insurance will arise on all gains. |

When considering introducing new share plans the remuneration committee should start a dialogue with investors at an early stage, bring the design of the share incentives within best practice and be ready to provide convincing explanations to shareholders about why new share incentive arrangements are constructed as they are. Best practice in this context is set out in both the UK Corporate Governance Code and the guidelines published by institutional shareholders (or their representative bodies, such as the IA or the PLSA) and is explored below.

## Share incentives: the UK Corporate Governance Code

The UK Corporate Governance Code affirms the general principle that performance-related elements of executive directors' remuneration (which executive share incentives invariably will be) should be transparent, stretching and rigorously applied. Code Provision D.1.1 requires the design of performance-related remuneration for executive directors to follow the provisions of Schedule A to the Code, the main provisions of which with respect to share incentives are set out below. Code Provision D.1.1 also requires provisions to be included that enable a company to recover sums paid or withhold the payment of any sum, and specify the circumstances in which it would be appropriate to do so.

- Traditional share option schemes should be weighed against other kinds of long-term incentive scheme and executive share options should not be offered at a discount other than as permitted by the LR.
- In normal circumstances, the right to exercise options and other rights should not vest in less than three years from grant. Subject to the need to finance acquisition costs or associated tax liabilities, directors should be encouraged to hold their shares for a further period after vesting/exercise, including for a period after leaving the company.
- New schemes should be approved by shareholders and preferably replace existing schemes or at least 'form part of a well-considered overall plan, incorporating existing schemes'.
- The total rewards potentially available 'should not be excessive' (but note that no specific participation limits are mentioned).
- Performance conditions including non-financial metrics, where appropriate should be relevant, stretching and designed to promote the long-term success of the company.
- Remuneration incentives should be compatible with risk policies and systems.
- Grants/awards under CSOPs or Long-Term Incentive Plans (LTIPs) should normally be phased, rather than awarded in one large block.

The provisions in LR 9.4.1R require prior shareholder approval to be obtained for any employees' share scheme involving the issue of new shares or the transfer of treasury shares and for any long-term incentive scheme in which one or more directors of the listed company is eligible to participate, unless the grants are made under a scheme where participation is offered on similar terms to all employees.

By LR 13.8.11, the notice to shareholders containing the resolution seeking approval for an employees' share scheme or long-term incentive scheme must include the full text of the scheme or a summary of its principal terms.

## Share incentives: IA and PLSA guidance

Remuneration committees must take account of what shareholders consider to be best practice for share incentives. Section C of the IA Principles covers shareholder expectations relating to variable remuneration including share incentive schemes. The main provisions of Section C insofar as it relates to share plans may be summarised as follows:

- simplicity in remuneration packages is preferred by investors and remuneration committees are encouraged to adopt the structure which is most appropriate for the implementation of their business strategy. No particular remuneration structure is prescribed or recommended;
- executive directors and senior executives are expected to build up a high level of personal shareholding in the companies for which they work and those shareholdings should be retained for a period after they leave;
- performance periods should be clearly linked to the timing of business strategy implementation, which should be no less than three years, and to the achievement of appropriately challenging financial performance which will enhance shareholder value. Shareholders would generally prefer performance periods to be longer than three years and the use of additional holding periods is now expected so that in total, the performance and holding periods span at least five years;
- sliding scales and graduated vesting profiles are considered a useful way of ensuring that performance conditions are genuinely challenging and full vesting should reflect exceptional performance. Retesting of performance conditions is not acceptable;
- new share-based incentives and/or any substantive changes to existing schemes should be subject to approval by shareholders by means of separate and binding resolutions. In particular any change in quantum should be fully explained and justified;
- where a substantial fall in share price could result in a windfall share or option grant expressed as a percentage of salary, some scaling back of grants to take account of this should be implemented;
- provisions should be included to allow for performance adjustment (malus) and/or clawback in specified circumstances which should be clearly disclosed;
- share incentive schemes should not lead to dilution of capital in excess of the limits acceptable to shareholders (essentially an all employee scheme limit of 10% share capital in a rolling ten-year period and an executive scheme limit of 5% the same period);

- executive share options should not be granted at a discount to the market price at the time of grant; and
- NEDs are encouraged to own shares in the company and may receive part of their fees in shares. Shareholders consider it inappropriate for chairmen and independent directors to receive incentive awards geared to the share price or corporate performance.

Where the IA has particular concerns over certain issues, it has written to remuneration committee chairman highlighting these. In October 2016, an open letter was sent to explain the change of focus in the (2016) IA Principles, following the report from the Executive Remuneration Working Group and to re-emphasise their thinking on levels of remuneration, bonus disclosure, policy renewals and use of discretion.

The PLSA publishes its own Corporate Governance Policy and Voting Guidelines, reflecting best market practice after consultation with its members. The PLSA supports the UK Corporate Governance Code and believes that remuneration policies should be closely aligned with the shareholder interests and drive long-term strategic success.

### Share incentives: institutional shareholder statements

The IA Principles and the PLSA Corporate Governance Policy and Voting Guidelines are now supplemented by statements on executive remuneration published by the governance teams of larger institutional shareholders. Remuneration committees must be mindful of the expectations of its major shareholders and the importance of regular dialogue and shareholder consultation cannot be overstated.

### Share incentives: performance targets

A particular point of evolving practice is with respect to performance targets. While for many years, performance targets were based upon increases in the company's earnings per share (EPS) or total shareholder return (TSR) over the performance period, the IA Principles recognise that the widely differing nature of business models and industry characteristics means that the appropriate performance targets for different companies may vary significantly. Appropriate performance targets should be set in the light of the specific business characteristics of the group. These should fully reflect the performance of the business as a whole and should be applied consistently. Performance targets have become more tailored to the business strategy and measures such as Return on Capital Employed (ROCE) are frequently used.

Both financial and 'non-financial' metrics may be used. What those non-financial metrics are likely to be will vary from company to company and sector to sector. They could, for example, include CSR targets, like for like sales or be linked to health and safety standards. In such cases the link to strategy and method of performance measurement should be clearly explained and, where appropriate, account should be taken of the IA Guidelines on Responsible Investment Disclosures.

## Share incentives: accounting treatment under FRS 102/IFRS 2

While there is not space here to examine in depth the applicable share-based payment accounting standards, the remuneration committee should be aware of their broad impact.

The accounting standards require all equity-based instruments, which include options and LTIP awards or equivalent share incentive rights, to be valued by reference to their fair value at the date of grant. For share-based awards, fair value is measured according to the market value of the shares at grant. For options, fair value is measured using an option pricing model which determines the fair value according to set assumptions, including the expected share price volatility. When determining the fair value at grant, vesting and performance conditions may need to be taken into account. The resulting expense (i.e. the value) is then spread over the relevant vesting period. The FRS also imposes various disclosure requirements aimed at enabling users of the company's financial statements to understand the nature and extent of share-based payments and the effect they have on the financial statements as well as the methodologies used in arriving at the relevant figures.

## Share incentives: design features

The remuneration committee will need to address the key design features of executive (and most other) share incentive schemes. Table 12.3 describes such design features, together, where relevant, with pointers as to the position set out in the IA Principles.

**Table 12.3** Share incentive schemes – IA Principles

| Design feature | Comment |
|---|---|
| **Legal structure of grants/awards** | Table 12.2 outlines the main types of executive plan. Plans can be designed to provide either a conventional market price option, or alternatively a nil cost option (or equivalent) where the full value of the share is awarded. Also, shares can be delivered by the company through new share issues, the transfer of shares out of treasury or out of an employee trust. The committee needs to determine such structural aspects with its advisers. |

**Table 12.3** *continued*

| Design feature | Comment |
|---|---|
| **Administration and decision making** | Particularly with executive plans, there is usually scope for discretion to be exercised at various points, e.g. grant, vesting, change of control. Various administrative processes must also be undertaken, e.g. dealing with the company secretarial team or trustees of an employee trust. Independent decision making by the remuneration committee is required under authority delegated by the board. |
| **Individual participation limits** | The plan should define who is eligible to participate on the total value of potential benefit. Participation should be limited to employees and executive directors and is typically subject to appropriate limits for individual participation, which should be disclosed. In practice, this is expressed as an annual limit by reference to basic salary, e.g. in any year, the value of shares subject to grants not to exceed one times basic salary. Where there has been a substantial fall in share price, grants made as a proportion of base salary should be adjusted so as to avoid windfalls. |
| **Share dilution limits** | The implementation of the scheme will involve either the commitment of shareholders' funds or the dilution of their equity. Under the IA Principles, dilution can be through new share issues or by transfers of treasury shares and should not exceed the following:<br>▪ Commitments to issue new shares or re-issue treasury shares under all the company's schemes must not exceed 10% of the issued share capital in any rolling 10-year period.<br>▪ Commitments to issue new shares or re-issue treasury shares under discretionary/executive schemes must not exceed 5% of the issued share capital in any 10-year period. This limit may be exceeded in circumstances where significantly more stretching performance conditions apply.<br>▪ Appropriate flow-rates should apply to the issue of new shares so that the total 10% overall limit is not used up in too short a period.<br>▪ The implicit dilution commitment should always be provided for at point of grant even where it is recognised that only a proportion of shares may in practice be used.<br>Note that market purchases of shares (e.g. using an employee trust) are not dilutive and should be considered if limits may be breached. In that case, however, the provisions within the IA Principles relating to the use of such trusts, including the disclosure and shareholding limits and voting restrictions, should be adhered to. |

**Table 12.3** *continued*

| Design feature | Comment |
|---|---|
| **Vesting triggers** | Vesting triggers are the events specified in the plan on the occurrence of which participants will become entitled to benefit, e.g. by exercising an option. The main vesting triggers for the remuneration committee to consider are as follows:<br>■ *Expiry of award period* – the IA Principles specify that the minimum period should be 3 years, with strong endorsement of longer periods and the use of additional holding periods.<br>■ *Participant leaves employment* – generally, vesting is allowed for 'good' leavers subject to achievement of performance criteria over the original performance period, but only at the discretion of the remuneration committee for 'bad' leavers, if at all.<br>■ *Death of participant* – the IA Principles require that options are exercised (or lapse) within 12 months.<br>■ *Change of control of the company* – the IA Principles state that there should be no automatic waiving of performance conditions. Vesting should be based on the level of performance achieved and pro-rated for time elapsed since grant. |
| **Pricing issues** | For conventional options the exercise price is a key factor. It must not be less than the market value immediately preceding grant. There must be no re-pricing (or surrender and re-grant) of 'underwater' options. |
| **Cost issues** | Shareholders bear the ultimate 'cost' of executive incentives, through dilution or use of shareholder funds, but expressing that cost is problematic. The IA Principles require that the cost of the incentive arrangements should be disclosed as follows:<br>■ the potential value of awards due to individual scheme participants on full vesting. This should be expressed by reference to the face value of shares or shares under option at the point of grant and expressed as a multiple of base salary; and<br>■ the maximum dilution which may arise through the issue of shares to satisfy entitlements. |

**Table 12.3** *continued*

| Design feature | Comment |
|---|---|
| **Accounting and taxation treatment** | The remuneration committee will need to take advice on these aspects, as the accounting and tax rules are very complex and the interrelation between the two can be critical. The following priorities arise for the company:<br>■ *Accounts*: to manage effectively the recognition of the cost of awards on the profit and loss account and any balance sheet impact.<br>■ *Corporate tax*: to secure corporation tax relief in relation to awards made in accordance with the tax legislation and to address any transfer pricing issues.<br>■ *Employment tax*: to be able under the plan rules to make deductions for PAYE income tax and employee national insurance and to manage employer national insurance. |
| **Amendment and lifespan of scheme** | The adoption of a new plan is subject to shareholder approval as are any 'substantive' amendments, e.g. relating to limits or performance targets. The lifespan of the plan should not exceed 10 years. |

### Share incentives: professional advisers

It is beyond the scope of this book to examine the complex legal, taxation and regulatory issues to be addressed in relation to share incentive arrangements. For the remuneration committee, it will be important to obtain expert advice in determining share incentive elements of the company's remuneration policy as well as the particulars of the plans themselves. They are likely to refer not only to remuneration consultants, but also lawyers and accountants. In using such advice, however, in particular the advice of remuneration consultants, the remuneration committee should be able to justify to shareholders that the level of remuneration is not excessive and is linked to sustainable long-term value creation. Both the IA and PLSA have highlighted these core principles. The respective competencies of advisers commonly overlap (e.g. larger accounting firms will usually offer a remuneration consultancy alongside their accounting service, specialist lawyers will have the capacity to design awareness plans and all the advisers will lay claim to the taxation advice), but, in broad outline, their particular roles and skills can be described as set out in Table 12.4.

The remuneration committee also needs to pay due attention to potential conflicts of interest that a remuneration consultant, or accountant may have, in particular those that arise from providing other services to the company.

The remuneration committee will also want to consider whether their chosen remuneration consultant has committed to adhere to the RCG Code of Conduct. As a final point, while the use of advisers is essential in such a complex area such as the design of incentive arrangements, the committee should ensure that those advisers are not involved in the decision-making process itself which is for the committee and board alone.

**Table 12.4** Share incentive plans – professional advisers

| | |
|---|---|
| **Remuneration consultants** | ■ Data on market practice/benchmarking<br>■ Plan design<br>■ Performance modelling and measurement |
| **Lawyers** | ■ Plan documentation<br>■ Shareholder circulars and regulatory issues<br>■ Taxation |
| **Accountants** | ■ Accounting treatment and taxation<br>■ Funding and cost issues<br>■ Financial modelling |

## Executive pensions

A company's pension arrangements for executives will be shaped to a significant degree by the group-wide pension policy and will need to be reflected in the company's remuneration policy. It follows that, where the company has an active occupational pension scheme for its employees, the committee's remuneration policy will normally provide that executives should become members of the company's pension scheme in the normal way (indeed, the statutory automatic enrolment regime may require that executives be automatically enrolled into the company's pension scheme). However, the committee should be aware that, in governance terms, pension provision is a particularly challenging element of the overall executive remuneration package. As now examined, the reasons for this include uncertainty about the overall pension cost and the reporting requirements and tax regime for executive pensions.

### Pension cost to the company

The final paragraph of Schedule A to the UK Corporate Governance Code states that, in general, only basic salary should be pensionable. While this means that the level of pension provided to executives is not usually determined by performance, nevertheless the cost to the company can be highly volatile and obscure to shareholders. It can also be very significant.

It is beyond the scope of this book to examine in any detail the various factors that determine the size and nature of the company's executive pension cost. However, the committee should be aware that providing defined benefit (or final salary) pensions to executives will present more challenges in this regard than providing defined contribution (or money purchase) pensions. In the former case, the value of the company's pension liabilities will need to be determined actuarially according to various factors. These will include the executive's individual pensions record (age, length of service, salary, transferred benefits); the nature of the benefits provided by the pension scheme (e.g. accrual rate(s), death benefits, pension inflation-linking); and the assumptions adopted in relation to investment returns on scheme assets (equities, bonds, gilts, property, cash), inflation and longevity. In addition, trust-based defined benefit schemes provide further challenges as UK pensions law will usually require the scheme trustees to be involved in the liability valuation process. In some cases, the trustees will have unilateral power to both value the liabilities and determine the company contributions required to meet those liabilities. While actuaries can bring much professional skill to the valuation process, the outcome for both the company and its shareholders clearly cannot be certain.

In apparent recognition of these cost factors, the final paragraph of Schedule A to the Code also requires the remuneration committee to:

> 'consider the pension consequences and associated costs to the company of basic salary increases and any other changes in pensionable remuneration, especially for directors close to retirement'.

To be able to do so it is evident that the committee will need to understand the nature of what is being provided by way of pensions to executives and the pension policy applicable to employees elsewhere in the company. The committee will also need to take appropriate actuarial advice from their pension consultants. Shareholders are similarly attuned to the issues, including the need to have regard to the pension benefits available to staff generally. The IA Principles state:

> 'The pension provision for executives should, where possible, be in line with the general approach to the employees as a whole. Any differences in pension contribution rates for executives and the general workforce should be disclosed and justified to shareholders.'

The IA Principles specify various other disclosure requirements aimed at ensuring shareholders have the complete picture and are able to make a properly informed decision on the appropriateness of executive pension arrangements including: information about any payments in lieu of pension scheme participation; incremental value accruing to pension scheme participation; and changes in pension benefit entitlements or transfer values reflecting significant changes in actuarial and other relevant assumptions. Where benefit entitlement changes or transfers are made at the discretion of the remuneration committee, this and the justification for doing so should be made clear.

One further clear message within the IA Principles is that pensions paid on early retirement should be subject to abatement (i.e. that pensions should be reduced where possible to reflect receipt of a severance payment).

## Pensions accounting treatment under IAS 19

UK listed companies are required to follow accounting standard IAS 19 when accounting for pensions. Most other UK companies have the choice between IAS 19 and the employee benefits section of FRS 102 (the Financial Reporting Standard applicable in the UK and Republic of Ireland).

While there is not space here to examine in depth the requirements of IAS 19, the remuneration committee should be aware of its broad impact.

Accounting for defined contribution pension schemes is relatively straightforward as the cost is normally equal to the contributions payable to the scheme in the relevant accounting period.

However, the position is more complicated for defined benefit schemes. IAS 19 requires the cost of the defined benefit obligations to be calculated using actuarial assumptions relating to demographics (including mortality and employee turnover) and financial variables (such as future salary increases). These assumptions and variables are fed into a valuation model and an actuary then determines the resulting defined benefit obligation.

IAS 19 requires defined benefit plan assets to be measured and accounted for, where possible, using a market-related approach i.e. assets are measured at their fair value. However, the definition of plan assets is strict such that only assets which meet that definition can be offset against the defined benefit obligation. The amount then recognised on the balance sheet will be the net amount of the difference between the defined benefit obligation and the plan assets which, in turn, results in a net surplus or net deficit.

While remuneration committees may conclude that the implications of IAS 19 extend well beyond their terms of reference, they should ensure that the accounting impact of their policies is taken into account and work with the audit committee as necessary.

## Tax regime for pensions

In 2006 fundamental changes were introduced to the tax regime applying to pensions. The main effects of the changes were to set:

- an annual allowance – this is the limit on how much tax-free pension savings an individual can make to tax-approved pension schemes in any one year, i.e. the maximum amount of member and company contributions that can be paid to defined contribution pension schemes and benefit value that can build up in defined benefit pension schemes, for tax relief purposes. The annual allowance is £40,000 for the 2017/18 tax year (although it may be a smaller amount for high earners). Any pension savings in excess of the annual allowance are taxed at the individual's highest marginal rate; and

- a lifetime allowance – this is the limit on the total amount of benefits that an individual can draw from tax-approved pension schemes – whether lump sums or pension income – without triggering an extra tax charge.

The lifetime allowance is £1 million for the 2017/18 tax year. If the cumulative value of an individual's benefits across all their pension schemes exceeds the lifetime allowance, the excess is taxed at a rate of 55% if taken as a lump sum and at 25% if taken in any other way, e.g. as pension income.

Given the significance of pension provision to the total remuneration package and the complexity of the subject, in considering what pension arrangements are appropriate, the remuneration committee will require the benefit of specialist advice from the company's pension consultants.

## Executive contracts and severance terms

When considering the terms of executive directors' contracts, the remuneration committee will need to pay particular attention to severance terms. In particular, the committee is tasked with ensuring that departing executives are not rewarded for failure or underperformance because of the way their service agreements were drafted when they were first appointed, or because of a failure to negotiate robust severance terms on behalf of the company when the agreement is terminated. Remuneration committees must take account of the approved remuneration policy, which will include limits on exit payments and the requirement to promptly publish a statement of the payments the departing director has received. Although legal advice clearly will be required for the drafting of the contract, useful general guidance is available in the ICSA *Guidance Note on Directors' Service Contracts* which takes account of the 2008 joint ABI (now IA)/NAPF (now PLSA) statement, *Best Practice on Executive Contracts and Severance.*

### Executive contracts: the UK Corporate Governance Code

Code Provision D.1.5 provides that notice or contract periods should be set at one year or less. If it is necessary to offer more than this to a new externally recruited director, the contract terms should revert to the standard notice or contract period of one year or less once the initial period of appointment has expired. Additionally, Code Provision D.1.4 provides that the remuneration committee should give careful consideration to what compensation commitments (including pensions) the directors' terms of appointment would entail in the event of early termination. In order to avoid 'rewarding poor performance' the committee should 'take a robust line on reducing compensation to reflect departing directors' obligations to mitigate loss'. The UK Corporate

Governance Code does not describe what steps can be taken by the committee to reduce compensation in this manner. There are several possibilities, the main ones of which are explored immediately below in the context of the joint ABI (now IA)/NAPF (now PLSA) Joint Statement on Executive Contracts and Severance.

### Executive contracts: ABI/NAPF Joint Statement

In their 2008 *Joint Statement on Executive Contracts and Severance* the ABI (now IA) and NAPF (now PLSA) endorsed the UK Corporate Governance Code's position by affirming that directors should be retained on contracts of 'one year or less' and recommending that 'a one-year period should not be seen as a floor'. The possibility of a longer initial period for a new executive is conceded. Such cases should be justified to shareholders and, as under the UK Corporate Governance Code, the longer notice period should reduce on a rolling basis.

The IA/PLSA are clear in their view of executive contracts and 'rewards for failure'. The conclusion to their Joint Statement sums up their sentiments in the following words:

> 'It is unacceptable that poor performance by senior executives, which detracts from the value of an enterprise and threatens the livelihood of employees, can result in excessive payments to departing directors. Boards have a responsibility to ensure this does not occur.'

Given the shareholder muscle represented by these two organisations, the remuneration committee should pay careful attention to the points highlighted. These fall under the following headings.

### Severance and compensation

The IA/PLSA identify the likelihood that unacceptable rewards will be paid to departing executives if the initial negotiation of the contract does not deal with this risk adequately. They emphasise that 'compensation for risks run by senior executives is already implicit in the absolute level of remuneration, which mitigates the need for substantial contractual protection'. As a result, severance payments for poor performance should be limited to basic salary. So as not to overlook the consequences of underperformance, when negotiating the contract terms, the remuneration committee should calculate the total potential cost of termination. Boards should 'consider and avoid the reputational risk of being obliged to make and disclose large payments to executives who have failed to perform'. The guidance is clear – there should be no entitlement to discretionary payments on termination for poor performance and moreover remuneration committees should consider providing for a right to reclaim bonuses in the event they are based on achievements which are 'subsequently found to have been significantly mis-stated'. This supports the similar requirement in Schedule A to the UK Corporate Governance Code.

The primary responsibility for setting directors' contracts is squarely placed on the shoulders of the remuneration committee. Although the need for the committee to have leeway in deciding overall policy and specific contract terms is acknowledged, the Joint Statement also emphasises the need for the remuneration committee to have a 'clear understanding of their responsibility to negotiate suitable contracts and be able to justify severance payments to shareholders'. With the introduction of the binding vote on remuneration policy, contract terms will clearly need to be within the scope of the agreed policy and, any payments that fall outside of the authorised policy will be potentially subject to repayment. This applies to all service contracts entered into since 27 June 2012. In the event that an unauthorised payment cannot be recovered, it will even be possible for the directors who authorised the payment to be held liable for any losses incurred as a result. The PLSA has also recently published its revised *Corporate Governance Policy and Voting Guidelines* (2017) in which it indicated that a shareholder vote against a remuneration policy may be warranted where it includes guaranteed termination payments. Any severance payment made to a director which is not consistent with an approved remuneration policy will require separate shareholder approval under section 226C of CA 2006.

## Liquidated damages clause in the contract

The IA/PLSA refer to the possibility of negotiating the amount of the severance payment at the outset, so that it is payable in all cases of removal from office, except for misconduct. The payment would be made under the contract, rather than (as is generally the case) as damages for breach of the contract caused by early termination of the employment. While certainty is achieved by incorporating a liquidated damages clause in the contract, the IA/PLSA express some concern about this approach because the damages will be payable as a contractual term and therefore not be capable of negotiated reduction to reflect underperformance. This is at odds with the obligation on the remuneration committee to ensure that the 'full benefit of mitigation is obtained'. For this reason, the IA/PLSA note that they are 'not supportive' of such an approach. A simple alternative is to specify in the contract a fixed cap on the level of damages (e.g. six months of basic salary).

## Link between pay and performance

A remuneration policy that provides a relatively low base pay and a higher proportion of variable pay is generally viewed as being a good way of linking remuneration to performance. With a view to minimising rewards for failure, a proportion of variable pay (e.g. bonuses) may be paid for retaining the executive, which would fall away in the event of severance. In the absence of such a provision, the courts will most likely take into account variable pay when determining the compensation payable to departing executives.

### Phased severance payments

In 1995, the *Greenbury Report* proposed the payment of compensation in instalments on a phased basis. This approach is endorsed by the IA/PLSA, on the basis that most executives will be motivated to seek additional employment during the payment period and thereby will exercise the directors' common law duty to mitigate. Other commentators suggest that the phasing of compensation payments may simply deter executives from seeking new employment.

### Objective setting

The IA/PLSA note that corporate objectives set for directors should be clear. With irrefutable logic, the Joint Statement points out that, 'the more transparent and understandable the objectives, the easier it is to determine how an executive has performed'. This statement is made in the context of preventing payment for failure but conversely the logic also applies to rewarding achievement. The objectives against which performance will be measured should be made public.

### Paying compensation in the form of shares

A further possibility is that the compensation payable should be expressed in terms of the price of a fixed number of shares, determined at the share price prevailing on the date the contract begins. This is not mentioned in the IA/PLSA Joint Statement, but it is a possibility for the committee to consider when negotiating the contract terms. The aim is to align the level of compensation directly to the extent to which the executive's performance has enhanced (or depressed) the share price during his or her term of office.

### Current best practice on executive contract terms: a summary

There are several established best practice principles on executive contracts and severance to be observed. These will be relevant both when considering the company's remuneration policy and at the point when the remuneration committee first negotiates the contract terms, but will also be relevant when it negotiates the compromise agreement entered into on termination of the contract. Table 12.5 summarises the position.

**Table 12.5** Executive contract terms

| Item | Best practice |
|---|---|
| **Contract notice period** | This should not exceed one year (save where necessary, for an initial period only, to attract a new external appointment). |
| **Choices on severance** | The committee should consider the structure of severance payments when negotiating the contract, e.g. liquidated damages and phasing. Where termination takes the form of early retirement, best practice demands that pensions are abated (see above). |
| **Cost of termination** | When negotiating the contract, the committee should calculate the potential liability on severance (including pension costs) and be ready to justify this to shareholders. |
| **Setting clear objectives** | To ensure executive performance is targeted and measurable, the committee must set and keep under review appropriate objectives. |
| **Performance and pay** | A material proportion of total remuneration should be in the form of variable pay, linked to performance targets set by the committee. |
| **Clawback** | Consideration should be given to provisions which permit the company to reclaim variable pay in the event that a material misstatement is subsequently discovered. |
| **Contract review** | Contract provisions should be reviewed periodically to ensure they remain in line with company policy and best practice guidelines. |

## Remuneration disclosure requirements

Narrative reporting requirements on executive remuneration and related matters are explored in Chapter 8. However, there are also a number of other reporting and disclosure requirements relevant to the remuneration committee.

Code Provision D.2.1 requires that:

> 'The remuneration committee should make available its terms of reference, explaining its role and the authority delegated to it by the board'.

This disclosure can be made through a company website and overlaps with the requirement of DTR 7.2.7R to disclose within the company's corporate governance statement a description of the composition and operation of the company's committees.

In addition, working with the company secretary, the remuneration committee should ensure that the appropriate notifications are made to the LSE whenever the granting or vesting of share-based incentives changes the interests of a director. The rules are complex and require careful attention. These are addressed in detail in Chapter 15 in the context of the wider notification requirements of the MAR.

Under Companies Act requirements (s. 430(2B)), where a director leaves the company for any reason, the details of any payment for loss of office will need to be made available 'as soon as reasonably practicable' on the same company website as that on which the company's annual report and accounts are made available. In practice, the company will also announce the same detail through a Regulatory Information System (RIS) announcement.

## Governance checklist

✓ Are the executive directors aware of their wider role?

✓ Does the chief executive enhance board effectiveness by taking the necessary steps to ensure high standards of reporting to the board and by implementing board decisions and good governance across the organisation?

✓ Is the finance director an effective partner for the chief executive, providing him or her with both appropriate support and challenge?

✓ Does the remuneration committee have the necessary skills and is it independent both in form and substance to meet best practice requirements?

✓ Does the committee obtain appropriate external advice? When appointing remuneration consultants, is an appropriate tender process used and are issues of independence and conflicts of interest adequately considered?

✓ Has the committee determined a coherent policy on directors' remuneration, taking into account the company's strategy, issues of risk, shareholder expectations and best practice? Does it keep the policy under regular review and satisfy itself that the policy remains 'fit for purpose'? Will the policy prove contentious when put to a shareholder vote?

✓ Does the remuneration committee apply the remuneration policy appropriately within its approved framework, taking account of the pay and employment conditions which prevail elsewhere in the company, the potential ratchet effect of over-reliance on peer-benchmarking, in particular when such comparisons are used too frequently and the need to align pay with the creation of shareholder value without introducing unnecessary complexity into executive pay packages?

- ✓ Are the executive share incentive schemes designed so as to align shareholder and executive interests, in compliance with the UK Corporate Governance Code and institutional investors' best practice guidelines?
- ✓ Are the performance targets attached to incentive schemes transparent and challenging, linking reward to the company's long-term strategy?
- ✓ Do the terms of directors' contracts address issues relating to rewards for failure on termination?
- ✓ Does the board have a coherent policy on executive pensions and is disclosure of the arrangements sufficiently transparent to enable shareholder scrutiny?
- ✓ Is the committee familiar with the requirements for shareholder approval for the remuneration policy, relevant share incentive schemes and the remuneration report? Does it seek shareholders' views at an appropriate stage and take account of shareholder feedback?

# 13 Non-executive directors

## NEDs and corporate performance

When Sir Derek Higgs was asked to review the role and effectiveness of NEDs, the belief was that stronger and more effective corporate boards would improve corporate performance and that NEDs were the individuals who would be central to securing the delivery of such a key economic outcome. Institutional investors share the Government's affirmation of the important role of non-executives in securing improved corporate performance, albeit from a slightly different perspective. To the institutional investor, the primary goal of the company is that it should be run in the long-term interests of its shareholders with a view to generating value for them. From this perspective, it is easy to conclude that NEDs are quasi-representatives of the shareholders, whose role in major part is to ensure that shareholder interests are taken into account in the strategic debate and decision making and to take the lead in areas where the executives are hindered by conflicts of interest. Institutional investor reactions to executive pay excesses and failures in the financial services sector illustrate the extent to which they expect non-executives to be, not only their eyes and ears, but also their representatives on the board.

Some detractors have suggested that, given the limitations on their time commitment and active participation in the day-to-day running of the organisation, the role now expected of non-executives – to act as both guardians of the public interest and representatives of shareholder interests – is unrealistic. Yet they are undoubtedly in a minority. Criticism of non-executives in the wake of the global financial crisis was addressed in the *Walker Report* and the role and potential effectiveness of non-executives reviewed. Despite acknowledging the lack of evidence-based guidance available from the economic and business school research which had been undertaken into the impact of non-executives, the report noted that 'it seems clear that the NED contribution was materially helpful in financial institutions that have weathered the storm better than others'. In so doing, the report affirmed the value of effective NEDs within the UK's corporate governance framework.

## The NED's role

The non-executive position and role was first given a significantly higher profile as a result of the publication of the *Cadbury Report* which highlighted the part that NEDs could play in controlling and monitoring the executive team, acting very much as the custodians of good governance on behalf of shareholders. At the same time, the *Cadbury Report* restated NEDs' contribution to the strategic leadership of the company as equal members of the board. There is potential for an inherent tension between the monitoring (or supervisory) role and the strategic role. The one implies the prudent application of checks and balances and the other purposeful entrepreneurial leadership. By the time of the *Hampel Report* there was a common perception that the monitoring role had been overemphasised as an 'unintended side effect' of the *Cadbury Report*'s reforms. Consequently, the *Hampel Report* made it clear that:

> 'Non-executive directors are normally appointed to the board primarily for their contribution to the development of the company's strategy. This is clearly right. We have found general acceptance that non-executive directors should have both a strategic and a monitoring function.'

The dual nature of the role was strongly endorsed by the *Higgs Report*. Noting the dangers of the two extreme polarities, it observed that an overemphasis on monitoring and control risks will cause NEDs to be viewed as 'an alien policing influence on the board' and an overemphasis on strategy may result in them becoming too close to the executive management. The inference is that the NED needs to keep the two aspects of the role in balance, thereby achieving a creative and valuable tension. While now superseded by the FRC *Guidance on Board Effectiveness*, much of the guidance found within the *Higgs* 'Suggestions for Good Practice' remains relevant. *Higgs* listed the responsibilities of NEDs in the following terms:

- To provide entrepreneurial leadership of the company within a framework of prudent and effective controls which enable risk to be assessed and managed.
- To set the company's strategic aims, ensure that the necessary financial and human resources are in place for the company to meet its objectives and review management performance.
- To set the company's values and standards and ensure that its obligations to its shareholders and others are understood and met.

Table 13.1 shows the key elements that Higgs outlined for the role of the NED in addition to these requirements.

**Table 13.1** Role of the NED – *Higgs*

| | |
|---|---|
| **Strategy** | NEDs should constructively challenge and help develop proposals on strategy. |
| **Performance** | NEDs should scrutinise the performance of management in meeting agreed goals and objectives and monitor the reporting of performance. |
| **Risk** | NEDs should satisfy themselves on the integrity of financial information and that financial controls and systems of risk management generally are robust and defensible. |
| **People** | NEDs are responsible for determining appropriate levels of remuneration for executive directors and have a prime role in appointing and where necessary removing executive directors and in succession planning. |

The role is complex and demanding and requires a range of commitment, skills, experience, knowledge and personal attributes. These are examined below.

## Attributes, skills and behaviours

Research prepared in support of the 2003 *Higgs Report* concluded:

> 'Effectiveness requires high levels of engagement . . . It is not sufficient just to turn up at board meetings. Instead individuals need to build their knowledge of the business through all sorts of informal contact with executives, as well as their work on board sub-committees. Only with this sort of engagement and understanding of a company can individuals make a credible contribution to board discussions.'

As might be expected, the Principles and Provisions set out in the UK Corporate Governance Code do not emphasise such 'softer' aspects, as they cannot be reduced to rules. However, the *Walker Review* elevated the issue by identifying that corporate failures had 'related much more to patterns of behaviour than to organisation'. The lack of comprehensive guidance on issues of boardroom behaviour was emphasised by ICSA in its submission on that issue to the *Walker Review*, pointing out that:

> 'appropriate boardroom behaviours are an essential component of best practice corporate governance; and that the absence of guidance on appropriate boardroom behaviours represents a structural weakness in the current system.'

In research appended (as Annex 4) to the *Walker Review*'s final recommendations, boards were urged to:

> 'take time to purposefully evaluate [the board's] behaviour and the implications on the effective functioning of the board'.

The FRC *Guidance on Board Effectiveness* addressed this apparent gap in the best practice guidance for directors and boards and contains much that is relevant to the skills and attributes necessary to performing a non-executive role effectively. It affirms the view that an effective board is one which embraces constructive challenge and debate and as a result 'should not necessarily be a comfortable place'. The Guidance points out that NEDs can be ideally placed to test the proposals of the executive team given their wider experience outside the organisation. Being less closely involved on a day-to-day basis with the company and the proposals being brought to the board, NEDs can bring a fresh perspective to issues. They need to be capable of suggesting changes and alternatives when appropriate.

Being aware of the views of shareholders and other stakeholders can enhance the ability of non-executives to bring contrasting views into the boardroom. The implication is that they have a valuable role to play in avoiding the tendency towards 'group think' – common when a board is too like-minded.

The benefits of ensuring diversity of psychological type, background and gender within the boardroom are discussed in Chapter 9. As part of a diverse board, NEDs will possess different personal attributes. The FRC *Guidance on Board Effectiveness* suggests these might include 'intellect, critical assessment and judgement, courage, openness, honesty and tact; and the ability to listen, forge relationships and develop trust'. In particular the Guidance advocates that non-executives uphold high standards of integrity and probity, 'instilling the appropriate culture, values and behaviours in the boardroom and beyond'.

The need for the board to define the company's culture and values and to demonstrate and promote ethical leadership throughout the organisation is a recurring theme within the FRC Guidance. Far from being immune from this collective responsibility, notwithstanding that the nature of the non-executive role means that as individuals they spend far less time working within the company than their executive colleagues, the role of non-executives in providing ethical leadership is emphasised in the Guidance.

In practice, however, there is evidence that not all NEDs are comfortable with this challenge. In the 2016 FRC report, *Corporate Culture and the Role of Boards*, it was observed that, while non-executives were generally supportive of the board's responsibility to define and embed the organisation's values, there was a degree of uncertainty about the role and ability of non-executives to implement those values within the company. The report noted that some 'felt this is not the role of the non-executives'

Strong interpersonal skills are required of NEDs. Much of their effectiveness will depend on their exercising influence rather than giving orders. The typical listed company NED will have experience elsewhere as a senior executive and will be familiar with leading and giving orders. Having to exercise a more consensual style of leadership, based on influence and persuasion, may prove challenging for some and is one area which can be assessed through annual evaluation and addressed through the board's induction and development programmes.

Part of the non-executive's job is, in UK Corporate Governance Code language, to 'constructively challenge' strategy and to 'scrutinise the performance of management'. However, with their involvement limited to a few days per month, non-executives can never have the same detailed knowledge of the business as the executives. Non-executives sitting on the boards of highly complex businesses, for example in the financial services sector, will be particularly disadvantaged if their skills are those of the generalist rather than the expert. This latter point was particularly pertinent to the *Walker Review* and was specifically addressed within the review's final report. The conclusion reached was that 'several banks whose strategies appear to have been determined by long-entrenched executives with little external input to their decision-taking appear to have fared materially worse than those where there was opportunity for effective challenge within the boardroom'. The review recommended that the best basis for ensuring an environment of effective challenge within the boardroom was to have the right mix of sector-specific industry expertise together with the critical perspective brought to the table by others with high-level experience in other major businesses.

## Support and resources

Despite confirming the value of more generalist experience, however, the disparity in detailed knowledge of the organisation between executives and NEDs can create real issues. In its October 2004 submission to Paul Myners' review of the governance of mutual life companies, headhunting firm Odgers, Ray and Berndtson proposed that non-executives should have their own dedicated and independent secretariat, which would gather and analyse information and provide the non-executives with the tools they need to do their job. While this proposal has not been adopted, the underlying idea that non-executives should have the resources they need to counter-balance their limited day-to-day involvement with the business has been accepted.

The UK Corporate Governance Code therefore includes as a Supporting Principle a requirement that all directors have appropriate knowledge of the company and access to its operations and staff. This should dilute the potential for executives to keep information from the non-executives, although non-executives will themselves need to take responsibility for raising concerns or requesting more detail if they feel they need more detail or clarification. Accordingly, the FRC *Guidance on Board Effectiveness* places the emphasis on non-executives to demand high-quality information sufficiently in advance so that they have adequate opportunity to consider issues prior to the meeting and can engage in 'informed debate and challenge' at board meetings. The clear implication is that NEDs must critically assess the support and access to resources made available in order to ensure they have what they require to perform their role effectively. In other words, NEDs must be active in ensuring that the company is providing them with sufficient detail that they can be well informed about the company and will have a good understanding of the issues under discussion in the boardroom. Ensuring they have a good command of such issues will also, the FRC Guidance suggests, 'generate the respect of the other directors'.

## The composition of the board

Code Principle B.1 requires that:

> 'The board and its committees should have the appropriate balance of skills, experience, independence and knowledge of the company to enable them to discharge their respective duties and responsibilities effectively.'

The 2009 review of the Code made it clear that this key principle should not be compromised by the need to comply with the related independence provisions accompanying it. In other words, for companies which do not find it possible to comply with both the Code Principle and the related Code Provisions, the Code Principle should prevail. In such a case, the overriding test is whether the board is fit for purpose and the board should be ready to provide a robust explanation for their decision to their shareholders.

The FRC *Guidance on Board Effectiveness* provides some pointers for boards intended to stimulate their thinking on how best to apply the Code's principles and provisions to their own circumstances and business needs. In determining the optimum composition for their board, the valuable skills possessed by the NEDs will need to be taken into account, in particular in relation to the company's strategic aims and current challenges. In addition, an important consideration will be ensuring that there are NEDs in office who possess the necessary technical skills and knowledge to enable them to effectively contribute to the work of the various board committees, including non-executives appropriate for the role of chairing those committees.

Naturally, smaller boards will less easily cover the range of skills, experience and diversity they need in their non-executive positions. At the opposite end of the spectrum, boards which have too many members can become unwieldy. The optimum size for a board is recommended to be 8 to 12 (Annex 4, *Walker Review*); however, while research on such issues might provide useful benchmarks for boards and their nomination committees, the needs of each company will vary, depending on factors such as the size and complexity of the organisation, the stage it is at in its development and the sector in which it operates. Boards should be focused on achieving a composition which meets the needs of their business.

### Independence

Code Provision B.1.2 is prescriptive as to the minimum requirements for a balanced board. It provides that, except for companies outside the FTSE 350, at least half the board, excluding the chairman, should comprise non-executive directors who are judged by the board to be independent. A smaller company should have at least two independent NEDs.

Under Code Provision B.1.1, the board must identify in the company's annual report whether a NED is independent, having been determined by the board to be 'independent in character and judgement' and also taking account of 'whether there are relationships or circumstances which are likely to affect or could appear to affect, the director's judgement'. These relationships or circumstances will be deemed to exist if the director:

- has been an employee of the company or group within the last five years;
- has or has had within the last three years a material business relationship, with the company either directly or as a partner, shareholder, director or senior employee of a body that has such a relationship with the company;
- has received or receives additional remuneration from the company apart from a director's fee, participates in the company's share option or a performance-related pay scheme or is a member of the company's pension scheme;
- has close family ties with any of the company's advisers, directors or senior employees;
- holds cross-directorships or has significant links with other directors through involvement in other companies or bodies;
- represents a significant shareholder; or
- has served on the board for more than nine years from the date of first election.

The relevance of the last of these criteria in particular was the subject of some debate during the 2009 review of the Combined Code. Some commentators argued that the length of tenure was too arbitrary a measure for assessing independence and that the nine-year rule could lead to a loss of directors who could otherwise continue to make a valuable contribution. In contrast, others considered the existence of NEDs with overly lengthy service as flagging the need for the board to be refreshed. In the event, the length-of-service criterion was retained, as were the references within the Code to the need to ensure 'progressive refreshing of the board'. However, it is interesting to note that research carried out by Manifest for the FRC's 2007 review of the Combined Code found that 'there was only a marginal difference in the outcome of votes on the re-election of NEDs who met the independence criteria in the Code and those who did not'. Such evidence might encourage boards and nomination committees to consider taking a more robust stance on whether to propose renewal of a highly valued non-executive's appointment at the end of a nine-year term in circumstances where they are in no doubt as to the relevant individual being 'independent in character and judgement' or to otherwise compromise the requirement for half the board (excluding the chairman) to be 'independent' NEDs. An analysis of 2012 UK Corporate Governance Code compliance for the Grant Thornton report *The chemistry of governance: a catalyst for change* found that the area of greatest non-compliance amongst FTSE 350 companies related to this independence requirement, with which almost one in five companies failed to comply.

If any of the relationships or circumstances mentioned above exists with respect to a NED identified as being independent, the board must explain in the company's annual report why it has reached such a conclusion. Ultimately, the determination of what is meant by 'independent in character and judgement' is a matter for the board. Where one of the listed relationships or circumstances exists, the board will be required to robustly justify its view if it is to satisfy shareholders that the director is truly independent. It should also be noted that, as circumstances change, the independence of an individual may be compromised. NEDs' independence should therefore be kept under review.

## Non-executive terms of appointment

A NED's terms of appointment will be set out in writing in an appointment letter. It should be noted that, under Code Provision B.3.2, the terms and conditions of appointment of NEDs must be made available for inspection at the company's registered office during normal business hours and at the AGM for 15 minutes prior to the meeting and during the meeting itself. ICSA publishes on its website (www.icsa.org.uk) a useful sample letter of NED appointment. The structure of appointment letter used by different companies may vary, but the main terms which it should include are laid out in Table 13.2.

**Table 13.2** Letter of appointment

| | |
|---|---|
| **Term of office** | The term of office and circumstances under which it can be terminated should be clearly described. These may include removal from office by shareholder resolution, the failure to achieve re-election or the occurrence of specified termination events (e.g. disqualification as a director or failure to perform duties properly). The initial appointment will normally be for a period of 3 years, subject to re-election by shareholders according to the company's articles of association and the requirements of Code Provision B.7.1 (re-election by shareholders). |
| **Time commitment** | As required by Code Provision B.3.2, there should be a statement as to the number of days per year that will be required of the NED and the letter should include an undertaking by the director that the director will have sufficient time to meet what is expected of him or her. An outline of the types of meetings and other events or visits which the director is likely to be expected to attend will help to clarify how the anticipated time committed to the role is likely to be spent. |
| **Duties** | The role should be described in terms of the strategy, performance, risk and people aspects. Clear links should be made to the regulatory and statutory obligations the director will have. |
| **Fees and expenses** | The director's fees should be specified, including, if appropriate, additional fees payable for work on board committees. Reasonable expenses properly incurred should be reimbursed by the company. As regards taxation, the company should reserve to itself the right to make appropriate deductions for income tax and national insurance contributions. |
| **Independence, outside interests and conflicts of interest** | It should be confirmed whether or not the board considers the NED to be independent for the purposes of Code Provision B.1.1. Guidance should be given about the holding of outside positions and the steps which should be taken in the event that the NED wishes to accept an additional outside interest or becomes aware of any additional or potential conflicts of interest. See Code Provision B.3.2 regarding the information on other appointments that directors are expected to share. |

**Table 13.2** *continued*

| | |
|---|---|
| **Confidential information** | The director's obligations in relation to dealing with confidential information should be reinforced by an express contractual requirement to preserve the company's confidentiality at all times. |
| **Price-sensitive information and share dealings** | The statutory requirements in relation to the disclosure of price sensitive information and the obligation to observe the requirements of the MARs should be reiterated. The company's own code in relation to dealing in the company's securities should also be supplied to the director. |
| **Induction, development and evaluation** | Arrangements for the director's induction and ongoing training should be outlined, together with confirmation of the board's evaluation processes. |
| **Independent advice** | It should be expressly stated that the NED can, as required by Code Provision B.5.1, at the company's expense, obtain independent professional advice if required in the performance of his or her duties. The board's policy for obtaining such advice should also be provided. |
| **Insurance and indemnity** | The provision of D&O liability insurance (Code Provision A.1.3) and any indemnity to be granted by the company for the benefit of the director should be specified. Full details are best covered in separate documents. |
| **Termination** | The requirement to return to the company upon termination any property, including papers, records and other documents, should be stated. A non-compete clause preventing the director from taking up any appointment with a competitor company within a reasonable period (say six months) of termination should be considered. |
| **Miscellaneous** | There will be various other clauses required relating to more routine matters such as data protection, the right of third parties and the law governing the letter of appointment. |

On being offered an appointment, the NED should undertake due diligence on the company (see Chapter 9) and would be well advised to take personal legal advice on the specific written terms. The relevant terms should be cross-checked with any service agreement held with any other company in which they hold office or employer to ensure that it will not be breached.

### Term of appointment

Code Provision B.2.3 provides that the NED's appointment should be for a specified term, subject to re-election by the shareholders and to statutory provisions relating to the removal of directors. For directors of FTSE 350 companies, re-election should be annual under Code Provision B.7.1. Code Provision B.7.2 places emphasis on the board informing shareholders why a new non-executive should be first elected and on proposed re-election the chairman must confirm that the individual's performance remains effective and that they have continued to demonstrate commitment to the role. This statement by the chairman should be informed by the formal performance evaluation processes undertaken by the board.

An initial term of three years is normal, with the expectation that the term will be extended by a second period of three years. Code Provision B.2.3 states that any extension of a NED's appointment beyond six years should be subject to particularly rigorous review and should take into account the need for 'progressive refreshing of the board'. If the term is to extend beyond nine years (i.e. more than three terms of three years), the board will need to determine whether the NED will then no longer be independent. This is implicit in Code Provision B.1.1. For such directors, even if their company falls outside of the FTSE 350, Code Provision B.7.1 imposes annual re-election.

### Time commitment

As well as preparing for and attending the AGM, board meetings and relevant committee meetings, NEDs might expect to attend board dinners, strategy away-days, meetings with the other NEDs, meetings with significant shareholders, site visits, training and development events and board evaluation meetings. As a result, the normal time commitment for a NED might be expected to lie somewhere between 15 and 30 days each year. For a chairman of the board or a committee the period will normally be considerably more. For example, the PwC *Monks Non-executive Directors Practice and Fees: Key Findings 2009* report found the average time commitment by board chairmen in 2009 to have been 110 days. In certain sectors, in particular financial services, the time commitment may also be greater. A 2016 report of the Bank Governance Leadership Network, *Clarifying Supervisory Expectations for Non Executive Directors and Boards*, observed that participants in their study reported spending two-to-five times as much time on large bank boards as they do on other boards, even boards of other large multinational companies.

For all NEDs there are likely to be periods of intense corporate activity when more will be required of them. Their time commitment will also vary, depending on their roles in the various main board committees, particularly the audit committee. New directors might expect to need to devote more time to their role while they become familiar, through the induction process and otherwise, with the key issues facing the company and its board.

The commitment by some NEDs of insufficient time to adequately fulfil their role was a concern addressed by the *Walker Report*. The UK Corporate Governance Code now includes as Code Principle B.3 the requirement that 'all directors should be able to allocate sufficient time to the company to discharge their responsibilities effectively'. The individual evaluation of NEDs will need to address whether each of them demonstrates sufficient time commitment in practice.

Clearly, one factor affecting a chairman's or NED's ability to dedicate sufficient time to the role is the existence of other significant commitments. For this reason, Code Provisions B.3.1 and B.3.2 require a new chairman or NED to disclose to the board before appointment any other significant commitments they may have and to report to the board any changes in such commitments as and when they arise. While suggestions by some that a strict limit should be imposed on the number of non-executive directorships which can be held simultaneously may not be well supported, a practical approach is required at the very least. In order to discharge their duties well, NEDs need to be satisfied they have sufficient time available to keep themselves adequately informed, to engage in appropriate development activity and to attend meetings and other company events. When considering the sufficiency of their available time, they should take account not only of whether they have sufficient time to deal with 'business as usual' but also to give additional time at potentially short notice in the event of a crisis.

### Non-executive fees

The level of fees payable will be a matter of negotiation and will reflect the going rate for the relevant board. In recent years, the trend in non-executive fees has been ever upwards, reflecting the heavier workload and enhanced responsibilities of non-executives. PwC's *FTSE 100 Non-Executive Director Fees* in 2015 found that the median FTSE 100 non-executive fee, exclusive of committee fees, was £65,000 per annum. The median FTSE 100 non-executive chairman's fees were reported as £393,000 per annum, with the highest paid receiving considerably more. The same survey found that chairing a committee would result in additional fees with a median of between £16,000 to £22,000 depending on the committee, with SIDs receiving a median increase to their basic fees of £20,000. PwC's similar study of FTSE 250 fees in 2015 found that levels were considerably lower.

Code Provision D.1.3 sets out governance expectations in relation to levels of non-executive remuneration, requiring fees to 'reflect the time commitment and responsibilities of the role'. Various surveys are published on a regular basis which may provide appropriate benchmarking data.

The ICGN updated its *Non-Executive Director Remuneration Guidelines* in 2016, in particular to more clearly define the expectation that non-executives will attain a significant holding in the company's shares. The best practice, in this regard, is to establish a holding that aligns the director's interests with those of shareholders without compromising independence and judgement. The IA Principles of Remuneration also confirm that shareholders encourage NEDs to own shares in the company. However the practice adopted by some companies of paying some or all of a NED's fees in the form of shares bought at market-price in lieu of cash raises some important legal issues for companies, at two levels.

First, under s. 678 of the CA 2006, a public company is prohibited from giving direct or indirect financial assistance in the purchase of its own shares. Secondly, under s. 19 of FSMA 2000, a company is prohibited from carrying out a regulated activity (unless authorised or within an exempt category) and under s. 21 of FSMA 2000, it is prohibited from making a financial promotion in the form of an invitation or inducement to engage in an investment activity. If adopting a policy of paying non-executives in shares the company must be careful to avoid being in breach of these rules, the penalty for which is the imposition of criminal sanctions. Accordingly, while particularly in the early stages of a company's development, payment in shares rather than cash may be desirable from the company's perspective, any proposal to pay non-executives in shares will need to be reviewed carefully by the company's legal advisers to ensure that there is no breach of these important rules.

The granting of non-executive fees in the form of share options or awards under other incentive schemes linked to share price or corporate performance is widely opposed by institutional investors, as confirmed in the ICGN Guidelines and the IA Principles of Remuneration, on the grounds that it is likely to compromise the recipient's independence under the terms of Code Provision B.1.1. Should it, on exceptional grounds, be proposed to grant options or other performance-related benefits to a NED, Code Provision D.1.3 requires that shareholders approve the grant in advance and that shares acquired on exercise should be retained for at least one year after leaving the board. The ICGN Guidelines in fact recommend a retention period of two years post termination for any shares held by non-executives. Beyond the fees discussed above and the provision of D&O insurance (see Chapter 4) no other benefits should be provided. This includes pensions, severance pay, company cars, etc.

## Evaluating NEDs

Code Principle B.6 states:

> 'The board should undertake a formal and rigorous annual evaluation of its own performance and that of its committees and individual directors.'

The chairman is responsible for taking forward the evaluation of the board, its committees and individual directors and for 'acting on the results' of that evaluation. In turn, the NEDs, led by the SID, are responsible for the evaluation of the chairman (Code Provision B.6.3). Evaluation of NEDs will require special consideration, but the following questions may form a useful starting point:

- How well prepared and informed are they for board meetings and do they attend all meetings unless prevented from doing so by urgent and unavoidable circumstances?
- Do they demonstrate a willingness to devote time and effort to understanding the company, its business and the key challenges it faces and a readiness to participate in events outside the boardroom, such as site visits?
- What has been the quality and value of their input at board meetings? Do they demonstrate a strong grasp of the key issues and the ability to test management proposals? Do they contribute well to board debate, providing constructive challenge and, where appropriate, suggesting alternatives?
- What has been their contribution to development strategy and risk management?
- How successfully have they brought their knowledge and experience to bear in the consideration of strategy?
- How effectively have they probed information, analysis and assumptions? Where necessary, how resolute are they in maintaining their own views and resisting pressure from others?
- How effectively and proactively have they followed up areas of concern?
- How well do their personal attributes fit with others as part of a diverse board? How effective and successful are their relationships with fellow board members, the company secretary and senior management? Does their performance and behaviour engender mutual trust and respect in the board?
- How well do they discharge their responsibility to uphold high standards of integrity and probity? Do they actively support the chairman and executive directors in instilling the appropriate culture, values and behaviours both inside and outside the boardroom?
- How keenly and successfully do they participate in development activities to refresh their knowledge and skills and are they up-to-date with:
  - the latest developments in areas such as corporate governance and financial reporting?
  - the industry and market conditions?
- How well do they communicate with fellow board members, senior management and others, for example shareholders? Are they able to present views convincingly yet diplomatically and do they listen and take on board the views of others who may provide a different perspective?

For the NED a uniquely important aspect of performance will relate to the various board committees. These will take up a significant proportion of the total time spent on the job and are the environment in which much practical governance takes place. The evaluation of a NED, therefore, will also extend to their performance in any committee roles they carry out as well as in relation to their membership and contribution to the board as a whole. The process of board evaluation is examined in more detail in Chapter 9, which addresses building and maintaining an effective board.

### NEDs' knowledge and experience

The area of most concern to NEDs is always the extent to which the courts will choose to have regard to the different knowledge and experience of the company's affairs that they possess when compared to executive directors. This would be relevant in particular to a non-executive seeking relief from liability under s. 1157 of the CA 2006 (by which the court can grant relief from liability in proceedings for negligence, default, breach of duty or breach of trust if it concludes that the director acted honestly and reasonably and that in all the circumstances ought fairly to be excused). ICSA has published a guidance note on a directors' duty to exercise care, skill and diligence which is available on its website (www.icsa.org.uk). This useful guidance acknowledges that, although all directors have the same legal duties and objectives as board members, their involvement is likely to be different. In particular, the time devoted to the company's affairs, while still significant, is still likely to be less for a non-executive. Likewise, the detailed knowledge and experience of the company's affairs that could reasonably be expected of a non-executive will also in most cases be less than for an executive director. The guidance makes the point that it is:

> 'up to each non-executive director to reach a view as to what is necessary in particular circumstances to comply with the duty of care, skill and diligence they owe as a director to the company'.

In order to reach this view, a NED will wish to undertake thorough due diligence prior to appointment, ensure he or she has a good understanding of their role, responsibilities and duties, take care to declare and otherwise deal properly with any conflicts of interest, familiarise themself with the company, participate fully in induction and development processes and ensure they receive adequate information and support. Key to doing so will be committing sufficient time to their role.

### NEDs and personal liabilities

Chapter 4 on directors' duties and liabilities addresses this subject for directors in general. It is noted in particular that the CA 2006 contains statutory directors' duties and provisions on the indemnification of directors and payment of their legal costs in respect of proceedings taken by third parties. These developments are of relevance to non-executives just as they are to executives and should be referred to accordingly. It is worth noting here, however, that Code Provision A.1.3 requires companies to maintain appropriate insurance cover in respect of legal action against its directors.

## Governance checklist

✓ Do the company's NEDs contribute to the strategic direction of the company, scrutinise the performance of management, review the risk management system and both appoint and set the remuneration of executives?

✓ Are the non-executives provided in a timely manner with sufficient information and resources to do their job?

✓ Do the non-executives have the right personal attributes, skills and experience and do they provide the right balance to board challenge and debate, demonstrating the intellectual capacity to effectively test management proposals and to suggest alternatives where appropriate?

✓ Are the non-executives active in assisting to define, embed and support appropriate values and culture in the company?

✓ Are at least half of the board members (excluding the chairman) considered independent, taking account of the independent criteria set out in the UK Corporate Governance Code? Are robust justifications provided to shareholders for any recommendation to re-elect a NED who does not meet those criteria but who nevertheless is considered by the board to be independent in mindset?

✓ Do the non-executives have clear terms of appointment set out in writing which determine key issues such as independence, the level of time commitment expected and their duties? Are non-executive fees set at an appropriate level?

✓ Is there a comprehensive and formal induction programme on appointment tailored to the needs of the new appointee and is there provision of continuous professional development for non-executives based on the findings of the annual evaluation process? Do the non-executives give sufficient commitment to such development activities and acknowledge the value of engaging in them?

✓ Are the NEDs aware of their general duties of care, skill and diligence under the Companies Act and do they perform their role in a way which is consistent with meeting those duties?

# 14
# Company secretary

## Introduction

This chapter is in two parts. It is principally taken up with the role and duties of the company secretary as the individual with primary responsibility for advising the board on corporate governance matters. Additionally, however, the second section considers the demand from boards for advice on the legal aspects of governance and compliance and the role which in-house counsel may usefully play in meeting those demands. In practice there is significant overlap between what is 'company secretarial' and what is 'legal' and the company secretary will, as a rule, have developed a significant amount of experience of legal issues even if not formally qualified as a lawyer. The two roles are complementary in many respects and are sometimes fulfilled by the same person, particularly in the medium-sized or smaller company where fewer senior managers means that each may have a wider remit. Neat demarcation lines between the two roles are therefore often unrealistic in practice, although, as will be seen, there are some potential advantages to be gained from separating them.

## Company secretary and corporate governance

Since the *Cadbury Report*, those both inside and outside company boardrooms have repeatedly affirmed the importance of the company secretary to good corporate governance. Along with the chairman, the secretary is the officer who sits at the hub of the governance process, providing support to the board and in particular the NEDs on their legal and best practice obligations. ICSA has expressed the point succinctly:

> 'As an officer of the company at the centre of the decision making process, the company secretary is in a powerful position of influence. The company secretary should assist and guide the directors in their pursuit of profit and growth but should also act with integrity and independence to protect the interests of the company, its shareholders and its employees. Today's company secretary should play a proactive and central role in the governance of the company.'

It might be said that historically, the company secretary's place in governance has perhaps been neglected. So, when the *Higgs Report* noted that 'the value of a good company secretary was a recurring theme amongst consultees', there was an implied suggestion that this was a theme which needed to be proclaimed more widely. Certainly, there is a sense that recent governance developments have shed some welcome light on the company secretary's unique and important position on the board. In 2012, the All Party Parliamentary Group for Corporate Governance commissioned Lintstock to carry out research into the role of the company secretary as part of its *Reconnecting the board to the business* series. The resultant 2012 report *Elevating the role of the company secretary* noted the 'breadth and importance of the role of the company secretary has increased markedly over the past five years' and that endeavours continued to ensure recognition of the company secretary as 'board advisor' with the unique position of being neither line management nor a member of the board itself. Reflecting this unique position, the company secretary is often described as the 'conscience' of the board. Part of the reason that the company secretary can carry out this role of corporate conscience is that he or she has the task of facilitating (and, in large measure, controlling) advice, good information flows and effective processes to the board and its committees.

The 2014 report commissioned by ICSA, *The Company Secretary, Building Trust Through Governance*, noted that 'the company secretary adds significant value as a go-between and helps facilitate the successful delivery of organisational objectives'. The report went on to describe the attributes needed to achieve that as being 'closest to those of the Chairman: humanity, humility, high intelligence, an understanding of agendas, negotiation and resilience'.

The UK Corporate Governance Code makes the central role of the company secretary clear in a variety of ways. For example, the Code requires that all directors 'have access to the advice and services of the company secretary' to whom the key responsibility for advising the board on all governance matters is assigned (Code Provision B.5.2 and Supporting Principle to Code Principle B.5). The FRC *Guidance on Board Effectiveness* notes that 'well-informed and high-quality decision making is a critical requirement for a board to be effective and does not happen by accident . . . Boards can minimise the risk of poor decisions by investing time in the design of their decision-making policies and processes'. The efficiency of the board relies very significantly upon the company secretary's capacity to contribute to the management of such processes. In summary, it is now recognised that an effective company secretary is a necessary requirement of effective corporate governance.

## Appointment of the company secretary

Unlike directors, for whom there is currently no statutory qualification requirement (although this may change if proposals described in the *Corporate Governance Review* Green Paper to extend governance requirements to larger private companies are implemented), the secretary of a PLC must be appropriately qualified. While other professional qualifications also meet the statutory minimum, the specialist Chartered Secretary, who qualifies through and is an associate member or fellow of ICSA, is often a board's first choice. One of the key findings of the report *The Company Secretary, Building Trust Through Governance* was that ICSA-qualified company secretaries deliver a more rounded governance and board member service than those who have come to the role via other professional routes.

In addition, under s. 273 of the CA 2006, the board must be satisfied that the secretary has 'the requisite knowledge and experience to discharge the functions of the secretary of the company'. So, for example, the board of a financial services company may consider that, beyond the professional qualification that a candidate for the role of company secretary holds, they require someone with specific knowledge and experience of financial services regulation.

The company secretary is responsible to the board, not to any individual director, and accordingly Code Provision B.5.2 provides that 'both the appointment and the removal of the company secretary should be a matter for the board as a whole'. While removal of the company secretary is a matter for the board as a whole, the resignation of the company secretary in circumstances in which he or she has concerns is not currently addressed by governance best practice. In a speech by Peter Swabey, ICSA's Policy and Research Director, on 15 February 2017, it was announced that, in its response to the *Corporate Governance Review* Green Paper, ICSA intended to propose that company secretaries be given a statutory right, similar to that of auditors, to provide a statement to shareholders regarding the circumstances in which they have ceased to hold office.

As the chairman is the leader of the board, best practice, as confirmed in the FRC *Guidance on Board Effectiveness*, is that the company secretary reports to the board through the chairman on all governance matters. If the company secretary has additional executive management responsibilities (e.g. on legal matters) he or she will report to the relevant member of senior management, probably the chief executive, in respect of such executive functions. Maintaining such distinctions in the reporting lines does not provide the company secretary with security of tenure or exempt them from criticism, but it does ensure that on key governance matters they are not accountable only to the executive directors.

The UK Corporate Governance Code does not make any provision for the terms that should apply under the company secretary's contract of employment. Best practice, again confirmed in the FRC Guidance, is that the main contract terms, including salary and benefits, should be settled by the remuneration committee.

## Attributes and skills

The CA 2006 requires that the secretary of a public company is 'a person who appears to [the directors] to have the requisite knowledge and experience to discharge the functions of the secretary of the company'. Additionally, the company secretary must meet one of a number of qualification requirements, one of which is membership of a recognised professional body such as ICSA.

Apart from possessing the requisite knowledge, experience and qualifications, the company secretary needs to be impartial and independent in the advice provided to the board. Although a member of the executive team, the company secretary occupies something of a middle position, which may at times require the making of difficult judgements and even challenging the board's line on a particular matter. Described in the Lintstock Report *Elevating the role of the company secretary* as the 'interface between the Board and management', the company secretary will often require strength of character as well as good interpersonal skills. In ICSA's *The Company Secretary, Building Trust Through Governance*, the 'careful choreography between board and executive' was described as requiring 'balance, independence and respected and valued judgement'. The report notes that one of the challenges which many company secretaries face is 'being considered "traitors" by the executive team'. Skills and attributes beyond technical knowledge will clearly be necessary to be able to stand up to a strong chief executive or to bring the non-executives to an understanding of their responsibilities in a particular respect, while at the same time retaining the confidence and trust of the whole board. As is noted in the *Higgs Report*, ultimately the value of a company secretary's contribution will be determined by the calibre of the individual concerned.

In the wake of the banking crisis, a view was offered by some that the effectiveness of the board and its NEDs in particular might be improved if the company secretary's reporting lines were changed so as to create greater independence from the executive. The extent to which company secretaries are largely viewed as already successfully performing their role with a sufficient degree of independence was illustrated by the lack of support for this suggestion.

## The company secretary's role and duties

The requirement to have an effective company secretary is a reflection of both the importance, and the demanding nature, of many aspects of the role traditionally fulfilled by the company secretary. To understand the context of the company secretary's specific interest in corporate governance matters, an overview of the wider role and duties is required.

### Fiduciary duties

Like a director, the secretary is an officer of the company and as such owes fiduciary duties to the company and its shareholders. As an officer, the company secretary must act in good faith and in what he or she considers to be the best interests of the shareholders, exercising his or her powers for a proper purpose. Also, they must avoid any circumstance where their duties to the company are in conflict with their own personal interests. The governance implications of these fiduciary duties are clear.

### Main secretarial responsibilities

The purely secretarial duties (as distinct from the additional duties outlined below) involve compliance with the numerous statutory and regulatory obligations the company must observe. Any breach of such obligations may cause the company's officers, including the company secretary, to suffer either civil or criminal sanctions or the censure of a competent regulatory authority such as the UKLA or the Takeover Panel. It is apparent, therefore, that the directors place considerable reliance on the company secretary's skill, knowledge and efficiency. Assuming the company is listed, the main secretarial responsibilities revolve around four core areas:

- The board – supporting the chairman and directors, providing advice and information before, during and after board and committee meetings and, based on an in-depth knowledge of legal, regulatory and governance requirements, best practice and the company's constitution, advising the board on appropriate governance arrangements.
- The Listing Regime – compliance with the Listing, DTR and PR and MARs.
- Shareholders – provision of information to the company's shareholders including managing general meetings.
- The company's statutory registers and returns.

Table 14.1 lists the main duties falling within these four core areas. Some of these duties will need to be replicated for subsidiary companies. Commonly the company secretary will be responsible for ensuring these statutory requirements are met for a multitude of entities found within a large, complex and possibly international group. Where overseas subsidiaries exist, diverse local regulatory requirements will need to be taken into account and managed. The issue of subsidiary governance is explored further in Chapter 16.

**Table 14.1** Main duties of the company secretary

| **1. Board and the company's constitution** | |
|---|---|
| **Corporate governance** | To provide independent and impartial advice to the board on governance matters including appropriate delegation arrangements; facilitating the induction, professional development and evaluation of directors. |
| **Board strategy** | Assisting the board to both plan and implement its strategy, ensuring that board decisions are actioned. |
| **Board/committee meetings** | Organising board/committee meetings; agreeing the agenda with the chairman and advising on which matters should be considered by the board and committees in accordance with the schedule of matters reserved to the board and relevant terms of reference, ensuring papers are of sufficiently high quality and are issued in good time to enable proper preparation for the meeting; taking minutes and preserving all company documents; facilitating the flow of information to the board and committees, particularly to the NEDs. |
| **Legal and constitutional requirements** | Being familiar with and ensuring that the company's constitutional documents, shareholder directions and company law requirements are observed at all times and advising/challenging the board accordingly where necessary. Advising on amendments to the constitutional documents in line with developments in legislation or best practice. |
| **2. Listed company obligations** | |
| **LR/DTR/PR** | Ensuring compliance with requirements (e.g. continuing obligations requirements, management of inside information and contents of listing particulars, circulars and RIS notifications). |
| **Dealings by persons discharging managerial responsibilities (PDMR)** | Overseeing directors' share dealings and ensuring compliance with the company's share dealing policy and code and FCA notifications; delivering notifications of dealings to the FRC and an RIS at the LSE. |
| **Takeover Code** | Monitoring the share register and drawing to the board's attention relevant movements and any related issues under the Takeover Code; leading discussions with the Takeover Panel when required. |

**Table 14.1** *continued*

| **3. Shareholder information** | |
|---|---|
| **Financial statements and annual report** | Ensuring the interim financial statements and the annual report and accounts are prepared and published in a timely manner; contributing in particular to the meaningful narrative in the strategic report, directors' report, remuneration report and the corporate governance report. |
| **Circulars** | Working with the company's advisers as necessary, preparing and, where required, obtaining UKLA approval of shareholder circulars. |
| **General meetings** | Convening and organising general meetings and sending out shareholder notices in a timely manner; supporting the board and preparing briefing notes, overseeing processing of proxy forms and voting; preparing meeting minutes. |
| **Shareholder relations** | Maintaining good relations with shareholders, organising the AGM and facilitating other meetings and engagement; managing shareholder activism issues on behalf of the board. Advising the board on investor expectations and best practice. |
| **4. Company's statutory registers and returns** | |
| **Statutory registers** | Managing the company's relationship with its registrars and ensuring maintenance of the company's registers (e.g. those relating to members, interests disclosed in shares, directors and secretary, directors' residential addresses, debenture holders, charges). Maintaining subsidiary company records, including those on people with significant control (PSC). Overseeing dividend arrangements. |
| **Statutory returns** | Filing the company's returns at Companies House (e.g. report and accounts, confirmation statement, return of allotments, company resolutions, appointment/removal/resignation of directors and secretary). |

## Additional duties

Additional to the specifically secretarial duties, the company secretary will play a leading role in supporting the board to implement its policies or to manage particular projects on its behalf. The list of additional duties may include responsibility for risk management, the administration of subsidiary companies, managing corporate transactions, overseeing the design and management of director and employee share schemes and compliance with all relevant legislation such as health and safety, data protection and employment law. To some extent, factors such as the size of the company and the personal skills of the individual will determine the nature of the full job description.

## Contribution to corporate governance

The company secretary provides a vital level of internal control to the board. The FRC *Guidance on Board Effectiveness* concludes that the obligations and responsibilities placed upon the company secretary by the Companies Act and UK Corporate Governance Code to support the chairman and assist the board and its committees to function efficiently, necessitate him or her playing a 'leading role in the good governance of the company'. While there are dangers of dissecting the role artificially into its 'governance' and 'non-governance' aspects, the sections below review the areas in which the company secretary makes a recognised contribution to the company's governance.

### Providing advice to the board

The company secretary is the key source of advice to the board on all aspects of governance. The Supporting Principles to Code Principle B.5 state that 'the company secretary should be responsible for advising the board through the chairman on all governance matters'. Similarly, Code Provision B.5.2 provides:

> 'All directors should have access to the advice and services of the company secretary, who is responsible to the board for ensuring that board procedures are complied with.'

The FRC *Guidance on Board Effectiveness* clarifies that this responsibility requires the company secretary, together with the chairman, to 'periodically review whether the board and company's other governance processes ... are fit for purpose and consider any improvements or initiatives that could strengthen the governance of the company'. In order to perform this role well, the company secretary must clearly not only have an in-depth understanding of existing governance arrangements and how they fit with regulatory and legislative requirements, best practice guidance and, above all, the needs of the board and company, he or she must also have the ability to critically assess those arrangements. That critical assessment will require good judgement and sometimes the application of fresh thinking to familiar issues. Often a degree of commercial acumen and professional cynicism will also be required.

In times of corporate stress, the company secretary needs to have the freedom to provide 'a discreet but challenging voice in relation to board deliberations and decision making' (ICSA *Guidance on Corporate Governance Role of the Company Secretary*). Particularly in such circumstances, but also when providing advice generally, the company secretary will need to have built strong relationships of mutual trust with board members and to have their confidence if they are to be able to influence the board's debate and decision making. It is evident that in order to provide such advice, the company secretary also needs to keep abreast of latest developments and should update the board from time to time accordingly. To fulfil this aspect of the role, it is important that the board does not exert undue pressure to achieve its own ends.

### Providing support and guidance to the chairman and NEDs

*The Company Secretary, Building Trust Through Governance* describes the 'triumvirate at the top' – the chairman, company secretary and CEO. This crucial three-way relationship requires parity of esteem and good teamworking. Similarly, the FRC *Guidance on Board Effectiveness* stresses the need for a close relationship between the company secretary and both the chairman and SID, as well as the non-executives more generally. Indeed the Guidance makes a clear link between the effectiveness of the company secretary and his or her ability to build 'relationships of mutual trust' with the non-executives while also maintaining the confidence of the executive directors.

The UK Corporate Governance Code emphasises more the whole-board outlook of the role, perhaps so as to avoid the company secretary being forced to 'take sides', to the possible detriment of the unitary board ideal. However, given the information deficit that can be suffered by the non-executives and their need from time to time for detailed understanding of aspects of the company's business and management, it is they, rather than other members of the executive team, who are likely to turn most readily to the company secretary for more information.

This is not to say that the executive directors will not also call upon the company secretary to support them. They will value the company secretary's experience of board matters and judgement on issues such as whether a decision needs to be referred to the board, preparing technical background information and advice on various quasi-legal matters and how and when to present their proposals.

There are a number of areas examined below in which the company secretary will work closely with the chairman. In particular, the chairman and company secretary will regularly work together preparing for and setting the agendas of board meetings as well as on issues of induction, director development and board evaluation. The chairman will rely on the company secretary to fulfil, on his or her behalf, their obligations under the Code in relation to these latter issues. The chairman will also rely heavily on the company secretary in the lead-up to the AGM, in particular if a difficult meeting is anticipated. The value of the 'continuously dependable support' provided by the company secretary to non-executives in particular was recognised in the *Walker Review* as unlikely to be bettered by external resource in most circumstances.

### Board information flows

The efficient running of the board and its committees is a core responsibility of the company secretary. Managing board procedures will involve assisting the chairman in the preparation of agendas, preparing and collating supporting papers, advising during meetings on board procedures and best practice, taking minutes and maintaining meeting records. While at first glance many of these functions may appear to be somewhat administrative or mundane, in fact many of these require fine judgement and intelligent application, and accordingly, their potential impact on the effectiveness of a board and its ability to take timely, well-informed and high-quality decisions should not be underestimated.

Take, for example, preparation of the agenda. The company secretary will, using their judgement and based on their knowledge of the matters reserved to the board, the company's annual cycle, past decisions and current issues, diarise matters which will require consideration at the next or a particular future meeting so that they are not inadvertently missed. The executive team will frequently seek guidance from the company secretary on whether a particular matter should be referred to the board and, if so, at what stage and via which route. The company secretary is uniquely placed to provide this guidance and to judge what matters are likely to warrant board attention and whether, for example, the matter should also be considered by a board committee. These will form the basis of the first draft of each agenda for discussion with the chairman and help ensure that matters referred to the board are appropriate and timely and that executive colleagues have adequate warning so that they can provide well-prepared papers. Ensuring, in this way, that agendas are appropriately focused is perhaps the first essential step in creating the right conditions for a board to be effective.

The provision of timely and relevant information to NEDs is made a governance objective under Code Principle B.5 and the accompanying Supporting Principles and Code Provisions. As the *Company Secretary, Building Trust Through Governance* set out in its key findings, company secretaries play a vital role by aligning the interests of different parties in the boardroom, facilitating dialogue and assimilating relevant information flows in order to enable effective decision-making. Accordingly, the FRC *Guidance on Board Effectiveness* tasks the company secretary with ensuring that the information provided to the board and its committees is of a high quality. The importance of carrying this out well is emphasised elsewhere in the Guidance, where the provision of high-quality board documentation is identified top of a list of factors which can facilitate good decision making.

As noted in the 2003 *Higgs Report*, information overload and the associated risk that important information is overlooked can be a problem for non-executives. A key part of the company secretary's role is to support the chairman to assess what information is required by the directors and how best to deliver that information without compromising clarity or transparency. Ensuring information is adequate without being excessive requires both judgement and a good understanding of the matter under consideration and the board's decision-making processes. Getting this balance right can be particularly difficult when the matter under consideration is complex or contentious.

In order to achieve this objective, it is worth remembering that the purpose of informing directors about the relevant issues is to enable them to meet their duties as directors, in particular their duties to exercise due skill, care and diligence and to promote success of the company. Retention of the information provided to directors as background to board decision making is important in order to evidence how the directors have fulfilled these responsibilities as well as creating a valuable archive. Copies should therefore be kept centrally with the minutes.

## Supporting board decision making

The FRC *Guidance on Board Effectiveness* highlights the challenge which boards face to ensure their decision-making processes are sound, particularly when considering complex matters. The guidance points out that 'the judgement of even the most well intentioned and experienced leaders can, in certain circumstances, be distorted'.

The company secretary is well placed to be alert to the potential for distortion of judgement created by the existence of conflicts of interest and to provide advice on the appropriate procedures and legal implications when such conflicts exist. He or she should also be ready to advise on alternative strategies for the presentation of information to the board and for decision-making processes which the chairman may wish to contemplate when more difficult issues are under consideration. In this context the FRC Guidance provides the following two useful examples of the additional steps which might reduce the risk of judgements being distorted by factors such as emotional attachment or inappropriate reliance on previous experience or decisions:

- describing in board papers the process that has been used to arrive at and challenge the proposal prior to presenting it to the board, thereby allowing directors not involved in the project to assess the appropriateness of the process as a precursor to assessing the merits of the project itself; or
- where appropriate, putting in place additional safeguards to reduce the risk of distorted judgements by, for example, commissioning an independent

report, seeking advice from an expert, introducing a devil's advocate to provide challenge, establishing a sole purpose sub-committee or convening additional meetings. Some chairmen favour separate discussions for important decisions; for example, concept, proposal for discussion, proposal for decision. This gives executive directors more opportunity to put the case at the earlier stages and all directors the opportunity to share concerns or challenge assumptions well in advance of the point of decision.

The FRC *Guidance on Board Effectiveness* commends to boards the benefits which can be derived from reviewing past decisions, particularly those with disappointing outcomes. Lessons can be gleaned not only from the decision itself but also from reviewing the decision-making processes employed. The opportunities for the company secretary to support this review process, as well as to learn from it, are self-evident.

### Minutes of meetings

The importance of minutes as the definitive record of the proceedings of directors and shareholders in meetings is well recognised and underpinned by the provisions of the CA 2006 that:

- require minutes of directors and shareholder meetings to be taken and kept for a minimum of ten years (ss. 248 and 355); and
- confirm that, once signed, minutes are evidence (unless the contrary is proved) that the meeting took place and that its proceedings were as described (ss. 249 and 356).

Following the publication of a PRA/FCA review into the failure of HBOS, the Treasury Select Committee noted in its 2015 report to Parliament that HBOS board and committee minutes were frequently not sufficiently full to provide a definitive record of what happened. ICSA was asked to provide guidance on minute-taking best practice.

While the resultant guidance confirmed that practice in different sectors, for example financial service companies and NHS entities, could be markedly different, the guidance suggested some principles that can be tailored to the particular circumstances and preferences of the company, the requirement of the company's Articles of Association and expectations of its regulators.

Importantly, the guidance emphasised that the taking of minutes is not merely an administrative task but rather a deceptively complex responsibility that is almost an art form. In law, the responsibility for ensuring that all board and shareholder meeting proceedings (or written resolutions) are properly recorded, rests with the directors (failure to do so is a criminal offence). In practice however, the role will be fulfilled by the company secretary.

While the degree of detail contained in the minutes will vary, as a minimum all minutes should detail:

- the time and date and place of the meeting;
- attendees, including those who are advisers, guests or who are attending in some capacity other than as one of the principal participants;
- apologies for absence;
- declarations of interest;
- a summary of the reports, documents and/or advice received by the meeting;
- the key points of discussion;
- the decisions taken and the reasons for them; and
- the actions that were agreed including details of any delegated authorities.

Above all, the record of proceedings set out in meeting minutes must be accurate, unambiguous, impartial and balanced. Minutes are not generally intended to be a verbatim record (although a shift towards more of a verbatim record is increasingly common in some sectors reflecting some regulators' wish for in-depth detail about the contribution made by each director).

Consistent with a unitary board's collective responsibilities, minutes are traditionally written in the passive voice ('the report was noted', 'the proposal was discussed', etc.) without attributing specific comments or views to any one individual. However, even where this approach is adopted, there will be occasions when particular individuals should be identified in the minutes, including:

- where information or a decision specifically relates to one or more individuals rather than more generally to a category of persons, e.g. an individual declaration of interests;
- one or more individuals disagrees with a majority decision to such a degree that it is appropriate to record their dissent or they choose to, or are required to, abstain from voting and their abstention needs to be recorded;
- an individual has presented a paper;
- an individual has been tasked with executing a particular action and/or been given delegated authority; and
- a personal item such as where an individual is appointed to the board or a committee, their remuneration is decided, performance appraisal discussed or re-election recommended.

The above list is not exhaustive but provides some examples where the naming of individuals is not only relevant, but sometimes essential in order for the minutes to be meaningful. Of relevance to listed companies in this context is Code Provision A.4.3 which requires:

> 'where directors have concerns which cannot be resolved about the running of the company or a proposed action, they should ensure that their concerns are recorded in the board minutes. On resignation, a non-executive director should provide a written statement to the chairman, for circulation of the board, if they have any such concerns.'

As has been noted, the writing of minutes is not necessarily a simple task to complete to a high standard. It is a skill that will certainly require training and practice and, for many company secretaries, arranging for a more junior member of the secretariat team to attend and minute meetings alongside them not only provides a useful development opportunity for that more junior team member, but also enables the company secretary to participate more actively in the meeting. Making notes of a discussion at the same time as contributing to it is surprisingly tricky to achieve! The attendance of a separate minute taker can therefore be of considerable benefit.

The full ICSA *Guidance on Minute Taking* covers these issues more comprehensively and, in highlighting a variety of different approaches, can be a useful tool for reviewing even the most experienced company secretary's minuting practices.

Flowing from the minutes, a clear set of agreed actions should be apparent. To a large extent, a board's effectiveness can be measured by the effectiveness of its decisions and their implementation. The use of minutes to record those decisions is therefore a key tool in translating board decisions into implemented actions. The first step in doing this well is to ensure that decisions and actions are recorded accurately and, to this end, the company secretary should always seek clarification at the meeting if a decision is unclear or not well understood.

Having first recorded the decisions in the minutes, the production of a separate actions list can be used:

- to communicate the board's decision to the appropriate people within the business;
- to track progress on implementation; and
- as the basis for consideration of matters arising from the minutes of the previous meeting.

### The company secretary and committees

The use of committees is mandatory for listed companies in respect of certain matters but can also be helpful in a number of contexts including to consider complex issues. The company secretary will have a key role to play in advising on appropriate terms of reference for special purpose and standing committees and in the periodic review of the latter as well as in providing support to key committees in a similar way as they do to the main board. Those terms of reference should set out the ongoing support role to be provided by the company secretary or company secretariat team. That support is likely to be similar to the company secretarial support provided to the full board.

### Facilitating director induction, training and evaluation

As is considered in more detail in Chapter 9, the induction, training and evaluation of the board and individual directors is now an established governance priority. Despite this, in the *Walker Review* it was noted (at least in relation to the banks and other financial institutions covered by the review) that 'practice and experience in respect of induction and training programmes appears to be quite variable'.

The chairman is primarily responsible for ensuring that new directors receive a full, formal and tailored induction and for agreeing and reviewing with each director their training and development needs (Code Principle B.4 and Supporting Principles and Provisions). However, the UK Corporate Governance Code also stresses the important role to be played by the company secretary as the facilitator of the induction and training programmes and this point is reiterated in the FRC *Guidance on Board Effectiveness*. That guidance points out that the company secretary can add value by managing the procurement of induction and development activity on behalf of the chairman and makes the point that, when doing so, care needs to be taken to ensure the activity is appropriate to the relevant director (i.e. it must be tailored to their needs), must have the objective of enhancing that director's effectiveness within their board or committee role and must be consistent with the results of the board evaluation process. Ensuring the board evaluation process is objective and rigorous in identifying areas requiring individual development is therefore essential.

For listed companies the UK Corporate Governance Code requires the board to engage the services of external board evaluation consultants at least every three years (Code Provision B.6.2). Where external board evaluation consultants are not used, the company secretary's impartial status on the board means they are ideally positioned to implement an evaluation programme and to collate and report the results without loss of anonymity. Ensuring anonymity encourages the sharing of open and honest views and thus enhances the value of individual contributions which might otherwise be undermined by loyalties, personal sensitivities or a reluctance to 'rock the boat'. Regardless of whether the evaluation is externally, or internally facilitated the company secretary will play a key role in its arrangement and in ensuring the action-plan that results from the process is presented to the board for approval, is subsequently implemented and progress tracked.

Although the Preface to the Code makes it clear that the company's chairman is expected to give a personal report on how the Principles in Sections A and B of the Code have been applied, it is usual for the company secretary to also play an active part in framing the reporting to shareholders required by Code Provision B.6.1. Having identified board performance as a contributory factor in the failure of some banks, the *Walker Review* recommended that a statement on board evaluation be included in the report and accounts every second or third year. While Code Provision B.6.1 is fairly undemanding as to the reporting of board evaluation, requiring only a statement in the annual report on how the performance evaluation was conducted, 'boilerplate' reporting in this regard will not be sufficient. Investors will wish the narrative to be sufficiently detailed that they can gain an insight into how the evaluation was carried out, how effective governance arrangements are and how gaps will be addressed. There is often a challenge in balancing the need for confidentiality while still being appropriately transparent. A best practice suggestion proposed by Legal & General Investment Management in its 2016 document 'Board Effectiveness Reviews: Guiding Principles' was that the party which led the board evaluation should agree and approve the disclosures.

These induction, training and evaluation tasks will require the company secretary to work with the chairman, who remains ultimately responsible for these areas and also the internal HR team. External board evaluation consultants and other external consultants might also be used to assist with evaluation, induction and development tasks. Whoever the company secretary is working with to deliver the induction, evaluation and training functions, he or she should ensure that any programmes take account of the particular needs of individual directors as well as the strengths and weaknesses of the board.

### Annual report and accounts

The company secretary will typically co-ordinate contributions to the annual report and accounts and manage the complex arrangements needed to ensure the report and accounts meet regulatory requirements but also support the company's external communication and engagement strategies. The company secretariat is custodian of much of the information required for the report and accounts, not only for the parent company but also for its subsidiaries. Providing and checking this information and ensuring timely board approval of subsidiary company accounts in advance of approval of the consolidated group accounts can, for large groups of companies, be a mammoth task in itself. It will require careful planning and a cool head in the face of the last-minute glitches which inevitably seem to occur.

Oversight and control of the content of the report and accounts, at least of the front 'narrative' part of the documents and arrangements for the production and issue of the report and accounts to members, will form a significant part of the company secretary's annual remit in line with their overall compliance responsibilities. The project, which will be closely linked to the AGM arrangements, will rely on significant planning and will involve a number of internal parties including finance, HR, communications, IR, directors, board and committees, as well as external parties such as the auditors, registrars, financial PR agencies, printing and mailing houses, design consultants and other advisers.

Working so closely with the board and its committees, the company secretary has a unique bird's-eye view of group-wide strategic issues and governance matters and as such is ideally placed to provide valuable input into much of the company's narrative reports including the chairman's statement, strategic report, the directors' report, the reports of the nomination, remuneration and audit committees and the corporate governance statement. In contributing to these reports, the company secretary should pay particular attention to the regulatory intentions behind the reporting requirements and draft them in such a way that they will provide useful and meaningful information to users of the reports and so help to enhance stakeholder trust and confidence in the company.

With their expertise and central role in the company's corporate governance practices, the company secretary will normally have particular responsibility for preparing the corporate governance statement. The company secretary, through his or her experience, knowledge and close involvement in the design of the company's governance practices, will be able to provide the clear and useful explanations which shareholders require in order to understand them properly. In particular, the company secretary's in-depth knowledge of the UK Corporate Governance Code requirements and the company's compliance with its provisions, he or she is ideally placed to prepare the 'comply or explain' narrative. The FRC's '*What Constitutes an Explanation under "Comply or Explain"?*' will be a useful source of reference. By producing a corporate governance statement which meets these shareholder information requirements, the company secretary can contribute greatly to securing the valuable support of investors. The requirements for the narrative reports are examined in Chapter 8.

### Shareholder relations and general meetings

Code Principle E.1 makes the board as a whole responsible for 'ensuring a satisfactory dialogue' with shareholders and Code Provision E.1.1 and the Supporting Principles to Code Principle D.2 give the chairman specific responsibilities for discussing governance, strategy and remuneration issues with major shareholders. However, the company secretary will have a significant part to play in support of these governance objectives, for example advising the board and chairman on the regulatory requirements in relation to key aspects of the company's narrative reporting, managing the IR part of the company's website, preparing shareholder circulars or answering investors' enquiries on forthcoming shareholder resolutions or governance standards. Shareholder engagement and dialogue best practice is discussed further in Chapter 5 but suffice to say at this point that the company secretary, as a minimum, will be closely involved in this activity.

The company secretary will be responsible for managing, with the assistance of the company's registrar, the preparation for and delivery of the company's AGM and other general meetings. Ensuring the timely giving of notice to all members for the meeting in compliance with the requirements of the Companies Act will be just one part of those preparations. Working with external advisers where required, in particular the company secretary will ensure that adequate explanations and details are provided in the accompanying notice of meeting as required by the relevant rules of LR13 and that, where circulars require prior UKLA approval, this is obtained. Particularly where there are difficult or potentially contentious issues anticipated at the meeting, the explanations and justifications provided in the accompanying documentation may need to go beyond that required by the relevant regulations and will certainly need to be drafted in a clear and readily understandable style.

For the meeting itself, practical and security arrangements will need as much thought as legal requirements and, as part of this, the chairman will rely on the company secretary to ensure he or she is adequately briefed. On the day, the company secretary will have an important role providing information about proxy votes and the processes required to take a resolution on a poll, as well as advising on matters of meeting procedure so as to ensure compliance with the company's articles of association and statutory requirements. After the meeting, the company secretary will need to ensure that information relating to the voting and resolutions is published on the company's website in a timely manner. Further details of these requirements are set out in Chapter 15.

For many private shareholders, the AGM represents their only opportunity to engage directly with the company's directors. The company secretary, through the key role he or she plays in determining the success of the event, can influence the extent to which the AGM delivers a genuine opportunity for retail investors to enter into dialogue and discussions with board members.

## Statutory registers and returns and LR obligations

Completion of the statutory registers and returns is a relatively routine matter, but nevertheless they are essential sources of information on the company's constitution, the shareholders and the board.

The LR and DTR require disclosures on vital governance information such as transactions relating to major interests in the share capital and directors' dealings and the announcement of interim or final results. The company secretary is responsible for ensuring that such information is notified to an RIS at the LSE within the relevant timescales. Under the LR 9.6.11R a company must notify an RIS at the LSE of any change to the board including:

- the appointment of a new director, stating the appointee's name and whether the position is executive, non-executive or chairman and the nature of any specific function or responsibility of the position;
- the resignation, removal or retirement of a director (unless the director retires and is re-appointed at a general meeting of the shareholders); and
- important changes to the role, functions or responsibilities of a director.

The notification must confirm the date the change takes effect and must be made as soon as possible, in any case no later than the end of the business day following the decision or receipt of notice about the change by the company. If the effective date is not known, the notification should state this fact and the company should issue a further notification as soon as it has been decided.

The company secretary will also need to guide the directors on requirements relating to misleading the market, and market abuse. In addition, the company secretary will ensure that disclosures required to be available on the company's website – copies of announcements, general meeting voting outcomes, gender pay gap reports and the like – are kept up-to-date and meet requirements. These issues are considered in greater detail in Chapter 15.

#### *Subsidiary governance*

Control of subsidiary companies is an important area in which company secretaries of larger groups will play an active and vital role. Some of the practical considerations are discussed in more detail in Chapter 16.

## In-house counsel and corporate governance

### Opportunity and challenge

The UK Corporate Governance Code has nothing to say about the role of in-house legal counsel. Instead, it is the company secretary who is given sole responsibility for acting as the main source of advice to the board on governance matters. Yet frequently the head of the in-house legal function will either be on the board or will be close to it and as such is well positioned to complement the skills and knowledge of the company secretary when providing advice to the board on their legal duties with respect to governance matters or on other legal issues. In short, in-house counsel will often also be required to act as a 'trusted adviser' to the board and to assist the company secretary in carrying out his or her governance responsibilities.

There have been several factors at work in recent years that have led to an enhanced profile and status for in-house counsel. Chief amongst these has been a perception by boards that their legal function can assist in managing risk and ensuring compliance at a time of far more burdensome regulation. This development has been particularly evident in the US, where the in-house counsel of large companies can command a very important place in the senior management team (with remuneration to match). The need to comply with the raft of new regulations in the wake of the Sarbanes-Oxley Act 2002, the challenges of managing legal compliance across jurisdictional boundaries and the increasing risk of class actions in the US have all caused the in-house legal function to shift closer to centre stage.

In major part, it is the fall-out of the more high-profile corporate governance scandals which has been instrumental in promoting in-house counsel's governance role in this manner. When Royal Dutch/Shell appointed US law firm Davis Polk & Wardwell to conduct an investigation into the over-statement of its oil reserves, one of its conclusions was the significant lack of involvement of the legal function within the business. The review recommended the attendance of general counsel at executive management meetings at the level of both the main board and the business units and that all in-house lawyers should report directly to the legal director (and not, for example, to a member of the executive management team).

While such developments have created an opportunity for in-house counsel, there are also some significant challenges. During the 1990s, in-house legal teams became more integrated with their businesses, with a clearer mandate to add value within the mainstream management structure. If the in-house legal team becomes the 'corporate governance policeman', this value-adding role will be jeopardised because they will spend a disproportionate amount of their time advising boards on their legal obligations. For example, the highly prescriptive nature of the Sarbanes-Oxley requirements makes it inevitable that boards will turn to their legal counsel, literally in this case, to 'keep them out of jail'. Even where the board is not subject to Sarbanes-Oxley, the risks to the business of failing to comply with regulatory requirements in areas such as competition and environmental law are such that the board will need to take legal advice on a regular basis. The challenge, therefore, is to be in a position to offer that 'trusted adviser' type of advice, while remaining fully integrated within the business and the senior management structure. Separation of the role of in-house counsel from that of company secretary can therefore bring benefits. A number of significant companies have reversed earlier decisions to combine the roles, perhaps recognising, if nothing else, that combining two extremely demanding roles risks compromising the execution of both.

### The governance role of in-house counsel

Since the *Cadbury Report*, corporate governance guidelines have principally focused on the roles of the board and company secretary. Particularly in the US, however, there has been increased recognition of the potential for in-house counsel to play a part in ensuring good corporate governance standards. There are several areas in which in-house counsel may play a governance role in their capacity as advisers to the board, as identified in Table 14.2.

**Table 14.2** Governance role of in-house counsel

| | |
|---|---|
| **Risk management** | Managing legal risk (both enforceability risk to an organisation's contracts and property rights and regulatory risk of breaches of statutory or regulatory requirements), creating adequate risk assessment processes for large projects, managing due diligence on mergers and acquisitions transactions, contributing to internal control systems to prevent financial and accounting fraud. |
| **Compliance** | Advising the board on the legal compliance requirements with respect to the key statutory and other duties (competition, environmental, health and safety, corporate manslaughter, etc.). |
| **Reputation** | Acting as part of the corporate conscience to maintain the company's reputation, warning of the potential damaging effect of a profit-at-all-costs approach. |
| **Litigation** | Handling class actions taken by shareholders against the board and also investigations by the regulatory authorities (including 'dawn raids'). |
| **External appointments** | Overseeing the terms of appointment for external advisers and consultants (e.g. the auditors), checking for transparency, and consistency in terms and potential conflicts. |
| **Business ethics** | Drafting the company's business ethics policy and leading on enforcement of the company's anti-corruption policies, as well as making judgements where necessary on whistleblowing. |

## Reporting lines, conflicts of interest and professional privilege

In-house counsel can fulfil multiple roles – at any one time they can be cast in the roles of employee, director, adviser to the board, corporate conscience and officer of the court – with the result that the potential for conflict positions to arise is material. The starting point is that in-house counsel owes a duty of loyalty to their employer. In practice, this should not be incompatible with the day-to-day requirement to serve and advise the board, particularly in a well-managed company. However, there may be occasions when conflict does arise, in which case it will be vital that there are clear reporting lines through which it can be discussed and resolved.

Within a large in-house legal function the reporting lines should lead up to the group general counsel and then normally to the chief executive. In the smaller function, the report may perhaps be directly to the chief executive. The senior legal adviser should generally have direct access to the board and its committees. In extreme cases the in-house counsel would be able to raise concerns with the chairman or, ultimately, to whistleblow. In this respect, the in-house counsel is no different from any other member of the senior management team. All senior managers, as employees, have a duty to the business and if they are directors, to the company. However, while this may be the case legally and ethically, the in-house counsel, as a matter of professional conduct, may also hold an important position (jointly with the company secretary) as an independent custodian of good governance within the company. The Solicitor's Code of Conduct, which applies to solicitors notwithstanding that they are in-house, sets out principles for in-house counsel to adhere to. The principles cover issues such as who is the in-house counsel's client, the obligations owed to that client, client confidentiality, conflicts of interest and legal professional privilege.

The issue of legal professional privilege for in-house counsel is complex and has been the subject of two key decisions in recent times. First, in 2004 in *Three Rivers DC v Bank of England* (No 6) ([2004] UKHL 48) the House of Lords allowed an appeal from an earlier Court of Appeal decision (*Three Rivers DC v Bank of England* (No 5) [2003] EWCA Civ 474) confirming that confidential communications between in-house counsel and the client will be protected by legal advice privilege when that advice is given in a 'relevant legal context' (in contradistinction to a 'business' context). However, the House of Lords' decision left open the issue of 'who is the client'. The Court of Appeal had held that a narrow definition of client ought to be applied, dictating that, for example, a communication from a junior employee who would not have the authority to seek advice directly from, or give instructions to, in-house counsel would not be a client. Therefore, any such communication (which might, for example, be on a whistleblowing matter) would not be protected by legal advice privilege. The Court of Appeal's narrow approach was recently affirmed by Hildyard J in *Re RBS Rights Issue Litigation* ([2016] EWHC 3161).

A practical solution may be for the board to clarify that a wide group of employees has the authority to seek and/or receive advice from in-house counsel. However, the court would no doubt carefully scrutinise whether any such authority was genuine if faced with this issue. Consideration might also be given to ensuring that internal communications to/from in-house counsel are not documented until the client has been properly identified, and, thereafter, appropriate steps are taken when sharing advice rendered by in-house counsel to avoid the risk of privilege inadvertently being waived.

The second key decision was given by the European Courts in a case brought by the Dutch multinational, Akzo Nobel, against the EC (C-550/07P, 14 September 2010). Akzo Nobel asserted that communications with in-house counsel which had been seized by the EC in a price-fixing investigation were subject to legal professional privilege. However, the European Court of First Instance decided that these communications were not subject to legal professional privilege and the European Court of Justice subsequently upheld this decision. One implication of this decision is that when dealing with competition investigations by the EC, communications between in-house counsel and other employees will not be subject to legal professional privilege. Therefore, amongst other things, in-house counsel should consider conducting sensitive investigations, or seeking advice on sensitive issues, regarding relevant matters through external lawyers.

## Conclusion

Responsibility for a company's governance does not rest with one single individual but is shared by the board, its company secretary and other advisers. As the board's principal governance adviser, the company secretary will inevitably wish to draw upon the expertise of other internal and external specialists from time to time, including in-house counsel. In doing so, the company secretary will need to ensure both that the involvement of the legal function is secured whenever appropriate and through processes that safeguard privilege and that the legal advice proffered is given proper consideration by the board.

## Governance checklist

✓ Are the company secretary's role and reporting lines well defined and does the board understand and support that role and take responsibility for the terms of appointment?

✓ Does the company secretary have the trust and confidence of the board and possess the necessary personal attributes and skills for the job?

✓ Does the board run efficiently and is high-quality and timely information provided to the board by the company secretary?

✓ Does the company secretary produce accurate minutes which reflect best practice, demonstrate the duties properly and record decisions and actions so as to support board effectiveness?

✓ Does the company secretary support the chairman as leader of the board, including providing director induction, professional development training and evaluation?

✓ Does the company secretary advise the board on all governance matters and, working with the chairman, periodically review the board and company's governance processes to ensure they are fit for purpose and recommend steps which could enhance or strengthen the company's governance as appropriate?

- ✓ Does the company secretary take responsibility for the coordination of the annual report and accounts and provide quality input to the directors' report, corporate governance statement and other reports required to be published?
- ✓ Does the company's IR programme take full advantage of the company secretary's experience and knowledge?
- ✓ If the company secretary's role is combined with another executive role, has the board taken steps to ensure that conflicts of interest are addressed?
- ✓ Is the in-house legal function available to assist the company secretary when appropriate in advising the board on governance matters, with a role that is not restricted to internal governance 'policeman'?
- ✓ Is the governance role of the in-house counsel well defined and is the identity of the client widely understood?
- ✓ Does the in-house counsel have clear reporting lines within the organisation and direct access to the board?
- ✓ Are appropriate procedures in place to safeguard privilege?

# Part 5

## Governance in Practice

# 15

# Governance of listed companies

## Introduction

Chapter 4 describes the duties and liabilities of directors generally. This chapter examines aspects of the additional responsibilities of directors of public companies whose shares are listed and traded on a public market, in particular those companies on the Official List and with some commentary for those traded on AIM. For such companies and their directors, the capacity to offer shares to the public gives a particular relevance to corporate governance matters owing to the evident shareholder protection issues. There is a significant layer of additional rules and regulations to be observed. The chapter begins with an overview of the regulatory environment for listed company directors and outlines the UK regime for the listing of securities.

Directors of listed companies should understand the regulatory framework within which they must work and need to be aware of developments in that regime as they occur. Within that broad regulatory framework, listed company directors will be faced with considerable complexity. So, for example, when dealing with such events as a fresh public offering of shares or a major corporate transaction, they will need to ensure compliance with the detailed requirements relating to the contents of listing particulars and prospectuses, the intricacies of the continuing obligation rules, and other relevant regulatory requirements. In practice, for such discrete and one-off transactions they will need to rely heavily on the company's sponsor and professional advisers, who will both identify the relevant areas for compliance and help to navigate a way through them.

Turning to their more everyday governance responsibilities, directors will be challenged by the rules applying to communications with shareholders and the wider market on price-sensitive matters, and also their personal dealings in the company's shares. These latter aspects are the subject of the main bulk of this chapter, the aim being to focus on the governance obligations for directors of public companies that are continuing and everyday – in contrast to those that are transaction-focused and 'set piece'. This chapter concludes with a section on the Takeover Code (which applies also to certain companies beyond those with a current listing) and directors' duties in a takeover or merger situation.

## An overview of the UK listing regime

### UKLA's responsibilities and objectives

Section 75 of the FSMA 2000 states that admission to the Official List may be granted only on an application to 'the competent authority' in such manner as may be required by the rules framed for this purpose. Part VI of FSMA 2000 imposes on the FCA the requirement to act as the competent authority for the listing of shares and gives it the powers to enable it to fulfil this function. In this capacity, the FCA is known as the UKLA. The UKLA's main responsibilities under Part VI of FSMA 2000 are listed in Table 15.1 below.

**Table 15.1** UKLA responsibilities under FSMA 2000

| | |
|---|---|
| **Admitting securities to listing and other applications** | The UKLA examines and approves prospectuses and listing particulars, taking into account the requirements of its rules and any special conditions it may impose. Note that directors have primary responsibility for the accuracy and completeness of these documents. |
| **Sponsor regulation** | Sponsors must be approved by the UKLA to provide relevant services to issuers, so ensuring compliance with the rules applying to them. Other advisers (e.g. reporting accountants and lawyers) have an important role in securing such compliance. |
| **Enforcing ongoing obligations on issuers** | The UKLA is required to ensure that standards are not only met on admission to the Official List, but also on a continuous basis through the disclosure of relevant information. FSMA 2000 gives the UKLA powers to impose penalties for breaches of its rules, both on issuing companies and any of their directors who are knowingly concerned in such a breach. |
| **Suspending and cancelling listing** | The UKLA can suspend securities from the Official List to protect investors from trading where there is insufficient information to ensure an orderly market. It can also cancel a listing where it believes there are special circumstances preventing normal dealings. |

The regulatory objectives of the UKLA are focused around the need to maintain the competitiveness of the UK market in listed securities and the desirability of facilitating competition in such securities and the confidence of investors generally.

### The UKLA Rules

In order to comply with its obligations, including in particular those arising under relevant EU regulation and FSMA 2000, the UKLA has created and maintains the UKLA Rules. The UKLA Rules are divided into the Listing

Rules, DTR and PR. This structure reflects the main EU Directives and Regulations which set standards for issuers of securities and in particular those trading on a 'regulated market' within the EU such as the Main Market.

The main reason for structuring the UKLA Rules in this manner is that EU regulation applies to a broader range of issuers than those admitted to the UK's 'regulated markets', e.g. the main market. For example, the Prospectus Directive imposes requirements relating to public offers of securities whether or not application has been made for admission to trade on an EU-regulated market, including where the securities are not traded at all. It follows, therefore, that some requirements also apply to issuers with securities listed on AIM, which is a 'multilateral trading facility' but not a 'regulated market'.

Table 15.2 sets out a brief summary of the scope and contents of the three rulebooks.

**Table 15.2** UKLA Rules – summary

| Rulebook | Summary of scope and contents |
|---|---|
| **LR** | ■ Contain rules and guidance for issuers of securities admitted (or seeking) admission to the Official List.<br>■ Focus on eligibility for listing and the continuing obligations of listed issuers and sponsors.<br>■ Also include the Listing and Premium Principles, based on recognised standards of corporate governance. |
| **PR** | ■ Scope extends to all issuers making public offers of securities.<br>■ Contain, together with FSMA, the rules and guidance outlining circumstances in which a prospectus is required and what that prospectus must contain.<br>■ Set out requirements applicable to the preparation and contents of prospectuses.<br>■ Incorporate the ability to passport prospectuses on a pan-European basis. |
| **DTR** | ■ Provide guidance relating to the publication and control of inside information in addition to the directly applicable provisions of MAR.<br>■ Stipulate the provisions on periodic financial reporting.<br>■ Establish the disclosures to be made by and in relation to major shareholdings and voting rights.<br>■ Regulate for the dissemination of information to shareholders.<br>■ Require the appointment of an audit committee and specify the minimum responsibilities of that body.<br>■ Set out the need for a corporate governance statement and its form and contents. |

As is evident from this summary, the UKLA Rules sit at the centre of a complex legal and regulatory structure, as illustrated in Figure 15.1.

**Figure 15.1** UK corporate legal and regulatory structure

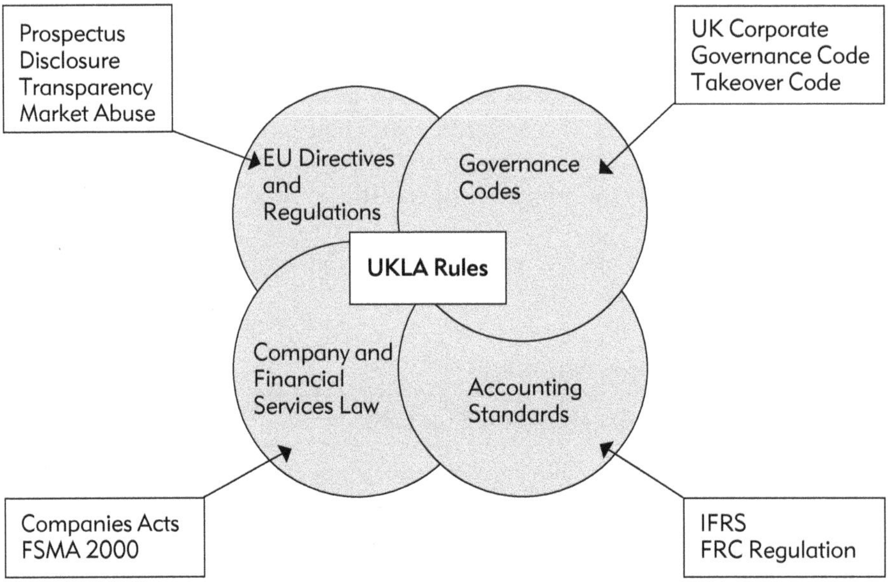

Prospectus
Disclosure
Transparency
Market Abuse

UK Corporate
Governance Code
Takeover Code

EU Directives and Regulations

Governance Codes

UKLA Rules

Company and Financial Services Law

Accounting Standards

Companies Acts
FSMA 2000

IFRS
FRC Regulation

## Premium and Standard Listings

The Listing regime has a two-tier structure with Premium and Standard listing segments. The two segments are then further divided into different categories based upon the type of issuer and securities listed.

UK companies are eligible for Standard Listing, similar in form to a secondary listing for non-UK companies. Overseas Standard Listed companies are required to comply with the EU Company Reporting Directive. Premium Listed companies, whether UK or overseas, are subject to the requirements of the UK Corporate Governance Code on a 'comply or explain' basis. These changes have created a level playing field for all listed companies regardless of their country of incorporation. For the purposes of this chapter, the requirements described will, in general, reflect the requirements for Premium Listed companies. For an understanding of the detailed contents and application of the rulebooks, reference should be made to specialist works and to the UKLA Rules themselves.

The following paragraphs highlight some of the requirements of the UKLA Rules which are particularly significant in governance terms. Later paragraphs in this chapter will address separately the insider dealing and market abuse rules and the rules relating to dealings by directors and other PDMR.

To address these issues, the main focus of the following sections is on the LR and the DTR.

## Premium Listing: 'super-equivalent' requirements

Premium Listing is only available to equity securities which meet the so-called 'super-equivalent' requirements – that is, requirements which go further than is necessary to achieve strict compliance with EU law. The requirements relate both to eligibility for listing as well as aspects of the continuing obligation regime, as now described.

On the eligibility requirements, the super-equivalent requirements include, amongst other things, the need for an applicant to provide consolidated accounts for the previous three years audited by independent auditors, a three-year revenue earning record for at least 75% of its business and evidence that the issuer has sufficient working capital for the next 12 months.

### Continuing obligations

As regards the continuing obligation requirements, of particular note is the obligation placed upon issuers with a Premium Listing to reinforce shareholders' rights in potentially dilutive circumstances to ensure their equal treatment. The pre-emption rights regime, the aim of which is to ensure that all shareholders have the right to subscribe for additional shares in proportion to their existing shareholdings, can be disapplied in the case of UK Companies as permitted by ss. 570 and 571 of the CA 2006, for the purposes of selling treasury shares to employee share schemes, to deal with fractional entitlements arising from a rights issue or open offer or to exclude shares held outside the UK from an offer where there are regulatory reasons which make excluding that territory necessary or expedient: LR 9.3.11R and 9.3.12R. For non-UK companies not covered by the CA 2006, the pre-emption rights requirement can be excluded by obtaining shareholders' consent (subject to certain conditions).

The continuing obligations for Premium Listed shares also cover certain types of significant transactions and transactions with related parties. A summary of these is set out in Table 15.3 overleaf.

Certain changes were made to the LR in May 2014. These included provisions relating to 'controlling shareholders' of Premium Listed companies, defined broadly as any person who exercises or controls on their own or with any person with whom they are acting in concert, 30% or more of the votes of the company. Controlling shareholders are now required to enter into a relationship agreement with the company, and the LR set out certain minimum criteria for such agreements to ensure the independence of the company from the controlling shareholder. Certain other protections were brought into the LR including disclosures in annual reports and a dual voting system for independent shareholders.

**Table 15.3** Continuing obligations

| Transaction type | Description of super-equivalent listing rule |
|---|---|
| **Significant transactions** | These are divided into two classes depending on the size of the proposed transaction relative to the size of the issuer proposing to undertake it (the class test provisions). A listed company is required to disclose a greater level of information for larger transactions and shareholder approval must be obtained and a UKLA-approved circular issued in the case of Class 1 transactions (i.e. where any of the specified percentage ratios is 25% or more) and reverse takeovers (i.e. an acquisition by a listed company of a business, an unlisted company or assets where any of the specified percentage ratios is 100% or more or which would result in a fundamental change in the business or in a change of the board or voting control of the listed company). The LR state that the class tests provisions are designed to cover transactions that are outside the ordinary course of business and/or have the potential to change a shareholder's economic interest in the assets and liabilities of the company (LR 10.1.4G). |
| **Related party transactions** | A related party transaction includes a transaction with a substantial shareholder, a director of the company or a group company, a person exercising significant influence or an associate of any of these parties ( LR 11.1.4R and LR 11.1.5R and exemptions set out in LR 11 Annex 1R). If a listed company proposes to enter into a related party transaction it must make an appropriate announcement, send a circular to its shareholders, obtain the shareholders' approval of the transaction and ensure that the related party does not vote on the resolution (LR 11.1.7R). |

## Listing Principles

LR 7.2.1R contains two Listing Principles and LR 7.2.1A contains six Premium Listing Principles. The Listing Principles and the Premium Listing Principles (together, the 'Principles') apply to every issuer of equity shares with a Premium Listing in respect of its obligations under the LR and the DTR. The responsible party is stated to be the issuer itself, not its directors. However, while there is no attempt to attribute to the directors personal responsibility for compliance, the line of responsibility runs directly to the boardroom. Table 15.4 and 15.5 set out the text of the Listing Principles and the Premium Listing Principles.

The Listing Principles are as follows:

**Table 15.4** Listing Principles

| Listing Principle | Text in the LR |
|---|---|
| Listing Principle 1 | A listed company must take reasonable steps to establish and maintain adequate procedures, systems and controls to enable it to comply with its obligations. |
| Listing Principle 2 | A listed company must deal with the FCA in an open and co-operative manner. |

The Premium Listing Principles are as follows:

**Table 15.5** Premium Listing Principles

| Premium Listing Principle | Text in the LR |
|---|---|
| Premium Listing Principle 1 | A listed company must take reasonable steps to enable its directors to understand their responsibilities and obligations as directors. |
| Premium Listing Principle 2 | A listed company must act with integrity towards the holders and potential holders of its Premium Listed shares. |
| Premium Listing Principle 3 | All equity shares in a class that has been admitted to Premium Listing must carry an equal number of votes on any shareholder vote. |
| Premium Listing Principle 4 | Where a listed company has more than one class of equity shares admitted to Premium Listing, the aggregate voting rights of the shares in each class should be broadly proportionate to the relative interests of those classes in the equity of the listed company. |
| Premium Listing Principle 5 | A listed company must ensure that it treats all holders of the same class of its listed equity shares that are in the same position equally in respect of the rights attaching to those listed equity shares. |
| Premium Listing Principle 6 | A listed company must communicate information to holders and potential holders of its listed equity shares in such a way as to avoid the creation of a false market in those listed equity shares. |

Such a high-level, principles-based approach is similar to the UK Corporate Governance Code. However, there is no 'comply or explain' process under the LR, and failure to comply with the Principles could lead to penalties or other enforcement action. Guidance to the LR makes it clear that, rather than expanding the scope or application of the underlying rules and guidance, the Principles should be interpreted in accordance with those underlying rules and guidance. The Principles are intended to assist issuers in identifying their obligations and responsibilities.

In order to enforce the Principles, the FCA will need to demonstrate that an issuer has been at fault and in doing so it will be expected to exercise its enforcement powers 'reasonably and on a proportionate basis'. The aim, therefore, would seem to be to pick up issuers who are persistently in deliberate breach of either the LR or the DTR.

Listing Principle 1 is subject to separate guidance. It relates to an issuer's systems and controls, and has an apparent linkage with the internal control provisions in the UK Corporate Governance Code and the related FRC guidance. The LR guidance emphasises that in particular issuers should ensure adequate systems and controls are in place in relation to LR 10 (significant transactions), LR 11 (related party transactions) and the timely and accurate disclosure of information to the market.

In relation to the last of these, further guidance clarifies not only that systems and controls should be in place to ensure proper identification of information that requires disclosure, but also that any such information is 'properly considered by the directors and that such consideration encompasses whether the information should be disclosed'. This emphasis, taken together with Premium Listing Principle 6, which requires an issuer to communicate with the market in such a way as to avoid creating a false market in its securities, is perhaps indicative of the importance placed by the UKLA on the need to set a high standard for market communications by issuers, requiring them to observe the spirit as well as the letter of the rules.

## Market communications, disclosures and dealings

Participants in the market are subject to disclosure and dealing requirements imposed under both civil and criminal law. The UK's regime, which has been something of a leader in EU terms, is now supplemented by the overriding requirements of EU law.

The UK's civil market abuse regime was largely superseded by the new EU MAR in July 2016. It sits alongside the requirements of the criminal law relating to insider dealing (contained in Part V of the Criminal Justice Act 1993). Taken together, these provisions and the associated rules and codes of practice issued by the FCA as the regulator of public markets, are aimed at ensuring a proper flow of information to the market and preventing (and, where relevant, detecting and punishing) abusive or manipulative use of such information. From the governance perspective, the investor protection implications are apparent. For directors of listed companies (and others in managerial positions), an understanding of their related duties and liabilities will have an everyday impact on their behaviour and decision making and should therefore be a priority.

The following sections of this chapter address the criminal and civil law regimes respectively. Further sections focus on provisions in the DTR.

## The criminal law framework: insider dealing and misleading statements

The fundamental purpose of the criminal law's insider dealing and misleading statements provisions is to ensure that investors can have confidence in the integrity of the securities markets by prohibiting and punishing inappropriate dealings by insiders and the deliberate misleading of market participators. The aim, therefore, is to ensure equal and timely access to accurate information that is of relevance to an investor so that participants in markets can make informed and unprejudiced decisions. In this respect, information is the key.

### Insider dealing

Under the provisions in Part V of the Criminal Justice Act 1993, insider dealing is a criminal offence punishable on conviction by an unlimited fine and/or imprisonment for up to seven years. It applies in circumstances (described here as 'specified circumstances') where an individual who is 'an insider' acquires or disposes (or procures the acquisition or disposal) of shares by a transaction on a regulated market or when making such a transaction relies on a professional intermediary or the 'insider' is acting as a professional intermediary.

A person is an insider for these purposes if they are in possession of information which they know to be 'inside information' that has been obtained from an inside source. Inside information is defined as information which relates to particular securities or a particular issuer (or issuers) of securities, is specific or precise, has not been made public and if it were made public would be likely to have a significant effect on the price of the securities. Information is obtained from an inside source if the person has obtained it through being a director, employee or shareholder of an issuer of securities or by virtue of their employment or profession or the source of their information has obtained it in either of such manners. The offence of insider dealing will be committed if:

- the person deals in securities that are price-affected securities in relation to the information knowing that the dealing would take place in the specified circumstances (described above);
- the person encourages another person to deal in securities that are price-affected securities in relation to the information, knowing or having reasonable cause to believe that the dealing would take place in the specified circumstances; or

- the person discloses the information, otherwise than in the proper performance of the functions of their employment, office or profession, to another person.

A key consideration for directors (and other potential insiders) is what constitutes price-sensitive information. It is only where information would, if made public, be likely to have a significant effect on the price of securities that it will be considered price sensitive. However, in practice, it has proved difficult to set out unequivocally when information would be likely to have such an effect.

There are several general and also special defences to an accusation of insider dealing. The general defences rely on the individual concerned being able to show that:

- they did not expect the dealing to result in a profit attributable to the fact that the information in question was price-sensitive information;
- they reasonably believed that the information had been disclosed widely enough to ensure that none of those taking part in the dealing would be prejudiced by not having the information; and
- they would have done what they did even if they had not had the information.

An individual is not guilty of insider dealing by virtue of a disclosure of information if they are able to show that they did not at the time expect any person, because of the disclosure, to deal in securities in the specified circumstances (as described above), or that, although they had such an expectation at the time, they did not expect the dealing to result in a profit attributable to the fact that the information was price-sensitive information.

### Misleading statements and impressions

Sections 89–91 of the Financial Services Act 2012 contain provisions imposing criminal sanctions relating to three separate offences:

- Section 89: making false or misleading statements;
- Section 90: creating a false or misleading impression; and
- Section 91: making false or misleading statements or creating a false or misleading impression in relation to specified benchmarks.

The offences in sections 89 and 90 of the Financial Services Act 2012 replaced the misleading statements and conduct offences regime in s. 397 of FSMA from 1 April 2013.

With respect to false or misleading statements, s. 89 applies if one of three circumstances arises. These are where a person makes a statement knowing, or being reckless as to whether it is false or misleading in a material respect or dishonestly conceals any material facts, whether in connection with a statement made by that person or otherwise.

In such circumstances, the person will commit an offence if they make the statement or conceal the facts with the intention of inducing, or are reckless as to whether it may induce, another person to enter or offer to enter into (or to refrain from doing so) a relevant agreement or to exercise or refrain from exercising, any rights conferred by a relevant investment.

An offence can be committed if a person makes a false or misleading statement 'recklessly', even though they do not realise that it is false or misleading. However, the concealment of a material fact can only involve an offence if the fact was concealed 'dishonestly', i.e. recklessness alone is not sufficient. Case law has established that a person is dishonest if they act in a way which they know ordinary people consider to be dishonest, even if they believe that they are justified in acting as they did.

With respect to false or misleading impressions under s. 90, any person who does any act or engages in any course of conduct which creates a false or misleading impression as to the market in or the price or value of any relevant investment is guilty of an offence, if they do so intending to create that impression and the case falls within at least one of two limbs:

- intending to induce another person to deal in or exercise any rights conferred by investments (or to refrain from doing so); or
- knowing or being reckless as to whether the impression is false or misleading and intending to (or being aware it is likely to) make a gain for the benefit of the person committing the offence or make a gain or cause a loss to another person or expose another person to the risk of loss.

As well as available defences for stabilisation activity and buy-back programmes in accordance with relevant rules, or conduct in conformity with control of information rules, a defence is available if the accused person can prove that they reasonably believed their conduct would not create a false or misleading impression.

Section 91 introduces the offence of making false or misleading statements or creating a false or misleading impression in relation to specified benchmarks. This offence was created in response to the Libor scandal and after the recommendation of a specific offence in the final report on the review of Libor by Martin Wheatley.

## The civil law framework: market abuse

### Prohibited behaviour

The market abuse regime is intended to address damaging behaviour (including inaction) by participants in the market which is not otherwise caught by the criminal law sanctions or the misleading statements and impressions offences. Its scope is broader than each of the heads of criminal law. In particular, the behaviour that it encompasses is more wide-ranging and there is no need for participants practising abusive behaviour to have knowledge, intent or recklessness and a person requiring or encouraging someone to engage in any prohibited behaviour can suffer the same sanctions as a person who actually commits that behaviour. Also, the lower burden of proof applying in civil law means that for the FCA, as the regulator, market abuse provides a particularly powerful addition to its regulatory weaponry.

The UK civil market abuse regime, set out in Section 118 of the UK FSMA, was originally implemented in 2001. It was amended in 2005 in order to implement the Market Abuse Directive (MAD), although various super-equivalent requirements were preserved. On 3 July 2016, this regime was largely superseded by the new EU MAR.

The spirit of the core components of the previous UK regime has remained in place following the coming into force of the new MAR regime on 3 July 2016, but much of the detail has been replaced by the new and more extensive MAR regime. MAR was designed to reduce interpretative discrepancies across EU Member States, as well as updating the regime to take account of emerging market practices such as algorithmic and high-frequency trading. While, with the exception of the commodities markets, MAR is unlikely to see a change in business practices, the net effect will almost certainly be an increased compliance burden on firms (at least those that engage in significant trading activity) and their staff.

The FCA's Code of Market Conduct as set out in MAR 1 of the FCA Handbook of Rules and Guidance has been substantially redrafted. It is no longer legally binding and has instead been recast as guidance with a much reduced scope.

The seven categories of abusive behaviour under s. 118 of FSMA 2000 have under MAR been reduced to three categories: insider dealing, unlawful disclosure and market manipulation (including an express prohibition on attempted market manipulation). The latter offence is extremely broad and captures most if not all manipulative or distortive behaviours prohibited by the existing rules, as well as capturing new practices including high-frequency trading and social media activity. Under MAR, the civil 'encouraging' offence has been removed in relation to market abuse offences other than insider dealing.

These three new offences are summarised in Table 15.6. Finally, it is worth noting that the remaining two categories of market abuse under the UK's legacy pre-2009 MAD regime which employed the 'regulator user' test have now expired.

**Table 15.6** Categories of abusive behaviour

| Areas of prohibition | Summary of MAR definition |
|---|---|
| **Insider dealing** | Dealing while in possession of inside information in financial instruments to which that information relates, includes using inside information in cancelling or amending existing orders, even where orders were placed before the person came into possession of such inside information. Recommending or encouraging another person to deal or cancel or amend an existing order and to deal in a financial instrument to which the information relates. |
| **Unlawful disclosure** | Where a person possesses inside information and discloses that information to any other person except where disclosure is made in the normal exercise of employment, profession or duties. |
| **Market manipulation** | Entering into a transaction that is likely to give false or misleading signals to the supply or demand for, or price of a financial instrument, related spot commodity contract or auctioned product based on emission allowances or secures the price of such instrument at an abnormal or artificial level. Employing fictitious devices/deception or disseminating false or misleading signals are also offences under the market manipulation head. Attempted market manipulation is also an offence. |

#### *Financial instruments*

All three offences must occur in relation to 'financial instruments' admitted to trading on an EU-regulated market or for which a request for admission to trading has been made. This includes shares, financial futures, options, swaps and any other derivative instruments traded on a prescribed market. The regime has been extended under MAR and now covers (to varying degrees) abusive behaviour in relation to: all Markets in Financial Instruments Directive 2004/39/EC (known as MiFID) financial instruments traded on multilateral trading facilities (MTFs) or organised trading facilities (OTFs) (which are to be introduced by the MiFID II legislation); and, in relation to market manipulation, emissions allowances; certain commodity derivatives and related spot commodities contracts; over-the-counter (OTC) derivatives-based activity with potential to affect traded instruments; and benchmarks.

As mentioned before, the benchmark manipulation offences were introduced in response to the recent Libor and FX manipulation scandals in the UK and elsewhere. The UK already prohibits benchmark manipulation activity under s. 91 of the Financial Services Act 2012.

#### *Territorial scope*

The territorial scope of the regime has also been extended: MAR covers acts or omissions occurring anywhere in the world, provided that they relate to the extended range of EEA-traded financial instruments and practices covered by the regime. Accordingly, the market abuse regime can apply to behaviour in the UK in relation to financial instruments traded on non-UK EEA-regulated markets and also to behaviour in the UK or abroad in relation to qualifying investments traded on one of the prescribed UK markets.

#### *Safe harbours and the FCA's Code of Market Conduct*

Certain types of 'legitimate behaviour' are relevant for the purpose of the insider dealing and unlawful disclosure offences. MAR sets out five specific instances of legitimate behaviour where, despite the fact that a person is in possession of inside information, they will not have engaged in market abuse by way of insider dealing or unlawful disclosure. These are:

1. a legal person while in possession of inside information where they have established and implemented effective Chinese walls to ensure that the natural person making the decision to trade does not possess such inside information;
2. market makers acting legitimately in the normal course of the exercise of their function as a market maker;
3. a person carrying out an obligation or transaction resulting from an order or to satisfy a legal or regulatory obligation that arose before the person concerned possessed the inside information;
4. a person will not have committed the offence of insider dealing where that person has obtained inside information in the conduct of a public takeover or merger and uses that information solely for the purpose of proceeding with such takeover or merger and provided that at the point of approval of the merger or acceptance of the offer such information is made public. Note that this does not apply to stake-building; and
5. a person does not commit the offence of insider dealing where they are simply carrying out their own intentions.

There is also an 'accepted market practices' exclusion for the market manipulation and attempted market manipulation offences. A person will not have committed an offence where they have undertaken the transaction or behaviour in question for legitimate reasons and conform to an accepted market practice established in accordance with MAR. A procedure is set out in MAR detailing how a competent authority may establish an accepted market practice.

The FCA's Code of Market Conduct continues to provide examples of situations in which, in the FCA's view, behaviour might or might not amount to market abuse.

### *Defences, enforcement and sanctions*

The penalties regime has not changed significantly under MAR as the UK has chosen to preserve its existing domestic civil sanctions regime (together with the separate criminal insider dealing regime as set out above).

The FCA has significant statutory powers allowing it to require the production of documents or to detain and interview suspects in relation to market abuse, as set out in its *Enforcement Manual*. Before exercising such powers, it has stated that it will apply certain tests when deciding whether to investigate or pursue enforcement action in relation to a particular matter. The tests include whether the alleged behaviour has had an impact on market confidence or has caused consumers financial loss.

Where the FCA decides to take action, its procedures will comply with those set out in its *Enforcement Manual*. This will include giving the relevant person a 'warning notice' before bringing the matter before its Regulatory Decisions Committee. If the Committee finds that market abuse has occurred, it will issue a decision notice. The person named in that notice may refer the matter to the Financial Services and Markets Tribunal, and beyond that may appeal to the Court of Appeal.

If a finding of market abuse is reached, the FCA can impose an unlimited monetary fine, make a public statement censuring the person concerned, require the making of restitution by that person and apply to the court to restrain behaviour by an injunction.

Some other key changes under MAR:

- **Cancellation or amendment of prior orders**: cancelling or amending existing orders following subsequent receipt of inside information now potentially amounts to market abuse.
- **Market soundings**: this refers to the scenario in which an issuer or its agents approach certain investors in order to gauge the likely success of a potential issue; formerly a grey area of the law, this practice is now extensively regulated, increasing the burden on issuers and recipients of market soundings.
- **Insider lists**: are governed by specific rules on content, format and surrounding procedures.
- **Delaying disclosure**: the obligations set out in MAR in relation to delaying disclosure of inside information are broadly in line with the previous

regime under the DTR. Delay by an issuer in announcing inside information on the basis of recognised legitimate interests does however, now require reasoned justification to be recorded and (if requested) notified to the FCA.

- **Management dealings**: the restrictions governing PDMR have been clarified; the timeframe for reportable transactions has been reduced to three business days. National regulators also have the discretion to increase the annual aggregate de minimis limit of €5,000 below which notification is not required (previously optional) to €20,000.
- **Dealing during 'closed' periods**: management of an issuer is formally prohibited from trading during the 30-day period preceding the publication of annual or interim financial results.
- **The Model Code**: has been removed on the basis that it is not compatible with MAR. Some areas formerly covered by the Model Code are now regulated by MAR (for example, dealing during closed periods). Companies may still wish, however, to adopt an appropriate share dealing policy and code (see below).

## The regulatory framework: the MAR and the Disclosure Guidance and Transparency Rules Sourcebook

With MAR having direct effect in the UK from 3 July 2016, the FCA amended the FCA Handbook to ensure consistency with MAR on implementation. The FCA's DTR were substantially amended, including the deletion of a number of rules replaced by signposts to relevant provisions of MAR. As a result, this part of the FCA Handbook has been renamed the Disclosure Guidance and Transparency Rules Sourcebook. The purpose of DTR 1, DTR 2 and DTR 3 is now to provide guidance on aspects of the disclosure requirements under MAR.

The inside information and PDMR (persons discharging managerial responsibilities) transaction disclosure regimes under MAR apply to issuers who have requested or approved admission of their financial instruments to trading on a regulated market or in the case of instruments only traded on a multilateral trading facility (MTF) (or from the implementation of MiFID II on 3 January 2018, an organised trading facility (OTF)), to issuers who have approved trading of their financial instruments on an MTF or an OTF or have requested admission to trading on an MTF. The MAR provisions therefore apply not only to companies with securities traded on the Main Market (a regulated market) but also extend to AIM companies (AIM being an MTF). The previous inside information and PDMR transaction disclosure regimes in DTR 2 and DTR 3 respectively did not apply to AIM companies who needed instead to comply with relevant provisions of the AIM Rules.

The FCA is the UK's competent authority for the purposes of MAR and can investigate and take enforcement action for breaches of MAR. It has a number of powers for the purposes of MAR and can impose significant penalties including fines, censures, trading suspensions and can require the publication of information and corrective statements and suspend or prohibit certain activities, e.g. permission to carry on regulated activities, dealing in financial instruments or managing an investment firm. It has a number of broad powers, including the power to gather any information or explanation the FCA reasonably requires to verify compliance with the public disclosure of inside information regime in Article 17 of MAR or the PDMR transaction disclosure regime in Article 19 of MAR.

## Disclosure and control of inside information by issuers

The rules relating to the disclosure and control of inside information in DTR 2 have been deleted and replaced with signposts to Article 17 of MAR. Similar to DTR 2, Article 17 requires relevant issuers to publicly disclose inside information as soon as possible.

The fundamental rule is that an issuer must inform the public as soon as possible of inside information which directly concerns it (Article 17(1) MAR). In the UK this is through a RIS. That disclosure must now clearly identify that the information communicated is inside information and comply with the other content requirements set out in Implementing Regulation 2016/1055. Inside information is as defined in Article 7 of MAR.

Under MAR, the definition of inside information has been expanded and modified in light of the regime's expanded scope to include commodities and emission allowances. The core elements of the test in relation to financial instruments are that the information:

1. is of a precise nature;
2. has not been made public;
3. relates directly or indirectly to one or more issuers or to one or more financial instruments; and
4. if it were made public, would likely have a significant effect on the prices of those financial instruments or as to the price of related derivative financial instruments.

The definition of inside information is slightly different for commodity derivatives and emissions allowances.

Intermediate steps in a protracted process may now also be deemed to be inside information under MAR. Consideration should therefore be given at each stage of a transaction as to whether new inside information has arisen that should be disclosed.

MAR defines 'likely to have a significant effect on the prices of financial instruments' as meaning 'information that a reasonable investor would be likely to use as part of the basis of his or her investment decisions'.

In the final analysis issuers will need to exercise their judgement, particularly where the decision as to whether or not a piece of information is inside information is finely balanced. It is not a case of blindly following the rules and the directors of the issuer are to monitor 'carefully and continuously' whether changes in the issuer's circumstances are such that an announcement should be made (DTRs 2.2.7G and 2.2.8G).

It is worth noting that inside information is defined differently under MAR and Part V of the Criminal Justice Act.

MAR has effectively codified the European Court of Justice's decision in the case of *Spector Photo Group and Van Raemdonck v Commissie voor het Bank-, Financie- en Assurantiewezen* (CBFA) (Case C-45/08) by making it clear that there is a rebuttable presumption that where a person deals while in possession of inside information they have used that information. MAR does, however, set out a number of circumstances in which legal persons are deemed not to have used the inside information in their possession when dealing.

The disclosure obligations for issuers are designed to ensure that there is prompt and fair disclosure of relevant information to the market. As explained in recital 49 of MAR, the disclosure obligations for issuers are essential to avoid insider dealing and ensure that investors are not misled. However that obligation may, under special circumstances, prejudice the legitimate interests of the issuer. In such circumstances, as an exception to the fundamental rule requiring immediate disclosure, an issuer may 'on its own responsibility' delay disclosure under Article 17(4) of MAR. There are three conditions to be met:

- that immediate disclosure is likely to prejudice the legitimate interests of the issuer;
- delay is not likely to mislead the public; and
- the issuer is able to ensure the confidentiality of the information.

Immediately after information that has been subject to a delay is disclosed to the public, the issuer must inform the FCA that disclosure was delayed using the specified FCA electronic form and if requested by the FCA, provide a written explanation of how the conditions in Article 17(4) MAR were met.

Guidance on what circumstances might constitute prejudice to the legitimate interests of the issuer is contained in ESMA's 'MAR guidelines on delay in the disclosure of inside information'. The guidelines provide a non-exhaustive list of example circumstances, being:

- ongoing negotiations, for example in relation to mergers and acquisitions and other transactions;

- the financial viability of the issuer is in grave and imminent danger;
- the issuer's management decisions and contracts need the approval of another body of the issuer (other than shareholders);
- jeopardy to the issuer's intellectual property rights for a product or an invention;
- jeopardy to the implementation of a plan to buy or sell a major holding in another entity; and
- the risk of affecting the ability of an issuer to meet conditions relating to a public authority's approval of a previously announced transaction.

Also where delayed disclosure of inside information is permitted, an issuer may selectively disclose that information to persons owing it a duty of confidentiality, provided such disclosure is in the normal course of the exercise of that person's employment, profession or duties (Article 17(8) MAR and see also DTR 2.5.7G for non-exhaustive examples of categories of recipients in addition to the issuer's employees who require the information to perform their functions).

MAR and the disclosure guidance in DTR 2 requires issuers to be careful to secure proper control of inside information. Accordingly, they must ensure that access to inside information is denied to persons other than those who require it for the exercise of their functions within the issuer (DTR 2.6.1G). However, guidance clarifies that the FCA recognises that an issuer may not be responsible for breach of the obligation relating to delayed disclosure under MAR if a recipient of inside information breaches their duty of confidentiality (DTR 2.6.4G).

***Insider lists***

The requirement to draw up and maintain insider lists is contained in Article 18 of MAR, with the FCA removing the obligations previously contained in DTR 2.8 and signposting Article 18. Issuers, or any person acting on their behalf or account, must draw up and maintain a list of all persons who have access to inside information and who are working for them under a contract of employment or otherwise performing tasks giving access to inside information such as advisers, accountants or credit rating agencies. The list must be provided to the FCA as soon as possible if requested.

An insider list must contain information on the identity of each person with access to the inside information, the reason for including that person on the list, the date and time each person obtained access to inside information and the date the list was created. Such lists must be in electronic form, updated promptly and retained for at least five years after being drawn up or updated. Mandatory templates for the format of insider lists are contained in Commission Implementing Regulation (EU) 2016/347.

The lists are to include deal-specific or event-based sections for different inside information but there can be a separate section for permanent insiders who have access at all times to all inside information. Permanent insiders must not be included in any deal-specific or event-based section. All reasonable steps must be taken to ensure that those on the list acknowledge in writing the legal and regulatory duties entailed. They must also confirm they are aware of the sanctions for insider dealing and unlawful disclosure of inside information.

The obligation to maintain and update insider lists requires careful attention to detail and the establishment of appropriate internal processes. Such processes should include proper and regular briefing of staff and others who have access to the issuer's inside information. Issuers should also ensure terms of employment adequately address the regulatory duties relating to the disclosure and control of inside information and that those on the insider list acknowledge their responsibilities as required by MAR.

### *AIM companies*

AIM companies must comply with the inside information disclosure provisions in Article 17 MAR and Rule 11 of the AIM Rules which requires disclosure of price sensitive information without delay. The Guidance to AIM Rule 11 states that compliance with MAR does not mean that an AIM company will have satisfied its obligations under the AIM Rules and vice versa. Therefore AIM companies must consider and comply with both sets of rules. Until MiFID II is implemented (scheduled for 3 January 2018) and AIM applies to become an SME growth market, AIM companies must comply with the full requirements to maintain and update insider lists in Article 18. If AIM is designated as an SME growth market, AIM issuers will not be required to draw up an insider list; however, this is on condition that they can provide one if requested by the FCA. They would also have to take all reasonable steps to ensure any person with access to inside information makes similar acknowledgements as to duties and sanctions as above but such acknowledgements will not need to be in writing. The FCA, as the competent authority for MAR in the UK, will be responsible for the investigation and enforcement of AIM company breaches of MAR.

## Transactions by PDMR

Article 19 of MAR has replaced the PDMR transaction notification rules in DTR 3. The FCA has deleted the notification rules in DTR 3, instead signposting Article 19 and keeping the remaining minimal guidance in DTR 3. To comply with the restrictions on dealings obligation in Article 19, the FCA has also deleted the Model Code from the Annex to LR 9.

The concepts of a 'person discharging managerial responsibilities' (PDMR) within an issuer and their connected persons remain similar under MAR, although connected persons are now called 'person closely associated' (PCA) (note the FCA has kept its use of the term 'connected persons' in the FCA Handbook). Article 19 sets out PDMR and PCA notification obligations in respect of transactions conducted on their own account in the shares or debt instruments of the issuer or in derivatives or other financial instruments linked to them. MAR extended the securities covered to include debt instruments.

The phrase 'person discharging managerial responsibilities' is defined in Article 3(25) of MAR as a person within an issuer who is a member of the administrative, management or supervisory body (i.e. in the UK, the directors of the issuer) or any other senior executive who has regular access to inside information relating directly or indirectly to the issuer and the power to take managerial decisions affecting the issuer's future developments and business prospects. Persons will be closely associated with a PDMR if they fall within the definition set out in Article 3(26) of MAR. In accordance with this definition, PCAs include the PDMR's:

a) spouse or partner considered to be equivalent to a spouse in accordance with national law (in the UK this includes a civil partner);
b) a dependent child in accordance with national law (in the UK this includes a stepchild and 'dependent child' means a child who is under 18 years of age, is unmarried and does not have a civil partner);
c) a relative who has shared the same household for at least one year on the date of the transaction concerned; or
d) a legal person, trust or partnership, the managerial responsibilities of which are discharged by a PDMR or by a person referred to in (a), (b) or (c), or which is directly or indirectly controlled by such a person, or which is set up for the benefit of such a person, or the economic interests of which are substantially equivalent to those of such a person.

The fundamental rule is that PDMRs and PCAs must notify the issuer and the FCA in writing of the occurrence of every transaction conducted on their own account relating to the shares or debt instruments of the issuer or to derivatives or other financial instruments linked to them, within three business days (Article 19(1) MAR). Although this includes similar 'on own account' wording as DTR 3, the examples of notifiable transactions under MAR are wider. Non-exhaustive examples of notifiable transactions are included in Article 19(7) MAR and Article 10 of Delegated Regulation 2016/522.

MAR has introduced a de minimis threshold, so there is no obligation to notify until transactions reach €5,000 (aggregated) per calendar year. However, because of the administrative burden and risk involved in calculating annual de minimis thresholds, some issuers are asking their PDMRs to notify all transactions in any event.

The notification must contain prescribed information, including details of the PDMR/PCA and the transaction and be sent electronically both to the issuer and the FCA within three business days. The Annex to Commission Implementing Regulation (EU) 2016/523 contains the prescribed template for notifications. The FCA has published this in an online form on its website to be used for notifications to the FCA.

The issuer must in turn announce the notification through a RIS within the same three-day timeframe, giving them little time to make the announcement when a PDMR or PCA makes notification late in the day. This has led many issuers to ask for PDMR and PCA notifications to be made to them in a shorter timeframe (i.e. one or two business days) to give them time to announce.

Under Article 19, issuers must notify their PDMRs in writing of their obligations and keep a PDMR and PCA list. PDMRs are required to notify their PCAs of the notification requirements in writing and to keep a copy.

#### *Restrictions on PDMR dealings*

As noted in earlier sections of this chapter, the freedom of directors and certain employees of listed companies to deal in their company's securities is restricted by statute and MAR, particularly by the insider dealing and market abuse rules. For directors, it is also restricted by the directors' duties relating to conflicts of interest and the making of a personal profit. Article 19(11) of MAR restricts PDMR dealings during closed periods. The previous restrictions on PDMR dealings for Premium Listed companies were contained in the Model Code which the FCA has deleted from the LR to ensure compliance with MAR.

#### *No dealings by PDMRs during a closed period*

Subject to certain exceptions to the basic rule, Article 19(11) requires that a PDMR shall not conduct transactions on its own account or for the account of a third party, directly or indirectly during a closed period. A closed period under MAR is the period of being 30 calendar days before the announcement of an interim financial report or a year-end report obliged to be made public under trading venue rules or national law (MAR closed periods). It has been confirmed by ESMA (and endorsed by the FCA) that if a company publishes a preliminary announcement of annual results this is sufficient to end the relevant closed period. Companies should remind their PDMRs of the closed period dates shortly before the start of the closed period.

Although Article 19(11) only covers closed periods, for periods where there is inside information consideration needs to be given to the insider dealing and other market abuse regimes. Some companies specifically include such periods as an additional prohibited period in their dealing code (as was the case in the Model Code).

Article 19(11) places the restriction on PDMRs not their PCAs, also there is no requirement on PDMRs to seek to prohibit dealings of their PCAs during closed periods as there was in the Model Code. Some companies have decided to retain such an obligation on PDMRs in their own dealing code or extend dealing restrictions during MAR closed periods to PCAs (even if this is difficult to enforce).

The deletion of the Model Code has left Premium Listed companies without a requirement for a dealing code or a policy where PDMRs seek clearance for dealings (outside MAR closed periods). ICSA, the GC100, the Quoted Companies Alliance and other market participants agreed that it would be of great benefit for listed and quoted companies to be able to turn to an equivalent version of the Model Code with a single, industry-led dealing code. Shortly before the implementation of MAR they jointly published a guidance note containing a specimen group-wide dealing policy, dealing code with templates for clearance to deal applications and notifications of transactions and a dealing procedures manual to assist the company when applying the dealing code and considering clearance to deal applications. The relevant guidance is available from www.icsa.org.uk. Some companies have adopted these dealing policy documents with a few amendments and others have adopted more bespoke dealing codes and policies. Company dealing codes must comply strictly with Article 19 of MAR during MAR closed periods but companies are left with a greater choice of what to include outside MAR closed periods.

### *Exceptions to the normal rule*

MAR includes limited exemptions where a PDMR is permitted to trade during a MAR closed period. Article 19(12) provides circumstances where an issuer may allow a PDMR to trade either:

- on a case-by-case basis due to exceptional circumstances such as severe financial difficulty; or
- trading related to an employee share or saving scheme, qualification or entitlement of shares, or transactions where the beneficial interest in the relevant security does not change.

More detail on the exemptions is included in Articles 7 to 9 of Commission Delegated Regulation (EU) 2016/522. In order to be able to trade under one of the circumstances in Article 19(12), a PDMR must also demonstrate that the transaction cannot be executed at another moment in time than during the closed period. When requesting permission to deal in exceptional circumstances, a PDMR must provide a reasoned written request and the issuer must take into account a list of factors when considering the request. Circumstances shall be considered to be exceptional when they are extremely urgent, unforeseen and compelling and where their cause is external to the PDMR and the PDMR has no control over them. Article 9 of the Delegated Regulation goes on to include a narrow list of permitted trades, however the precise extent of the exemptions to dealing in a MAR closed period is not clear as the list in Article 9 is not exhaustive.

*AIM companies*

To ensure consistency with Article 19 of MAR, the LSE amended the AIM Rules removing the corresponding notification rules from AIM Rule 17 and replacing the restriction on dealings obligations in AIM Rule 21, as well as signposting Article 19. AIM companies are required to have a reasonable and effective dealing policy in place under AIM Rule 21, resulting in AIM companies being obliged to have a dealing policy when Main Market companies are not required to (although most will adopt a dealing code in any event).

## The Takeover Code

The Takeover Code is published and administered by the Panel on Takeovers and Mergers (the Takeover Panel). This is an independent body responsible for regulating the conduct of the parties to takeovers or mergers to ensure that there is a 'level playing field' and that all shareholders in the public company which is the subject of the takeover or merger are treated equally. The Takeover Panel has been designated as the supervisory authority to carry out certain regulatory functions in relation to takeovers pursuant to the Directive on Takeover Bids. Its statutory functions are set out in Chapter 1 of Part 28 of the CA 2006, as amended.

Broadly, the Takeover Code applies to offers for all public companies and Societas Europaea resident in the UK (including the Channel Islands and the Isle of Man) which have any securities traded on a UK-regulated market or multilateral trading facility or Channel Islands or Isle of Man stock exchange. It also applies to offers for UK-registered and managed private companies and Societas Europaea whose shares have been listed, publicly traded or offered to the public in the UK in the previous ten years. Consequently, the Code may impact on companies which would not otherwise be subject to the normal governance requirements that apply to listed companies.

Following the controversial takeover of Cadbury by Kraft in 2010, prior to which Kraft announced its intention to keep open Cadbury's Somerdale factory but after the takeover confirmed that it would be unable to do so, a consultation on certain aspects of the Takeover Code was carried out. The consultation focused on proposals to strengthen the measures designed to ensure that the offeree company is not disadvantaged during a bid process, particularly when that process is lengthy, to recognise that parties other than the offeree company's shareholders can have a legitimate interest in the bid and to address the disproportionate influence on the outcome of the bid which can be exerted by short-term investors. Following the consultation, the Code Committee of the Takeover Panel proposed amendments to the Takeover Code to:

- increase the protection for offeree companies against protracted 'virtual bid' periods;
- strengthen the position of the offeree company;
- increase transparency and improve the quality of disclosure; and
- provide greater recognition of the interests of offeree company employees.

These amendments were adopted in September 2011 amid concerns that potential offerors might be deterred by the changes but the revised Code, when reviewed a year later, was found to be working well.

The provisions of the Takeover Code are set out as six general principles, which mirror the general principles set out in the Directive on Takeover Bids. The general principles are supported by more specific rules. Much emphasis is placed on observing the spirit, and not simply the letter, of the Takeover Code's provisions, with participants in relevant transactions encouraged to consult the Takeover Panel where uncertainties exist. The importance to corporate governance matters is self-evident.

### Directors' responsibilities

The Takeover Code places numerous specific responsibilities on the directors of both a target company and a company making or considering a takeover offer. However, the Takeover Code also provides guidance on the overriding general duties and responsibilities of directors whose companies are parties (or potential parties) to such transactions. Appendix 3 to the Takeover Code reminds directors of their collective responsibility within a unitary board structure. The 'board as a whole must ensure that proper arrangements are in place to enable it to monitor' day-to-day conduct of an offer, notwithstanding that such conduct may be delegated to individual directors or a committee of directors. To keep directors abreast of developments, board meetings should be held as and when necessary throughout the period of the offer. The guidance also specifically recommends that arrangements should ensure that:

- the board is kept up-to-date with all documents and announcements published by the company in relation to the offer and with details of all share dealings made by the company or its associates;
- those directors to whom day-to-day responsibility for the offer is delegated should be able to justify to the board all their actions and proposed actions; and
- the board has access to the opinions of the company's advisers.

Directors are obliged to consult with the Takeover Panel if they are concerned about the propriety of any action and the Panel expects all directors to give them their full co-operation with requests for information or documents in their possession.

*Public announcements*

In accordance with General Principle 4, the boards of both the offeror and offeree companies must be careful to ensure that false markets are not created. This requires secrecy to be maintained prior to any announcement, so that potentially price-sensitive information is disclosed only on a strict 'need to know' basis to persons to whom the need for such secrecy is emphasised.

Rule 2 of the Takeover Code sets out specific circumstances in which an announcement is required. These include upon the receipt by the offeree company of notification of a firm intention on the part of the offeror to make an offer, when rumour or speculation give rise to untoward movements in the company's share price and when an acquisition of an interest gives rise to an obligation to make an offer under Rule 9.1. Rule 9.1 prescribes the percentage interests held by a person or persons acting in concert which, if exceeded, must give rise to a mandatory offer for the target company.

Until the board of the target company is approached, the primary responsibility for making announcements rests with the offeror. Accordingly, the offeror should actively track the share price of the offeree company in order to be alert to any untoward share price movements that might be the result of rumour or speculation as well as to the need for a mandatory offer, should the percentage limits in Rule 9.1 be exceeded. Once an approach has been received, much of this responsibility switches to the offeree, regardless of whether or not the approach leads to an offer.

The announcement that an approach has been received from a potential offeror (other than one which has been unequivocally rejected) or that the offeree company is in talks with a potential offeror must identify the potential offeror. Furthermore, this announcement will trigger the commencement of the offer period and an automatic 28-day put-up-or-shut-up period. By the end of that time, unless an extension is granted by the Panel, the potential offeror must either announce their firm intention to make an offer or they will be prevented from making any more such approaches for six months.

Once a firm intention to make an offer has been confirmed, the required announcement must detail, amongst other things, the terms of the offer, including any conditions to which the offer is subject, the identity of the offeror and confirmation by the financial adviser that the offeror has sufficient resources to enable it to satisfy any cash element of the offer. It follows that a cash offer, or offer where an element of the consideration will be settled in cash, should not be announced until the offeror has ensured that the cash commitment can be fulfilled. In addition, the announcement must include a summary of the provisions of Rule 8 (disclosure requirements of the Code) and the form which that summary is normally expected to take is published on the Panel's website. Directors of the target company should also be aware of the requirement of Principle 2 that, where the board of an offeree company advises the holder of securities, it 'must give its view on the effects of implementation of the bid on employment, conditions of employment and the locations of the company's places of business'.

When making the announcement of the firm intention to make an offer, employees or employee representatives and the trustees of any defined benefit pension scheme operated by the target company must be informed. They will have a right to receive the same information and circulars as shareholders and may provide the offeror with opinions as to the effect of the offer on employment or the pension scheme to be appended to the offer circular. This makes it necessary in practice to start liaising with employees (or their representatives) and the relevant pensions scheme trustees at an early date.

Also at the time of the announcement, a number of documents must be published on a website. The Code emphasises the need for announcements to be absolutely clear and unambiguous, in particular avoiding giving any impression that a party has committed themselves to any course of action such as accepting the offer when they have not in fact done so. It should be noted that the highest standards of care are expected in the preparation of all announcements, statements and documents published (see Rule 19.1) and the need for careful drafting will therefore be paramount.

### *Recommendations*

Once an offer has been made, the target company's board will need to assess the bid. When doing so, as required by General Principle 3, the board must act at all times 'in the best interests of the company as a whole and must not deny the holders of securities the opportunity to decide on the merits of the bid'. Rule 3.1 requires the board of the offeree company to take 'competent independent advice' and to make the substance of that advice known to its shareholders.

The target company's board will normally give a recommendation as to acceptance or rejection of a bid. Such recommendation is particularly important where there are competing bidders and must be made in good faith after careful consideration of the company's interests, taking into account all relevant factors. The wording used for the recommendation should make it clear that the board has been advised by its independent advisers accordingly. Where it has not been possible for the advisers to make a recommendation or the board has failed to reach consensus or to agree with their advisers, an explanation of the important factors in the arguments for and against the proposed takeover must be provided (see notes on Rule 3.1) which also address the circumstances where the offer is a management buy-out or is made by the company's controllers or where there is uncertainty about financial information.

### *Share dealings*

The Takeover Code imposes obligations in relation to share dealings (Rule 4) and disclosures (Rule 8) during the offer period. The broad effect of the dealing rules is that those apart from the bidder who have confidential information about the bid (including in particular the directors involved) should not deal in shares in either the bidder or the target company. Also, the directors must not deal in their shares in a manner that is contrary to the advice given to the shareholders. For such purposes, the directors will be deemed to be 'acting in concert' with their company and accordingly subject to the same restrictions and obligations. Similarly, trustees holding shares in trusts of which the directors are beneficiaries will be considered concert parties for such purposes.

As for the specific rules, these include restrictions on the build-up of shareholdings (i.e. stake building) by holders of less than 30% and between 30% and 50% of the voting rights (Rule 5.1). Additionally, a mandatory offer for the target company's shares must be made by any person who, falling in either category, breaches the relevant 30% or 50% limit (Rule 9). If the bidder does buy shares in the target company during the bid period then it must increase its offer to the price paid and, where it has bought shares in the three months before the bid, the bid price must not be less than the price paid. These and similar rules are designed to protect shareholders and market confidence in accordance with General Principle 1 which states:

> 'all holders of the securities of an offeree company of the same class must be afforded equivalent treatment; moreover, if a person acquires control of a company, the other holders of the securities must be protected'.

Directors must be careful to observe the rules, both on behalf of themselves, their deemed concert parties and their company. They should be aware that, in addition to the Takeover Code, the insider dealing and market abuse rules and the requirements of MAR and company share dealing codes described earlier in this chapter will be relevant to share dealings conducted during a bid period.

### *Documentation*

General Principle 2 requires shareholders of an offeree company to be given 'sufficient time and information to enable them to reach a properly informed decision on the bid' and the Takeover Code sets out obligations on both bidding and target companies in relation to the public documentation they must issue. The principal documents are the initial announcement of the bid, the bidder's offer document and any reply or defence documents issued by the target. Such documents must be prepared to the highest standards of care and accuracy and the information contained in them must be adequately and fairly presented (Rule 19.1). There are also various requirements regarding how documents are to be published, including the requirement to publish various documents on a website.

Every document or advertisement published by the offeror or offeree companies must contain an appropriate directors' responsibility statement (Rule 19.2). The statement should confirm that they take full responsibility for its contents and that, to the best of their knowledge and belief, having taken all reasonable care to ensure such is the case, the information set out in the document is accurate and does not omit anything of relevance. The stringency of this requirement reinforces the need for robust verification processes to be employed in the preparation of such documents and emphasises the accountability of the directors for ensuring the adequacy of the information disseminated to the market. Failure to do so may leave directors liable to a claim for misrepresentation or a charge of market abuse.

#### *Enforcement and sanctions*

As mentioned above, the Takeover Panel has statutory functions under the Companies Act. In order to carry out those functions, it has power to require certain information and documents, although a person is entitled to resist such requests on the grounds of legal privilege. Breach of the Takeover Code may result in a compensation ruling, the issue of a censure statement or referral of the matter to the FCA which has the power to impose a fine. The existence of such sanctions gives the Takeover Code the 'teeth' which it previously lacked.

## Conclusion

Clearly the additional responsibilities of directors of public companies whose shares are listed and traded on a public market are considerable. For directors of companies with a dual listing, particularly if also listed on a US market, the responsibilities will be even greater. The aim of this chapter has been to provide an overview of the regulatory environment in the UK, with particular reference to the listing regime, the insider dealing and market abuse rules, the inside information and dealing disclosure requirements of MAR and the rules applying on takeovers and mergers. While in practice affected directors will need to rely heavily on the company's sponsors and professional advisers to ensure that they avoid breaches of the rules and regulations, the requirement placed on the board to maintain its effectiveness means that it should ensure that its members have access to effective professional development and training. Governance best practice would suggest that the curriculum to be covered should ensure that directors have an appropriate knowledge and understanding of the regulatory regime outlined above.

## Governance checklist

- ✓ Are the directors familiar with the role and responsibilities of the UKLA as the competent authority with respect to the Official List?
- ✓ Are the directors familiar with the structure of the UKLA Sourcebook, containing the LR, DTR and PR?
- ✓ Are the directors familiar with the MAR?
- ✓ Do the directors have a sound knowledge of the company's continuing obligations under the LR?
- ✓ With respect to market communications and dealings, do the directors have a working knowledge of the criminal law regime relating to insider dealing and misleading statements?
- ✓ Is the board satisfied that the internal procedures for complying with the notification and continuing obligations requirements under the LR, DTR and the MAR respectively are sufficient for the task?
- ✓ In particular, does the company have a share dealing code and are proper controls in place to monitor and enforce meaningful compliance?
- ✓ Will the directors' familiarity with the principles contained in the Takeover Code ensure that they both identify relevant market events and seek professional advice where necessary?
- ✓ Do the directors have access to the resources that they require to meet their obligations in the listed company context, both internally (company secretary and in-house legal) and externally (professional advisers)?

# 16

# Governance of private companies

## Introduction

A company, regardless of the size of the business, may have many stakeholders, from those directly affected such as shareholders, employees, creditors and suppliers, to others from the wider community with less obvious and concrete links but still with a legitimate interest in the company and its activities. The need for effective governance is, therefore, not only an issue of legitimate public interest in respect of listed companies, but also for private companies and, in particular, larger businesses.

The furore over large private equity acquisitions which reached a peak in 2007 illustrated this point well. Demands to open up the traditionally opaque world of private equity led to the development of the British Venture Capital Association's (BVCA's) Walker Guidelines imposing voluntary reporting requirements on the larger private equity firms.

More recently, the 2016 Green Paper, *Corporate Governance Reform*, has shone a light on the disparity between the corporate governance expectations applied to listed companies and those of non-listed businesses which can, in some cases, be just as large. The Green Paper seeks views on whether some features of the listed governance regime should be extended to larger non-listed companies and it seems likely therefore that some form of more formal corporate governance requirements may be introduced to larger private companies in the medium term.

Regardless, however, of what pressures, influences and requirements may or may not apply to a privately owned enterprise, adherence to good standards of compliance and corporate governance standards is an aspiration of potential benefit to any organisation.

## Regulatory framework

The demands placed upon large listed companies will inevitably not all be relevant to smaller entities and this need for proportionality is reflected by reductions or exemptions from many of the statutory requirements that apply to listed or larger companies. A look through relevant legislation reveals, for example:

- exemptions from various accounts and audit requirements for small and medium companies;
- relaxations to the share capital change processes that only private companies can take advantage of;
- exemptions from environmental and CSR-related statutory provisions, in particular transparency and narrative reporting requirements such as carbon emission, modern slavery and gender pay gap disclosures for businesses with smaller turnovers or employee numbers; and
- simpler shareholder rights and exemption from the need to hold an AGM for private companies.

However, such exemptions are the exception rather than the rule. The majority of legislation and obligations apply equally to all companies. Businesses will therefore need to comply with a range of company law and stakeholder statutes including employment, health and safety, environmental protection, anti-corruption, tax and competition laws to name but a few. For small businesses, despite Government red-tape cutting initiatives, compliance can present considerable challenges and directors of such entities may therefore need to be even more alert to the risks of non-compliance in order to properly fulfil their responsibilities.

## Board governance role and organisational culture

For boards of unlisted companies giving consideration to what governance arrangements might be appropriate, a good starting point is the joint IoD and ecoDa *Corporate Governance Guidance and Principles for Unlisted Companies in the UK*. This guidance sets out nine common-sense principles for all unlisted companies plus an additional five principles which are applicable only to larger and/or more complex organisations. Additionally, the guidance draws links between the CA 2006 provisions and good governance practices on issues such as director's duties and conflicts of interest. While the corporate governance demands placed upon unlisted companies may be modest compared with those applying to companies on the Official List, elements of best practice will nevertheless add value in many instances.

The *Corporate Governance Guidance and Principles for Unlisted Companies in the UK* set out a board's governance role in the following terms:

> 'Every company should strive to establish an effective board, which is collectively responsible for the long-term success of the company, including the definition of the corporate strategy.'

The Guidance sets out key points which are relevant to boards seeking to understand how to carry out their responsibilities in practice, including recommendations that they should:

- provide leadership including setting the company's values and standards;
- set the company's strategic objectives and ensure that adequate resources are in place to enable the company to meet them;
- monitor and evaluate management performance;
- ensure that the company's obligations to shareholders and other stakeholders are understood and met; and
- ensure the company complies with its articles of association and all regulatory and legal requirements.

## Subsidiary governance in groups of companies

Within a group of companies, thought needs to be given to the process necessary to ensure that the group operates as a cohesive organisation and that controls are adequate and appropriate across the group.

Subsidiary governance regimes are likely to consist of:

- controls over appointments to subsidiary boards and corporate structures;
- imposition of group policies, processes and internal control frameworks;
- budget and business plan approvals;
- restrictions on authorities, for example banking arrangements, debt facilities, charges over assets, the giving of guarantees and management of litigation; and
- implementation of consistent group-wide values and culture.

The starting point for determining the delegations to subsidiary companies will be the schedule of matters reserved to the ultimate parent company board. Matters outside of the list may be delegated, including to the board of subsidiaries. A balance will need to be struck between ensuring adequate group-wide control and stifling the ability of the subsidiary company's management team to run the subsidiary company's business.

Where subsidiaries are based in another jurisdiction, the framework will also need to take account of local requirements.

The rationale for retention of each subsidiary company should be well understood and an active approach taken to dissolving those that are no longer required, as to retain companies longer than necessary increases both the group's costs and potential risks.

A modified approach may be required when dealing with joint venture companies. Where joint venture entities are not under the control of the group (i.e. the group holds a minority stake) imposition of group standards is likely to be more difficult in practice. In all cases, careful thought should be given to the necessary governance, control and oversight arrangements when preparing and approving the relevant joint venture agreement.

To provide assurance on the efficacy of subsidiary governance frameworks, a series of checks and reporting measures should be implemented such as:

- risk management reporting and risk aggregation processes;
- audit and reporting of legal compliance;
- monitoring of management accounts, financial projections and progress against financial and non-financial business objectives; and
- audit of statutory accounts.

Care needs to be taken so as to avoid inadvertently creating a 'shadow director' scenario whereby group directors effectively become directors of a subsidiary by virtue of the subsidiary board acting generally in accordance with their directions or instructions. However, the Companies Act (s. 251) does clarify that a holding company will not be treated as a shadow director for the purposes of applying the Companies Act sections relating to general duties of directors, transactions requiring members' approval or contracts with a sole member who is also a director. While a board of directors cannot ignore the directions given to it by its shareholder(s), key to managing the shadow director risk is the exercise of independent judgement by each subsidiary board. In exercising that judgement it is likely to be entirely reasonable, however, to take account of the negative consequences for the subsidiary that might be expected to arise from failure to comply with group practices or to support group strategy. Taking account of parent company wishes is therefore generally consistent with the need to 'promote the success of the company'.

## Board composition and resources

Many of the ideas expressed in the FRC *Guidance on Board Effectiveness* can be applied to any board, regardless of the size or complexity of the organisation. Few would argue that all boards need to perform a leadership role or that they need to provide direction to management. However, where boards of smaller entities are likely to differ from those of larger listed companies is in the composition of the board and the roles performed by individual directors. The *Corporate Governance Guidance and Principles for Unlisted Companies in the UK* recognises these differences and provides some practical thoughts on how boards of smaller companies can still implement effective measures without creating a disproportionate regime.

The guidance establishes what it calls the 'key concepts' for good governance – delegation of authority, checks and balances, professional decision making, accountability, transparency, conflicts of interest and aligning incentives – and, while recognising the challenges of implementing these in real-world situations, encourages companies to adopt appropriate governance structures and processes, using a phased approach where necessary. Practical checklists are suggested to help directors determine, for example, the schedule of matters reserved to the board, the authority delegated to management and committees (if any), a list of key compliance responsibilities and the sort of subjects that might be included in a company-wide code of conduct. Practices which can be adopted by even the smallest board, such as regular meetings, the advance circulation of a proper agenda and supporting papers to enable attendees to prepare in advance, the recording of formal minutes and the adoption of guidelines on how the board will be run, are advocated. Where the company is too small to provide sufficient in-house resources to meet these needs, the option of appointing external advisers such as a consultant company secretary is suggested as a viable alternative.

Considering the importance of the board's role to any organisation, it is indisputably logical to devote some time and energy in ensuring that the board is composed of the right individuals. For smaller companies, these individuals can often primarily comprise investors and/or family members and there may, therefore, not be the same degree of freedom to shape and develop the board's composition as might be available to larger organisations. This, however, should not be taken as an excuse to disregard the issue entirely. A phased approach – perhaps forming an advisory board without decision-making authority, considering whether there are skills gaps which could be addressed by the appointment of additional NEDs, taking an active approach to succession planning and agreeing the approach to be used in board recruitment are potentially helpful measures which can be adopted towards establishment of a full, independent main board. Appointing the right people to the right roles on the board is key to ensuring the board is well resourced to deliver the company's strategy and to drive the business forward. The next sections examine those roles and related issues.

## Chairman

The IoD *Corporate Governance Guidance and Principles for Unlisted Companies in the UK* recognises that, while the role and responsibilities of the chairman of a smaller company are much the same as they would be for a larger, listed company, in smaller companies the roles of chairman and chief executive are often combined as the appointment of an additional independent chairman may not be commercially viable. In such circumstances, however, the guidance cautions that 'the person holding both roles should remember that the responsibilities of chairman and CEO are distinct and should be viewed separately'. As discussed in Chapter 11, the leadership attributes of a good chairman are quite different from the attributes of a senior executive. For the chairman of a smaller entity combining the role with that of chief executive and possibly also wearing other 'hats', the challenge is all the greater. This can be particularly important in family-run businesses where the distinction between ownership and directorship can also be quite blurred.

The chairman of a small company, together with any other independent NEDs, may have a more hands-on role to play in determining executive remuneration, developing succession plans and leading board recruitment activity than would be the case in a larger company with more formal governance structures and greater access to specialist resources. Particularly where there is no company secretarial support, the role may be more demanding than the size of the company might otherwise indicate. He or she will need to ensure they can commit adequate time to their responsibilities as chairman if they are to discharge their role well.

In the absence of other NEDs who can collectively appraise the chairman's performance, it is recommended that, nevertheless, regular board evaluations are undertaken and used to provide, amongst other things, feedback on the chairman's effectiveness. That evaluation process will also be used to appraise the performance of other board members and the chair will have a key role to play in recognising strengths and addressing development needs to encourage improvement.

## Executive directors

Senior appointments are valuable, and often scarce, resources for smaller businesses. To maximise their value, roles should be clearly defined and set out in job descriptions. In order to ensure a company is led effectively, smaller companies should ensure a chief executive (or managing director) is appointed to direct the executive team and the day-to-day running of the business.

The role of the chief executive may, as above, often be combined with the role of chairman although, as the company grows and steps may be taken to introduce independent members of the board, thought should be given to separating the role. Where the roles are combined, the individual fulfilling both should, as a minimum, be cognisant of the distinction between the two and be aware of when he or she is acting in their capacity as chairman and when they are acting as chief executive.

Another key role will be that of the finance director. For micro businesses, external accounting arrangements may be a necessary and/or acceptable alternative.

### Management delegation

For smaller companies, a tendency to more informal structures and procedures may result in a lack of clarity over individual roles or authority. However, even in a smaller company, those matters which are not reserved to the board and which are delegated to management should be clearly defined. *Corporate Governance Guidance and Principles for Unlisted Companies in the UK* provides a suggested list of the matters that might be delegated in this way, covering, for example, the preparation of strategic plans, proposals and budgets, the execution of strategy and board decisions, operation of banking and financial arrangements, the signing of legal and regulatory documents, operating adequate systems of control and risk management, staff recruitment, health and safety and remuneration.

### Executive remuneration

As with all companies, there is a need to align the pay of the executive team members with the interests of shareholders and to ensure remuneration is reasonable. The *Corporate Governance Guidance and Principles for Unlisted Companies in the UK* suggests that in designing their executive remuneration arrangements, companies aim to:

- achieve a balance between fixed and variable pay, linking variable pay to pre-determined performance targets with some portion of the variable pay deferred;
- impose a minimum vesting period where shares are granted, together with a requirement to retain some proportion of those shares until the conclusion of employment;
- provide for a clawback of variable pay paid on the basis of data which subsequently proves to be manifestly misstated; and
- limit severance pay and provide for non-payment of severance pay in cases of poor performance.

In framing their remuneration policies, many companies will wish to seek external advice. However, care should be taken to ensure the remuneration policy adopted is one which reflects the company's needs and objectives. A one-size-fits-all approach is rarely helpful.

## Independent NEDs

While for some companies, the appointment of a first NED may be required as a condition of the provision of a bank loan or some other form of capital injection, for others, such a development may be seen as part of the company's evolution as it grows and develops. The IoD's *Corporate Governance Guidance and Principles for Unlisted Companies in the UK* observes that for unlisted companies 'a key stage in opening up the company to external scrutiny is taken by the appointment of independent (non-executive) directors'. The appointment of the first such non-executives therefore can often be seen as a transformational stage, perhaps moving the company away from its owner-manager roots towards a more open, potentially more sustainable form and the effectiveness of such a transformation will be reliant to a great extent on the appointment of the right person(s).

For companies where the appointment of one or more NEDs seems too radical a move, the IoD Guidance suggests the appointment of an advisory board without any formal decision-making powers, as an interim solution. While lying outside of the company's formal governance structure, advisory board members can bring expertise, experience and, often most importantly, a useful network of contacts.

Particularly where the appointment of an advisory board or NED signals a new way of working, with all-powerful owner-managers in some cases required to operate in a more consensual manner than they may hitherto have been used to, the establishment of well-defined processes and structures will be necessary to ensure that individual board members, whether executive or non-executive, have clarity over individual as well as collective roles and responsibilities.

So that all directors have the same understanding of the company's strategy, business plan and objectives, these matters should be documented and the directors provided with access to appropriate advice to support them working effectively. The introduction of such measures can be an important part of formalising governance processes which may hitherto have been more casual. Such formalisation is just one example of how the process of bringing in external independent directors can influence the development of a more mature governance framework for the business and so ensure the existence of appropriate structures to support the company as it grows into a larger and possibly more complex organisation.

The role of the non-executive or independent director of a small unlisted company is similar to that in larger entities. Essentially the director is required to provide constructive challenge to their executive colleagues, to support the development of proposals, bringing their own expertise to bear where appropriate and to monitor and scrutinise performance including financial performance. A NED will have a particular role to play in relation to verifying the integrity of the financial information and will play a key oversight function of the financial controls and risk management systems so as to provide a degree of independent assurance of their effectiveness and adequacy.

### Non-executive remuneration

Remuneration of NEDs will normally be on the basis of a fixed-fee arrangement. Share options or similar incentives will not normally be offered as to do so might compromise the independence of the NEDs' perspective although there is no hard and fast rule and shareholders may take an opposing view about the potential for share-based arrangements to align directors' interests with their own. Whatever the arrangements, the quantum will need to reflect the total time commitment of the director, including that spent on committee meetings and other activities. Issues such as time commitment as well as the initial term of the appointment will need to be clearly set out in the letter of engagement.

## Company secretary

Private companies are not required by statute to appoint a company secretary, although the compliance functions traditionally carried out by the company secretary remain. In the absence of a company secretary, under s. 270, CA 2006, the directors are responsible for ensuring that adequate arrangements are in place to meet these compliance requirements, either by carrying them out themselves or by authorising some other person to carry out those functions on their behalf. In larger private companies and groups of companies, it is still likely to be beneficial to retain the role, even if combined with other responsibilities or outsourced to an external specialist consultant.

In smaller businesses, the role of company secretary is often undertaken by one of the executive directors, typically the finance director. The *Higgs Report* noted that around 40% of companies outside the FTSE 350 combined the roles in this manner. Where this is the case, the board needs to be aware of the potential for conflicts of interest and steps may need to be taken to ensure that the non-executives in particular receive the impartial information that they require. In addition, for a public company, even if not listed, the person appointed needs to be appropriately qualified as required by s. 273 of the CA 2006.

In a smaller company, an in-house company secretary is likely to have a particularly wide range of additional duties, as it is unlikely that there will be a significant internal specialist resource to cover each individual area. An affordable practical alternative for smaller companies is to outsource company secretarial compliance functions to a specialist company secretarial service provider. Such providers are able to offer a flexible service tailored to the needs of the company and to provide varying degrees of assistance depending on the compliance needs of the business at that particular time. This can be particularly useful given that compliance needs will certainly fluctuate at different times of the year, for example when preparing for the company's AGM (if it has one) and are also likely to change at different stages of the company's development, for example when the company is preparing to enter into transactions, share capital changes or to pursue an initial public offering (IPO) to list its shares on a stock exchange (see below).

For smaller companies which are growing and developing, the governance expertise and discipline that can be brought to the business by an experienced company secretary should not be underestimated. A company secretary should therefore not be seen as someone who can merely take notes of directors' meetings and carry out basic administration to ensure the company makes appropriate filings at Companies House, but rather as a highly skilled professional who, by guiding and supporting the board in its governance processes, can contribute to the formation and delivery of strategy and ensure the board's effectiveness is optimised for the benefit of the business.

In particular, the company secretary may play a vital role in carrying out an evaluation of the board's effectiveness. This useful practice, which need not require the services of an external adviser but will require openness, honesty and a willingness to apply fresh thinking, often provides thought-provoking results which can be a catalyst for change, development and improvement.

## Use of committees

The *Corporate Governance Guidance and Principles for Unlisted Companies in the UK* makes the valid point that for many smaller companies, a single individual may often be investor, director and manager so that the distinct roles of shareholders, the board and the executive team may be more difficult to distinguish. To assist the shareholders and boards of such companies in establishing an appropriate delegation structure, the Guidance contains example lists of which matters might typically be reserved for decision by the company's members or its full board or delegated to management. Such lists will always require a degree of adaptation in order to meet the particular needs and circumstances of a specific entity, but they do at least provide a sensible starting point for considering the establishment of an appropriate regime.

As part of that regime, committees can be a helpful tool to assist boards of smaller companies to discharge their governance responsibilities in an effective way. The committee structure needs, of course, to be proportionate; however, the guidance recommends that most larger unlisted companies will require nominations, remuneration and audit committees, although combining nominations and remuneration responsibilities within a single committee can also offer a practical alternative. As well as establishing and regularly reviewing written terms of reference for its committees, the board should ensure that all committees have sufficient resources to carry out their remit. For companies with independent non-executives on their boards, those directors are likely to play a key role within the committees. For companies which have no non-executives, an alternate possibility is to co-opt individuals with particular skills or knowledge onto a committee in order to bring external perspective and oversight to the committee's work without necessarily appointing them as directors.

## Director's duties and liabilities

The duties of directors described in Chapter 4 will equally apply to the directors of private companies. However, for smaller and unlisted companies, the distinction between owners and managers may be more blurred, with board members often owning a more significant stake in the company than is likely to be the case with a larger listed entity or owing their appointment to one or more shareholders to whom they might therefore feel a particular responsibility. An increased likelihood for conflicts of interest, difficulty in exercising independent judgement when faced with potential pressure from a significant shareholder and temptation to promote the interests of one party to the detriment of those of the company as a whole can all easily arise where circumstances of this nature exist.

In such cases the challenges for the directors in adhering to their general duties, which of course apply regardless, are heightened. The *Corporate Governance Guidance and Principles for Unlisted Companies in the UK* recognises these issues, which can be a particular feature of family-owned businesses, joint ventures and group subsidiaries, and the extent to which, if not properly managed, governance processes can be undermined as a result. A particular awareness on the part of directors will be required and appropriate procedures implemented to ensure that directors can act – and can robustly demonstrate that they do act – in accordance with their statutory duties.

In relation to specific compliance duties, while directors of smaller and less complex businesses may have the advantage of being closer to the company's operations and therefore benefit from a greater degree of direct knowledge of the organisation's compliance activities, where a smaller business lacks the level of compliance resource that would be available within a larger organisation, the risk of non-compliance can be increased. Pressure on, or non-availability of, dedicated or expert resources can result in compliance arrangements being compromised and directors may need to take particular care to ensure this is not the case.

Notwithstanding that smaller and unlisted companies may lack the high profile and more intense regulatory pressures of listed companies, the potential for directors to find themselves personally liable for breach of general or specific duties will remain. Directors of such companies will therefore wish to assure themselves that appropriate indemnity and insurance arrangements are in place to cover such eventualities.

## Report and accounts

A smaller company may have exemptions available to it under the Companies Act enabling it to prepare micro-entity accounts; however, regardless of the form of the statutory accounts, the board will want to ensure it has access to complete, timely and accurate financial information, including financial management data such as cash flow projections and management accounts. They will need to be mindful of the statutory requirement to produce accounts which give a 'true and fair view' and will in particular need to assess whether the company is a going concern and can prepare accounts on that basis.

Notwithstanding differences in size and complexity that may exist between their companies and listed companies, the directors of smaller businesses have the same responsibilities for keeping accounting records and for preparing and approving their company's report and accounts. Ensuring the report and accounts give a 'true and fair view' will require appropriate processes, systems and safeguards to be in place, proportionate to the size and nature of the business. Certainly robust financial controls will become necessary if the company wishes to secure external financing or capital.

The report and accounts is the primary document by which companies communicate on progress of the business with their shareholders. Narrative reporting is considered next.

## Narrative reporting

While statute sets certain requirements for the disclosure of information to external shareholders and other stakeholders, particularly for small companies, those requirements are potentially quite undemanding and uninformative. Companies may choose, however, to make additional voluntary disclosures, for example if the board wishes to gain the confidence and commitment of external stakeholders. For some companies, an immediate shift to full transparency may be a step too far and in such cases the phased introduction of an enhanced reporting and dialogue regime may be more appropriate. The board should not forget, however, when making such disclosures and entering into dialogue with external parties, that all shareholders should be treated equally.

Statutory narrative reporting requirements will vary depending on the size of the company as exemptions are available under the small companies regime but, even in cases where the company is not required to produce a strategic report and directors' report, the board may wish to consider, as part of the company's external communications strategy, making voluntary disclosures in order to present useful information to shareholders and other stakeholders. *Corporate Governance Guidance and Principles for Unlisted Companies in the UK* suggests that boards may wish to consider including the following in their narrative reports:

- the company's vision and values;
- an outline of the company's business strategy and the likely risks associated with that strategy;
- a review of the company's activities and performance and a forward-looking assessment of its business environment; and
- a statement of its corporate governance principles, the extent to which it has complied with a specific corporate governance code (if any) and additional governance information, including:

- how the board operates, a high-level outline of the types of decisions taken by the board or delegated to management;
- the names of all the directors, including the chairman, the chief executive and the chairmen and members of any committees;
- the names of the NEDs confirming if the board considers them to be independent and if so why;
- details of how any evaluation of the board, its committees and its directors has been conducted; and
- activities, for example community projects, of particular interest to stakeholders.

As the company develops, it may wish to enhance its reporting and the *Corporate Governance Guidance and Principles for Unlisted Companies in the UK* suggests the annual report and accounts, as the primary document for communicating with shareholders, might be expanded. Website disclosures may, however, provide a more flexible mechanism with greater potential to communicate with a wider audience. The full narrative reporting requirements described in Chapter 8, perhaps diluted to make the reporting more proportionate, may provide ideas from which the board can draw their inspiration when determining their own company's transparency priorities. And compliance, where required, with gender pay gap reporting and modern slavery disclosures, will also be relevant for companies which exceed the relevant employee number and turnover thresholds.

### Role of independent directors in reviewing financial statements

Once the company has attained the size to warrant the appointment of independent directors, NEDs should be tasked with satisfying themselves of the integrity of financial information and relevant controls. The need for, and implementation of, an appropriate system of internal controls is explored further below but suffice to say at this point that it should not be forgotten that such controls need to extend beyond purely financial matters to encompass operational, legal and reputational matters. For unlisted companies of sufficient size to have independent directors or an audit committee, while they should take a lead on the items listed above, this does not detract from the unitary board's collective responsibility for these matters.

Where an audit committee is established, its remit should be set out in formal terms of reference approved by the board. Ideally the audit committee should consist wholly of independent NEDs and have at least one amongst its members with relevant financial experience, for example an accountancy qualification. The committee will need to consider what sources of assurance are available to it and whether it needs additional sources of assurance, in particular if there is no internal audit function.

## Financial controls

The starting point for an appropriate framework of financial controls will be to reserve high-level control over finances and related matters to the board. The IoD's *Corporate Governance Guidance and Principles for Unlisted Companies in the UK* recommends that such matters include, amongst other things, approval of:

- corporate plans;
- operating and capital budgets;
- major corporate actions (e.g. acquisitions, disposals, commencing or terminating of business activities);
- financial statements;
- borrowings or creditor guarantees (possibly above a certain amount); and
- authorities delegated to management.

Below this, as indicated by the latter item, authority will be delegated to management to deal with day-to-day financial management issues, for example the operation of bank accounts. The terms of the authority delegated should be well defined, identifying who can exercise the authority and any applicable limits, whether financial or otherwise. Such delegations should be regularly reviewed to ensure that they remain appropriate to the structure, size and complexity of the company and its activities.

Accountabilities should reflect this delegation hierarchy and processes to facilitate effective oversight implemented. Such over-sight will need to be supported by an appropriate level of reporting and is likely to include scrutiny in the form of the external audit and, where relevant, transparent reporting to the company's external shareholders and other stakeholders.

*Corporate Governance Guidance and Principles for Unlisted Companies in the UK* recommends that boards maintain a schedule of the various financial requirements that must be completed and who is responsible for dealing with each item. Such a schedule can be a simple but effective control mechanism to ensure that the preparation and filing of financial statements, tax compliance requirements and loan and capital requirements and covenants are considered, actioned and delivered appropriately and on time. For the smallest companies, these requirements may be met by an external accountant although as the company develops and grows the employment of an in-house specialist is likely to become an increasingly attractive option.

## Risk management

Risk is of course inherent in business, but, in order to protect shareholder value, company boards should take steps to understand the risks which their business faces and to reduce or remove unnecessary or unacceptable risks through appropriate risk management processes. Establishing the system of internal controls and risk management will be the responsibility of management but the board should be clear that it retains oversight of those controls and will need to satisfy itself that the controls and processes are adequate and effective. To this end, the *Corporate Governance Guidance and Principles for Unlisted Companies in the UK* recommends that the board carry out a periodic check on the effectiveness of the company's approach towards internal control ensuring that their review covers all material financial, operational and compliance controls and risk management systems.

For smaller organisations, risk can often be managed in a relatively informal way, but starting to formalise the processes as the company develops, commencing with documentation of strategic, financial and operational risks and assessing them through a risk mapping exercise or simple SWOT analysis is recommended in *Corporate Governance Guidance and Principles for Unlisted Companies in the UK* as a sensible first measure. Without creating bureaucratic processes, such measures help to focus management attention on the risks the business faces and to place risk management clearly within the business's decision-making processes.

Information on risks, including a description of the key risks, the scale of the potential impact, probability of the risk occurring and a summary of the mitigating actions, can be recorded in a straightforward risk register which can then form the basis of the board's regular consideration and review of risk matters. Such basic processes can be developed and refined, drawing where appropriate on specialist advice, as the company grows and becomes more complex or in order to satisfy banks or other funders. The chief executive will be responsible for ensuring these processes, whether of a basic or refined nature, are embedded through the implementation of appropriate policies (financial controls, records management, anti-bribery, whistleblowing, data protection, health and safety, etc.) and clear delegation limits are adhered to throughout the business.

## External audit

Audit exemptions may apply depending on the size of the company's business but, in such cases, voluntary appointment in order to provide the board with additional assurance on the financial statements should still periodically be considered. The appointment of the external auditor will be a key consideration and an important element of the company's systems of control as well as a source of assurance to the board and the company's shareholders. Where an auditor is appointed, it is vital that an appropriate relationship with the external auditors is established in order to support the board as it, amongst other things:

- monitors the integrity of the financial statements of the company;
- reviews the company's internal controls and risk management systems;
- monitors and reviews the effectiveness of the company's internal audit function (if it has one);
- considers the appointment or removal of the external auditor and the auditor's remuneration and terms of engagement;
- reviews and monitors the external auditor's independence and effectiveness and determines a policy on the supply of non-audit services by the auditor;
- reviews risks and the adequacy of risk management processes; and
- reviews whistleblowing arrangements.

### Audit role and resources

If there is no internal audit function, the assurance provided by the external auditors on financial controls in particular will be all the more important. Starting with the external audit plan, the board (or audit committee) should ensure that, as well as standard risks covered by audit, they seek additional comfort on any areas of concern.

Where there are internal audit resources, it is important to ensure that the working relationship between the two sets of auditors makes efficient use of the total audit resources so as to maximise their effectiveness.

The audit committee or in smaller companies the board itself will need to regulate the relationship with the auditors, recommending the appointment or removal of the auditors to shareholders and approving the terms of engagement. The directors will also be responsible for ensuring the auditors have access to all relevant information and that there is a culture of co-operation with the external auditors.

Feedback from the audit can prove valuable to the business in indicating where its controls can be enhanced and developed. Additionally the auditors will be able to provide advance notice on changes to accounting standards so that the implications for the business can be understood and preparations made to introduce the necessary changes.

## Shareholder engagement

Principle 7 of *Corporate Governance Guidance and Principles for Unlisted Companies in the UK* states:

> 'There should be a dialogue between the board and the shareholders based on a mutual understanding of objectives. The board as a whole has responsibility for ensuring that a satisfactory dialogue with shareholders takes place.'

The key points of guidance suggested to accompany this principle are:

- the board should keep in touch with shareholder opinion in whatever ways they find to be most practical and efficient;
- the chairman in particular has responsibility for effective communication between shareholders and the board, which should include discussions of corporate governance and strategy;
- while the chairman is the primary means of ensuring that the views of shareholders are communicated to the board, other directors should have the opportunity to meet with shareholders; and
- one of the chairman's key roles is to set the agenda for the AGM, even for private companies which are not required by law to hold them, but the relationship with shareholders should not be limited to an annual formal meeting and should instead be viewed as a continuous process.

Such dialogue opportunities may be of particular value to shareholders of unlisted companies, whose ability to sell their shares may be quite limited in the absence of a liquid market. By engaging in such discussions, investors can exercise a degree of influence over the company's direction and strategy to ensure it remains aligned with their own objectives. The nature of the dialogue will need to be structured to reflect the needs of the company and its shareholders, for example whether it is a family concern or one in which the shareholders are largely also directors. Additional care may be needed in such cases to ensure that the lines of responsibility and respective roles of the parties do not become blurred.

Even where the law does not require an AGM to be held, the meeting can offer an important engagement opportunity, particularly where the company has a large number of shareholders. As well as reviewing the past year's activities and performance and discussing the future prospects of the company, the meeting can be used to exchange information and views more generally.

Whatever engagement strategy is adopted, however, it must ultimately be suited to the circumstances of the company and its shareholders.

For family companies where there is a need to address particular family interests, the engagement and information sharing arrangements should reflect this. *Corporate Governance Guidance and Principles for Unlisted Companies in the UK* makes the following suggestion for a mechanism by which extended families can co-ordinate and unify their interests in the company:

> 'A family assembly may meet once or twice per year, and brings together all members of the family. It allows family members to stay informed about the business and furnishes them with the opportunity to voice their opinions. It helps avoid potential conflicts that might arise due

> to an unequal access to information and other resources. A family council is a small group of family members or family representatives that acts as the primary decision making body of the family vis-à-vis the company. It is also the main communication link between the family and the company and has a crucial role in conveying the expectations of the family owners to the board. It is normally elected by the family assembly. Family institutions can play a useful role in co-ordinating and unifying the interests of extended families'.

Whatever the shareholder structure or range of the company's stakeholders, establishing channels for the provision of candid feedback and complaints and ensuring the processes surrounding these channels provide confidence that such issues will be addressed without compromising their position is an important measure which the board should consider. This should include a formal whistleblowing policy and also extend to facilitating discussion of shareholder concerns, for example about proposed changes or recent performance that, if left unaddressed, could result in a loss of shareholder confidence to the longer-term detriment of the business. Directors may wish to initiate such discussions at times of significant uncertainty or change.

In the context of ensuring that the directors are engaging with the 'right people' it can be useful to understand the underlying ownership and control of the company's shares. Recent legislation described below places a responsibility on the directors of non-listed companies to establish a register of 'Persons with Significant Control' which may extend beyond the shareholders registered as members of the company. Those requirements are examined next.

## PSC

A new Part 21A and Schedules 1A and 1B to the CA 2006 were introduced under the SBEEA 2015 and brought in the requirement for companies to have a register of PSC (the PSC register). The PSC register is a register of individuals or legal entities that have significant control over UK companies and UK LLPs. It was introduced with the purpose of identifying the ultimate beneficial owners and controllers and making their holdings public. The requirements are intended to increase corporate transparency with the aim of combatting money laundering, the financing of terrorism and tax evasion. The PSC register sits alongside the usual company registers including the register of directors and the register of shareholders and the information in the PSC register must be filed at Companies House. There are a number of obligations under the new regime for companies, LLPs and PSCs any breach of which is a criminal offence. Sentences range from a fine to up to two years imprisonment.

The requirement for all UK incorporated companies and UK LLPs to have a PSC register came into force in 2016. It covers companies limited by shares, companies limited by guarantee (including community interest companies), societates europaeae (SE), wholly owned subsidiaries and dormant companies. The only exception is for UK companies that are subject to Chapter 5 of the FCA's DTRs and companies with voting shares admitted to trading on a regulated market in the UK or EEA (other than the UK) or on specified markets in Switzerland, the USA, Japan and Israel as listed in Schedule 1 to the Register of PSC Regulations 2016 as these companies are subject to other transparency rules. Overseas entities operating in the UK might be subject to requirements in their home country but are not subject to the requirements to hold a register. However they might still be required to disclose their ownership or control of companies, SEs or LLPs which have to have their own PSC register. This section covers the requirements for companies though there are similar provisions for LLPs.

## What is a PSC?

A company's PSC is a person who meets one or more of the specified conditions, namely:

i) holds directly or indirectly more than 25% of the company shares;
ii) holds directly or indirectly more than 25% of the voting rights;
iii) has the right to appoint or remove the majority of directors;
iv) has the right to exercise, or actually exercises, significant influence or control over the company; or
v) has the right to exercise, or actually exercises, significant influence or control over the activities of a trust or firm which is not a legal entity but would itself satisfy any of the first four conditions.

## Significant influence or control

A company will only need to identify where a PSC or RLE (see below) meets conditions (iv) or (v) if they do not meet one or more of conditions (i) to (iii). There is statutory guidance on the meaning of 'significant influence or control' over companies in the context of the PSC register published by the Department for Business Innovation & Skills. Control indicates that a person has the right to direct the policies and activities of a company, whereas significant influence allows a person to ensure that the company adopts the policies and activities that the person desires. Control and significant influence are alternatives and neither concept depends on the person seeking economic benefit from the exercise.

The statutory guidance does not provide an exhaustive list but rather a number of principles and examples which would be indicative of holding the right to, or actually exercising, significant influence or control. It also gives a non-exhaustive list of the types of roles and relationships which a person might have with a company which would not, on their own, result in that person being considered to have significant influence or control. This includes people such as directors, lawyers and accountants.

### Relevant legal entities

A PSC is by definition an individual but a legal entity's details must be put on the PSC register if it is both relevant and registrable in relation to the company. A legal entity is relevant in relation to a company if it meets any one or more of the conditions (i) to (v) and:

- it keeps its own PSC register; or
- it is subject to Chapter 5 of the FCA's DTRs; or
- it has voting shares admitted to trading on a regulated market in the UK or EEA (other than the UK) or on specified markets in Switzerland, the USA, Japan or Israel as listed in Schedule 1 to the Register of PSC Regulations 2016.

A relevant legal entity (RLE) is registrable in relation to a company if it is the first RLE in the company's ownership chain.

Section 790C (12) of the CA 2006 deems the following to be individuals for the purposes of the PSC regime so should be entered into the PSC register if they satisfy one or more of conditions (i) to (v):

- a corporation sole. This is an office held by a single person that has a separate legal existence from the person occupying the office. Examples of a corporation sole include certain ministers of the Crown, the Information Commissioner, the Treasury Solicitor and the holders of various ecclesiastical offices such as archbishops and bishops;
- a government or government department of a country or territory, or a part of a country of territory;
- an international organisation whose members include two or more countries or territories (or their governments); and
- a local authority or local government body in the United Kingdom.

### Indirect holdings

Shares and rights in the company may be held indirectly. This happens when a legal entity holds the shares or the rights in the company and someone has a majority stake in that legal entity. That person is not required to be entered on the company's register unless the legal entity they hold their interest through is not an RLE. When a legal entity is not an RLE it cannot be registrable and so cannot be entered on the PSC register. A legal entity might not be an RLE because it is a UK legal entity which is not a company, LLP or SE or it is a non-UK company or other legal entity that is not a RLE. If shares are held indirectly the company must look at the ownership and control of the legal entity to identify any individuals or RLEs who have a majority stake in that legal entity. Someone will hold a majority stake if:

- they hold a majority of the voting rights in the legal entity;
- they are a member of the legal entity and have the right to appoint or remove a majority of its board of directors;
- they are a member of the legal entity and control a majority of the voting rights by agreement with the other shareholders or members; or
- they have the right to exercise or actually exercise dominant influence or control over the legal entity.

If there is an individual or RLE with a majority stake in that legal entity then that individual or RLE's details must be entered on the PSC register. If there is another legal entity which is not an RLE but which has a majority stake, the company must look through that legal entity until it finds either an individual or registrable RLE with a majority stake. If there is no one who meets these criteria then this fact must be entered on the PSC register.

If shares or rights in the company are held by a nominee the shares should be treated as if they were held by the person for whom the nominee is acting. If that person is a PSC or registrable RLE their details must be entered on the register. If two or more persons hold the same shares or rights in the company then they are treated on the basis that each of them holds the total number of shares or rights held by all of them. If there is a joint arrangement where two or more people arrange to exercise all or substantially all of their rights arising from their shares jointly in a way which is predetermined each of them is deemed to hold the total number of shares held by all of them.

## Identifying a PSC

A company must take reasonable steps to identity its PSCs as failure to take reasonable steps is a criminal offence. The non-statutory *Guidance for Companies, Societates Europaeae and Limited Liability Partnerships* published by the Department for Business Innovation & Skills (April 2016 publication) outlines the steps a company should typically take to identify its PSCs or registrable RLEs. The guidance is not definitive or exhaustive and further action may need to be taken by a company depending on its circumstances. Some companies may not have any PSCs or registrable RLEs whereas some may have multiple. A company which has identified that it does not have any PSCs or registrable RLEs will still need to keep a register. A PSC register cannot be empty so while a company is working through its reasonable steps it must enter this fact and, where appropriate, where in the stage the company has reached. Failure to keep a PSC register up-to-date is also a criminal offence. Annex 2 of the non-statutory guidance gives the official prescriptive wording that must be used in the company's PSC register. All the applicable conditions that the PSC fulfils must be recorded on the PSC register. Information about both PSCs and registrable RLEs must be complete before it is entered on the PSC register. Information about a PSC must be confirmed by the PSC before it can be added to the PSC register; however, information about a registrable RLE does not need to be confirmed by the RLE. Once information about a PSC or registrable RLE is complete it must be entered on the PSC register even if the company does not have all the information it needs about any of the other PSCs or registrable RLEs. If a company has reason to believe that there is a PSC or registrable RLE in relation to the company but has not been able to identify them the company should consider serving notices requesting information on anyone it knows or has reasonable cause to believe knows the identity of the PSC or legal entity or trust or firm or could know someone likely to have that knowledge. This could include intermediaries or advisers known to act for them, such as lawyers, accountants, banks, trust and company service providers or any other contacts such as family members, business partners or known associates. If the company is owned by a foreign entity, notice can be served on the foreign entity, to ask for any information on PSCs or registrable RLEs which may sit above the foreign entity in the claim. Notices served require a response within one month. Anyone who fails to respond (without a valid reason) commits a criminal offence. If they also fail to respond to an additional warning notice and the addressee has a relevant interest in the company the company may consider imposing appropriate restrictions on any shares or rights such entity or person holds in the company.

## Duty to disclose

There is a duty on individuals or legal entities who think they should be on a PSC register to tell the company or LLP and provide it with the necessary information. Such a PSC or registrable RLE must notify the company or LLP of their status, when there is any change to their status and when they cease to be registrable. Failure to notify the company or LLP is a criminal offence.

Each register is open to public inspection and the information has to be filed at Companies House and is freely available online. The information needs to be confirmed to Companies House every 12 months. When a company, SE or LLP is incorporated a statement of initial significant control will have to be registered at Companies House alongside the other documents required for an application required to incorporate. The residential addresses and day (but not the month or year) of the date of birth of individuals will be suppressed and will not therefore be available on the public record. Applications can be made to keep PSC information private but only if there is a risk of people being put at risk of serious violence or intimidation, as a result of them being PSCs of the relevant entity, in the event that the information is public.

### Future changes to PSC regime

The law is stated as at 15 June 2017 and where possible we have attempted to outline prospective changes of which we were aware at the time of writing. Article 30 of the Fourth Money Laundering Directive ((EU) 2015/849) (MLD4) will require all corporate and legal entities incorporated in the UK to keep information on their beneficial owners. This will require the government to extend Part 21A of the CA 2006 with key changes that MLD4 will require being:

- From 24 July 2017 extending the scope of the PSC regime to capture, among other entities Scottish limited partnerships and general Scottish partnerships, unregistered companies and open-ended investment companies which would come under the MLD4 regime.
- From 26 June bringing in AIM and NEX companies within the scope of the PSC regime as MLD4 does not expressly exclude from the scope of Article 30 companies listed on prescribed markets.

Article 30(4) of MLD4 requires that information held in the central register must be adequate, accurate and current. As entities subject to Part 21A need only notify Companies House of changes in the PSC register once a year through a Confirmation Statement, which may potentially mean that a change is not notified for 11 months, a change to the existing regime (under which any change to the PSC register must be made on the register within 14 days of the change occurring and must be notified to Companies House 14 days thereafter on new Companies House forms) is being considered and would be enforced from 26 June. This would apply to both existing entities within the scope of Part 21A and to new entities to be brought within scope as part of the implementation of MLD4.

## Corporate social responsibility (CSR)

Even private companies have to operate in an environment in which there is growing scrutiny over corporate behaviour and an increased awareness of the responsibilities of business to the communities in which they operate. Businesses can suffer significant reputational and, as a result, financial damage if they fail to meet the expectations of stakeholders and society at large. The size or legal structure of the business has no bearing on the damage which can be done to a company which fails to operate in an appropriately responsible way and therefore CSR is an issue of relevance to all businesses.

Small unlisted companies are subject to many of the same CSR-related statutory requirements as larger businesses. Laws covering the environment, employment, health and safety, bribery and corruption, supply chain and modern slavery, whistleblowing, data protection, product safety, advertising and labelling may all apply depending on the nature of the company's activities and appropriate processes and safeguards will be needed to ensure the business complies as required. In addition, the directors of the company should be mindful of s. 172 of the CA 2006 which requires directors to consider the following factors (amongst other matters) when making decisions, all of which must be in the context of promoting the success of the company for the benefit of its members as a whole:

- the likely consequences of any decision in the long term;
- the interests of the company's employees;
- the need to foster the company's business relationships with suppliers, customers and others;
- the impact of the company's operations on the community and the environment;
- the desirability of the company maintaining a reputation for high standards of business conduct; and
- the need to act fairly as between members of the company.

This requirement firmly places the need to have regard to the wider needs of society at the centre of directors' decision making.

### CSR strategy

As with other aspects of the company's strategy, the starting point is to understand the motivations for the strategy, which may include perceived business benefits such as better management of risk and resources, improvements to legal compliance, meeting stakeholder expectations or the pursuit of personal values and beliefs. Having established those motivations, existing CSR practices (for example the company's code of conduct, anti-bribery policy or charity partnership) can be identified and target changes set and prioritised to establish a roadmap to implement further appropriate initiatives.

Steps may be quite simple – the use of recycled stationery, the installation of more efficient heating and lighting or insulation, more environmentally friendly travel and transport policies – or could involve a more ambitious product re-design, move to new premises or audit of the supply chain. Overriding these targets should be the need to align them with business objectives. Highly visible 'quick wins' can be particularly effective in engaging employee support and getting the message out into the business. A business of smaller size may benefit from the greater flexibility and 'local knowledge' it has to identify and implement relevant initiatives. As with all strategic issues, leadership from the board and regular review to ensure ongoing relevance are essential.

## CSR resources for smaller businesses

With much of the economy made up of smaller businesses, the impact that can be made by them collectively by behaving in an ethical and responsible manner is being increasingly recognised and specific resources are being prepared for smaller businesses as a result. Examples include:

- the EC's *My business and human rights: a guide to human rights for small and medium-sized enterprises based on the United Nations Guiding Principles on business and human rights*;
- the EC's *Tips and tricks for advisers: CSR for small and medium-sized enterprise*;
- Defra's *Small Business User Guide: Guidance on how to measure and report your greenhouse gas emissions*;
- ISO 14001 Environmental management systems. An easy-to-use checklist for small business;
- the EC's *Opportunity and Responsibility: How to help more small businesses to integrate social and environmental issues into what they do*;
- the Business Council for Sustained Development's *A business case for CSR in SMEs*, developed with the support of the EC employment and social affairs directorate; and
- the UK Government's *Transparency in Supply Chains etc. A Practical Guide.*

## CSR reporting

Although the requirement to produce a strategic report applies to all UK companies other than small companies (for which there is an exemption), the requirement to include information on environmental matters, employees, human rights and social issues as well as gender data for directors, managers and employees applies only to quoted companies. This, however, is not to say that the boards of smaller unlisted business should dismiss the need for any CSR reporting. The KPMG report *International Survey of Corporate Responsibility Reporting 2011*, which found that bigger companies were generally better at CSR reporting, noted that this analysis also pointed 'to a significant opportunity for smaller businesses to leverage their corporate responsibility reporting as a competitive differentiator'; in other words, to give their business the credibility of a larger business by behaving like a larger business.

*Corporate Governance Guidance and Principles for Unlisted Companies in the UK* makes a different point with regards to the benefits of CSR reporting, noting that CSR projects often offer a potential point of engagement with stakeholders and that, as such, CSR activities should be integrated into the company's activities and included in and consistent with the reported strategic goals of the business. Obtaining the feedback of stakeholders is essential to understanding their views and priorities so as to maximise the chances of securing their support. Such views are all the more difficult to obtain on the type of non-financial matters typical of CSR activities unless positive steps are taken to elicit them through an active consultation strategy. It is helpful in this regard to make contact details for an appropriate individual available for stakeholders to approach in the event of comments or concerns.

Some reporting on certain CSR issues will, in any case, be mandatory for some businesses, for example:

- gender pay gap reporting for business employing 250 or more employees; and
- modern slavery disclosures for companies with a turnover greater than £38m per annum.

Further details on these requirements are provided in Chapter 8.

## Preparing for an IPO

The final section of this chapter considers the position of private companies which may look to go public and obtain a listing of their shares on one of the UK equity capital markets.

The process of a company coming to market and undergoing an IPO is complex and will involve many aspects beyond the remit of this book; however, corporate governance is a key element of the process and it is never too early for companies to consider starting to implement appropriate procedures and corporate governance policies.

The LSE's guide to corporate governance notes:

> 'the relationship between companies and their shareholders has never been more important. With an ever increasing range of global investment options, companies need to focus on building long-term relationships with investors, founded on trust and regular communications. In doing so, companies will maximise the full benefits of being publicly listed. Corporate governance is central to this process'.

It is clear that in recent years corporate governance has become a key factor in the decision-making process for potential investors and can have an impact on the overall success of an IPO or the ultimate valuation achieved upon listing. The ability of a company to demonstrate good governance practices and procedures will assist with giving comfort to potential investors. There are inherent risks in the success of an IPO and, where markets are suppressed or where fund managers are seeing multiple IPO candidates, good corporate governance may provide the balancing factor in an investor's decision whether to invest.

The FRC's annual report, *Developments in Corporate Governance and Stewardship 2016*, published in January 2017 noted that while in 2015 there were lower levels of compliance amongst new market entrants, most of the companies that were listed in 2016 appear to have ensured their governance arrangements were in place ahead of listing.

Becoming a publicly listed company involves significant change to the entity, its constitution and board. A vital part of the process is understanding the new regulatory requirements and guidelines that will become applicable and educating those involved as to the corporate governance expectations both during the IPO process and after listing.

Much of the earlier content of this book covers the ongoing corporate governance considerations relevant to listed companies but the following sections highlight some of the key areas that will need to be considered at the time of an IPO.

## The board

Structuring an effective board is essential for the ongoing success of a listed company ensuring effective risk management and oversight. The board composition will need to be reviewed and it is likely that significant new appointments will be made in particular strengthening the balance of non-executive directors on the board.

The service contracts of any new executive directors and appointment letters of any new NEDs, together with the levels of remuneration and benefits will need to be reviewed. Any existing service contracts may not be suitable for a director of a listed company and new contracts will need to be negotiated and agreed.

Ultimately at the time that an IPO goes live, all members of the board will need to take full responsibility for the listing documentation and no distinction will be drawn between the executive and non-executive members of the board. It is therefore crucial to start the process of identifying potential new board members early in the process in conjunction with the company's advisors so that, by the time the IPO goes live, they are in a position to sign off on, and take responsibility for, the listing documents alongside the incumbent executive team.

The appointment of a new non-executive will be a two-way process with prospective directors wanting to understand the business and carrying out their own due diligence. Identifying prospective non-executive candidates, ideally with relevant industry experience, can take time and although the formal appointment to the board may only occur shortly before the listing goes live, investors will want to understand the composition and make-up of the board as part of the marketing process.

The company will also need to consider the make-up of the various corporate governance committees, identify the proposed chairman of the board, as well as which of the board members will be deemed to be independent and identifying one of these as the senior NED. The corporate governance committees are considered in more detail in Chapter 2.

In addition, the IPO documentation will usually include a list of matters reserved for the full board and identified procedures in the event that the non-executive directors need to obtain independent legal advice. These matters are considered in more detail in Chapters 3 and 9–14.

### Compliance with regulatory and governance requirements

As part of the transition from private to publicly listed company, both the company and the board will find themselves subject to an additional layer of statutory and regulatory requirements and guidelines. This regulatory framework is considered in more detail in Chapter 2.

Companies will need to consider how to best comply with the requirements of the UK Corporate Governance Code and will need to give consideration to the key areas of leadership, effectiveness, accountability, remuneration and relations with shareholders. While the provisions of the UK Corporate Governance Code do not strictly apply to companies listed on AIM, it is seen as good practice to comply with the UK Corporate Governance Code as far as is practicable given the nature and size of the company in question.

One particular area which will require significant thought as part of the IPO process will be ensuring compliance with the market abuse regime as governed by the MAR (Regulation 596/2014) which came into effect in July 2016. As a listed company, it will be necessary to demonstrate that systems are in place to identify potential inside information that may require disclosure to the wider market. This may involve the establishment of a disclosure committee (see Chapter 3). Once listed, a company will need to maintain insider lists.

As part of the preparation for listing, the company will need to adopt a share dealing code and identify who from amongst its employees will be classed as PDMRs. Such persons will need to be notified to ensure that they understand and acknowledge their obligations under the market abuse regime and that they will comply with the share dealing code. PDMRs will also be asked to identify and notify persons closely associated to them. Depending on the size and nature of a company's workforce, a company may decide to extend some or all elements of the share dealing code to all employees. Further details of MAR are set out in Chapter 15.

## IPO process

Feedback from investors has regularly shown that companies do not provide enough emphasis on corporate governance or that attention to this area is given too late on in the IPO process. Other criticism can arise where new non-executive appointments are only identified at a late stage or where matters such as risk management or shareholder protection mechanisms are not addressed as part of the pre-IPO engagement and meetings.

Practically, the IPO process will require the implementation of necessary governance procedures and systems, briefings of employees and the board of all relevant new rules and obligations. In addition adoption of relevant policies including anti-bribery, whistleblowing, health and safety should be considered and where appropriate implemented. These will form part of the significant documentation involved in the IPO process.

The formal prospectus (or admission document) will need to include full disclosure of the applicable corporate governance regime and set out the detailed arrangements that the Company is adopting including details of the board, board committees, PDMRs, related party arrangements and controlling shareholder arrangements (see below).

## Significant shareholders

Depending on which market a company chooses to list on, there may well be requirements as to the percentage of shares that must be in public hands so as to ensure sufficient free float and liquidity in the company's shares. Notwithstanding this, it is not unusual for the pre-existing shareholders in the private company to maintain a significant holding in a listed company albeit that this may gradually dilute over time. Corporate governance becomes even more important in instances where new shareholders coming in at the time of the IPO will be in a minority position. A robust corporate governance framework and good ongoing communication with shareholders will be essential.

Where any single shareholder (or connected persons) holds 30% or more of the share capital upon listing, the LR (in the case of a premium listed company) require that a form of controlling shareholder or relationship agreement is put in place effective from admission to govern the relationship between the company and the major shareholder. As well as providing the company with certain protections and comfort, the agreement would also require the major shareholder to confirm that any arrangements between it and the company post-listing would be entered into at arm's-length and on normal commercial terms. In addition, going forward the LR also require two forms of shareholder approval on certain matters, one of which will exclude the significant shareholder. Further details of these requirements are set out in Chapter 15. Although no formal requirement in this regard exists under the AIM rules, it is standard market practice for a similar form of agreement to be entered into when listing on AIM.

### Constitutional matters

Aside from the more general governance matters mentioned above, there will need to be significant changes made to the constitutional documentation of a company considering a listing. First and foremost, a private company will need to convert to a PLC or alternatively create a new public holding company which will become the listed entity. In addition, long form plc articles will need to be adopted and the share capital of the company restructured to ensure a single class of listed share. It is not uncommon for private companies to have multiple classes of shares with differing rights attaching to them. Upon listing, it is usual for any special share rights to be removed. Such changes will require a shareholder meeting to be convened which will need to be taken into account in the listing timetable. The US markets have seen examples, particularly amongst some of the larger tech IPOs of dual class share structures with investors acquiring non-voting or limited voting shares with the founders holding voting or enhanced voting shares – examples include Facebook and Google. While the UK has no overt ban on such structures (and a few examples may still be found amongst a handful companies which originally listed over 40 years ago), it is unlikely that the relevant UK regulatory bodies would approve such structures from an eligibility perspective. It is also clear that commercially, institutional investors have no appetite for such structures not least as they would appear to fly in the face of governance best practice and the equal treatment of all shareholders.

## Conclusion

The absence of mandatory corporate governance codes should not mislead the board of unlisted companies into thinking good governance is neither relevant nor necessary. In order to fulfil their duties as directors, board members should pay close attention to governance arrangements and ensure oversight and leadership of the business is both proportional and effective. As the business continues to develop, those governance arrangements should also develop in order to remain appropriate and therefore such arrangements should be kept under critical, periodic review.

## Governance checklist

✓ Does the board provide strategic leadership that is in line with the company's strategic objectives, obligations towards shareholders and other stakeholders and complies with regulatory and legal requirements?

- ✓ Have adequate steps been taken to ensure effective governance of any subsidiary entities?
- ✓ Notwithstanding the limits of board composition of smaller companies, is appropriate evaluation of the board undertaken to identify any gaps? Is feedback given on the effectiveness of the chairman, and are areas of required improvement identified?
- ✓ Are executive roles well defined and is the remuneration policy appropriate?
- ✓ Are NEDs adequately ensuring the effectiveness of financial controls and risk management systems?
- ✓ Does the company secretary support the board in its governance process and ensure that the board works effectively?
- ✓ Does the board make effective use of committees in order to discharge their responsibilities?
- ✓ Do directors act in accordance with their statutory duties, including in relation to financial and narrative reporting?
- ✓ Has the appointment of an external auditor been thoroughly considered?
- ✓ Has the board identified its PSCs and RLEs and taken steps to include them on the PSC register and to the details at Companies House?
- ✓ Does the board take responsibility for ensuring that there is satisfactory and productive dialogue with their shareholders?
- ✓ Does the company comply with all relevant CSR-related disclosure requirements and identified and implemented CSR practices which align with the company's business strategy?
- ✓ If the company may consider a future IPO, are early steps being taken to embed good corporate governance practices which will enhance the chances that the company will be attractive to potential investors?

# Glossary

**AIM company** A company which has shares or other securities admitted to trading on the AIM market. AIM is a multilateral trading facility operated by the LSE, offering smaller, growth companies access to the benefits of having securities which are publicly traded but within a less onerous regulatory regime. AIM is not a regulated market.

**Audit committee** A committee of the board, consisting entirely of independent NEDs, with responsibility (among other things) for monitoring the integrity of the financial statements, the quality of the external audit and the company's relationship with external auditors.

**Board committee** A committee established by the board of directors, with delegated responsibility for a particular aspect of the board's affairs. For example, audit committee, remuneration/compensation committee and nominations committee.

**Board succession** The replacement of a senior director (typically the chairman or CEO) when they retire or resign.

**Cadbury Code** A code of corporate governance, published by the Cadbury Committee in the UK in 1992 (now superseded by the UK Corporate Governance Code).

**Chairman** Leader of the board of directors. Often referred to as the 'company chairman' in companies and 'chair' in public bodies and voluntary organisations.

**Chief executive officer (CEO)** The executive director who is head of the executive management team in an organisation.

**Corporate governance** The system by which a company is directed, so as to achieve its overall objectives. It is concerned with culture, influences, relations, structures, processes, information flows, controls, decision making and accountability at the highest level in a company.

**Corporate social responsibility (CSR)** Responsibility shown by a company (or other organisations) for matters of general concern to the society in which it operates, such as protection of the environment, health and safety and social welfare.

**Dealing code** A code of conduct for directors and senior managers of listed companies, stating when they should (in normal circumstances) avoid buying or selling their company's securities, including clearance procedures for dealings.

**Disclosure Guidance and Transparency Rules** Part of the FCA's Handbook including guidance on disclosures and rules on periodic financial reporting and corporate governance that listed companies are required to comply with. The rules (like the LR) are issued and enforced by the FCA.

**Executive director** A director who also has executive responsibilities in the management structure. Usually a full-time employee with a contract of employment.

**Limited company** The most common form of a company, in which the liability of members for the debts of the company is limited – either to the amount of share capital for which they have applied (a company limited by shares) or to a specific amount guaranteed in the event of a winding-up (a company limited by guarantee).

**Listed company** A company whose shares are listed by the FCA on the Official List of the UK and admitted to trading on the LSE or NEX Exchange listed markets. The term 'listed company' is also used colloquially to refer to a company which has shares listed on other markets and is sometimes used in that context within this publication.

**Market abuse** Market abuse is a civil offence regime under MAR. It prohibits the misuse of precise non-public information concerning issuers that would havc a significant effect on the price of issuers' shares or related financial instruments. The regime creates three offences: insider dealing, unlawful disclosure of inside information and market manipulation. There is a separate criminal regime for insider dealing under Part V of the Criminal Justice Act 1993 and misleading statements and impressions, including in relation to benchmarks, under sections 89–91 of the Financial Services Act 2012.

**Nomination committee** A committee of the board of directors with responsibility for identifying potential new members for the board. Suitable candidates are recommended to the full board, which then makes a decision about their appointment.

**Non-executive director** A director who is not an employee of the company and who does not have any responsibilities for executive management in the company. NEDs participate in the decision-making process of the board and are expected to constructively challenge board performance and decisions and help develop strategy.

**Quoted company** For the purposes of the CA 2006, a company whose equity share capital has been included in the Official List in accordance with the

FSMA 2000, or is officially listed in an EEA state, or is admitted to dealing on either the New York Stock Exchange or NASDAQ.

**Remuneration committee** A committee of the board of directors, with responsibility for deciding remuneration policy for top executives and the individual remuneration packages of certain senior executives, for example all the executive directors.

**Traded company** A company where any of their transferable securities that carry voting rights are admitted to trading on a regulated market in an EEA state (this excludes AIM companies).

**UK Corporate Governance Code** The code of corporate governance issued by the FRC in the UK, which is applied to companies with a premium listing of equity shares. Formerly (until 2010) called the Combined Code. In this publication, unless the context suggests otherwise 'Code' generally refers to the UK Corporate Governance Code and the terms 'Code Principles' and 'Code Provisions' are used to refer to the Principles and Code Provisions respectively of the UK Corporate Governance Code.

**UK Listing Rules** The LR are part of the FCA's Handbook. They lay down minimum requirements for the admission of securities to listing on the Official List and the continuing obligations of issuers after admission, including the 'comply or explain' rule on compliance with the UK Corporate Governance Code.

# Directory

## Legislation, reports and codes of practice

*Advertising Standards Authority Codes*, ASA
http://www.asa.org.uk/Advertising-Codes.aspx

*A Review of Corporate Governance in UK Banks and Other Financial Industry Entities (Walker Review)*, Sir David Walker HM Treasury, 2009
http://webarchive.nationalarchives.gov.uk/+/http:/www.hm-treasury.gov.uk/d/walker_review_261109.pdf

*Best Practice Principles for Shareholder Voting Research & Analysis*
http://bppgrp.info/wp-content/uploads/2014/03/BPP-ShareholderVoting-Research-2014.pdf

*Committee on Corporate Governance: Final Report (Hampel Committee report)*
Gee Publishing, 1998
http://www.ecgi.org/codes/documents/hampel_index.htm

*Corporate Governance Guidance and Principles for Unlisted Companies in the UK*
https://www.iod.com/news-campaigns/press-office/details/Corporate-Governance-for-Unlisted-Companies

*Corporate Governance Policy and Voting Guidelines*, PLSA, 2015/16 update
http://www.plsa.co.uk/PolicyandResearch/DocumentLibrary/0556-2016-Corporate-Governance-Policy-and-Voting-Guidelines.aspx

*Directors' Remuneration: Report of a Study Group chaired by Sir Richard Greenbury (Greenbury Committee Report)*
Gee Publishing, 1995
http://www.ecgi.org/codes/code.php?code_id=131

*FRC Guidance on Audit Committees*
FRC, 2016
https://www.frc.org.uk/Our-Work/Publications/Corporate-Governance/Guidance-on-Audit-Committees-(2).pdf

*FRC Guidance on Board Effectiveness*
FRC, 2011
https://www.frc.org.uk/Our-Work/Publications/Corporate-Governance/Guidance-on-Board-Effectiveness.pdf

*FRC Guidance on Risk Management, Internal Control and Related Financial and Business Reporting*
https://www.frc.org.uk/Our-Work/Publications/Corporate-Governance/Guidance-on-Risk-Management,-Internal-Control-and.pdf

*Implementing the Recommendations of the Sharman Panel: Revised Guidance on Going Concern and revised International Standards on Auditing (UK and Ireland) – November 2013*
https://www.frc.org.uk/Our-Work/Publications/FRC-Board/Feedback-Statement-Implementing-the-recommendation.pdf

*Internal Control: Guidance for Directors on the Combined Code (the Turnbull Report)*
FRC, Croner CCH, 1999 and updated 2005
http://frc.org.uk/Our-Work/Publications/Corporate-Governance/Turnbull-guidance-October-2005.aspx

*The Investment Association Principles of Remuneration*
The Investment Association, October 2016
https://www.ivis.co.uk/media/12445/Principles-of-Remuneration-2016-Final.pdf

*King IV Report on Corporate Governance*
South African Institute of Directors, November 2016
http://www.iodsa.co.za/page/KingIVReport

*OECD Guidelines for Multinational Enterprises, OECD*
www.oecd.org/dataoecd/56/36/1922428.pdf

*OECD Principles of Corporate Governance*
OECD, 2004
www.oecd.org/corporate/ca/corporategovernanceprinciples/31557724.pdf

*Pensions and Lifetime Savings Association Corporate Governance Policy & Voting Guidelines 2015/16*
http://www.plsa.co.uk/PolicyandResearch/DocumentLibrary/0556-2016-Corporate-Governance-Policy-and-Voting-Guidelines.aspx

*Principles for Corporate Governance in the Commonwealth: Towards Global Competitiveness and Economic Accountability*
Commonwealth Association for Corporate Governance, 1999
http://www.ecseonline.com/PDF/CACG%20Guidelines%20-%20Principles%20for%20Corporate%20Governance%20in%20the%20Commonwealth.pdf

*Report of the Committee on the Financial Aspects of Corporate Governance*
Cadbury Report Gee Publishing, 1992
www.ecgi.org/codes/documents/cadbury.pdf

*Report on Board Effectiveness: Updating progress, promoting best practice*
December 2012
www.ivis.co.uk/media/5920/ABI-Report-on-Board-Effectiveness-2012-Final.pdf

*Review of the Role and Effectiveness of Non-Executive Directors (the Higgs Report)*
BIS, 2003 Sarbanes-Oxley Act of 2002, H.R. 3763
www.ecgi.org/codes/documents/higgsreport.pdf

*Solicitors' Code of Conduct – Guidance to Rule 13 In-house Practice etc*
Solicitors Regulation Authority
www.sra.org.uk/solicitors/code-of-conduct/rule13.page

*Turner Review: A regulatory response to the global banking crisis*
FSA, March 2009
http://www.fsa.gov.uk/pubs/other/turner_review.pdf

*UK Corporate Governance Code*
FRC, 2016
https://www.frc.org.uk/Our-Work/Publications/Corporate-Governance/UK-Corporate-Governance-Code-April-2016.pdf

*UK Stewardship Code*
FRC, 2010
https://www.frc.org.uk/Our-Work/Codes-Standards/Corporate-governance/UK-Stewardship-Code.aspx

## Further reading

### Governance

*A Fine Line – Further Guidance to In-House Lawyers in England and Wales on Ensuring Good Corporate Governance in your Organisations*, CIG Corporate Governance Committee, July 2006
www.cigroup.org.uk/images/file/fine_line.pdf

*A Practical Guide to the UK Listing Regime* 4th edition, Herbert Smith Freehills LLP ICSA Publishing Limited, 2017

*Cases in Corporate Governance*, Wearing, R., Sage, 2005

*Corporate Governance* 5th edition, Mallin, C., Oxford University Press, 2015

*Corporate Governance* 5th edition, Monks, A. G. and Minow, N. (eds), John Wiley and Sons, 2011

*Corporate Governance and Accountability* 4th edition, Solomon, J. F., John Wiley and Sons, 2013

*Corporate Governance and Chairmanship: A Personal View*, Cadbury, A., Oxford University Press, 2002

*Corporate Governance: Accountability, Enterprise and International Comparisons*, Keasey, K. (ed), John Wiley and Sons, 2005

*Corporate Governance: Principles, Policies and Practices of Corporate Governance* 3rd edition, Tricker, R. I., Oxford University Press, 2015

Hermes Investment Management 'UK Corporate Governance Principles January 2017'
https://www.hermes-investment.com/wp-content/uploads/2017/02/UK-CG-Principles-Jan-2017-1.pdf

*Keeping Better Company: Corporate Governance Ten Years On*, 2nd edition, Charkham, J., Oxford University Press, 2008

*Theories of Corporate Governance*, Clarke, T., Routledge, 2004

### Directors

*GC100 Companies Act (2006) – Directors' duties* GC100, February 2007
www.practicallaw.com/8-378-8813

*GC100 Guidance on Directors' Conflicts of Interest Authorisation Process*
GC100, August 2008
https://uk.practicallaw.thomsonreuters.com/8-380-1895?_lrTS=20170404135242794&transitionType=Default&contextData=(sc.Default)&firstPage=true&bhcp=1

*Rights and Duties of Directors* 15th edition, Bruce, M., Bloomsbury Professional, 2016

*The Female FTSE Report 2016*
Cranfield University School of Management
https://www.cranfield.ac.uk/som/~/media/images-for-new-website/centres/school-of-management-centres/global-centre-for-gender-and-leadership/female-ftse-board-report-2016.ashx?la=en

*The ICSA Director's Guide* 5th edition, Bruce, M., ICSA Publishing Limited, 2013

## Boards and committees

*Boards That Deliver*, Charan, R., John Wiley and Sons, February 2005

*Building Better Boards: A blueprint for effective governance*, Nadler, D. A., John Wiley and Sons, March 2006

*FT-ICSA Boardroom Bellwether survey*, published twice a year
www.icsa.org.uk/knowledge/research

*Inside the Boardroom*, Leblanc, R. and Gillies, J., John Wiley and Sons, June 2005

*Running Board Meetings* 3rd edition, Dunne, P., Kogan Page, 2007

*Thin on Top: Why corporate governance matters and how to measure and improve board performance*, Garrett, R., Nicholas Brealey Publishing, 2006

*Voluntary Code of Conduct for Executive Search Firms*
https://www.gov.uk/government/publications/standard-voluntary-code-of-conduct-executive-search-firms

## Audit

*Audit Firm Governance Code*
FRC, July 2016
https://www.frc.org.uk/Our-Work/Audit/Audit-and-assurance/Audit-Firm-Governance-Code.aspx

*ICAEW Guidance for Audit Committees – The internal audit function*
ICAEW, March 2004
http://www.icaew.com/-/media/corporate/files/technical/audit-and-assurance/audit/guidance-for-audit-committees/the-internal-audit-function.ashx?la=en

*Position Statement: The Role of Internal Audit in Enterprise-wide Risk Management*
IIA, 2009
https://www.iia.org.uk/media/78513/the_role_of_internal_audit_in_enterprise_risk_management.pdf

*The Investment Association Guidelines on Audit Tenders*
https://www.ivis.co.uk/media/12498/Audit-tenders-guidelines.pdf

## Remuneration

*Code of Conduct in relation to Executive Remuneration Consulting in the United Kingdom*, Remuneration Consultants Group
www.remunerationconsultantsgroup.com

*Hermes EOS and NAPF – Pay Principles*
http://www.plsa.co.uk/PolicyandResearch/DocumentLibrary/0290_0290-Hermes-EOS-and-NAPF-Pay-Principles.aspx

*Non-executive director fees review*
Incomes Data Services, March 2013
http://www.incomesdata.co.uk/wp-content/uploads/2014/06/IDS-NED-fees-2014.pdf

*PwC FTSE100 Non-executive directors fees in 2015*
http://www.pwc.co.uk/human-resource-services/assets/ftse-100-review-of-ned-fees-january-2016.pdf

*Recommendations on directors' remuneration 2004/913/EC and 2005/162/EC*, EC Commission
http://ec.europa.eu/internal_market/company/directors-remun/index_en.htm

*Reforming Remuneration Practices in Financial Services*, FSA
www.fsa.gov.uk/pubs/policy/ps09_15.pdf

*Statement of Best Practice on Executive Contracts and Severance*, ABI/NAPF
https://www.ivis.co.uk/media/5896/ABI_NAPF_Joint_Statement_14feb2008_2_v_5.pdf

The Investment Association Principles of Remuneration, October 2016
https://www.ivis.co.uk/media/12445/Principles-of-Remuneration-2016-Final.pdf

## Reporting

*Comply or Explain: Investor expectations and current practices*, December 2012
www.ivis.co.uk/media/5923/ABI-Report-on-Comply-or-Explain-Investor-Expectations-Dec-2012.pdf

*FRC What constitutes an explanation under 'comply or explain'?*
February 2012
http://www.frc.org.uk/getattachment/590dd61a-d3b1-4a2e-a214-90f17453fa24/What-constitutes-an-explanation-under-comply-or-explain.aspx

*Guidelines on Responsible Investment Disclosure*
ABI, January 2007
www.ivis.co.uk/media/5893/ABI_RID_guidelines.pdf

*Lab project report: A single figure for remuneration*
June 2012
http://www.frc.org.uk/getattachment/5310093d-c092-45e1-8106-278ae7ac1a4b/Asingle-figure-for-remuneration.aspx

*Louder Than Words*
FRC, 2009
http://frc.org.uk/getattachment/7d952925-74ea-4deb-b659-e9242b09f2fa/Louderthan-words.aspx

*Reporting Statement: Operating and Financial Review*
ASB, 2006
www.frc.org.uk/Our-Work/Publications/ASB/UITF-Abstract-24-Accounting-for-start-up-costs/Reporting-Statement-Operating-and-Financial-Review.aspx

## Shareholders and shareholder relations

*Enhancing Stewardship Dialogues*, ICSA, March 2013
https://www.icsa.org.uk/knowledge/resources/enhancing-stewardship-dialogue

*EU Directive and Consultation on Shareholder Rights*
http://ec.europa.eu/justice/civil/company-law/corporate-governance/index_en.htm

*The Hermes Responsible Ownership Principles*
Hermes, 2015
https://www.hermes-investment.com/wp-content/uploads/2015/09/the-hermes-corporate-partnership.pdf

*Improving Corporate Governance and Shareholder Engagement*
https://www.ivis.co.uk/media/5929/ABI-Report-Improving-Corporate-Governance-and-Shareholder-Engagement.pdf

*Institutional Investment in the UK: A Review*, Myners, PHM Treasury, 2001, updated 2008
http://webarchive.nationalarchives.gov.uk/+/http:/www.hm-treasury.gov.uk/d/consult_myners_response_pu632.pdf

*Institutional Shareholders' Committee 'code on the responsibilities of institutional investors'*
https://www.theinvestmentassociation.org/assets/components/ima_filesecurity/secure.php?f=industry-guidance/isc-01.pdf

*London Stock Exchange: Investor Relations – A Practical Guide*
https://www.londonstockexchange.com/home/ir-apracticalguide.pdf

*Responsibilities of Institutional Shareholders and Agents – Statement of Principle*, Institutional Shareholders' Committee, 2002, and revised 2007
www.ivis.co.uk

*A Review of the Impediments to Voting Shares*
Paul Myners, November 2005
www.bba.org.uk/policy/article/review-of-the-impediments-to-voting-uk-shares-2004/custody-and-stock-lending/

*The Takeover Panel Practice Statement No. 26 – Shareholder Activism*
The Takeover Panel
http://www.thetakeoverpanel.org.uk/statements/practice-statements

*UK Corporate Governance Voting and Engagement Policy*
Jointly issued by the Railway Pension Trustee Company and Universities Superannuation Scheme, February 2010

## Corporate social responsibility

*AA1000 series of standards, Accountability*
www.accountability.org

*Communication from the Commission to the European Parliament, the Council and the European Economic and Social Committee, implementing the Partnership for Growth and Jobs: Making Europe a Pole of Excellence on Corporate Social Responsibility*
http://www.jussemper.org/Resources/Corporate%20Activity/Resources/IMPLEMENTINGPARTNERSHIPJOBS.pdf

*Green Claims*, Defra
http://www.defra.gov.uk/publications/files/pb13453-green-claims-guidance.pdf

*GRI G4 Guidelines*, Global Reporting Initiative
https://www.globalreporting.org/Pages/default.aspx

*Human Rights Translated – A Business Reference Guide*, International Business Leaders Forum
https://www.unglobalcompact.org/docs/news_events/8.1/human_rights_translated.pdf

*International Labour Organisation's Declaration of Principles and Rights at Work*
http://www.ilo.org/declaration/lang--en/index.htm

*KPMG International Survey on Corporate Responsibility Reporting*, KPMG
www.kpmg.co.uk

*Sustainability – Are Consumers buying it?* PricewaterhouseCoopers
http://pwc.blogs.com/files/pwc-sustainability-pamphlet13_06_08.pdf

## Magazines, journals and newsletters

*CSPOnline Newsletter*
Weekly newsletter from ICSA covering news and case law on corporate governance, company law and other issues

*Governance and Compliance*
Magazine published ten times a year by ICSA, featuring regular updates and articles on a variety of corporate governance topics

*Global ProxyWatch*
International corporate governance newsletter, available by email

*Governance*
International monthly newsletter on issues of corporate governance, boardroom performance and shareholder activism

## Web resources

AccountAbility21, www.accountability.org

Business for Social Responsibility, www.bsr.org

Business in the Community, www.bitc.org.uk

Calpers, www.calpers.org

Committee on Standards in Public Life, www.public-standards.gov.uk

Council of Institutional Investors, USA, www.cii.org

CSR Europe, www.csreurope.org

Deminor (scorecards), www.deminor.com

The Department for Business, Energy and Industrial Strategy (BEIS), https://www.gov.uk/government/organisations/department-for-business-energy-and-industrial-strategy

EIRIS (Ethical Investment Research Service), www.eiris.org

European Corporate Governance Institute, www.ecgi.org

EU Sustainable Investment Forum, www.eurosif.org

Financial Conduct Authority, www.fca.org.uk

Financial Reporting Council, www.frc.org.uk

Global Reporting, https://www.globalreporting.org/Pages/default.aspx

Hermes, www.hermes-investment.com

ICAEW Audit Quality Forum, http://www.icaew.com/en/technical/audit-and-assurance/audit-quality-forum-aqf

Institutional Shareholder Services (ISS), www.issgovernance.com

Institutional Voting Information Service, www.ivis.co.uk

International Corporate Governance Network, www.icgn.org

International Organization of Securities Commissions, www.iosco.org

The Investor Responsibility Research Centre, www.irrcinstitute.org

Manifest, www.manifest.co.uk

OECD, www.oecd.org

Office for Public Management, www.opm.co.uk

Pensions & Investment Research Consultants Limited, www.pirc.co.uk

Pensions and Lifetime Savings Association, www.plsa.co.uk

Public Concern at Work (Whistleblowing), www.pcaw.co.uk

Quoted Companies Alliance (QCA), www.theqca.com

The GoodCorporation, http://www.goodcorporation.com

The UK Listing Authority, http://www.fca.org.uk/firms/markets/ukla

## Professional bodies and useful organisations

The Institute of Business Ethics, www.ibe.org.uk

The Institute of Chartered Secretaries and Administrators (ICSA), www.icsa.org.uk

The Institute of Directors, www.iod.com

The Institute of Risk Management, www.theirm.org/

The Investment Association, https://www.theinvestmentassociation.org/

Investor Relations Society, www.irs.org.uk

Pensions and Lifetime Savings Association, www.plsa.co.uk

UK Shareholders' Association, www.uksa.org.uk

UK Sustainable Investment and Finance Association, http://uksif.org/

# Index